Critical Communication

Critical Communication

Glen Lewis and Christina Slade

Prentice Hall Australia
Sydney   New York   Toronto   Mexico   New Delhi
London   Tokyo   Singapore   Rio de Janeiro

Front Cover: Ethel Spowers
Australia 1890–1947
The gust of wind, 1931 colour lithograph on paper 22.0 x 16.6 cm (composition only).
Collection: National Gallery of Australia, Canberra.
Reproduced by permission of the Australian National Gallery, Canberra.

© 1994 by Prentice Hall Australia

All rights reserved. No part of this publication may be reproduced, stored in a retrieval system, or transmitted in any form or by any means, electronic, mechanical, photocopying, recording, or otherwise, without written permission of the publisher.

Acquisitions Editor: Joy Whitton
Production Editor: Katie Millar
Cover and text design: Nuttshell Graphics
Typeset by: The Type Group

Printed in Australia by Star Printery, Erskineville, NSW

1 2 3 4 5 98 97 96 95 94

ISBN 0 7248 0208 8

National Library of Australia
Cataloguing-in-Publication Data

Lewis, Glen
 Critical communication.

 Includes index
 ISBN 0 7248 0208 8.

 1. Communication. 2. Communication — Problems, exercises, etc. 3. Communication — Australia. 4. Communication — Australia — Problems, exercises, etc. I. Slade, C. M. (Christina M.). II Title.

302.2

Prentice Hall, Inc., *Englewood Cliffs, New Jersey*
Prentice Hall of Australia Pty Ltd, *Sydney*
Prentice Hall Canada, Inc., *Toronto*
Prentice Hall Hispanoamericana, S.A., *Mexico*
Prentice Hall of India Private Ltd, *New Delhi*
Prentice Hall International, Inc., *London*
Prentice Hall of Japan, Inc., *Tokyo*
Prentice Hall of Southeast Asia Pty Ltd, *Singapore*
Editora Prentice Hall do Brasil Ltda, *Rio de Janeiro*

Prentice Hall
A division of Simon & Schuster

Contents

Preface xi
Acknowledgments xiii

1 Theories and models of communication   1

The familiarity and difficulty of communication 3
    The study of communication 4
Models and theories of communication 6
    Transmission theories and models of communication 8
    Meaning-based theories of communication 12
    Communication, power and cultural relativism 14
Research methods and communication 17
Summary 21
Discussion questions 21
Further reading 22
References 22

2 Language in context   25

Languages and definitions 26
Levels in the analysis of language 28
    The level of significant sounds and words 28
    At the level of sentences 31
    At the level of pragmatics 33
    At the level of discourse 35
Semiotic analyses of language 39
Gender and language 42
Summary 46
Discussion questions 47
Further reading 47
References 48

3 The codes of nonverbal communication   51

The importance of nonverbal communication 52
The codes of nonverbal communication 56
    Kinesics 56
    Haptics 57
    Proxemics 58
    Chronemics 59

Contents

	The functions of nonverbal communication	60
	Taxonomy of nonverbal behaviour	61
	Context, culture and gender	62
	Semiotic accounts of visual codes	65
	Summary	71
	Discussion questions	71
	Further reading	72
	References	72

4 Critical thinking 75

The importance of reason 76
Clarity in communication 79
   Facts and inferences 81
Logic 83
   Deductive and inductive arguments 85
   Necessary and sufficient conditions 86
Fallacies 88
Reasoning with others 91
Summary 94
Discussion questions 95
Further reading 96
References 96

5 Interpersonal communication 97

Dimensions of the self in communication 98
   Self-concept, self-image and self-esteem 99
   Self-disclosure, self-presentation and self-monitoring 101
Interpersonal perception 104
   Implicit personality theory and stereotyping 105
Communication apprehension and social involvement 109
Communication in social relationships 111
Social approaches to communication and subjectivity 114
Summary 116
Discussion questions 117
Further reading 117
References 118

6 Intercultural communication 121

Definitions of intercultural communication 122
   Host and minority cultures 123
   Subcultures 124
   Multiculturalism 125
   Cross-cultural communication 127

Principles of intercultural communication 128
    Social distance and ethnocentrism 130
    Stereotyping, discrimination and prejudice 131
    Acculturation 133
Intercultural communication accommodation theory 135
Intercultural communication competence 137
Summary 140
Discussion questions 141
Further reading 141
References 142

7 Communicating in multicultural Australia 145

Anglo-Australian culture 146
    History, language and values 147
    Anglo-Australians and multiculturalism 150
The first Australians 152
    Aboriginality and the land 153
    Language and interpersonal relations 155
The new multicultural communities 157
    Southern Europeans: Italians and Greeks 158
    Arabs: Lebanese and Turks 159
    Asians: Chinese and Indochinese 161
Post-multiculturalism? 165
Summary 166
Discussion questions 167
Further reading 168
References 168

8 Small group communication 171

The nature of small group communication 172
    Factors shaping group effectiveness 174
    Group size and stages of group development 175
Membership and leadership roles in groups 178
    Group task roles 180
    Group maintenance roles 181
Group problem solving 182
Dealing with group conflict 185
Group decision making 189
Summary 192
Discussion questions 192
Further reading 193
References 193

9 Organisational communication (1) Structure and culture   195

- Australian organisational communication contexts 196
  - Functional and meaning-centred theories of organisations 198
  - Career paths: organisational entry and assimilation 199
- Organisational structure 202
  - The external environment 203
  - Organisational goals, resources and outcomes 203
  - Technology and the internal environment 204
  - Three dimensions of organisational structure 205
  - Organisational structure and communication 206
- Organisational culture 208
  - Organisational communication climate 208
  - The origins and uses of organisational culture studies 210
  - Levels of analysis in organisational culture studies 213
  - Communication and organisational culture 215
- Summary 216
- Discussion questions 216
- Further reading 217
- References 217

10 Organisational communication (2) Networks, gender and power   219

- Organisational communication networks 220
  - Social networks and job searching 220
  - Organisational communication network properties 222
  - The uses of communication network concepts 225
- Gender and communication at work 228
  - Managerial stereotypes and gender-typed organisations 228
  - Gender equity issues in the public and private sectors 231
  - Australian EEO programs 232
- Power and communication in organisations 234
  - Coalitions, influence strategies and resource dependency 234
  - Industrial Democracy programs 238
- Summary 240
- Discussion questions 241
- Further reading 241
- References 242

11 Analysing television   243

- TV criticism and TV research 244
- Analysing TV form 249
  - Media texts and intertextuality 249
  - Narrative discourse and TV genres 251

TV, identity and difference 253
    TV and personal identity 253
    TV and national identity 254
    TV and gender identity 259
Summary 262
Discussion questions 263
Further reading 263
References 264

Globalisation/Kokusaika 国際化 267

12

Modernisation, the media and development 269
    From modernity to modernisation: Asia and Latin America 272
From modernisation to globalisation 275
    Four key elements of globalisation 275
Globalisation and media politics in South-East Asia 277
Media and modernisation debates in Japan and Australia 280
    The 1950s and 1960s 281
    The 1970s and 1980s 282
    Current communications policy issues 284
Globalisation and Australian identity 286
Summary 286
Discussion questions 287
Further reading 288
References 288

Teaching appendix 291

Glossary 307

Name index 319

Subject index 323

About the authors 329

Preface

This text introduces the discipline of communication studies to first year tertiary students. Communication is now taught at many Australian universities as a degree in its own right, as an integral part of communications-related courses, such as media, public relations, journalism, advertising and marketing, professional writing, and organisational communication or as a service course in health, welfare, administration or business.

Our aim has been to write a text that could be used in first year courses in any of these programs, but which also has enough depth to be useful to students in the later years of their degree. The book covers some of the key areas in communication studies, has a variety of exercises, comprehensive current references, a glossary of key terms separated into chapters, and a teaching appendix with instructor's guide.

Scope

There are several differences between this text and others currently available. Australian texts, some of which are adaptations of American ones, have concentrated mostly on the media or on interpersonal and business communication. There are also many American and British texts available in these and other areas. In contrast, *Critical Communication* has several distinctive features:

- It aims to introduce a variety of theoretical approaches sympathetically, without caricaturing or exaggerating any particular viewpoint. The text is critical *about* communication and its theories.
- The account of language (Chapter 2) incorporates philosophical and linguistic approaches.
- The text emphasises the importance of critical thinking (Chapter 4).
- Its scope is considerably wider than that of traditional texts in that it covers aspects of both interpersonal, small group, organisational and mass communication (Chapters 5, 8, 9–10 and 11).
- It has two chapters on intercultural communication that deal specifically with Australian multiculturalism in the 1990s (Chapters 6 and 7).
- It has a final chapter that discusses international communication in terms of Australia's experience with globalisation and the uses of new communication technologies in the South and North-East Asian region.

Assumptions

Communication is a hybrid discipline in which different topics require different methodologies. We attempt to present topics in terms of the appropriate methodology, while encouraging students to think critically about the topic. Accordingly, an analytic approach to language and nonverbal communication is presented early in the book, whereas the chapters on interpersonal and small group communication are relatively functionalist.

Throughout *Critical Communication,* ethical dilemmas are treated in the context of situations in which they arise. North American texts tend to present ethical issues as a separate exercise at the end of a chapter. We have chosen not to do this. A variety of views about advertising standards, misrepresentation in the media, ethnic discrimination and gender equity programs in organisations, for example, are presented in the text. Students and instructors may locate these topics in the context of their own professional specialisations and debate their own view of ethical standards.

While most of the communication theories outlined in this text come from North American, European and British sources, they need to be located in an Australian context. Multiculturalism is one distinct feature of Australia, as is the unique experience of Australian Aboriginal society, and attention to neighbouring Asian cultures. We have attempted to be aware of these varying cultural perspectives. But equally distinctive, if often harder to define, is our Anglo-Australian culture which has developed over the past 200 years. This gives Australians and New Zealanders an outlook, style and sense of humour which is distinct from that of their British and European ancestors.

Critical Communication does not aim to teach 'communication skills' by a series of rote exercises. A considerable number of exercises are included, but our purpose is to clarify the often confusing multidisciplinary sources of communication theory and to demonstrate the applications of communication theory to a diverse range of communication contexts. There is nothing so practical as good theory.

Finally, we are aware of a number of postmodernist debates, which have had a strong impact on social theory. Postmodernism has made us sensitive to multiple perspectives both within and between theories. While we accept some of the new perspectives offered by recent theorists, we also consider students may appreciate a survey of communication studies which seeks to balance both critical and functional perspectives and is not ashamed to speak with an Australian accent.

Acknowledgments

Many people have assisted. We are grateful for their help. They bear no responsibility for mistakes we have made. For a critical reading of chapters or portions of the text, we thank Professors Belle Alderman, Peter Forrest, Bill Mandle, Errol Martin, Philip Pettit, Jack Smart, Brian Stoddart, Bill Ticehurst; and Michael Booth, Alice Caffarel, William Grey, Robert Hamilton, Peter Haynes, Sarah Hollis-Bennetts, Deborah Jenkin, James Kesteven, Jennifer Kitchener, Michael Leigh, San McColl, Ian McDougall, Peter Menzies, Jenny Millea, Denis Robinson, Rob Schaap, Jane Simpson, Diana Slade, Ruth Sless, Bill van der Heide, Sun Wanning and Jing-Huey Wei.

For discussion and support, we also thank Professors Don Aitkin, Malee Boonsiripunth, Myles Breen, Patricia Gillard, Harry Irwin, Elizabeth More, Graeme Osborne, John Penhallurick, John Passmore; and Michael Anderson, Elisabeth Auvillain, Pauline Bannerjee, Bob Boynes, Diana Bromley, Kathy Burns, Pru Goward, Carole Kayrouz, Ki-Sung Kwak, Susan McDougall, Mandy Martin, Satendra Nandan, Suzanne O'Neill, Bobby Patton, Ricky Puru, Diana Rahmin, Anne Ross-Smith, Siti Solikhati, Lee Thayer and Mary Vincent.

For other assistance, we thank Peter Cruttenden, Louise Elliott, Joan Lawson, Yvonne Lipscombe, Margaret Pasfield, Michael Tutalo, Helene Walsh and Sue Wright.

We particularly wish to thank Geoff Pryor of the *Canberra Times* for allowing us to use his fine cartoons, Xu Bai-ming for his photographs, the University of Canberra Research Committee for assistance which has contributed to the preparation of this book, the Board of Studies of New South Wales for permission to reuse material in Chapter 4, Joy Whitton and Katie Millar of Prentice Hall for exemplary editorial assistance and the Prentice Hall manuscript readers for their suggestions.

Theories and models of communication

Objectives

After completing this chapter you should be able to:

- understand the way communication models represent different facets of communication;
- describe a range of transmission theories of communication;
- describe meaning-based accounts of communication;
- recognise that there are relationships between communication, power and culture;
- identify research methodologies in terms of the communication contexts to which they are appropriate.

Chapter 1

He is, they tell me, the one surviving speaker of his tongue. Half a century back, when he was a boy, the last of his people were massacred. The language, one of hundreds (why make a fuss?) died with them. Only not quite. For all his lifetime this man has spoken it, if only to himself. The words, the great system of sound and silence (for all languages, even the simplest, are a great and complex system) are locked up now in his heavy skull, behind the folds of the black brow . . . It is alive still in the man's silence, a whole alternative universe, since the world as we know it is in the last resort the words through which we imagine and name it; and when he narrows his eyes, and grins and says 'Yes, boss, you wanna see me?', it is not breathed out . . .

The Only Speaker of His Tongue, *David Malouf*

'The only speaker of his tongue' is an Australian Aboriginal man who works in a road gang. The men he works with are English speakers. His own mother tongue will disappear with his death, since the rest of his tribe were massacred. David Malouf in this story movingly portrays a man cut off from his own language. The man who is 'the only speaker of his tongue' can communicate in English: he answers questions, for instance. Yet, in another sense, he cannot communicate fully, as he could in his mother tongue. Those modes of speaking and interacting with others are cut off from their source, no longer embedded in the society that gave rise to them. Is communication just getting a message across, or is it more — understanding another person well enough to grasp how they see and talk of the world? Can we ever 'understand' someone whose language is unrelated to our own?

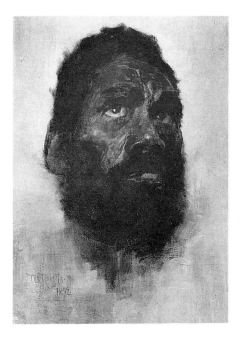

Aboriginal Head, Charlie Turner, *1892*
Tom Roberts, Australia 1856–1931, oil on canvas on paperboard, 39.4 x 29.8 cm, Art Gallery of New South Wales, purchased 1892. Used with permission.

When we think of communication, we think of people chatting over coffee; of a radio broadcast; of spoken or written language. We are told that there is a communication revolution; that the world has become a 'global village'. News is transmitted almost instantaneously, via satellite or cable; New York will soon have 150 cable television channels, some interactive; there are virtual reality games in most cities and the developed world keeps in contact by phone or fax or electronic mail. Yet communication is more than the ways we communicate: it affects how we act in and perceive the world.

The familiarity and difficulty of communication

We are so familiar and dependent on communication that it is difficult to identify what communication is. Just as we are made aware of how important our eyes or our toes are when they do not function, so unexpected breakdowns in communication make us aware of how important communication is in our lives. Communication can break down in many ways. The complete annihilation of a language is an extreme case. The image of a communicator whose language can no longer be used to communicate, like Malouf's Aboriginal man, is a shocking one, in part because of the violence implied by the destruction of an entire tribe, but also because we are aware of the isolation that a man would feel, cut off from his language. It is a feeling which, in a lesser way, we all sometimes experience.

Consider a range of different cases. Communication breakdowns happen when we lack a common language, when travelling for instance. Even then, using gestures or maps, we can often communicate. Yet gestures and maps may not suffice. Once, lost in the last Aramaic speaking town of Syria, we hauled out a map to ask for the road to Damascus, *Shams* in Arabic. The response was startling: the map was turned up and down, handled, laughed at, but never interpreted as a map. Even *Shams*, said with a querying tone, failed to elicit an arm wave. The Aramaic speakers did not understand our conventions of maps and direction asking.

At another level, communication often fails between English speakers, when it is not just a matter of misunderstanding the words. Many mother tongue English speakers have great difficulty in understanding the Australian accent — indeed, in the 1970s some Australian films were dubbed for the North American market! Within languages, too, it is not just a matter of understanding the words. An anecdote was reported by an English teacher of a recently arrived overseas student who was relatively fluent in English. The student had met an Australian at a party who said, on leaving: 'Well, great to meet you. You must come over some time and have a meal.' A week later the recent arrival went to the English teacher in distress and asked how he might have offended his new Australian friend. 'He asked me for dinner last week and has never said when I should go.' The recent arrival failed to know that in Australian English the form of words: 'You must come over for a meal some time', is more a formula to signal farewell than a direct invitation.

Communication may fail when there is no obvious source of incomprehensibility. Sometimes technology fails us — such as a bad telephone line, an unclear fax, or interrupted reception on a television. Sometimes, there is a misfit between our expectations and those of the people we communicate with. In a job interview, an overconfident applicant may think she has done well, while the interviewing panel may regard her behaviour as pushy. It is not just how the applicant speaks, but how she moves and holds herself, which gives her away and communicates.

Chapter 1

Even within the family, where there is a shared language and an understanding of behaviour patterns, communication breakdowns are endemic. A teenage child comes home, walks into the house and slams the door. He is upset and doesn't reply when asked by his mother how he is. 'Why can't she work it out?' he wonders. He goes to his room, turns his radio on very loudly. 'What's the matter with you?' his mother asks, hoping to help. He yells 'Nothing' over the noise of the radio. 'What do you mean?' she replies. 'You're obviously upset.' He mutters to himself 'No one understands me.' Both mother and son feel misunderstood, isolated, unable to communicate. The very words each of them use seem to have different meanings. Yet each would like to be able to communicate clearly. It is not easy to identify just what has gone wrong. They speak a common language, know each other well and have a fund of experiences to draw on in interpreting each other. There is no straightforward technique to solve this communication breakdown.

Communication breakdowns are the rule, rather than the exception. Even when we understand more about communication, we may not be able to avoid communication breakdown. Having a theoretical knowledge of communication does not guarantee that we can communicate better than someone else who does not have that knowledge, but it does mean that we understand better what communication is. This text sets out to identify and show how to circumnavigate some pitfalls in communication, and to explain, in the process, how we can conceptualise the processes of communication.

Exercise 1.1 Communication breakdowns
Note down an example of communication breakdown that you have encountered recently. What was it that caused the breakdown?
   Was it language, technology, culture or some other factor?
   What could have been done to prevent the communication breakdown?

The study of communication

Only connect.
Passage to India, *E.M. Forster*

According to the *Shorter Oxford English Dictionary*, communicate, from the Latin meaning to 'impart' or 'share', has inherited those meanings and has broadened to mean 'converse', 'transmit' or even 'open into', as in 'two rooms communicate with each other'. **Communication** is the sharing of ideas, knowledge or feelings. So defined, communication is something done by people, not by machines. We could not convey ideas or knowledge unless it were understood, so the definition assumes there is more than one person involved and that understanding is, to some extent at least, achieved. **Communications** in the plural has a different sense. It has come to refer to the technologies and media used to transmit ideas, information and entertainment. Notice that this definition refers to machines, to the hardware and software they involve and does not assume any more than that ideas, information and entertainment are transmitted.

Communication theory is about both communication and communications. Very often the two concepts are conflated, so that what is true of machines, which is called the **mechanistic** approach, is assumed true of people. The

---

communication
The sharing of ideas, knowledge or feelings.

communications
The technologies and media used to transmit ideas, information and entertainment.

mechanistic models of communication
Models based on the idea that human communication resembles communication between machines.

difficulty is that the two notions are difficult to separate entirely. People use machines to communicate and machinery itself does not communicate — it only aids people. Consider mass communication. Some theorists concentrate on print and the audiovisual media. Other researchers investigate the emerging technologies of cable television, interactive computers and virtual reality. They are interested in *communications*. Others are interested in advertising and 'ratings'; others again are interested in who owns the media and their economic implications, while others concern themselves with how the media influence the way audiences understand the world. Here, the audience is conceived as people, communicators understanding the world, rather than as elements of a technical and technological process. The focus is on *communication* and the way people acquire knowledge.

The academic discipline which focuses on communication is known variously as **communication studies**, communication and communications. The topics dealt with in the discipline are very wide-ranging, covering theories of communication, processes involved in communication and the contexts in which communication occurs. At one extreme, communication studies merge with cultural studies; at the other, with information science. Between these extremes, communication studies draw on a variety of disciplinary sources, ranging from literary theory and philosophy through social psychology to the computer sciences.

communication studies
The disciplinary field concerned with the study of communication.

In this text, we concentrate on people communicating, in language and nonverbally, agreeing and disagreeing, producing reasons, communicating between themselves, in small and larger groups, across cultures and within their own culture, interacting with the mass media. People act to fulfil their goals on the basis of reasons determined by the social, physical and personal contexts in which they find themselves. One focus will be communication between people, in which we include theories about language, nonverbal communication, reasoning, and small group and intercultural communication. Another focus is organisational, mass and international communication. In approaching these **contexts** or settings of communicative acts, this introductory chapter will explain how the broad field of communication can be understood in terms of distinguishing theories of communication (see Table 1.1).

contexts
The setting of communicative acts.

Table 1.1 *Contexts of communication*

Intrapersonal communication	• Communication with oneself
Interpersonal communication	• Communication between individuals
Small group communication	• Communication in groups
Organisational communication	• Interpersonal and group communication in organisations
Intercultural communication	• Interpersonal and group communication between people from different cultures
Mass communication	• One-way broadcast or print communication

Models and theories of communication

Models, whether in communication or in other fields, serve certain purposes. Models of the same thing are justifiably different if they serve different purposes. Think of models of aircraft. A paper plane models certain aerodynamic properties of gliders — a good paper plane glides. Wooden and plastic models resemble aircraft in another respect — they resemble the external appearance of the planes, perhaps a World War II bomber, but are a different size and often do not fly. Flight simulators resemble aircraft in yet another respect: they model the machinery and controls of the cockpit for the purpose of training pilots. It would be ridiculous to say the flight simulator was a bad model, because it failed to fly, or because it did not resemble the external appearance of a real plane.

Notice that, while models often represent the object they model, whether in two or three dimensions, not all representations are models. This painting by Bob Boynes is called 'Flyover and Tower'. It represents a freeway and a tower block, but does so quite differently from a town planner's drawing. Boynes' painting is similar in certain respects to a real flyover, but his purposes are complex. He wishes to suggest that life rushes past as cars rush along the freeway, and his tower's isolation represents the isolation of people. The purposes served by the painting may not be exhaustively specifiable.

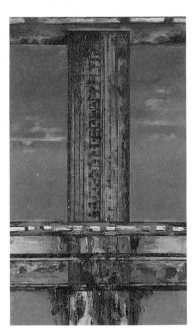

Flyover and Tower, *1990.*
Oil on canvas, 214 x 120 cm.
Courtesy of the artist, Bob Boynes.

communication model
A simplified representation of some feature of communication which is similar in some crucial and specifiable respects to an original; models simplify, aid in prediction or explain complex events.

A **communication model** is a simplified representation of some feature of communication which is similar in some crucial and specifiable respects to an original. As McQuail and Windahl (1981: 1) point out, 'a model seeks to show the main elements of any structure or process and the relationships between them'. Models are often presented as two-dimensional diagrams. However, no model can represent all features of the modelled object or process without being

Theories and models of communication

an exact replica. Models serve to simplify, so as to make understanding easier. They may aid in prediction, as economic models are supposed to; or may be designed merely to organise or explain complex events. There is a tendency to think of one model of communication as correct or complete and all others as incorrect. It may be true that there is one best model for satellite traffic, but it is unreasonable to expect one unique model for the entire range of communication and communications. In so far as models simplify, they omit features of the original. There is always a danger that a model might simplify too far, and distort the original.

Communication models serve as the basis of theories of communication. **Communication theories** are extended representations of communication processes that seek to explain or classify essential features. What both communication models and theories have in common is that they imply that there are regularities in the communication process which can be studied systematically. Without models and theories there can be no way to understand the complexity of communication. Unlike models, however, theories purport to give a complete account of the phenomena described. A theory articulates the generalisations that may be implicit in a model, but are not explicitly stated. Chaos theory, for instance, is a set of statements about the nature of the world: one which states that a butterfly moving its wings in one corner of the world can have catastrophic consequences in another. This is the theory on which Pryor's cartoon is based: he suggests that the Mabo dispute, about native title to land in Australia, could, like a butterfly fluttering, split the country. His cartoon represents the theory, but is not itself a theory: the theory is a set of statements.

communication theories
Extended representations of communication processses that seek to explain or classify essential features.

Chaos theory.
Source: G. *Pryor,* The Canberra Times, *8 June 1993. Used with permission.*

We take the view that it is best to draw on a range of communication theories and models derived from a variety of other disciplines. In the next section, we turn to models and theories of communication based on the mechanistic models of communication. These are useful in certain contexts, but are not the best models for communication between people. In the following section, we look at models and theories of communication based on the notion of communication as meaning — the idea that in communication people attempt to understand each other. For convenience, the terms 'models' and 'theories' will sometimes be used interchangeably, though it should be remembered that a theory is an extended explanatory account of communication, while a model is essentially a simplified representation of the theory.

Exercise 1.2 Models of communication
Consider the purposes that a model of communication will serve for you. Are you planning to work in advertising, public relations or nursing? Do you need to conciliate, or work in groups or an organisation? Will you work with language or with images in the media? List the aspects of communication likely to be of most interest to you. Keep the list — you may find you have omitted aspects which you later find interesting.

Transmission theories and models of communication

Communication, claim Rue and Byars, is the 'transmittal of understanding' (1980); Dessler talks of the 'exchange of information' (1982) (both quoted in Axley, 1984: 430). Someone completely unaware of communication theory may say: 'He just cannot put his thoughts into words.' Each of these remarks about communication already encapsulates a model of communication. It is a model of communication that sees communication as a form of delivery. The assumption of all these definitions is that there is something that communication delivers or, in the case of communication breakdown, fails to deliver. From this perspective, **transmission models of communication** map the pathways communication takes, and assume that information, understanding and thoughts travel along those paths as if they were objects.

In fact, historically, just such models of communication have dominated early versions of communication theory. In part, this was a result of communication theory serving to describe communications — the emerging technologies that enabled instantaneous communication over distances. For instance, communication was often equated with transport (Osborne, 1982). It was the effort to describe how transmitters such as the radio sent 'messages' and how they were 'received', successfully or not, that led to the development of formal models of communication. At their crudest, such models of communication identified a **sender** (the transmitter), a **receiver** and the **medium** through which the message passed. **Noise** is anything which interferes with the successful reception of the message.

transmission models of communication
Models that map the pathways communication takes, and assume that information, understanding and thoughts travel along those paths as if they were objects.

sender
The transmitter or source of a message.

receiver
The person or object that receives a transmitted message.

medium
The particular channel through which messages, converted into signals, are sent.

noise
Any element that interferes with the successful reception of a message.

```
                    message
     sender ─────────────────────────▶ receiver
       +              medium              +
     noise                              noise
```

In the case of radio, the medium is the atmosphere through which the electromagnetically encoded sound waves passed. Noise could be the crackle of an atmospheric storm, or the hum due to a fault in the receiver or transmitter. In the case of a newspaper the medium is the newsprint that constitutes the newspaper. For a newspaper, a sender is the journalist or editor, the receiver anyone who reads the news and noise anything that interferes with the transmission of the message, such as a blot of ink.

Notice that, even in describing the mechanical processes of communication, this model is overly simplistic. Even to describe the most basic forms of machinery, such as a Morse code machine, used for early telegraph, we need the notion of code. A **code**, in this context is a system of signs (see O'Sullivan et al., 1983, for alternative definitions). The notion of code has been taken over into communication theory somewhat uncritically, as if codes were meaningful messages in themselves. As we see in the next section, this is already a simplification. The machine does not take a message as input. It takes a coded form of another message, originally in language, turned into dots and dashes. The receiver then decodes. We need to add another stage to the model:

code
A system of signs.

```
                        message
sender–encoder ─────────────────────────▶ decoder–receiver
       +                medium                    +
     noise                                      noise
```

The radio transmitter transfers sound waves into another form and the receiver turns them back into sound. But sound itself is still not meaningful, except in so far as it exists in a language known to the receiver. At some level there is a further coding process, into a language. In adapting these models based on machines to illustrate interpersonal communication, one fundamental adaptation is necessary. People both send and receive messages, so each source, or sender, is also a receiver.

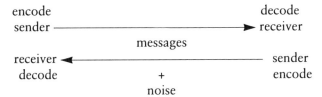

In these models of interpersonal communication, people are seen as encoders and decoders, senders and receivers. Noise is anything that may interrupt the flow of information: an accent that is difficult to interpret, or a setting that makes the transfer of information difficult, whether that is a literally noisy train station, say, or a difficult situation, such as an interrogation, where psychological factors intervene. The medium is talk or writing or gesture — whatever we use to communicate.

This model treats people as machines which have a coded set of information they pass from one to the other. It is a model which existed implicitly long before communication theory and which has been made explicit by communication theorists. Shannon and Weaver's (1949) model is an instance of this type of model. Carey (1989) followed a long tradition of calling such models 'transmission models'.

Lasswell (1948) presented the transmission model in the form of a question. Since the model describes the way information or understanding is transferred, we can identify the major parts of the process, according to Lasswell, by asking:

Who	(sender)
said what	(message)
in which channel	(medium)
to whom	(receiver)
with what effect?	(function)

> **functional models of communication**
> Models that define the communicative process in terms of the functions — or effects — of communicative acts.

Notice that this question adds an emphasis on the function of the message. **Functional models of communication** define the communicative process in terms of the functions — or effects — of communicative acts. The notion of an effect specifically separates the message sent from the effect it produces. This is important, as we don't always interpret the behaviour of others or even their words as they intend them to be interpreted. In the mechanistic models this is a surprising fact, which can only be due to noise or the receiver's misunderstanding of the code. Yet, as we know, communication is a far from reliable business, even under wellnigh perfect conditions.

> **process models of communication**
> Models that identify communication as a series of messages to which the receiver responds, and to which the sender may then in turn respond.

Process models of communication are models which identify the communication as a series, or loops, of transmitted, received, interpreted messages, to which the receiver responds, and to which the sender may then in turn respond with feedback. The model treats the gap between the intended and received message as an explicit facet of the model. Let us define the intended message as that intended and sent by the sender. The perceived message is the message as received by the receiver. This may often be very different from the intended message.

> **feedback**
> The message the source receives when their original message is received, interpreted and responded to by a receiver.

Feedback models of communication build in the process of reinterpretation, much like a computer program or a cybernetic model. **Feedback** is the message the source receives when their original message is received, interpreted and responded to by a receiver. Communication then consists of a spiral: an intended message is encoded into a spoken message, that is received and decoded into a perceived message, to which the receiver produces an intended response. This is then encoded as a spoken response, which is in turn decoded by the original sender into perceived feedback, to which the original sender then formulates an intended response, encodes it as a spoken response which is decoded again as a perceived feedback and so on. The important insight of such models is that the effect of a message may differ from the intended effect (Figure 1.1).

sender(**S**) ➤
  S's intended message **M1**➤
    S's encoded message **M2**➤
      Hearer's (**H**) decoded message **M3**➤
        H's perceived message **M4**➤
          H's intended response to M4, **R1M4**➤
        H's encoded response **R2M4**➤
      S's decoded version of H's response **R3M4**➤
S's perception of H's response **R4M4 (feedback)**

Figure 1.1 *Feedback and process models*

> **context dependence of communication**
> The fact that the setting of communicative acts affects the import or meaning those acts have.

Sophisticated versions of these models of communication allow for a wide variety of factors. The context of the communicative act needs to be recognised. Some models do allow that communication is **context-dependent** — in so far as the setting of communicative acts determines the import or meaning those acts have. People do not talk the same way in a night club and a church; the style and topics of talk at a formal dinner are very different from the forms of talk and topics in a university refectory. The intended audience is also an important factor — the way you talk with a friend is not the appropriate way to talk to a professor. A further important factor is the background of the communicators. Their beliefs will make a difference both to what they communicate and how they interpret others. The basic model, however, is one in which information, understanding, meanings or thoughts are transferred and modified in the process of communication. While the process and feedback models allow for modification of the message, the underlying assumption is that messages are specifiable objects which can be passed back and forth, while being modified in the process.

These models of communication model the transfer of information. It is not surprising that these models often resemble flow charts or wiring diagrams or, in the sophisticated versions, cybernetic diagrams, since they are based on the assumption that communication involves sending messages along a path, or channel. Of course, except when machines are being used, communication does not literally use channels or pathways. The communicating brain may be modelled as a pattern or network of channels, but that too is a model. What is more, the information or understanding or thoughts we 'convey' when communicating are not objects of a familiar kind at all. Meanings, if they *are* objects, are not physical entities which can be transported.

We do, of course, speak of 'getting our meaning across' and of 'having our ideas blocked', much as if meaning were physical objects. But this is a way of speaking, which cannot be spelt out literally. Michael Reddy (1979) labels this sort of image 'the conduit metaphor' — a metaphorical way of talking about communication which, according to him, systematically misleads our understanding of the process of communication. The 'conduit metaphor' treats meanings as passing along conduits, or channels: it is a certain type of model of the communication process that we have called the transmission model.

There are many circumstances for which the transmission models are entirely appropriate. Indeed, managers who are interested in, say, how memos move through an organisation, or a computing specialist who wishes to track a fault in the system, require a transmission model of the flow of information. Process and feedback models of communication are both elaborate and sophisticated versions of transmission models which, by allowing for the modification of messages, succeed in modelling aspects of interpersonal communication. Moreover, the very clarity and power of the transmission model has meant that it has dominated the way that communication — and communications — are conceptualised by governments, media and communicators themselves.

Exercise 1.3 Chinese Whispers

Those of you who are familiar with the game of Chinese Whispers, so-called because few English speakers understood Chinese, will recognise the distinction between intended and perceived messages. Try it. Members of a group — at least eight members are best — sit in a circle. One person begins with a simple message, which they whisper to their neighbour, and so on around the circle. When it comes back to the originator, compare the two messages. Now illustrate the path of the message using the process model of communication, labelling the intended and perceived messages. What is feedback in this game? What is the conduit, or channel, of communication? Do you think we are surprised by the distortion of the message in this game because we believe the conduit metaphor?

Meaning-based theories of communication

Transmission models of communication concentrate on the communication process and the paths messages may take. In contrast, theorists from a number of different fields begin their enquiry into the nature of communication with questions about meaning and understanding and how it is that ideas and thoughts arise and are identified. These various approaches are couched in the language and structures of different disciplines and are sometimes incompatible with each other. We deal with them here as models that see communication as the sharing of meaning.

Meaning-based theories of communication give a central place to the notion of meaning in communication although they define 'meaning' in many ways. How do meanings arise in a group? Some theorists argue that meanings are relatively stable products of social interaction, having the force of conventions. One can imagine a convention arising in a group, say, that a wave means farewell. Suppose that on one occasion, someone raises an arm in farewell, and others see that the person then departs. Among the same group, the next raised arm may well be recognised as signalling a farewell and become a convention in the group.

Conventions occur when a group adopts a form of activity either by explicit agreement, or by implicit and possibly unconscious accord. Many conventions are non-linguistic, such as waves; others are linguistic, such as a cry of 'help'. Conventions have the force they do because, consciously or not, those party to the convention don't just recognise the particular convention, say that 'help' means help or a wave means farewell. They also recognise that others will expect them to use the convention meaning help by crying 'help' or say goodbye by the wave; and they expect others to make sense of what is done in the light of those conventions. The very fact that others are believed to conform to the convention is, in itself, a reason for conforming (Lewis, 1969). Thus, conventions are essentially social — they are embedded in the context of the social groups who adhere to the rules they give rise to (Pearce & Cronen, 1980).

Some theorists, such as Kress (1988: introduction), suggest that meanings are negotiated in each conversation, in each social interaction. Meaning then is conceptualised as flexible but, presumably, with a core of stability — as if, to use Aristotle's image, the boat is rebuilt as it floats, with each plank of meaning replaced in turn. Postmodernist theorists (McGuigan, 1992) think of meaning as essentially indeterminate. Yet other theorists conceptualise meaning as representable in terms of a complex calculus of descriptions of the world.

Transmission accounts are also concerned with meaning, to some degree. Feedback and process models of communication, for instance, describe how each act of communication involves the modifying of meanings. However, these models differ from meaning-based approaches in that they assume that speakers have already formed intended messages which they then encode into a language. But the questions arise: How are these intended messages understood? Is there a language of thought, as some theorists suppose? Is that language similar to the spoken language?

The questions involve a debate between transmission and meaning-based views about the order of explanation. Can we assume meanings, then explain communication in terms of intentions, or do we need to explain meanings to

---

meaning-based theories of communication
Accounts that give a central place to the notion of meaning in communication.

conventions
The behaviour arising when a group adopts a form of activity either by explicit agreement, or by implicit and possibly unconscious accord.

specify the intentions in the first place? Transmission models often assume that meanings are decided by individuals, independently of context, and can be produced and altered at will. For transmission theorists, the meaning is independent of the channel of communication, whether that be language or a telephone line. For meaning-based theorists, on the other hand, language is itself a social activity, located in a context which is defined within a speech community and responsible to it. We, as speakers and interpreters, cannot intend or perceive meanings that are totally divorced from the understandings of others. Meaning itself is a product of the social groups which adhere to accepted conventions and is hence in part defined by the channel of communication. The very objects we perceive are defined by interaction and language.

A story by the Argentine novelist Borges, *Averröes' Search,* vividly presents the relation between perception and social and linguistic context. The tale is set in Spain at the time of the Moorish occupation, when Aristotle was being translated into Arabic by Averröes, as he is known in English. It was by this route that Aristotle's work reached Western Europe. Averröes is translating a section that deals with drama — comedy and tragedy. However, Averröes comes from a culture in which the representation of people in art was forbidden, so he cannot conceive of the meaning of the word 'drama'. Even when he sees from his window small boys pretending to be a *muezzin* calling worshippers to prayer, he cannot imagine what a drama might be. The perceptions available to Averröes are limited by his upbringing and his language, so that he is literally unable to perceive the world in the way that we, with an acquaintance with drama, are able to.

The point is that perception of objects is not a straightforward recognition of things. It is a learned process, in which the way we see the world is inculcated by parents and community. The forms of communication, the ways we act and explain our own and others' actions (Pettit, 1993), themselves establish the objects we recognise. Perception is not a passive process, whereby the world passes us by and we lie back and watch the passing show, as if it were a particularly absorbing television program. Perception is an active process of learning, then structuring the elements of our world. The sociologists, Berger and Luckman (1966) used the catchy phrase 'the social construction of reality' to describe this aspect of perception. The American symbolic interactionist sociologist, Goffman (1959; 1974) uses the phrases 'the definition of the situation' and 'frames'.

For many theorists, the argument that perception is a function of social interaction can be carried over to an even stronger claim, that the world we see is determined by the language we speak. This is a contentious and much debated view, called **linguistic relativism**: the claim that each language embodies a way of conceptualising the world, and no one way is correct. This claim has often been associated with Whorf (1956), and is frequently expressed as the view that the understanding of the world implied by possession of a particular language is accessible only to speakers of that language.

Certain Aboriginal groups of Central Australia use a language of spatial reference very differently from the fashion common to Indo-European language families (Levinson, 1992). Instead of referring to directions in the familiar way, translated as 'right of here', 'left of here', they always use cardinal directions,

linguistic relativism
The claim that each language embodies a way of conceptualising the world, and no one way is correct.

translated as 'to the north', 'to the west-south-west' and so on. In describing an object in a store, they will not say 'It's to the left of the counter', but instead refer to its being, say, in the north-east corner of the store. For a learner of these languages, a complex calculation must be done each time they receive a direction — where is north, they wonder. For speakers of these tongues, on the other hand, there are different problems. They must first orient a map to their true north before they can understand it, for instance. According to many theorists, the very idea of how the world is — how space is defined — is different for speakers of the Central Australian languages than it is for the Indo-European groups.

David Malouf was making this point when he said, in the passage quoted previously, that 'the world as we know it is in the last resort the words through which we imagine and name it'. He was suggesting that the use of language defines the world. Of course, this is a theoretical view, and one that has been challenged. Many theorists question the extreme versions of this claim, asking whether this means that no one can ever understand concepts from a new language — or even new concepts. Among specialists in Aboriginal languages there is a more specific concern: that claims of linguistic relativism may be used to exclude Aboriginal people from working as, for instance, engineers, since they lack conventional Western concepts of space and time.

A more reasonable claim of linguistic relativism is that some concepts are language specific. The weaker claim is defensible, because there are groups whose concepts and perceptions, 'frames' in Goffman's (1974) terms, differ from our own. But it does not in any way suggest that we cannot acquire or come to understand others' concepts; nor indeed does it mean that we cannot weigh up and assess the truth of ideas in other languages translated into our own. What it does suggest is that we must be wary of too simplistic a view of the concepts expressed in other languages, and too ready a belief that we understand.

Exercise 1.4 Language and meaning

Consider again David Malouf's story at the beginning of this chapter. Will the death of the last speaker of a tongue mean that concepts from that language have disappeared? Do we need to be completely fluent in a language to understand the concepts used in that language? Can new concepts and new languages be created in isolation from a group?

Related questions arise in the following:

'When I use a word,' Humpty Dumpty said, in a rather scornful tone, 'it means just what I choose it to mean — neither more nor less.'

'The question is,' said Alice, 'whether you can make words mean so many different things.'

'The question is,' said Humpty Dumpty, 'which is to be master — that's all.'

Alice Through the Looking Glass, *Lewis Carroll*

Can Humpty Dumpty use words as he chooses? Can anyone create their own language?

Communication, power and cultural relativism

Many theorists of communication — and in particular of the mass media — are concerned not so much with primarily linguistic accounts of meaning, but with the issues arising from the question of how language and meaning are controlled by those in positions of economic or political power. Underlying this concern is the belief that ideas and therefore people can be manipulated by feeding only certain types of information to them — 'thought control'. For instance, control of the mass media in the former Soviet Union was intended to have the effect of regimenting the ideas of Soviet citizens. As Lenin said: 'Why should a government which is doing what it believes to be right allow itself to be criticised? It would not allow opposition by lethal weapons and ideas are much more fatal than guns.'

The assumption is that the way the mass media present events will inevitably limit people's views of the world. Many theorists adopt this view in order to criticise the presentation of the world given by the media. For example, McQueen's *Australia's Media Monopolies* (1977) argued that the commercial media were dominated by large monopolistic groups and that advertising was the central purpose of the media. His view was that the media therefore presented the world in the advertisers' terms, and that consumers subsequently swallowed that world view uncritically.

Such accounts share with early transmission accounts the assumption that the source alone determines the meaning and impact of the message conveyed: unlike more sophisticated transmission and meaning-based approaches. Windschuttle (1984) modified this determinist view of the functions of the media in his book *The Media*, and argued that TV news was not an objective form of reality, but a form of popular culture like entertainment and drama. Most recently, Australian theories of the media have moved further away from the transmission model assumption of a passive audience to the view that audiences actively interpret the media (Nightingale, 1993). These views have been influenced by feminist perspectives which have directed attention to previously little studied areas of popular culture on television, and to the way, for instance, that women engage with, rather than merely view, soap operas (Ang, 1985).

Other theorists have extended the wave of discussions generated by McLuhan's (1968) claim that the new media would alter the world into a 'global village', in which the rapid dissemination of news and the common cultural products, such as American soap operas, would overtake home-grown products. Here, **culture** is conceived not as 'high culture' in the sense that the opera is culture, but as the ideas, beliefs and practices of a group and the products they engender (Williams, 1961). There is a concern that cultures and subcultures will disappear under pressure of globalisation. **Cultural relativism**, the view that meaning is relative to a culture, is often associated with this concern. If cultures determine meaning, then globalisation affects not just superficial aspects of a culture, but how people think and speak. Awareness of cultural relativism has made us reluctant to question the social mores of another culture unless we understand it fully. However, cultural relativism in its stronger forms has distasteful consequences. There are actions, such as infanticide or female circumcision, or the sentencing to death of British writer Salman Rushdie by Iran's Ayatollah Khomeini in 1989, that we wish to insist are wrong whatever the internal practices of a culture might be. The extreme cultural relativist would be committed to allowing each culture its own assessment of such actions.

culture
The ideas, beliefs and practices of a group and the products they engender.

cultural relativism
The view that meaning is relative to a culture.

Chapter 1

administrative communication models
Models that draw on traditions of US communication research that aim at applying the results to the benefit of business or government.

critical communication models
Models that take the purpose of communication research to criticise in the public rather than in the private interest.

The complex relations between language, communication, culture and thought have interested theorists from a wide range of disciplines and traditions. Communication and cultural studies have drawn on a range of intellectual traditions, including both the social sciences and humanities, from computer science, psychology, history, economics and philosophy. As well as drawing on different disciplines the field has been strongly influenced by feminism, Marxism and postmodernism (Milner, 1991). In that context, the very possibility of communication has been questioned (Easthope, 1990: 82–83). However, certain broad categorisations of approaches to the study of communication are current.

Frequently, transmission models have been identified as North American, or **administrative**, since these models draw on traditions of communication research used in the United States with the aim of applying the results to the benefit of business or government. On the other hand, meaning-based models are often identified as European or **critical**, as these models take the purpose of communication research to criticise in the public rather than in the private interest. Such research has often been critical of business and government. Although these distinctions are helpful, they are also too simple, as there are critical North American communication scholars (Grossberg, 1989) and flourishing schools of cultural studies in the United States. There is also a long-established American emphasis on communication as linked with studies of speech and persuasion (Barnett Pearce, 1990). Similarly, there are a number of administrative British and European communication researchers who prefer to rely on quantitative research methods (Gunter, 1987).

The tradition of both the transmission models of communication and of the meaning based theories, however, concentrates on American and Western experience. Dissanayake (1988), a Sri Lankan scholar, makes us aware of the new directions communication theories may take when the full impact of non-European theories and modes of understanding the world is taken into account. He argues that non-Western and Asian societies should adapt Western communication theories to rich local cultural traditions rather than directly importing them. The Asian Mass Communication and Information Centre (AMIC) has firmly placed Asian communication studies on the wider global agenda and regional issues have become the focus of recent research in Australia (Slade & Applebee, 1993). Whether or not we accept the principle of cultural relativism, it is essential to consider non-Western views of communication and communications (Lewis & Osborne, 1993).

Exercise 1.5 The conduit metaphor
Much of the discussion of the links between power and communication is framed in terms of the conduit metaphor, explained earlier. Does the quotation from Lenin at the beginning of this section assume a transmission model of meaning and the conduit metaphor? The conduit metaphor is ubiquitous — you will find it in the newspapers, on the television and in ordinary conversation. Take one half-hour segment of television or radio, or casual conversation, and note down instances of the conduit metaphor. A group might allocate each member one area to look at and compare the examples they come up with.

Research methods and communication

We have drawn a contrast between two types of theories of communication: on the one hand transmission models, on the other hand meaning-based theories. Associated with these alternative views of communication are different research methods and underlying **methodologies**, or views of how research should be conducted. Transmission approaches to communication characteristically develop research methods which aim to measure whatever they are examining — interpersonal perceptions or organisational climate, for instance. Very often these methods will be **quantitative**, and use statistical measures to understand society. The assumption is that the observer does not disturb the data, that is, that the observer can record objective data.

These methods are frequently also decompositional, in that studying a communication process will be broken down into studies of each stage of the process — the coding, the reception, the feedback and so on. Most research of any sort must be decompositional in so far as it identifies categories in terms of which the analysis proceeds. The transmission models are decompositional in a particular sense, in that they identify categories which are suitable for numerical quantitative analysis. So, for instance, High Definition Television is developed as a means of encoding messages more efficiently. Optical fibre offers a technological medium of delivery less liable to noise than other forms, while satellite delivery is an alternative medium. Research might compare and evaluate the costs and consumer preferences for these technologies. Similarly, television or radio ratings give the numerical measure of choices between programs, essential knowledge for advertisers.

The actual content of the messages sent by television can also be measured. Cultivation analysis (Gerbner & Gross, 1976) is a form of content analysis which, together with self-reporting, counts how often certain topics occur on television in terms of the proportion of content. Other theorists measure the impact of television in terms of the changes in behaviour that might ensue. The psychologist, Albert Bandura (1967), for instance, used laboratory-based measures of violence to test whether children would hit a doll directly after watching a violent program (Lowery et al., 1988: 306). Underlying these methods is often the methodological view that communication can be **decontextualised**, that is, considered in isolation from the social context in which it occurs. Moreover, the research methods of transmission theories are typically reductive, that is, there is an assumption that the study of these processes can proceed in a piecemeal fashion, spelling out and reducing the processes of communication to its components.

Not all decompositional accounts need be reductive or decontextualised. Indeed, many contextually sensitive accounts proceed by identifying features of the situation or levels of analysis by which to organise material. Meaning-based models often assume that meaning must be located in a culture and that methods for understanding meaning must appreciate the role of social influences. In this sense, rather than being reductive, meaning-based theories are often holistic — they look at the role of communication primarily from the perspective of the entire culture. These analyses are generally highly **contextualised** in so far as the events described are set in the physical, social and cultural context of which they form a part. It follows that these methodologies

methodologies
Views of how research should be conducted.

quantitative research
Research that uses statistical measures to understand society.

decontextualised research methods
Those that consider acts in isolation from their social context.

contextualised research methods
Those that consider acts in the physical, social or cultural context of which they form a part.

Chapter 1

qualitative research
Research that uses non-numerical techniques for understanding society.

reflexive research methods
Those that take the researcher to be part of the research and see the researcher's purposes as crucially affecting the data.

are frequently **qualitative**, because they use techniques for understanding society which are not statistical. For example, in the analysis of television, methods are used which are similar to those used in anthropology: observation and description of the activities of television viewing as if those activities were part of an alien culture. Moreover, such methods are frequently **reflexive** in so far as the researcher is regarded as part of the research, and the researcher's purposes as crucially affecting the data.

Much recent audience research (Palmer, 1986), for instance, concentrates on the role of the television in the home, how it is used — whether as a background noise or as children's entertainment or as concentrated adult viewing — and the social circumstances of television users. The approach is to identify the role of television in a culture or subculture, to see whether it is an alternative to other forms of entertainment, and to locate the viewers as an 'active audience', not just passive receivers. Other theorists (Cranny-Francis, 1988) look at the meanings engendered by television programs, the cultural role of those meanings and the views of the world implicit in programs. Television is seen as an important component in culture, rather than as just one set of processes among many. Recent studies of other elements of communication, such as the telephone, have emphasised the context of telephone use, rather than technological data. Moyal (1992) shows how essential the telephone can be for social contact between isolated women. The telephone is more than the equipment: as the cartoon shows, it, too, belongs in context.

Telephones are used in context. Source: *G. Pryor,* The Canberra Times, *2 June 1991. Used with permission.*

Table 1.2 summarises the broad differences between the two approaches.

Some theories cut across the divisions, and not all theorists subscribe to every element of the characterisation. Indeed, modern theory tends to draw on a variety of models. However, the classification serves the purpose of simplifying a range of communication research. The appropriate methodology for a communication research project needs to be determined in part by the aims of

Table 1.2 *Two approaches to communication*

Transmission	Meaning-based
Transfer of meanings	Creation and negotiation of meaning
Quantitative	Qualitative
Decontextualised	Contextualised
Reductive	Holistic
Objective	Reflexive

study. It would be absurd to try to assess the 'noise' level of satellite-transmitted programs, relative to those sent by optical fibre, without using quantitative measures. Equally, it is difficult to imagine an account of the meaning of television programs which did not, explicitly or implicitly, make reference to the culture of which it is part.

Certainly, there are substantial disagreements between those who subscribe to one or the other view of communication. Yet in many cases, the two approaches are complementary, not alternatives. A full understanding of the effect of television violence, for instance, requires quantitative information about the levels of violence, an anthropological understanding of the role of television viewing in the lives of people and of how television characters influence behaviour, and a rigorous analysis of how these factors interact (Tulloch & Tulloch, 1992).

We have called this text *Critical Communication* because we aim to make the assumptions of models of communication apparent and open to question. Far too often in communication studies, a contrast is drawn between two alternative approaches to communication — the administrative and the critical, the quantitative and the qualitative — as if there are no other views (Fiske, 1982). While we have in this chapter replicated this to some extent, we do so only because it offers a useful introductory classification of theories of communication. In understanding communication we need a variety of theories for a variety of purposes. The following chapters will aim to explain and assess each approach relative to its purposes.

We begin with language, as the most powerful of our communication systems. We then turn to nonverbal codes and reasoning. Thus, we implicitly accept the claim of meaning-based theorists that an account of meaning is prior. We next approach issues of interpersonal, intercultural and multicultural communication and the analysis of small groups. We look at communication in organisations, at the media and the international context in which we communicate. While we approach each topic in terms of its own purposes, we adopt a critical, sceptical and deflationary attitude to theory. We thus take what is itself a theoretical position, a reasoned critical view of theory.

Exercise 1.6 Two views of communication
Divide into groups of three. Read Tables 1.3 and 1.4 and one excerpt each from the sources listed in 'Further Reading'. Now allocate roles to each student — one to defend a meaning-based approach, another a transmission approach and the third, a

compromise. Draw a sketch of the model of communication you defend. Then individually attempt the writing exercise, aiming to present succinctly the ideas you have discussed in your groups.

Table 1.3 *Transmission models*

Level	Interpersonal/ small group	Organisational	Mass
Models	Relationships considered in terms of social exchange	Organisations considered as mechanisms or systems	The effectiveness of media programs in winning maximum audience share
Topics	Persuasion and compliance gaining Communication competence	Communication flows Network links Structure	Quantitative audience measurement Demographics Ratings
Skills	How to analyse, participate in and manage communication in interpersonal, group, and intercultural settings	How to analyse, participate in and manage communication in organisations	How to make radio, TV and film programs How to write and market stories

Table 1.4 *Meaning-based models*

Level	Interpersonal/ small group	Organisational	Mass
Models	Relationships considered in terms of the interpersonal creation of meaning	Organisations considered as cultures	The social and cultural uses audiences make of media
Topics	Gender differences Communication	Organisational culture	Qualitative audience research
Skills	Theories of language Reasoning	Interpretive theories	Ethnographic studies Media analysis techniques

Writing exercise

Very briefly summarise the debate between transmission and meaning-based views of communication and defend the one you prefer. Your exercise should have the structure:

- Introduction — definitions of the two views.
- Describe the transmission approach — advantages and disadvantages.
- Describe the meaning-based approach — advantages and disadvantages.
- State your preference and reasons.

Summary

1. Communication scholars study a range of topics, from issues related to how people communicate in groups, to the communication structures of large organisations and the mass media, through to communications technologies. Communications refer to the technologies whereby people communicate or share ideas and knowledge.
2. There is a variety of contexts of communication studies, namely: interpersonal communication; small group communication; organisational communication; intercultural communication; mass media and telecommunications; and international communication.
3. Historically, communication research developed from studies of machines used to communicate over a distance and models of communication resembled models of the machines — they were mechanistic.
4. Transmission models of communication model the process of moving information. Such models range from the simple to the complex, and have been used mainly to model mass communication. Transmission models are appropriate for the description of a range of communication activities, are frequently reductive and use quantitative methodologies.
5. Meaning-based models are designed to model meaning. Meaning-based models are often holistic and use qualitative methodologies. Both types of models will be used in this text.
6. The different topics of communication research require different models of communication and different research methodologies. American research approaches may be labelled as administrative, and Anglo-European as critical, although these labels are simplifications.
7. The development of Australian and Asian perspectives on communication study is relatively recent. Australian approaches currently are a hybrid of the dominant American and European schools.

Discussion questions

1. Are breakdowns in communication necessarily failures in communication?
2. Should we try to communicate with others in the same way as they communicate with us?
3. Can you identify your own model of communication between people?
4. List some of the features which differentiate mass and interpersonal communication. Can you represent those differences in a model?
5. Do you have a model of mass communication — of the newspapers or the television news, for instance? What is it?
6. The transmission model is sometimes described as the 'hypodermic needle' model of communication. Can you suggest why?
7. Notions of meaning are notoriously difficult to specify. Artificial intelligence models meaning on computers. Do you think there may be theories of communication which develop the idea that our minds are like computers? Would they be transmission or meaning-based or both?

8. Can a dog make a mistake and know that it has?
9. A term which is often used in discussing alternative theories is Kuhn's (1962) notion of 'paradigm'. Kuhn argues that scientists are not objective seekers after truth, but set their research agenda — and their research methods — in terms of the subculture, or paradigms, of their scientific community. He then suggests that there is no point in comparing different paradigms. Does this hold true of communication research paradigms?
10. What research methods seem most suitable for the area of communication you are interested in?

Further reading

Civikly, J. (1981) *Contexts of Communication* New York: Holt.
Dissanayake, W. (ed.) (1988) *Communication Theory: An Asian Perspective* Singapore: AMIC.
Kress, G. (ed.) (1988) *Communication and Culture* Sydney: UNSW Press.
McQuail, D. & Windahl, S. (1981) *Communication Models* London: Longman.
Reddy, M. (1979) 'The Conduit Metaphor', pp. 284–324 in A. Ortony, (ed.) *Metaphor and Thought* Cambridge: Cambridge University Press.

References

Ang, I. (1985) *Watching Dallas* London: Methuen.
Axley, S. (1984) 'Managerial and Organisational Communication in Terms of the Conduit Metaphor', *Academy of Management Review* 9 (3): 428–37.
Bandura, A., Ross, D. & Ross, S. (1967) 'Imitations of Film Mediated Aggressive Models', *Journal of Abnormal and Social Psychology* 66: 3–11.
Barnett Pearce, W. (1990) 'The Historical Context of Communication as a Science', pp. 1–21 in G. Dahnke, C. Fernandez-Collado & G. Clatterbuck, (eds) *Human Communication* Belmont, CA: Wadsworth.
Berger, P. & Luckman, T. (1966) *The Social Construction of Reality* New York: Doubleday.
Carey, J. W. (1989) *Communication as Culture* London: Unwin Hyman.
Cranny-Francis, A. (1988) 'The Moving Image: Film and Television', pp. 157–80 in G. Kress, (ed.), (1988).
Cunningham, S. (1992) *Framing Culture: Criticism and Policy in Australia* Sydney: Allen & Unwin.
Cunningham, S. & Turner, G. (eds) (1993) *The Media In Australia* Sydney: Allen & Unwin.
Dessler, G. (1982) *Organisation and Management* Virginia: Reston.
Easthope, A. (1990) ' "I gotta use words when I talk to you": Deconstructing the Theory of Communication', pp. 76–88 in I. Parker & J. Shotter, (eds) *Deconstructing Social Psychology* London: Routledge.
Fiske, J. (1982) *An Introduction to Communication Studies* London: Methuen.
Gerbner, G. & Gross, L. (1976) 'Living with Television: The Violence Profile', *Journal of Communication* 26 (2): 173–99.

Goffman, E. (1959) *The Presentation of the Self in Everyday Life* Harmondsworth, UK: Penguin.
Goffman, E. (1974) *Frame Analysis: An Essay on the Organisation of Experience* New York: Harper & Row.
Grossberg, L. (1989) 'The Contexts of Audiences and the Politics of Differences', *Australian Journal of Communication* 16: 13–36.
Gunter, B. (1987) *Television and the Fear of Crime* London: Libbey.
Kuhn, T. (1962) *The Structure of Scientific Revolutions* Chicago: University of Chicago Press.
Lasswell, H. (1948) 'Communication in Society', in L. Bryson, (ed.) *The Communication of Ideas* New York: Harper.
Lealand, G. (1988) *A Foreign Egg in our Nest? American Popular Culture in New Zealand* Wellington: Victoria University Press.
Levinson, S.C. (1992) 'Language and Cognition: the Consequences of Spatial Description in Guugu Yimithirr', Working Paper no. 13, *Cognitive Anthropology Research Group*.
Lewis, D. (1969) *Convention* Cambridge, Mass: Harvard University Press.
Lewis, G. & Osborne, G. (1993) 'Asian Communication Studies in Australia', *Electronic Journal of Communication* 3 (3 & 4).
Lowery, S. & DeFleur, M. (1988) *Milestones in Mass Communication Research*, New York: Longman, 2nd edn.
Malouf, D. (1985) 'The Only Speaker of His Tongue', *Antipodes: Stories* London: Chatto & Windus.
McLuhan, M. & Fiore, Q. (1968) *War and Peace in the Global Village* New York: Bantam.
McGuigan, J. (1992) *Cultural Populism* London: Routledge.
McQueen, H. (1977) *Australia's Media Monopolies* Melbourne: Widescope.
Milner, A. (1991) *Contemporary Cultural Theory: An Introduction* Sydney: Allen & Unwin.
Moyal, A. (1992) 'The Gendered Use of the Telephone: An Australian Case Study', *Media, Culture and Society* 145: 51–72.
Nightingale, V. (1993) 'Media Audiences', pp. 267–96 in S. Cunningham & G. Turner, (eds) *op. cit.*
O'Sullivan, T., Hartley, J., Saunders, D. & Fiske, J. (1983) *Key Concepts in Communication* London: Routledge & Kegan Paul.
Osborne, G. (1982) 'Communication' — see Transport, pp. 153–68 in G. Osborne & W. Mandle, (eds) *The New History: Studying Australia Today* Sydney: Allen & Unwin.
Palmer, P. (1986) *The Lively Audience: A Study of Children Around The Television Set* Sydney: Allen & Unwin.
Pearce, W. & Cronen, V. (1980) *Communication, Action and Meaning* New York: Praeger.
Pettit, P. (1993) *The Common Mind: An Essay in Psychology, Society and Politics* New York: Oxford University Press.
Rue, L. & Byars, L. (1980) *Management: Theory and Application* Homewood, Illinois: Irwin.
Shannon, C. E. & Weaver, W. (1949) *The Mathematical Theory of Communication* Urbana: The University of Illinois Press.

Slade, C. & Applebee, A. (1993) *Media Images of Australia: Cross Cultural Reflections* Canberra: Canberra Centre for Information Research.
Tulloch, J. & Tulloch, M. (1992) 'Tolerating Violence: Children's Responses to Television', *Australian Journal of Communication* 19 (1): 9–22.
Whorf, B. (1956) *Language, Thought and Reality* Cambridge: MIT Press.
Williams, R. (1961) *The Long Revolution* New York: Columbia University Press.
Windschuttle, K. (1984) *The Media* Melbourne: Penguin.

Language in context

Objectives

After completing this chapter you should be able to:

- understand a variety of definitions of language;
- recognise four levels of linguistic analysis
    — significant sounds and words
    — sentences
    — pragmatics (sentences in context)
    — discourse (extended passages of language use);
- explain theories of the sign as they apply to language;
- discuss gender differences in the use of language.

Chapter 2

Language is like a cracked kettle on which we beat out tunes for bears to dance to, while all the time we long to move the stars to silence.

Madame Bovary, *Gustave Flaubert*

We communicate in many ways. We call out, we wave, we sit deep into the night over coffee discussing our feelings or we elaborate our ideas according to a plan in a debate or a university essay. We identify ourselves by the way we speak, by the way we move, by the way we dress: each move we make or fail to make may have meaning to others. Of all forms of communication, however, it is language which is the most remarkable. As Flaubert says, language may be intractable and inadequate to our purposes; nevertheless it is immensely powerful.

The changes in the way we view language are themselves an indicator of how important language is. Foucault's (1973) *The Order of Things* describes how changing linguistic models reflect our conception of how we find out about the world. Language used to be thought of as almost magical, as if just knowing words for objects gave power over them. In the mediaeval fairy story of Rumpelstiltskin, for instance, the princess is given a task: of discovering the curious and uncommon name of the anti-hero, who will then be in her power. Guessing someone's name seems to us now an absurd task, since names do not really 'belong' to their bearers. Yet, in mediaeval times, finding the correct word for an object would, it was thought, enable people to understand the object and thus the secrets of the world. The code of language was seen as reflecting the inner structure of the world.

We now no longer think that names belong to their bearers. We know that we could call a horse by another name, *cheval*, maybe, or *ma*, if we spoke French or Chinese. Yet we also believe that different languages classify the world in different ways, and that it may not be possible to translate a word or phrase completely into another language. All too often, English speakers assume that they can make themselves understood anywhere, as if language were transparent. The previous chapter should make us wary of such simplifications.

In spite of the sophistication of international structures, comprehension across linguistic barriers is immensely difficult. The biblical story of the Tower of Babel tells the mythic tale of the origin of a multiplicity of languages. Disturbed that the peoples of the world, sharing one language, could build to the heavens, God destroyed the Tower and 'did there confound the language of all earth'. It is not merely different languages that create problems. There are problems of incomprehension between speakers of one language or even one dialect. Indeed, it *is* as if language were magical. Understanding the language of a group does give you power. Politicians rise and fall with the force of their rhetoric, their ability to speak persuasively. Speaking the right way gets you the job you long for, social entrée or the respect your ideas merit. Language is the most powerful, but also the most complex, of communication systems. In this chapter we shall consider some aspects of language as a communication system.

Languages and definitions

Definitions of language focus on various aspects of language. Lewis (1974) describes two broadly different types of approach. On the one hand, there are

Language in context

Tower of Babel, *1563, Pieter Bruegel, the Elder, Kunsthistorisches Museum, Vienna. Used with permission.*

definitions of languages as systems that assign meanings. In communication theory, such definitions describe languages as codes, or systems of rule-governed symbols — sounds, words, sentences, pragmatic features, discourse structures — to which meanings are assigned.

On the other hand, language is described as a social phenomenon or, as Kress (1988: 183) puts it, 'the most fully articulated of all media of human communication ... a socio-political construct, encoding cultural values'. Language influences how we see the world and the way we act in it and the second type of definition aims to articulate these facts. What is the connection between these two types of view of language?

We can draw a link by appeal to the notion of convention. Recall the definition from the first chapter. Conventions are rule-governed activities, in which a group adopts a form of activity either by explicit agreement, or by implicit and possibly unconscious accord. In the case of language, there is an implicit agreement to use particular words with the meaning they have in our language community. However, we do not separately subscribe to a series of conventions, allocating each word its meaning, since words have meaning only in the context of the language of which they are part. Words take their meaning from the sentences and contexts in which they are used. Indeed, a language has no force outside the group of people who are party to the convention, who use the language for their particular purposes. Speaking a particular language is a matter of convention (Peacocke, 1976). Thus, we can go some way to reconciling the two types of definition. A **language** is a system which gives resources for people to assign meanings to words, sentences and discourse structures, by virtue of being used in interaction.

Apart from the broad differences in types of definition of language, there are several competing accounts of how to analyse language. Philosophers, psychologists, linguists and communication scholars each approach the task of analysing language from different perspectives and with different purposes. Certain philosophers, for instance, wish to draw out the logical structure of language; others to 'deconstruct' or uncover the assumptions built into particular ways of talking about the world; a social psychologist might wish to

language
A system which gives resources for people to assign meanings to words, sentences and discourse structures, by virtue of being used in interaction.

27

emphasise how language reveals personality through social interactions; some linguists attend to the functions or the grammatical relations within language, while sociolinguists and ethnographers look at the use of dialects within social groups.

Communication scholars have used all these approaches. We begin with an overview of different levels at which we might choose to concentrate in analysing language, from the narrowest level of sounds to the broadest social context. This approach is in essence a decompositional approach, as characterised in the previous chapter. Nevertheless, it is important to recognise that only at the broadest level do we have an account of meaning.

Exercise 2.1   Pronunciation
Can you identify some differences of pronunciation within the group you are working with? You may consider accents of those of non-English-speaking background (NESB), and regional differences of Australasian students. Is there a contrast between students from city and country regions? Do you think men and women speak differently? In what respects? Prepare a list for discussion.

To what extent do you judge educational level and likely occupation from different accents? Listen to a talkback radio program or watch a soap opera, and guess occupation and educational levels. Now think about how you judge people by their accents. Discuss whether accent is always a reliable guide to education and occupation.

Levels in the analysis of language

Frail colonial poetry . . . the very italics in which it was printed had the charm of fine wheat. It fell delicately onto the mind and sprouted there.

The White Topee, *Eve Langley*

In an extended metaphor, the Australian novelist, Eve Langley, decomposes a poem into 'the very italics in which it was printed'. It is not usual to think of a poem at the level of the typescript, though certain poets, notably e. e. cummings, have insisted on a certain visual presentation of their poems. What Langley is doing is to move from one level of analysis, of the sense or meaning of the poem, to another, of the typescript. The idea of different levels of linguistic analysis has been much used by linguists, although they have rarely concentrated on typescript. Instead, linguists have conceptualised the analysis of language in levels.

The level of significant sounds and words

A spoken language consists of sounds. They are written down as letters but, as we know all too well in English, the way a letter is written is not a reliable guide to sound. The 'a' in 'all' is quite different from the 'a' in 'apple'; the 'p' in 'put' is entirely different from that in 'philosophy'. The very first task in a systematic account of sounds is to devise a reliable system of writing the sounds. Most languages are written phonetically, in terms of the sounds: English, Arabic, Hindi, Indonesian, Russian, Tagalog are. Chinese, on the other hand, is written with pictographs, which are not phonetic.

Devising a phonetic alphabet is not the end of the problem. Consider English. An 's' sound can vary from a hiss at the end of a word to a softer sound at the beginning. Do we need to represent the 's' differently? The answer is: only if the differences in sound make a difference to the meaning of words containing it. In English, there is a significant difference between 'p' and 'b'. That is clear because we have a minimal pair, 'pin' and 'bin', differing only in one sound, here between 'p' and 'b', which mean different things. We say that /p/ and /b/ are different phonemes in English, and write them between slashed lines.

A **phoneme** is a sound which makes a significant difference in a language. Notice that the definition of a phoneme uses the notion of a significant difference — one that makes a difference to the meaning. We define this level of language using the higher level of meaning. We do not reduce meaning to the lowest level. The difference between 'p' and 'b' is not phonemic in Arabic because there are no words differing only in that sound which have different meanings. Monolingual Arabic speakers have difficulty in hearing the difference. Indeed, this is why, in the capital of Yemen, Sana'a, a sign proudly announced 'Parper' to label a barber's shop: for Arabic speakers, the distinction between /p/ and /b/ is very difficult to discern.

The Australian version of English differs phonetically from New Zealand, British, North American and Indian English. In particular, the vowel sounds we use in Australia differ from the English and North American versions. Characteristically 'broad' Australian vowels are formed by adding an extra 'eh' within syllables. New Zealanders have a different /i/ sound from Australians, so that the number six is pronounced rather like 'sex'. Within Australia and New Zealand, there are further variants in pronunciation, depending on where you come from and where you have been educated.

The **morphemes** of a language are those sounds or sound complexes that are meaningful. 'Flimp' is not a meaningful word in English although it is phonetically possible; 'slump' is. There are meaningful syllables which are not whole words — some are grammatical, such as the particle 'ing' as in 'stopping', 'racing' and so on; while others modify meaning, as 'un' meaning 'not' in 'unable'. The grammatical and meaning-modifying morphemes of a language stay relatively constant over time, but the particular words used in a community can change rapidly. For instance, in Australia there are variations in the names used for the apparel worn when swimming: 'bathers' in South Australia, 'swimming costume' or 'cossie' in New South Wales. Communities tend to develop their own specialised vocabulary or jargon. Jargon can be necessary as a form of shorthand for complex concepts and for speed of communication. In this chapter, for example, it is useful to use the notion of 'convention' rather than spell out at length the definition used above. It is academic jargon. Jargon can also be used to exclude or create a social group — indeed, academic jargon often serves this purpose as well. While communities tend to create new words — to neologise — in order to simplify and create social bonds, there is the converse tendency to harmonisation with the common language. This is imposed by the necessity to communicate, by the media and by the entire process of schooling, which teaches a standard literary form to all. In Australia, radio and television have been factors acting against regionalisation of our vocabulary.

phoneme
A sound which makes a significant difference.

morphemes
Those sounds or sound complexes that are meaningful in a language.

> **sense**
> The particular way a name identifies an object.
>
> **referent**
> The object referred to.
>
> **denotation**
> The core object to which a word refers.
>
> **connotation**
> The overtones, or colouring, of a word.
>
> **metaphor**
> Where the literal meaning of a word is not so much altered as used falsely.

Two commonly used distinctions are those due to Frege (1952): between **sense** (the particular way a name identifies an object) and **reference** (the name of the object it refers to, or its **referent**); and between denotation and connotation. The **denotation** of a name is its core referent, but **connotation** refers to the overtones, or colouring, of the word. For us, the name Pluto for a dog is faintly ridiculous, since the connotations are those associated with a comic strip character. Connotations can be far more dangerous, particularly when pejorative expressions for social groups are considered. 'Bitch' and 'female dog' have, in their primary meaning, the same denotation, but different connotations: to call someone a 'female dog' may not be offensive.

Many accounts of meaning stop at the level of words. Dictionaries do just this — they define the meanings of words. However, a dictionary is only of use to someone who already speaks and reads at least some of the language. If you did not know some words of a language, a dictionary would be useless. Moreover, even if you understand many words of a language, a dictionary might be useless for discovering the meaning of an unfamiliar word. That is certainly so if the unfamiliar words are defined in terms of other unfamiliar words, which are themselves defined in terms of the first unfamiliar word. Dictionaries simply cannot avoid some degree of circularity in their definitions.

Even were this not so, dictionary definitions cannot exhaust the meaning of words. Language is used in many ways and words alter their meaning too, not only as a function of context but also in turns of speech such as **metaphor**. In metaphorical uses of words, the strict and literal meaning of a word is not so much altered as intentionally used falsely. When we say of someone: 'He's a pig', what we say is false, but we understand the import of the remark, that is, in some respect the person behaves badly. Metaphor makes us aware that, while dictionary definitions generalise meaning across a range of contexts, we cannot exhaustively define the meaning of words independently of the sentences in which they occur.

The notion of metaphor has been much discussed. Metaphorical thought is very wide-ranging, so that abstract and complex ideas are often understood *via* metaphor (Lakoff & Johnson, 1980). This is in itself neither good nor bad; however, in certain situations, the use of metaphors can obscure issues. Lakoff (1991) argues that the predominance of metaphors from economic theory and from spectator sports in describing the Gulf War literally prevented our understanding war as related to death. When the costs and benefits of war are analysed constantly in economic terms, it is as if lives were commodities. When commentators talk of winning or losing as if war were a football match, it is easy to forget how much more serious the consequences of losing a war are — loss of life and of national sovereignty are worse than a lost football match. Like euphemisms, in which literal expressions such as 'She died' are replaced by indirect formulations like 'She's passed away', metaphors enable us to soften a painful truth.

On the other hand, abstract thought would be impossible without some metaphorical element. Much scientific language is inherently metaphorical, exploiting the fact that metaphors give us a framework in which to classify thought, just as models can create a framework for thinking about the world (pages 6–16). When we think, metaphorically, of light as waves, we are able to design experiments that we could not even conceive of without the metaphor. The metaphors which dominate our thought are not superficial and eliminible features of thought — they are essential to the thought itself.

Exercise 2.2 Jargon and specialised language
Is there a group whose jargon you are familiar with but which is probably unfamiliar to others in your class? You may know surfie jargon or that of graffiti artists or the language of a specialised area: film crews, medicine, sports and so on.

Write a series of six sentences using the jargon. Exchange with your neighbour and get them to translate into familiar terms. Sentences your neighbour does not understand should be set as an exercise for the entire group. When the problem sentences have all been translated, try to identify the reasons for the difficulty in understanding. Is the language highly technical? (Medical language is technical, but so are terms describing complex skating manoeuvres.) Is the language intended to exclude others? What is the difference between jargon which is slang and jargon which is respected? Is there one?

Discuss these issues in class.

At the level of sentences
Sentences, or their spoken analogues, **utterances**, are the smallest complete units in language. While words have meanings, only at the level of sentences are meanings complete. This point can be emphasised by considering the meaning of 'the' or 'a' or 'only'. We cannot give these words a meaning except in the context of sentences in which they occur. We can, however, spell out the difference in meaning between the three sentences below with very little difficulty, by examining their use in context.

> The president smokes.
> A president smokes.
> Only presidents smoke.

Although we may think of words as having meanings, they do so only because we understand them in sentences. We often think that a word like 'dog' means the object (or set of objects) it refers to: namely those four-legged animals that bark. This is a simplification. In interpreting the one-word sentence, 'dog', we assume that it has the meaning of the fully structured sentence 'This is a dog' or 'These are dogs'. 'Dog' uttered alone with different intonations may have a number of different meanings: 'I hate dogs'; 'I love dogs'; 'That dog!'; 'What a dog!' or even 'What a sexually suggestive person you are' (as in 'You old dog'). To use Frege's (1952) tag, words have meaning only in the context of a sentence.

Semantics is the study of meanings. Formal semantics shows how the meaning of sentences is constructed from the meanings of the elements of the sentence. Most formal semantics define meaning directly or indirectly in terms of conditions under which sentences would be true. The meaning of *The dog barks* is given in terms of conditions under which animals referred to as 'dogs' do make the noise known as 'barking': that is, when it is *true* of the dog that it is barking. This appears to be as circular as dictionary definitions and, indeed, there are those who object to some formal semantics on these grounds. Nevertheless, any account of meaning must draw a connection between the utterances of sentences and their acceptability in terms of truth or a related

sentences
The smallest complete unit in language.

utterance
The spoken analogue of a sentence.

semantics
The study of meanings.

notion and 'true' is best defined within a language. The apparent circularity is resolved in classical truth theoretic accounts of meaning by explaining that to give the definition:

The dog barks is true when real animals referred to as 'dogs' do make the noise known as 'barking'

is not to repeat the sentence itself. Instead, the definition spells out meaning by referring to things in the world: certainly things which are themselves identified linguistically — but that is exactly what we want, since without language and the categories it provides we could not define truth at all.

> **syntax**
> The structures that bind words into sentences.

The **syntax** of a language is its grammar: the structures that bind words into sentences. Those structures may depend on word order, as they do in English, or on morphology, as in Latin or Australian Aboriginal languages. A sentence consists of parts which are bound together by the syntactic relations. So, for instance, in a sentence like *The dog barks* a subject, 'the dog', is described as doing something, namely barking. It is the combination of subjects and predicates, nouns, verbs and so on that creates a sentence. The work of Chomsky (1957) revolutionised the study of syntax in linguistics. Chomsky pointed out that it was possible to simplify the description of language, and explain speakers' competence, by showing how syntactic forms were related to one another. He used the concept of a **transformation**, or **movement rule** — a systematic alteration of the syntactic form. Questions in English, for instance, are regularly formed:

> **language transformation**
> The systematic alteration of the syntactic form of sentences.

You have been swimming becomes *Have you been swimming?* by inversion of word order. That transformation is readily described. However, when the verb is in the simple present, *He walks to work* it is necessary to add 'do' to form a question: *Does he walk to work?*

The adding of 'do', sometimes called 'do support', to the verb happens elsewhere in English — with negations and tag questions, for instance: *He walks to work, doesn't he?*

The description of the language is simplified by giving one abstract rule for all these cases.

Such accounts, by concentrating on narrowly defined rules, undervalued meaning. It is the interplay between syntax and semantics at the level of the sentence that is responsible for what is often described as the unique power of language. Language as a sign system goes beyond one-word sentences in so far as it is structured and generative. The structure of language is the semantic and syntactic structure that holds parts of the sentences together. This structure enables us to create new sentences. Let us suppose we understand two sentences: *The cat is grey* and *The man is bald*. Then, by a simple process of re-glueing, we may create or generate a new sentence: *The cat is bald*. We may never see a bald cat, but we can invent and understand the new sentence in virtue of our understanding of the earlier sentences.

Thus, the structure of natural language has two unique features. First, it enables us to generate and understand a potential infinity of new sentences on the basis of the understanding of a finite number of components of the sentences. Secondly, it enables us to generate and understand untrue and nonsense sentences. These two features are a consequence of the interweaving of two aspects of language: syntax and semantics. The meanings available in sentences depend on the structures we can use in generating meanings. As finite beings, we are not capable of grasping or learning an infinite number of meanings. However, we are capable of learning a finite list of vocabulary and a finite list of syntactic rules, which jointly enable us to generate and understand an infinite number of meanings. Meanings relate to the world: to the context. It is the interplay between the strict structures of our language and the rich contextual situation in which our view of the world is negotiated that gives language its immense force.

Exercise 2.3 Sign languages

Is language just another code? What about sign languages? The neurophysiologist, Oliver Sacks' (1989) book on the deaf, *Seeing Voices*, asks why the blind have always been able to take a full role in society, while the deaf were, until the invention of sign languages based on spoken languages in the eighteenth century, literally 'deaf and dumb'. Children who became deaf after first learning a spoken language were not deaf and 'dumb' in this sense: they were able to learn to lip read and function in society. The deaf always had sign languages, with gestures meaning 'yes' and 'no', 'go away', 'food' and so on. But their sign language was limited to one word sentences or commands. Once a sign language develops, a whole new range of meanings become possible for the deaf and they are no longer 'dumb'. Can you explain what the congenitally deaf acquire, that they lack with primitive sign languages, in terms of the account of language above?

At the level of pragmatics

We have explained that the interplay of syntax and semantics at the level of sentences gives language its unique generative power. But the syntax and semantics leave aside the context of utterances, the actual uses we make of language. Even to understand whether a sentence like *I'm hot here* is true we need to know when and where and by whom it is spoken. Context determines truth and falsity in utterances like this one, which refer to the time, or place of the actual utterance, or to the speaker. Such contextual features are sometimes incorporated into semantics. However, they are often called **pragmatics** — that is, the study of features of utterances which depend on the linguistic and non-linguistic context.

A range of different features of language have been labelled pragmatic. Austin's classic work *How to do Things with Words* (1962) explored the notion that language can be used for a variety of purposes, and that speech involves action. Searle's (1969) project was to list the variety of types of acts performed by language use by categorising what he called 'Speech Acts' and describing when, say, a promise or an order had been successful.

For some theorists, an account of the way language interacts with context is best explained in terms of a general account of human rationality. Consider the following example, based on Grice (1975). An academic is asked for a reference by a pupil of little merit. The reference is given, saying only: *Mr X has good handwriting*. Anyone receiving the reference would have doubts about Mr X's academic ability, since the referee chose not to commend it: in effect, the referee manages to condemn the student while remaining polite. Yet the referee's words do not literally mean that the student is inadequate. It is a result of a rational process of interpretation to come to the conclusion that the referee has a

pragmatics
The study of features of utterances which depend on the linguistic and non-linguistic context.

Chapter 2

implicature
Conclusions derived from a statement on the basis of contextual knowledge.

'hidden' message. Grice calls this conclusion an implicature. It is not an implication, since it does not follow from the statement. The **implicature** is the result of contextual knowledge about what referees normally say, the conventions that references should be polite and a maxim — that one ought to be as relevant as possible. Understanding all these things, a reader of the reference can work out the hidden message.

Sperber and Wilson (1986) have developed a theory of pragmatics which describes how principles of maximal relevance are used in understanding language, using the insights of Grice and Searle. In the following conversation between two Sydney-siders, for instance, we must think through why certain responses are made, in order to make sense of the utterance at all.

A: *What do you think about winning the Olympic Games?*
B: *I'll never afford a house now.*

At first blush the reply is quite inadequate and irrelevant to the question. But using the maxim that the speakers are both party to, that one ought to be relevant in language use, A can set about interpreting B and possibly come to believe that B believes that Sydney's winning the Olympics will cause an elevation in house prices. This weakens B's prospects of buying a house and hence B is not pleased about Sydney winning the Olympics. Notice, too, that B's reply is more informative than a direct 'I'm not pleased', since it gives the reasons for the response with the least output of words.

We can use the resources of the maxim of relevance to explain why certain types of speech acts, such as polite requests, have the force they do. Polite requests are, strictly speaking, questions, such as *Can you pass the salt?* Nevertheless, the force of the act is as a request, having the meaning, *Pass the salt, please!* English has a large number of such speech acts which serve, conventionally, a purpose other than that apparent from the grammatical form.

Not all features of utterances in context are of the sort readily transcribed in written language. Stress, intonation, and rate of speech, for instance, can make a great deal of difference to the meaning of sentences, but are difficult to transcribe. For this reason such factors are often called **paralinguistic** features of utterances — features that alter or change the unmodified conventional meaning. They are often talked of as pragmatic or, with less justice, as nonverbal. Strictly speaking, intonation is actually not paralinguistic, but linguistic, and the stress and the rate of speech are genuine features of spoken language, as integral to the message as the written question mark.

paralinguistic features of utterances
Those features that alter or change the unmodified conventional meaning.

Take for instance the three sentences in Figure 2.1.

Off to the cinema?   Off to the cinema!   Off to the cinema?????

Figure 2.1 *Differences in intonation*

In the first, a normal question form with rising sentence intonation gives the sentence an interrogative sense. In the second, a downward sentence intonation gives the meaning of a statement or command. In the final sentence a combination of rising sentence intonation and stress on the first syllable of the final word gives the meaning of incredulity.

Australian and New Zealand speakers of English have been noted for their unusual use of the rising sentence intonation. Even when making a statement, they tend to use the question intonation pattern. So, for instance, someone may appear to be asking 'I'm feeling awful?' because of the rising intonation. It is not normally a question to which others know the answer better than the speaker. In the British context, this tendency of Australians and New Zealanders labels them uncertain of their own minds. In fact it is more likely to be a paralinguistic cultural difference between speakers. In British English, the rising sentence intonation has the force of a question, whereas in Australian and New Zealand English it is used for statements.

Exercise 2.4 Determining meaning

Look at an English or American soap opera. Find an extract in which participants are arguing or joking. Now transcribe a short section of the dialogue. Give the script to students from another cultural background to read through several times and audiotape their version. Try to persuade the students to tape their version without looking at the script.

Now compare the two versions during a class discussion. Do you agree on the meanings and implicatures of what has been said? What are the differences of intonation patterns between students and the original? Would it be easier if the original segment were of shopping?

At the level of discourse

We use language for purposes, to express ourselves and to fulfil our aims in society. In isolation, commands, requests and statements, however well formed in a language, do not make a language: it is the patterns of **discourse**, which we shall first define here as extended passages of language use, that constitute the language. (The notion of discourse is a complex one, and two further definitions will be offered in this chapter.) Discourse is organised in **texts** which are the smallest meaningful passages of social language (Halliday, 1985; Halliday & Hasan, 1985). Texts may be written, but primarily they are spoken passages of discourse (Penman, 1993). Language is a facet of human intentional social activity and must be seen in that context. The previous section emphasised the importance of context to understanding utterances; studies of discourse locate

discourse (1)
Extended passages of language use.

texts
The smallest meaningful passages of social language.

Language is a social process.
(Photo: *Robert Hamilton*)

the linguistic phenomena in a still wider context of human social behaviours, with what one author calls 'sociopragmatics' (Blakemore, 1992: 47).

Discourse is not normally one speaker informing or talking to others: more often we have dialogue between speakers. Language is a social process. Talking and listening, writing and reading, are equally facets of language. This obvious factor about language reminds us that it is not just speaking or writing in a monologue that makes meaning. It is speaking and writing in order to communicate to others that creates meaning. The type of discourse depends not merely on context, but also on purpose. Much discourse serves the purely social purpose of making others feel at ease, what is known as **phatic communication**. 'How do you do?' or the far less formal 'How ya goin'?' is not meant as a request for information — they are merely greetings. Some discourse structures are strictly defined: the interview has a different structure, different listening and speaking behaviours, different grammatical strategies and different meanings from a relaxed chat over dinner, and interviewees ignore those distinctions at their peril.

Some differences depend less on an externally imposed structure than on differences in linguistic style deriving from contextual constraints on language, particularly on syntax and semantics known as differences in **register**. While there are a number of different definitions of register (cf. Kress, 1993: 35), registers are generally agreed to be types of style. For instance, the polite forms of words used in a university lecture differ in register from forms of talk among students. Speakers of a language use a variety of registers, altering the way they talk, their vocabulary and, in written language, the structure of paragraphs, from more formal to casual contexts.

Bernstein (1977) makes a useful distinction between elaborated and restricted codes. An **elaborated code** is the language used with strangers or in formal situations, in which ideas are made fully explicit. The elaborated code tends to have complex syntax and precise vocabulary. Opposed to this, when with groups with whom we are familiar, we tend to use a more **restricted code**, in which we make assumptions about shared knowledge and do not need to spell out ideas in such detail. The restricted code tends to use less complex syntax. Written forms are often based on the elaborated, not the restricted, code. We all use both codes, but certain social groups place less emphasis on the acquisition of the elaborated code, through schooling and at home, than others. Access to the elaborated code facilitates life in the public sphere, where it is the appropriate code. The elaborated code thus gives access to power.

A further useful concept in distinguishing differences between different sets of discourses is the application of the notion genre to linguistics (as described for example in Kress, 1993; Martin, 1985). A **linguistic genre** is the set of principles governing discourse in a particular context of interaction. More strictly speaking, a genre is a staged, goal-oriented social process. Formal and informal talk are different genres; so are scientific articles and historical articles; children's fairy stories and true stories; or soap operas and serious drama. Those differences are a function of the purposes of the type of action and are spelt out in the different ways the genres are organised in stages. To use another form of words, the differences are a result of the structural conventions which govern the production of the articles or stories; conventions which arise because of the role those articles or stories play in social contexts. The conventions governing

---

phatic communication
Communication that serves purely social purposes.

register
Differences in linguistic style deriving from contextual constraints on language.

elaborated code
Language used with strangers or in formal situations, in which ideas are made fully explicit.

restricted code
Language that makes assumptions about shared knowledge.

linguistic genre
The set of principles governing discourse in a particular context of interaction.

each genre are rarely made explicit, but we all know, hearing 'once upon a time' that we have an untrue story; or reading an academic article arranged under headings like 'Aim', 'Method' and so on that we are in the scientific genre. We all tailor our writing and speaking to the conventions governing the type of situation we are in.

In order to describe a generic type it is necessary to describe the stages of a type of discourse and relate them to the purposes they serve. Each type of writing has its particular structure. In Table 2.1, the stages of a technical report are described (Baylis et al., 1993: 3). At each stage, certain types of language are appropriate: an abstract generally summarises what the report is about, and what has been concluded. The introduction states what the context of the report is. The theoretical background uses the present tense in defining terms and discusses what has been argued or shown in the past. In scientific and social scientific reports, methods and results are described, and the conclusion then summarises what has been established. Recommendations suggest what may be done in future.

Table 2.1 *The stages of a report*

Stage	Purpose of stage	Status
1. (Abstract)	• to give the reader general information about what is in the report	(Optional)
2. Introduction	• to state what area of the company the report concerns • to identify the problem to be investigated • to explain the reasons for the investigation • to state the purpose and scope of the report	Obligatory
3. (Theoretical background)	• to define the conceptual background of the investigation • to define and explain key technical terms terms and concepts	(Optional)
4. Methods and procedures	• to provide the rationale for the investigation • to describe the method of data collection and methodology used	Obligatory
5. Findings	• to present, discuss and interpret the findings of the investigation — involves both assessment and evaluation of the results	Obligatory
6. Conclusions	• to sum up the findings and relate them to the original statement of the problem or hypothesis • to present conditions or constraints for the recommendations to follow	Obligatory
7. (Recommendations)	• to make recommendations based on the earlier findings	(Optional)

Source: Baylis, Joyce and Slade (1993) *Improving Your Report Writing* Sydney: Centre for Workplace Communication and Culture.

In different languages, particular discourse strategies are used and considered appropriate for different ends. Many misunderstandings are a consequence of this fact. Misunderstanding register or discourse structures can have disastrous consequences, partly because we find it difficult to allow for failures at this level. If we do not know the word for coffee in another language, we at least know we don't know. If we misunderstand the conventions governing verbal discourse in another culture, we may never know what we have done to offend. So, for instance, all languages have forms which serve as jokes, or which are appropriate for gossip, but the particular ways a joke is structured so as to get the laugh, or what can be gossiped about and how, are culturally specific.

An account of discourse within one culture relies on a general grasp of language use within the culture. Studies from historical and sociological perspectives of the varieties of languages, language families, dialects, sub-dialects, sociolects and idiolects serve to classify social groupings (Montgomery, 1986; Hymes, 1974). English belongs to the language family of Indo-European languages, which includes languages as different as Sanskrit and Latin and German. Historical linguists have shown that these languages share a common underlying structure and even similarities in vocabulary. Arabic and Hebrew belong to a different group — the Semitic languages. There are several very broad divisions of types of English: British, North American, Indian, Australian, African. Within Britain, there are a number of dialects or versions of English which may be mutually incomprehensible.

There are not such extreme differences in Australia and New Zealand, but there are variants. About thirty years ago, Mitchell and Delbridge (1965) did a survey of the speech of Australian adolescents and classified three groups of accent, by vowel sounds. These groups they labelled Cultivated Australian, spoken by roughly 11 per cent of the population; General Australian, spoken by 55 per cent of the population; and Broad Australian, spoken by roughly 34 per cent of the population. They argued that the differences were not so much regional as educational. Accents within each capital city ranged from broad to cultivated, depending approximately on the level of education. However, country people had broader accents than their city peers. The differences they identified have been overlaid by far more complex webs of linguistic styles, with changing patterns of immigration and a more buoyant sense of an Australian national identity. Multilingualism carries its own complex linguistic strategies (Gumperz, 1970; Kalantzis, Cope & Slade, 1989).

Within dialects, there are variations. Sub-dialects may be formed by sub-groups in a society, using particular jargons. Age, gender and social groups have different sociolects; indeed, particular people have their own characteristic ways of talking or idiolects. Nevertheless, no idiolect can differ too greatly from the norm, precisely because a language is a mode of communication. The identification of the subgroup in terms of jargon is just one aspect of the processes of language change, which in turn depend to a great degree on the relations of social and political power. The language of the conqueror may completely displace the languages of the conquered, as in most of Australia, or it can profoundly modify the indigenous language, as French did to the language of England after William the Conqueror. Language is intimately linked to power. Modern studies of language draw explicit links between the power relations of groups or subgroups in society and the modes of talk available (Roberts et al., 1992).

Gender, ethnicity and social class are all defined by and define modes or ways of addressing others, not just phonetically, syntactically and pragmatically, but also in terms of the discourse. The notion of **discourse** used here is slightly different from that used previously. It is a systematically organised set of statements that describes and delimits what it is possible to say. Using this framework, van Dijk (1989) summarises a decade of studies on the link between power and discourse structures. His own work on media discourse showed that ethnic minority groups in first world countries, as well as the entire populations of certain developing countries, are typically reported on in the press in condescending fashion. They were treated stereotypically as a 'problem', assumed to be deficient as compared to our norms and goals and hence in need of outside help. When these stereotypes are presented, it is impossible to take comments from a member of an ethnic minority seriously. Fairclough (1989) extends the model to a systematic study of media discourse during the Thatcher years; Australian studies (e.g. Kalantzis & Cope, 1993) have investigated teaching practices and interethnic relations. The interplay between language, power and society provides at once the most fertile and least easily categorised of the levels of language.

Notice that the levels of language cannot be described independently of each other. Each level of description requires others to be understood. In terms of the distinctions described in Chapter 1, an adequate account of language must be contextualised. Many theorists go further, and claim we need holistic accounts of language. As Wittgenstein (1953) puts it, 'a language is a form of life'. A language is part of a society, and words do not have meaning in isolation from the social context and the purposes they are used for. Meanings are a product of social interaction.

discourse (2)
A systematically organised set of statements that describes and delimits what it is possible to say.

Exercise 2.5   The genres of writing

There are strict conventions governing how written work is structured, both at the level of how the written work is planned and at the level of how sentences are constructed and related within paragraphs. A number of different conventions govern academic writing: an article in history differs from one in physics and both differ from the report writing cited in Table 2.1.

In groups of four, go to the library. Each group should choose one communication journal, such as *Media Information Australia*, *Journal of Communication*, *Australian Journal of Communication*, *Media Asia*, *Media, Culture and Society*, *Cultural Studies* or other journals appropriate to your field. Look at the back or inside the front cover for the instructions on presentation for contributors. They will give you guidelines on conventions of presentation in the field.

Then each read one article from that journal and examine how the introduction, the body of the article and the conclusion relate. Compare with the structure of Table 2.1. Note down any unfamiliar words or syntactic structures. Compare your results within the group and then discuss your findings with the class.

Semiotic analyses of language

The approaches to language analysis above take as their focus different levels of language. This section deals with alternative approaches to language, which are

Chapter 2

semiotic theories of language
Theories that treat language as a system of signs.

at times incorporated into models of discourse analysis. They are **semiotic theories**. Semiotic theory treats language as a system of signs.

C. S. Peirce (pronounced 'purse', 1960), the great nineteenth century pragmatist, distinguished three ways that signs of any type could relate to an object: as an index, as an icon or as a symbol, as in Figure 2.2.

Figure 2.2 *Index, icon and symbol*

index
A sign that indicates or points to its object.

icon
A sign that resembles its object.

symbol
A representation of an object or idea where the connection between the object and the sign is arbitrary.

An **index** indicates or points to an object. So, for instance, the English word 'this' is often used to specify an object, and is called an indexical. An arrow is an index, since it points in the direction of the angle of the arrowhead. An **icon** resembles its object, as a photograph resembles the object photographed in certain respects. Other icons are the use of 'baa' to represent the sound of a sheep or of a curve on a road sign to indicate that the next section of road is winding. A **symbol** is purely arbitrary. Notice that indices and icons often require conventions to be interpreted. An arrow could be used to point in the opposite direction from the normal reading; a picture of a winding road could be read to mean 'snakes in the area'. There is a symbolic component of every sign.

Modern semiotic theory takes as its starting point the work of Saussure (1966) which treats language as a sign system. He argued that linguists have two quite incompatible tasks: the diachronic historical analysis of the development of language and the synchronic analysis of language as a sign system at a particular time. This distinction has set the agenda for modern linguistic theory. Saussure drew a further distinction, that between *langue* and *parole*. When we speak, we often speak in broken sentences and incomplete utterances. For Saussure, it is not our actual words (*parole*) but the underlying knowledge of language (*langue*) that linguists should analyse. Chomsky (1957) followed Saussure in distinguishing between our performance and competence, which allows us to interpret the utterances as meaningful entire sentences. This distinction is one of which some linguists are now wary, suggesting as it does that the actual performance of speakers is less important than some abstract knowledge they possess.

sign
This consists of two components, the signifier, or actual token of a sign, and the corresponding signified concept evoked by its use.

signifier
The actual token of a sign.

signified
The concept evoked by the use of a signifier.

Saussure thought of all **signs** as consisting of two components, the **signifier**, or actual token of a sign, say the word 'cat', and the corresponding **signified** concept evoked by its use — in this case, my concept of a cat. For Saussure, the actual object, a cat, does not enter into the description of the sign (see Figure 2.3).

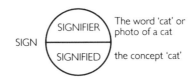

Figure 2.3 *Sign, signifier and signified*

Saussure also talked of **syntagmatic relations** in language — those relations that bind elements of the sentence together. It is these relations which we have called syntactic in the previous section. Saussure contrasts syntagmatic and paradigmatic relations. **Paradigmatic relations** are defined by contrasts within a set of members of a category. At the level of phonemes, for instance, English has a paradigm of dental consonants in which /t/ and /d/ are contrasted; another of labial consonants in which /b/ and /p/ are contrasted. At the level of sentences, paradigmatic relations are the relations between possible alternatives for the same role in a sentence. For instance, in the sentence:

Mary dances well.

the links between 'Mary, 'dances' and 'well' are syntagmatic, whereas 'dances' comes from a paradigm of action verbs, and is opposed to alternatives such as 'walks' or 'sings' or, with respect to tense, to the past form 'danced'. The adverb 'well' comes from a paradigm of adverbs of manner, opposed to alternatives such as 'badly'. Notice that this approach is decompositional, in so far as it identifies elements of language, but not reductive, since the notions of syntagm and paradigm are defined using a higher level of language.

The models and techniques derived from Saussure's linguistic theories have been widely applied to the products of the media — to advertisements, to the products of print and radio and television and to the economic and other factors that influence those products. **Social semiotics** describes the role of signs in society and how social practices constitute signs. Accents, for instance, and particular uses of language serve not only to communicate content but to identify social background. Hodge and Kress (1988) apply semiotic methods to spell out the meaning of a cartoon in which Bob Hawke, a galah, and a crocodile representing the ACTU (Australian Council of Trades Unions) are discussing South Africa. Hodge and Kress (1988: 92) show how a variety of factors in the cartoon contribute to the meaning of each character.

> The ACTU monster is represented as a crocodile, a large, dangerous and primitive reptile (one of the very few survivors from the age of the dinosaurs). It has a number of differences from crocodiles, including a hair-style that is parted in the middle, which seems to be 'short back and sides'. This style, in Australia in 1985, was a sign of both class and generation, referring to 1950's male working class, or middle-aged people who have not modified their style since then.

They go on to discuss the force of particular accents in the cartoon: the ACTU monster uses the broad Australian pronunciation, with open vowels, the characteristic addition of the 'eh' sound and unvocalised consonants ('bewdy' instead of 'beauty', with /d/ instead of /t/), representing the worker class. Hawke's use of the so called closed form of 'Yes', namely 'yep' is seen to contrast with the more laconic 'yair' and suggest decisiveness or pigheadedness. The difficulty with such analyses is that they tend to rely on one or two people's analyses of the force of signs. Many informed readers would spontaneously disagree with the analyses. If, as we have argued, signs take on meaning in a social context, then such analyses must be constrained to what informed readers would agree on.

Semiotic theories drawing on Saussure have since proliferated, passing through structuralism to postmodernism. Saussure's claim was that meaning derives from contrast within a paradigm. Structuralism (Pettit, 1977) generalises the Saussurean view that meaning derives from contrast within a

syntagmatic relations
Those relations which bind elements of the sentence together.

paradigmatic relations
Those defined by contrasts within a set of members of a category.

social semiotics
Linguistic theories that describe the role of signs in society and how social practices constitute signs.

paradigm. Postmodernism, however, rejects the conception that the theorist is in a position to categorise how the structure is organised for others. Derrida (1976; 1977), for instance, rejects the notion that signs have meaning in virtue of signifying meanings as if meanings were objects — what he calls 'transcendental signifieds'. How could we understand such signs? If a sign gains its meaning from the structures or relationships one sign has to others in the paradigm, then, Derrida supposes, there is inevitably one member of the paradigm that is privileged. This gives rise to the 'artificial' privileging implied by analysing language in terms of binary oppositions: for instance, 'good' and 'bad'; 'male' and 'female', one of which is preferable — in this case, the good, the male. Derrida used the French neologism *différance* to describe these binary oppositions. The role of the critic is not to encode these structures, but to **deconstruct** — to lay out the oppositions and displace or reverse the privileged one of the pair.

> **deconstruction**
> The laying out of oppositions and displacement or reversal of the privileged one of the pair.

Other postmodernists have rejected the privileged position of the analyst: our own assessments of others' signs are shot through with our own world view. As Foucault (1973) puts it, we must perform an 'archaeology of knowledge' and discover the **discourses** — the ways of knowing which are the products of social, historical and institutional frameworks, by finding what startles and surprises us about an attitude or a procedure for investigating the world. His own inquiry into the history of thought treated linguistics and the theory of knowledge itself in just this way.

> **discourses**
> The ways of knowing which are the products of social, historical and institutional frameworks.

Exercise 2.6   Analysing language in a cartoon

Consider the cartoon on page 43, which appeared after the amendment to the Mabo legislation, designed to give indigenous Australians very limited rights to native land title, by members of the Green party, holding crucial Senate seats. The images are based on a famous Australian children's story about gum nut babies, written by May Gibbs just after the first war.

How would you analyse the significance of the language used? To what extent could the audience be expected to understand the signs used? Is there any significance in the use of the repeated 'very' ? What is the point of representing politicians as gum nut babies? Write down in note form the relevant definitions, then the factors you find interesting about the cartoon. Prepare to discuss in class.

Gender and language

The discussion of gender and language is a vivid example of how linguistic theory can be used in understanding communication and the difficulties that may arise. Differences in linguistic behaviour are presumably learned rather than due to physiology. Those differences which cannot be traced directly to biological difference are labelled **gender differences**. Most of the evidence relating to gender differences in linguistic behaviour is based on Western societies, although recent studies have generalised the results.

> **gender differences in language use**
> Those differences in use of language which cannot be traced directly to biological difference.

We will present this issue in terms of the levels of linguistic analysis introduced above. Jennifer Coates summarises the evidence in her book, *Women, Men and Language* (1986). Women — and girls — speak a language which is distinctive from that of men at each level of linguistic description. At

Mabo legislation.
Source: *G. Pryor,
The Canberra Times,
25 November 1993.
Used with permission.*

the phonetic level, women tend to use standard or dominant forms, while men tend to use dialectal variants, possibly as a means of identifying with a subgroup (Romaine, 1984). Women use a much wider pitch range than men, and exploit paralinguistic variants more heavily. Similarly, at the level of vocabulary, women tend to use standard or socially acceptable words as well as certain diminutives, while men tend to older forms, slang and expletives. In an extreme form, this is evident in the role of women in adopting an entirely new language. Studies have shown that women have been crucial in the replacement of Provençal by standard French, for instance.

At the level of syntax, women's language differs substantially from men's. Robin Lakoff's classic (1976) study of English, *Language and Women's Place* shows that women use far more tag questions in statements than men. Thus, for instance, we find forms like *The weather's been wonderful, hasn't it?* where the final tag asks for an affirmation. While men also use these forms, women use them far more frequently, possibly indicating a need for affirmation. Women are less likely to use the unmodified imperative ('Do . . . !'), but prefer modalised forms ('We could do . . .'). In rejecting others' claims, they use concessive phrases, such as 'I think . . .' rather than bold negations. More recent studies on this topic are reported in Holmes (1993), where evidence of Maori usage is included.

Perhaps the most interesting and evocative work in the analysis of gender-based distinctions in language use is at the higher level of discourse structures. Deborah Tannen's recent book *You Just Don't Understand* (1991) has received intense attention in the media. She argues that women and men talk differently, women preferring self-disclosure in their intimate conversations, whereas men talk aggressively, in order to dominate conversations. Tannen's examples are almost exclusively North American. A closer analysis of discourse structures in the Australian context can be found in Poynton (1985). Other studies (Ochs, 1992) make it clear that among Samoans, for instance, men are more polite and less verbally aggressive than women, at least on our measures of politeness.

Sociolinguists have documented a range of conversational strategies which differ from men to women and which are liable to cause miscommunication. Coates (1986: 152–5) lists a number of causes of miscommunication. For instance, there are differences in the meaning of questions for men and women. For men, questions are seen as direct requests for information, whereas women use and interpret questions as facilitating the flow of conversation. This difference may explain women's greater use of tag questions, cited above. There are differences in links between speaker turns: men break in with their own opinions or even new topics, whereas women tend to acknowledge previous contributions and listen to others as they take turns. There are differences in attitudes towards self-disclosure, which is an exception in male–male conversation and normal in female–female talk. Coates summarises the differences by classifying men's talk as competitive and women's talk as cooperative.

In the educational context, differences in linguistic style have been widely remarked, and the deleterious effects on girls have received much attention. A range of studies (Gilbert & Taylor, 1991) discusses the implications of the domination of classroom talk by boys. In mixed classes, even in the primary school, boys talk more, and more aggressively, are given more attention — both positive and negative — by teachers and are permitted a wider range of response strategies. For instance, girls are more often asked 'closed' questions, in which the response is a choice of a limited range of responses, whereas boys are more often asked 'open' questions. Stereotypical expectations are fashioned in the talk of the classroom, so that passive 'feminine' behaviour is already implicit in the style of interaction of the primary school. On the other hand, mothers develop particular modes of talking to their children, using restricted vocabulary and simple syntax (Ochs, 1992), which reinforce the gender differences children perceive.

Underlying the differences of forms of talk of men and women and of boys and girls is a social structure in which women have traditionally had less access to the public domain, to the forums in which decisions affecting their lives are taken. There is a social context which is at the heart of the divide between the way men and women talk. In the language of semiotics, our very notion of the feminine — the concept signified by the female — has made it impossible for women to talk like men, by associating the feminine with the concessive forms of language, with listening rather than speaking, with answering closed rather than open questions, with speaking cooperatively rather than competitively. The myth of the feminine is created and reinforced by the presentation of women in literature, in the media and in the characteristic literary genres of romance and soap opera (Cranny-Francis, 1993).

It is because of social injustices that feminist theorists have urged the replacement of forms of language and literary modes which, according to them, reinforce those injustices. Gender as a grammatical categorisation is often assimilated to social difference. These points are made forcefully by Dale Spender (1980), who labels this phenomenon 'he man language'. She cites the following contrasts in meaning: *He's a professional* has overwhelmingly positive connotations — he is a lawyer or a doctor, perhaps. On the other hand, *She's a professional* means she is on the streets, as a prostitute. This may now be changing. In the following list, all the masculine forms have a positive connotation, whereas the feminine forms, while originally having the sense of being a female version of the male form, have changed in meaning, or developed new meanings with pejorative, often sexual, connotations.

Masculine form	Feminine form
governor	governess
master	mistress
king	queen
lord	lady
sir	madam
courtier	courtesan
dog	bitch

You can construct your own examples. For our purposes, it should be clear that underlying social distinctions between men and women are evident at various levels of analysis of language, and can be analysed according to a number of different theories. Among a variety of analyses, Lloyd's (1993) is a study of the historical and philosophical roots of the conception that women are irrational; others explicitly analyse the discourse of power which has made rejection of subjugation literally unsayable.

Perhaps the most interesting recent example is the case of whether pornography in the United States should be protected under the First Amendment as an instance of 'free speech'. Catherine MacKinnon (1987) of the University of Michigan Law School, has argued that pornography, while it is defended on the grounds of freedom from censorship, makes freedom of speech impossible for women. Her argument is that pornography influences some men to misinterpret women and hence literally prevents women from being able to say 'no' to sex, since 'no' is interpreted as a coy 'yes'.

It may not be possible 'to move the stars to silence', as Flaubert puts it, through language. But language is more than mere grammar, or the description of how we speak. Language is the window through which we glimpse the world; and it is the window through which we are seen. Language is a shared activity, apt 'for bears to dance to', to quote Flaubert again, able to mislead, but also to describe and serve our purposes in the world with some accuracy. It is the locus of power, of thought, of communication and action.

Exercise 2.7 Analysing radio talk

Erving Goffman (1981) discusses the particular characteristics of radio talk. It is a conventional language quite different from ordinary conversation. In groups of four, analyse two segments of talk on the radio that are similar in all respects, except that in one, the presenter is male and in the other, female. (The presentation of the news or current affairs are interesting cases. ABC's Radio National Daybreak program is presented by a man and a woman.) Are there characteristic differences between the two in presentation styles traceable to gender differences in language use? Does your analysis confirm or disconfirm the evidence of this section?

Prepare notes on your ideas, allocating the aim of your analysis and general theoretical background to one student, definitions from Goffman and from an account of gender differences in language to another, the description of the material you have chosen to another and the analysis of differences and conclusions to the last. You should prepare a bibliography and reference the material carefully. Present your conclusions to the entire group together with a written summary.

Exercise 2.8 Media texts
Choose three items from the press (newspapers, magazines) and television or radio, which refer to the same event or controversy. You might like to consider a front page story, an editorial and a letter to the editor in the same newspaper; a series of letters to the editor, or front page stories in three different newspapers or magazines; a series of radio reports or television current affairs programs dealing with the same issue; or three items from different media.

Consider the differences and similarities in the presentation of ideas, the assumptions made, in the three cases. Refer in particular to the language used (the use of sub-language and registers peculiar to the medium, the use of jargon, the appeal to signifiers of particular import, the discourse structures and genres and social setting). You may wish to use the different levels of linguistic analysis in your comparison.

Write an essay on the basis of your work. Your essay should be structured as a formal essay. It should begin with an introductory paragraph stating the aim or purpose of your study. You should then describe the materials you have chosen to examine, which should, if appropriate, be included in an appendix. Next you should describe the model of language you wish to apply in your analysis and give suitable definitions. The body of the essay will consist of the comparisons you draw. You should conclude the essay with an explanation of the differences you discern, if possible. A full bibliography will be required, using any acceptable convention (that used in this text is suitable, but there are others) and all references to materials used in the essay should also be noted, either with footnotes or using the shorter form of the Harvard convention (used in this text).

Summary

1. Human language is a means of communication: it is essentially a social phenomenon. A language gives resources for people to assign meanings to words, sentences and discourse structures, in virtue of being used in interaction and thought.
2. Language is also uniquely powerful as a mode of communication because of the fact that the syntactic structure of the language allows speakers to generate new sentences. Nevertheless, language takes its force from context — the uses of language determine its meanings.
3. Analysis of language may take place at a number of levels: at the level of significant sounds (phonemes) and words (morphemes), of sentences, of pragmatics, and of discourse. The significance of an utterance depends on its context.
4. Language considered at the level of sounds and words can be analysed phonetically and morphemically. Dictionary definitions do not exhaust the meaning of words.
5. Language considered at the level of sentences can be analysed in terms of its semantics and syntax. The interplay between syntax and semantics gives language its generative power.
6. Language considered at the level of pragmatics can be analysed in terms of

the features of utterances, which depend on the linguistic and the non-linguistic context.
7. Language may also be considered at the level of discourse. Discourse, or extended passages of language use, is studied in terms of linguistic genres — which categorise the stages of discourse in a particular context.
8. Semiotic theories, based on Saussure, have been influential in recent accounts of language. Such analyses, while using different terminology and structure, have been adopted in modern social semiotics.
9. Applying our understanding of language to the differences between how men and women talk, and listen, can enable us to understand that failures of communication may be due not only to disagreement but to gender differences in discourse structures.

Discussion questions

1. Is there ever a good reason for judging people by the way they talk?
2. To what extent do you alter the way you talk according to context? Is it wrong to do so?
3. Would an illiterate have a different attitude to language from a literate person? What of someone who has never encountered a written language?
4. Do bilingual or multilingual people have a different understanding of each particular language from monolinguals?
5. Is jargon ever acceptable? What roles do jargons play?
6. Do social groups or even families within one linguistic group have different paralinguistic styles? Can you identify any?
7. Could there ever be one universal language — as Esperanto was intended to be?
8. In general, speakers use only a small proportion of the language they know — the active vocabulary is much more restricted than the passive vocabulary. Should we try to alter this?
9. Should we alter all our documents so that 'he-man talk' is avoided?
10. Can we imagine a life without language?

Further reading

Coates, J. (1986) *Women, Men and Language* London: Longman.
Corner, J. & Hawthorn, J. (eds) (1980) *Communication Studies: An Introductory Reader* London: Edward Arnold.
Duranti, A. & Goodwin, C. (eds) (1992) *Rethinking Context: Language as an Interactive Phenomenon* (Introduction), Cambridge: Cambridge University Press.
Kalantzis, M. & Cope, B. (1993) *The Powers of Literacy: A Genre Approach to Literacy* London: Falmer.
Kress, G. (1993) 'Genre as Social Process' in Kalantzis & Cope, *op. cit.* pp. 26–37.
Tannen, D. (1991) *You Just Don't Understand: Men and Women in Conversation* New York: Ballantine.

Chapter 2

References

Austin, J. (1962) *How to do Things with Words* Oxford: Clarendon.
Baylis, P., Joyce. H. & Slade, D. (1993) *Improving Your Report Writing* Sydney: Centre for Workplace Communication and Culture.
Bernstein, B. (1977) *Class, Codes and Control* London: Routledge & Kegan Paul, 2nd edn.
Blakemore, D. (1992) *Understanding Utterances* Oxford: Blackwell.
Chomsky, N. (1957) *Syntactic Structures* The Hague: Mouton.
Cranny-Francis, A. (1993) 'Gender and Genre', pp. 90–115 in M. Kalantzis & B. Cope, (eds).
Derrida, J. (1976) *Of Grammatology* Baltimore: Johns Hopkins University Press.
Derrida, J. (1977) *Limited Inc: abc . . .* Baltimore: Johns Hopkins University Press.
Fairclough, N. (1989) *Language and Power* London: Longman.
Flaubert, G. (1972) *Madame Bovary* in Editions Gallimard, Paris, p. 254.
Foucault, M. (1973) *The Order of Things: An Archaeology of the Human Sciences* Vintage: New York.
Frege, G. (1952) 'On Sense and Reference', pp. 56-78 in P. Geach & M. Black, (eds) *Translations from the Philosophical Writings of Gottlob Frege* Oxford: Basil Blackwell.
Fromkin, V., Rodman, R., Collins, P. & Blair, D. (1990) *An Introduction to Language* Sydney: Holt, Rinehart & Winston, 2nd Australian edition.
Gilbert, P. & Taylor, S. (1991) *Fashioning the Feminine: Girls, Popular Culture and Schooling* Sydney: Allen & Unwin.
Goffman I. (1981) *Forms of Talk* Oxford: Blackwell.
Grice, H.P. (1975) 'Logic and Conversation', in P. Cole & J. Morgan, (eds) *Syntax and Semantics* New York: Academic Press.
Gumperz, J. (1970) 'Verbal Strategies in Multilingual Communication', *Monograph Series on Language and Linguistics* Georgetown University, pp. 129–48.
Halliday, M. (1985) *An Introduction to Functional Grammar* London: Edward Arnold.
Halliday, M. & Hasan, R. (1985) *Language Context and Text: Aspects of Language in Social Semiotic Perspective* Waurn Ponds, Vic.: Deakin University Press.
Harman, G. (ed.) (1974) *On Noam Chomsky: Critical Essays* New York: Anchor.
Hodge, R. & Kress, G. (1988) *Social Semiotics* Oxford: Polity Press.
Holmes, J. (1993) 'Women's talk: the Question of Sociolinguistic Universals', *Australian Journal of Communication* 20(3): 125–49.
Hymes, D. (1974) *Foundations in Sociolinguistics: An Ethnographic Approach* Philadelphia: University of Pennsylvania Press.
Kalantzis, M., Cope, B. & Slade, D. (1989) *Minority Languages and Dominant Culture* London: Falmer.
Kress, G. (ed.) (1988) *Communication and Culture* Sydney: UNSW Press.
Lakoff, G. (1991) *Metaphor and War* e-mail.

Lakoff, G. & Johnson, M. (1980) *Metaphors We Live By* Chicago: University of Chicago Press.
Lakoff, R. (1976) *Language and Women's Place* New York: Harper.
Lewis, D. (1974) 'Languages, Language and Grammar' in G. Harman *op. cit.* 253–66.
Lloyd, G. (1993) *The Man of Reason: 'Male' and 'Female' in Western Philosophy* London: Routledge, 2nd edn.
MacKinnon, C. (1987) *Feminism Unmodified* Cambridge, Mass: Harvard University Press.
Martin, J.R. (1985) *Factual Writing: Exploring and Challenging Social Reality* Waurn Ponds, Vic: Deakin University Press.
Mitchell, A. & Delbridge A. (1965) *The Speech of Australian Adolescents* Sydney: Angus & Robertson.
Montgomery, M. (1986) *An Introduction to Language and Society* New York: Methuen.
Ochs, E. (1992) 'Indexing gender', pp. 335–58 in A. Duranti & C. Goodwin, (eds) (1992) *op. cit.*
Peacocke, C. (1976) 'Truth Definitions and Actual Languages', pp. 162–88 in G. Evans & J. McDowell, (eds) *Truth and Meaning: Essays in Semantics* Oxford: Clarendon.
Peirce, C.S. (1960) *Collected Papers* vol. 7, A.W. Burks (ed.) Cambridge, Mass; Harvard University Press.
Penman, R. (1993) 'Conversation is the common theme: Understanding talk and text', *Australian Journal of Communication* 20(3): 30–43.
Pettit, P. (1977) *The Concept of Structuralism: A Critical Analysis* Berkeley: University of California Press.
Poynton, C. (1985) *Language and Gender: Making the Difference* Waurn Ponds Vic: Deakin University Press.
Roberts, C., Davies, E. & Jupp. T. (1992) *Language and Discrimination* London: Longman.
Romaine, S. (1984) *The Language of Children and Adolescents* Oxford: Blackwell.
Sacks, O. (1989) *Seeing Voices* London: Picador.
Saussure, F. (1966) *Course in General Linguistics* London: McGraw-Hill.
Searle, J. (1969) *Speech Acts* Cambridge: Cambridge University Press.
Spender, D. (1980) *Man Made Language* London: Routledge & Kegan Paul.
Sperber, D. & Wilson D. (1986) *Relevance: Communication and Cognition* Oxford: Blackwell.
Thorne, B., Kramarae, C. & Henley, N. (1983) *Language, Gender and Society* Rowley, Mass: Newbury House.
van Dijk, T. (1989) 'Structures of Discourse and Structures of Power, pp. 18–59 in J. Anderson (ed.) *Communication Yearbook 12* Newbury Park, CA: Sage.
Whyte, J., Deem, R., Kant, L. & Cruikshank, M. (1985) *Girl Friendly Schooling* London: Methuen.
Wittgenstein, L. (1953) *Philosophical Investigations* New York: Macmillan.

The codes of nonverbal communication

3

Objectives

After completing this chapter you should be able to:

- define nonverbal communication;
- differentiate kinesics and proxemics as the two main codes of nonverbal communication;
- recognise the functions of nonverbal signals with respect to other codes;
- appreciate the cultural and gender relativity of nonverbal communication;
- apply semiotic theory to the analysis of visual communication.

Chapter 3

He that has eyes to see and ears to hear may convince himself that no mortal can keep a secret. If his lips are silent, he chatters with his fingertips; betrayal oozes out of him at every pore.

Collected Papers, *Sigmund Freud*

Speaking is not the only way to communicate. Very often our spoken words are contradicted by the way we move, or the way we dress or even the seat we pick out in a lecture theatre. As Freud says, our secret thoughts are betrayed even when we do not speak out, by the way we move, glance or hold ourselves. Sometimes the very buildings people occupy 'communicate', so that grand buildings impose importance on their occupants. This chapter will examine a range of nonverbal communication: communication that is not in words.

We all recognise the impact of nonverbal communication. In *Out of Africa*, the author, Karen Blixen, describes an experience of going into Nairobi on the day when a close friend of hers, Denys Finch-Hatton, had crashed his plane and been killed. Her acquaintances were reluctant to tell her the news, so she sat through a lunch at Government House, unknowing. Her feeling, 'that everybody was turning away from me', she writes, 'grew so strong that I wondered if I were beginning to go mad'. Her acquaintances avoided all verbal communication about the tragedy, but they communicated their distress nonetheless, through their body language.

When verbal and nonverbal cues conflict, it is generally the nonverbal cues we trust. This is because nonverbal cues, such as body language, are more difficult to mimic and less likely to be misleading than language. Nevertheless, when there is conflict between the two, the interpreter may be left in an extremely ambiguous situation, unable fully to understand what is being communicated. So acute was the misfit between verbal and nonverbal communication for Karen Blixen in Nairobi that she felt almost mad.

The importance of nonverbal communication

We are all fluent speakers and interpreters of at least one language other than our mother tongue, and that is the body language of our own culture. Generally, we are not conscious of this second language. Arguably, body language is not really a language at all. It is certainly, however, a very powerful code of communication, which we use and interpret all the time. Most of us are adept, too, at 'reading' other codes: we know surfies by their clothes; we may be able to identify others' relationships from where and how they choose to sit and we obey a myriad of rules governing the use of territory — not barging into the lecturer's office, for instance. In this chapter, we will examine these codes in order to reach a better understanding of how they are used.

Nonverbal codes are codes which are not dependent on spoken languages. Some linguistic codes are not spoken, but written. Written English and morse code English are still forms of communication which are ultimately derived from and parasitic upon spoken languages. However, many nonverbal codes are not versions of spoken English, or any other spoken language, but are entirely independent codes. We might explain the meaning of a nonverbal code in English, but we do not have to in order for it to be understood. A **nonverbal code** is one which is independent of spoken forms.

nonverbal code
One that is independent of spoken forms; nonverbal codes are conventional and culturally specific.

The codes of nonverbal communication

Body language is a subclass of nonverbal codes. Body language includes not just the use of our hands, our shoulders, our feet but also, most importantly, the use of the eyes and face. It can be described at the macro level, such as when we say of someone that they were slumped or defensive. At the other end of the range, we may describe the flicker of a glance as meaningful. **Body language** is the entire range of nonverbal codes circumscribed by the use of the body.

Understanding nonverbal codes, whether they are gestures or images, relies on an implicit grasp of the rules governing the use of that type of code: nonverbal codes of communication are conventional. When we wave or kiss goodbye, we do not fling our arms or act randomly: however unconsciously, we do so intending to be interpreted as 'saying' goodbye. We expect others to understand and act in the same conventional way. Even in France, where it is conventional to kiss the cheek (or cheeks) of those you farewell, there appears to be some confusion about how many times you kiss: once, twice, thrice. As a newcomer, one only wants to get the convention right. Nonverbal codes are not spontaneous.

body language
The entire range of nonverbal codes circumscribed by the use of the body.

The Social Kiss,
*Desmond Digby, private collection.
Used with permission.*

Conventions are often explicit in nonverbal communication. Traffic lights are a particularly clear case, since the convention is a matter of law. The ruling global convention is that a red light means 'stop', an amber light 'caution' and a green light 'go'. It could have been otherwise: there is no reason that red should have the meaning it does. The same holds for the vertical order of the signals: the caution light could be on the top. Even though the convention governing traffic signals holds all over the world, it is clearly not a natural law that traffic lights be arranged that way. There are, too, cultural and subcultural differences in the interpretation of amber. In Sydney, for instance, amber means 'speed up', whereas in Canberra it means 'slow down'. When it comes to the side of the road on which we drive, there are two different conventions. Neither is better — but it is crucial that people within one country adhere to the same one. Many nonverbal codes are arbitrary in this way.

Other nonverbal codes arise naturally, rather than by agreement, or by law. Smiling is a conventional way to express pleasure, sympathy and greeting in our culture, but it is not something we all agree to do. Smiling is part of a code that we inherit from the apes, and which children learn instinctively. It is not a convention on which we have agreed, but it is part of the code nonetheless, because we use it to communicate intentionally. Conventions vary from one culture to another. If we went to continental Europe and drove on the left, we would have an accident. The same sort of errors can occur even with smiling. We expect female flight attendants on planes to expect us to expect them to smile. That is true of the vast majority of airlines, but not of all. When that nexus is broken, either by flight attendants who do not expect to have to smile, or by fliers who regard a smile as out of the ordinary, then misinterpretation ensues.

This is another feature of nonverbal codes: the codes you use depend on the society to which you belong, and to the subgroups of that society. We tend to forget this obvious fact, precisely because nonverbal codes like body language seem to be universal. No matter how hard we try, non-Russian speakers cannot understand spoken or written Russian, yet we tend to believe we can understand the body language of Russians. Whole articles were written, after the tumultuous first session of the Russian Parliament after Gorbachev's release from the Crimea, about Boris Yeltsin's 'overbearing' body language. The journalists assumed that his nonverbal codes were universal.

Some forms of body movement *are* universal, and hence not purely arbitrary. We all sweat with fear, cry out or grimace in pain and have characteristic patterns indicating sexual arousal. Such body movements scarcely deserve to be treated as a code at all, since they are not within our control. Of course, we interpret others' sweating as a sign of fear, their grimaces as a sign of pain, but it does not follow that they communicate their pain using a code. We need to distinguish, as Grice (1957) did, different senses of 'meaning'. There is a contrast between natural and non-natural meaning. We say that a smoke 'means' fire and, indeed, smoke is a reliable indicator or sign of fire, all else being equal, precisely because smoke is caused by fire. Natural meaning like this occurs when there is a causal connection between the sign and what is meant. Utterances in a language, such as a person's yelling 'fire', are quite different. There is no natural causal connection between the word 'fire' and the smoke, or indeed the fire itself, although of course the person was caused (or may have been caused) to yell by the fire. We say such connections are non-natural. Sweating is a natural sign of fear, just as smoke is a natural sign of fire. It is not an act of communication using a code, since someone sweating in fear did not intend, consciously or unconsciously, thereby to communicate.

When it comes to body language the line between natural and conventional meaning is blurred. We share with the higher primates a repertoire of movements for expressing, above all, our emotions: we stroke those who are distressed, laugh with joy, hunch our shoulders and lower our heads in submission. These actions are part of a communicative code. For human beings, as for the apes, these actions are powerful tools of communication. They are fundamental modes of expressing our emotions, a code which the higher primates share with humans. Part of the code may be born with us, and innate. Even profoundly deaf children laugh and cry, yet they could not intend to make such noises or learn to do so from others. However, the vast majority of body language, which we learn to interpret with such subtlety, relies on conventions and is culture bound.

This fact has important consequences. Precisely because there are universal elements in body language, we forget the cultural component. Failure to be aware of cultural conventions can be disastrous. In the Lebanon, as in many Mediterranean countries, a nod of the head does not mean 'yes', as it does for English speakers, but 'no'. Interpret the bus driver's nod, in answer to the question about where the bus is going, as meaning 'yes', and you can end up lost. On the other hand, it is exceedingly rude in an Arabic culture to offer anyone anything using the left hand, since that is the hand used for sanitary purposes. Get this wrong and you may, unwittingly, be very offensive. It is all too easy to forget that conventions may differ.

Notice, too, that in interpreting body language, we do best when we know the person concerned. We are sensitive to the tapping finger of a friend, which we would ignore in another. Indeed, one person screaming or swearing might indicate a degree of anger which another could convey by a slight clearing of the throat. Understanding body language depends on recognising idiosyncratic personal variations in the conventions. The characters we watch often on television acquire the familiarity of close friends, just because we've learnt their conventions. Australians and New Zealanders, when dealing with North Americans, can call on their knowledge of countless mutual television 'friends' in interpreting body language. We tend to forget that North Americans have no such clues in interpreting *us*.

Nonverbal communication has three major features:

1. it involves codes which are not derived from spoken languages;
2. these codes are conventional and are culturally specific;
3. the meaning of nonverbal interaction is influenced by context.

This suggests that we cannot isolate the nonverbal code and explain its significance independently of the context in which any action occurs.

Communication scholars draw on a variety of approaches when investigating nonverbal codes, some reductionist and decompositional, some holistic and decompositional and some semiotic. Semiotic analyses have been widely used for art and media. We begin with a decompositional approach, then turn to more contextual approaches.

Exercise 3.1   Interpreting body language without spoken language

This exercise is designed to give a measure of accuracy in our reading of body language. Students work in pairs, one viewing a certain TV program with the sound, and the other without, and each notes what is happening. In a large group, a selection of types of programs should be viewed, ranging from familiar soap operas to a current affairs program, such as *Sixty Minutes*. A film or cartoon not originally in English would be worth including.

How accurate were the interpretations that were based solely on movement? Were certain types of television program easier to interpret than others? What factors determined the ease of interpretation? Did it depend on how well you knew the program? Was there a difference between accuracy of interpretation of communication about emotions and communication of content?

Chapter 3

The codes of nonverbal communication

There is a range of approaches to the codes of nonverbal communication: we shall deal in turn with kinesics (the code of gesture and body movement), haptics (the code governing touch), proxemics (the code relating to the use of space) and chronemics (the code relating to the use of time).

Kinesics

Body language is called a 'language' because gestures communicate alone as well as in relation to, and supplementing, spoken language. **Kinesics** is the study of gesture as a meaning system. There is a variety of generalisations about body language, each depending on a different system of interpretation. Some describe the impact, or feeling, that body language of a particular type may engender. Others give clues for reading the body language of others, and altering your own, so as to create a particular effect. Who said body language can't lie?

Face and eyes
When we 'read' another person, the very first thing we do is assess their eyes and face: the eyes above all are a 'window of the soul'. Facial expression is immensely complex, culturally loaded and often contradictory. The process of spelling out the meanings of a flicker of an eyebrow is itself daunting. When we consider that, in reading an expression, we, as ordinary communicators, combine our interpretation of the eyebrow flicker with the angle of the mouth and the glitter in the eye and the shrug, it is evident that our communication skills are complex.

Some studies have concentrated on eye movements. In a work context, subordinates are more likely to seek to initiate eye contact with their superior and less likely to cut it off, for instance (Exline et al., 1975). The further apart we are, the more likely we are to seek eye contact; when physically close in a social situation, we tend to avoid eye contact (Baker & Shaw, 1980). When relaxed about a topic, we are more likely to initiate eye contact than when tense. If holding the floor in a conversation, we avoid looking at an interlocutor until we are ready to hear their opinion. Eyes are the major method of signalling turn-taking in conversation; they can be used to encourage and discourage intimacy and for a variety of other purposes (Argyle et al., 1981).

Eye movements are also culturally determined. What may seem to us ordinary direct behaviour with our eyes may seem shockingly forward to other cultures and vice versa. In Arabic culture, for instance, polite behaviour requires direct eye contact between men. Japanese culture has it that lowering the eyes is polite. That difference is likely to complicate business dealings between the groups.

Open and closed body language
One categorisation distinguishes between the receptiveness of bodily attitudes: arms and legs crossed, shoulders hunched, eyes and face down creates an unwelcoming impression. We say that the body language is *closed*. On the other hand, a relaxed posture, arms akimbo and head and eyes up would be a more receptive *open* attitude. If you wish to impress an interviewing committee in our culture, you would normally aim to look open — shoulders relaxed, head up, body leaning slightly forward, without appearing overconfident — not spreadeagled over a chair, for instance.

kinesics
The study of gesture and body movement as a meaning system.

Very often, interviewing committees are trained to interpret the body language of candidates. Characteristically, we cover or twist our mouths or noses when unsure of a response or lying. A trained interviewer will pick up such signals and go in with further questions. Salespeople are taught to distinguish receptive postures from unreceptive, so as to pick when to strike. Of course, the body language cues are specific to cultures and subcultures, and are frighteningly easy to misread. The person picked as dishonest may have chronic hayfever! Other categorisations concentrate on body movements in courtship rituals. When someone of the opposite sex sits with legs pointing towards you in a night club, this may be part of a courtship ritual and indicate sexual interest; a woman's preening by touching her face or hair may have a similar meaning.

Closed body language indicates defensive attitudes.
(Photo: *Helene Walsh*)
Used with permission.

Haptics

The study of the conventions governing touch is known technically as **haptics**. Touch is particularly important in courtship, and the taboos on touch are accordingly very strict. They do, however, differ among cultures, and even within one culture. In Latin and in some Asian cultures, men typically walk down the streets holding hands, as do pairs of women. On the other hand, it is very rare to see mixed pairs holding hands. In Anglo-Australasian culture, this pattern is reversed. In the past, it was acceptable for men to touch the arms of women who were working for them. In recent years, awareness of sexual harassment in the workplace has made such actions, however well intentioned, risky.

Taboos to do with touch can cause intense offence. Buddhist cultures forbid touching the head of another person and in Thailand even to keep your head at a level higher than a photograph of the King may be impolite. Indeed, in India, with its centuries-old caste system, the lowest social group were called 'untouchables', while in Japan another 'untouchable' outgroup, the *burakamin*, were stigmatised because they were considered to have been defiled by their traditional responsibility for killing animals in slaughterhouses. Australians and

haptics
The code relating to the use of touch.

New Zealanders may find that their nonverbal behaviour causes them to be labelled pushy in Britain and northern Europe, cold in the south of Europe and intolerably familiar in some parts of Asia.

Proxemics

Even when we are not touching others, the distance we keep away from them is strictly conventionally regulated. We may have come across the person who seems short-sighted, and just gets too close all the time, so that a conversation with them involves backing away. Other people are always edging away, and seem cold. What is happening is a misfit between the distances which each of the pair think suitable for social conversation.

Edward Hall (1966) has discussed the distances used when communicating according to the social relations to which they are appropriate. The study of distance as a meaning system is known as **proxemics**. His classification, while produced for a North American sample, appears to hold good in Australia. He distinguishes four major social relations signalled by distance:

> **proxemics**
> The study of the use of space as a meaning system.

1. Intimate   10–30 cm   Very close family or trusted friends
2. Personal   30–100 cm   Casual relations at party with friends
3. Social   1–2.5 m   Business or impersonal relations
4. Formal   > 2.5 m   Public situations as in lectures

While these categorisations may not apply precisely in our own social groups, and are culturally highly specific (Watson, 1970), the general approach is convincing. The distances between us and our acquaintances are a rough guide to our relations. Indeed, changing the distance relation is a sure signal that someone wants to alter the personal relationship. When we say of someone that they are 'moving in on' another we are not only speaking metaphorically.

Interestingly, the converse relation also holds. The distance at which we see others regulates how intimate we feel towards them. Television gives us a view of newsreaders and politicians and the heroes of soap operas magnified as if they were twenty centimetres from us. That is well within the intimate distance. Repeated exposure to those images makes us feel we are indeed intimate with the characters we see. Should we see the local newsreader in the street, it would then be natural to draw ourselves into their intimate space. This may well be the cause of the frequently bemoaned fate of newsreaders and stars of being treated as intimates by strangers. Politicians are more likely to exploit the spatial potentialities of television. A camera shot that is taken from above, for instance, puts the viewer in a superior position to the interviewee. Politicians will avoid being below the camera, and will aim to be on a level ('equals') or above the cameras, thus appearing all knowing.

The spatial distances that we maintain extend to the spaces we occupy. A young child may feel its personal space has been invaded when its drawer has been opened by someone else. People working in an open-plan office have very strict lines marking out their territory, sometimes delineated by bookshelves, sometimes invisible, but rigid nonetheless. **Territoriality** or **micro-territoriality** (Scheflen, 1981) is the area of space over which rights are held. Territoriality is familiar in the animal world, where birds mark out their trees by singing, and cats take over backyards (Ardrey, 1966). It applies equally among human animals, modified by social practice and convention.

> **territoriality**
> The tendency to defend an area of space.

Territories may be transitory. A dedicated cook may resent incursions into the kitchen while cooking, but not at other times: most of us prefer to have the bathroom to ourselves while we are there, but only a favoured few have a personal suite. These spatial empires that we build sway and change, but as with animals the territory is a marker of power and command. If you have ever settled into a student residence or group house — or even a room in a holiday resort — you could have observed the negotiation for space, the tacit battle for the best chair by the television, or the best lounge by the pool. Next time you are in such circumstances, watch carefully.

Chronemics

Chronemics is the code relating to the use of time. We are all aware that the patterns in the use of time differ across cultures and within cultures. There are differences between the time acceptable between utterances: some groups require a quick reply; others, such as philosophers, may allow long periods of silence. There are also different interpretations of the accuracy of time expressions — to say an order will be ready 'tomorrow' may be absolutely accurate in some cultures, while in others it may mean anytime in the next week or month.

The use of time relates both to the cultural context and to the expressions of tense. For instance, in Aboriginal languages, certain tenses used for referring to the mythical Dreamtime are not past, nor present nor future, but refer to the 'everywhen' (in Stanner's 1979 evocative phrase). The language describing the Dreamtime and the nonverbal behaviour appropriate to reverence for the Dreamtime, such as reverence for certain sites in the landscape, need to be understood in this context of a time outside the ordinary pattern of past, present and future (Rose, 1992; Swain, 1988).

For instance, John Rudder's (forthcoming) discussion of the time reference systems of Yolngu deals with the detail of tense in an Arnhem Land language. His hypothesis is that traditional accounts of Yolngu tense mistake the force of the distinctions, by imposing a 'Western' theory of time. By 'Western' theory of time, Rudder means an account of time which is of a homogeneous continuum, directional and spatialised. The Yolngu time is not of this type, he suggests. He distinguishes three different Yolngu types of time: 'cyclical' time (the events that recur through the seasons); continuum time (the Western conception used to describe the life of a person or events in living memory); and mythological time, which is eternal and recurrent. The Aboriginal Dreamtime is of the last sort — a time that is really a 'dream space' defined by sacred sites, not by the passage of time. Rudder's thesis is that time itself is defined culturally. Whether we accept this view or not, it is evident that chronemic codes only apply within a cultural context.

chronemics
The code relating to the use of time.

Exercise 3.2 Kinesics, proxemics and chronemics in a debate
Take three controversial topics for each group of three students:
1. There should be no tertiary student fees.
2. Australia should immediately stop all immigration.
3. Alcohol should be illegal (or marijuana legal).

Each topic should be debated between two of the students, while the other takes notes on eye movements (turn-taking), body language, the use of time and proxemic behaviours of the debaters. Each student has a chance to be notetaker. The notetaker may wish to vary the proxemics of the debaters, by ruling that debaters must be abnormally far apart, or closer than normal. Report the findings back to the group.

The functions of nonverbal communication

We learned . . . to interpret the hand language that accompanies any discussion of deadlines. When a Provençal looks you in the eye and tells you that he will be hammering on your door next Tuesday for certain, the behaviour of his hands is all important. If they are still or patting you on the arm reassuringly, you can expect him on Tuesday. If one hand is held out at waist height, palm downwards and begins to rock from side to side, adjust the timetable to Wednesday or Thursday. If the rocking develops into an agitated waggle, he's really talking about next week or God knows when, depending on circumstances beyond his control. These unspoken disclaimers . . . seem to be instinctive and therefore more revealing than speech.

A Year in Provence, *Peter Mayle*

The interpretation of body language, either within or between cultures, often involves the functional roles Peter Mayle discerns in this interpretation of the tradesmen of Provence. The hand movements in these cases may reinforce or contradict the verbal message. These two broad categories — matching and cancelling — are the main types of relationship between verbal and nonverbal messages.

The tradesman's still arms, or a reassuring pat, tell Peter Mayle he really means what he says; the gestures reinforce or repeat and strengthen the words. Similarly, a wave as we say goodbye reinforces the message of farewell. If we wave without actually saying 'goodbye', the wave substitutes or takes the place of the verbal message. In this case, the clear meaning of the nonverbal signal is equivalent to a verbal message. If someone asks where the bus stop is we might say 'Towards the shops', then reinforce and complement the message by pointing in the direction of the shops. The gesture adds to the message.

When we are talking about emotions, complementary gestures become very important. Australian and New Zealand women signal their sympathy to another woman by leaning forward, possibly making the sound of sympathy transcribed 'Tst'. Men in Australia and New Zealand are more likely to lean back, or lightly slap the shoulder of a mate in trouble. Children reinforce and complement unfriendly remarks by poking out their tongues, or worse. Without the complementary gestures, many verbal expressions of emotion appear quite hollow.

Peter Mayle's tradesman modified his promise to be there on Tuesday with the characteristic Mediterranean hand quiver, meaning maybe. A more agitated movement means, according to Mayle, a definite contradiction. Likewise, we may modify enthusiastic praise with a shrug, or contradict it with a raised eyebrow. When we receive mixed messages, we tend to believe the nonverbal, not so much because it is instinctive, as because it is less readily used to mislead.

There is another important function that body language plays with respect to verbal communication: it acts as a *regulator*, as the nonverbal signals provides cues for the verbal. For instance, turn-taking in conversations is, to some extent, dependent on verbal cues like 'What do you think?' To a far greater extent, turn-taking depends on visual signals, and the attitudes of arms and heads of the interlocutors. The speaker generally looks away from the audience while holding the floor: to glance up at an interlocutor is to invite an interjection. An attentive angle of the head encourages a speaker; restless hand and arm movements show a desire to break into the conversation. While our conforming to these rules is unconscious, any alteration to them causes immense unease.

The functional roles here applied in particular to the way body language modifies the verbal code also apply to other forms of nonverbal communication. Consider a traffic signal at a pedestrian crossing. The linguistic sign WALK may be accompanied by the loud beeping sound which alerts the seeing disabled that they may walk. Here the beeping sound reinforces the road sign.

Taxonomy of nonverbal behaviour

The degree of control that people have over their nonverbal behaviour determines how they present themselves to others. In interpersonal dealings, or in making judgments about the sincerity of public figures on TV, we often fall back on our reading of nonverbal clues to assess honesty or deceptiveness. Various signs of deception (called 'leakages') are more likely to appear in body clues than in facial expressions. Speech is another possible sign of deception. Experiments showed that deceitful speakers made more speech errors, spoke for shorter time periods, and spoke at a higher pitch, with fewer gestures than honest ones (Ekman, 1988). Such evidence is highly culturally specific.

Ekman and Friesen (1969) have suggested a further taxonomy of five types of nonverbal communication. The first of these is **emblems**. These are usually gestures that have a direct verbal translation and are performed quite consciously. So, for example, one universal emblem is to place your forefinger vertically in front of your mouth to instruct others to 'Be quiet!' Another is to place your cupped hand behind your ear and to incline your head, meaning 'I can't hear you'. The second type are called **illustrators**. These are nonverbal behaviours we use to illustrate what we are saying. Our use of illustrators is to some extent conscious, but we are likely to have several unique personal mannerisms in our use of illustrators — e.g. pauses in speaking, saying 'um' at mid or end of sentence, or the use of the hands — which we are not usually conscious of until we see or hear ourselves on video or audiotape.

The third kind is **affect displays**. This is the way our facial expressions, or sometimes our body movements, reveal our emotions. In informal, social situations in Western culture most people do not monitor their own affect displays, but they may be likely to do so in formal or public contexts. Some jobs require employees to present happy, smiling faces — McDonald's counter-attendants or airline stewards — no matter how tired they may be. Hochschild describes these kinds of jobs as requiring 'emotional labour' (1983).

Fourth, there are **regulators**, such as gaze direction and duration, nods, vocal pitch, head position and raised eyebrows. We often have little awareness of our own use of regulators, but are likely to notice them in others, especially if that person is saying too much or too little. Finally, there are **adaptors**. These are mostly nervous, unconscious mechanisms that we have little awareness of. 'Doodling' on paper in meetings or on the phone, picking your nose in traffic in the assumed privacy of your car, playing with your hair, or scratching, are all adaptors.

emblems
Gestures that have a direct verbal translation and are performed quite consciously.

illustrators
Nonverbal behaviours we use to illustrate what we are saying.

affect displays
The way our facial expressions, or sometimes our body movements, reveal our emotions.

regulators
Nonverbal signals that provide cues for verbal interaction.

adaptors
Nervous, unconscious nonverbal displays.

These varying types of nonverbal communication interact with each other to provide a dense and interlocking web of communication. Effective communication involves tailoring your nonverbal and verbal codes so that they reinforce each other and achieve what you wish. In order to do so we need to look more carefully at the various codes.

Exercise 3.3 Observing nonverbal codes in public
This is a preliminary observation exercise. Divide into groups of four. Each group is to observe the use of nonverbal codes in a public place: the refectory, a restaurant, a night club. Be careful not to be obtrusive or to embarrass others.

Note the variety of nonverbal codes used, and observe the differences due to gender and culture. Look for patterns in dress, hair and body language. Do similarly dressed groups have typical forms of greeting?

Now discuss your observations. Did you have a clear focus for your observation, or should you have been more precise before you began? How could you refine your observations? Should you begin with a specific hypothesis? Did you pick your target group — the subjects — clearly enough? Should you record your observations while you are on the site? How?

Context, culture and gender

The kinesic and proxemic codes provide a repertoire of actions which can be used to communicate, either in concert with or independently of spoken language. The account thus far is decontextualised. Communicative acts are, however, always performed in a context. As in the linguistic case there is a narrow and a broader conception of context, corresponding to the intricacies of the particular interactional context on the one hand, and the broader sociocultural context on the other hand.

Consider first the immediate context of communication. It is essentially interpersonal: more than one person is involved in a communicative action. Each participant brings to the situation an understanding of how acts of that type develop and are used. Contextualisation occurs when those interacting draw on their knowledge — and what they assume to be the others' understanding of the situation — to make sense of the action. In Goffman's (1974) terms, interactions create a 'frame' in terms of which the meaning of a particular action is determined. In the course of an interaction, the meanings of particular actions can then be modified.

To take one example: the patterns of interactions and the ways one uses the repertoire of eye movements in interaction has its own dynamic. Throughout passages of interaction, for instance, certain eye movements will take on meanings which they would not otherwise acquire. Kendon (1981a) spells out an example in his article 'Some functions of the face in a kissing round', in which he minutely dissects the meanings of minor facial movements and the ways they come to have a new significance.

Many recent theorists argue that not only do we need to locate codes in the contexts in which they occur, but also suggest the much stronger case, that nonverbal codes are meaningless independent of the entire web of codes. We need to set the account of meaning in any nonverbal code against related cultural codes. For instance, the Japanese tea ceremony is a fine-grained and peculiarly Japanese ritual, but to analyse the elements of nonverbal communication in it, we need to explain how the features of behaviour of the participants in the ceremony are also found in other Japanese nonverbal behaviours. The level of explanation may be very general, as it is when it is suggested that Japanese attitudes opposed to the importing of rice are a consequence of a reverence towards Japanese food and food rituals, of which the tea ceremony is also witness. It may, on the other hand, be very detailed. Japanese TV advertisements have features which are highly formalised and indirect, in just the same way, it may be suggested, as the tea ceremony is indirect.

Ramsey (1985) reports two studies of Japanese nonverbal behaviour. The first considered the relations between proxemics and privacy in Japanese public bath houses, and the second, the dress, body ornamenting and dancing style of young Japanese nightclubbers. She argues that Japan is a 'high-context' culture, where meaning is frequently communicated through the environment and behaviour, rather than linguistically. Japanese self-identity, which is usually defined in relation to a group, a school, a role or a situation is very sensitive to nonverbal context. In each of these, nonverbal behaviours are likely to be carefully regulated, just as Japanese business people rely on the strategic use of their *Meishi* (business cards). She concludes that much of Japanese nonverbal behaviour is concerned with establishing a sense of synchrony — 'agreeing with others'. In contrast, Western attitudes value individuality. Dressing alike, joining in *radio taiso* morning exercises, or group toasts at a party: all are Japanese rituals of synchrony that reaffirm certain group boundaries.

It is interesting to note that many of the features Ramsey discusses of Japanese nonverbal codes with respect to the body are relatively recent, at least among the non-governing classes. Nomura's (1990) study of the role of nakedness in Japan during the nineteenth century shows profound changes in the body images of Japanese. In a predominantly peasant society, it was usual to remove clothing after leaving the fields. It was a result of the Meiji Government policy of modernisation that nakedness became less acceptable, and that forms of behaviour became standardised. In this case there is an explicit link between power and nonverbal codes. Power relations profoundly determine the nonverbal codes, if rarely as explicitly as in this case.

The accounts of nonverbal codes we have cited above are essentially decompositional in the sense used in Chapter 1. We have emphasised the importance of the interactions of the various codes, but each code is described as if it were an independent system from which, in principle, we as communicators are free to choose any element. Yet as we dress for an interview, we take on not only the clothing, but also the typical body movements of an interviewee. Those postures are in turn dictated by the power relations between members of the interviewing panel and the supplicant for a job. Nonverbal behaviour is part of a manifold of behaviour within society, and must be interpreted in context.

Within our society, as in most societies, the largest divide between nonverbal behaviour patterns is based on gender. Women and men have distinct body languages. How a woman uses her eyes, her hands, holds her body, sits at dinner and even how she walks is vastly different from a man of a similar social background. American studies show that women smile more frequently than men and are expected to do so. Indeed, unsmiling women are viewed far more negatively than unsmiling men. Women are less likely than men to initiate touch, they use less space than males and they are less likely to interrupt than men. Our society is divided into the two groups of men and women not so much by their physiological differences, which are generally concealed, as by their different forms of verbal and nonverbal communication.

In this cartoon, a middle-aged conservative Australian female politician is seen lobbying for support among members of her electorate of similar age and class. Notice the verbal and nonverbal stereotypes. Source: *G. Pryor,* The Canberra Times, *8 November 1993. Used with permission.*

The gender differentiation of body language begins very early. In an extraordinary series of experiments performed for a BBC television documentary of 1987, toddlers were shown to recognise the gender of other children from their movement alone. Toddlers, it had been established, copy like-gender toddlers. In the experiment, this finding was exploited. The elbows, shoulders, hips and knees of a young girl and boy were fitted with reflectors. The two children were then filmed in such a way that only the movement of the reflectors was visible. Female toddlers copied only the girl, when shown the film, and male toddlers only the boy. The conclusion was that toddlers recognise the gender of movement patterns.

It is a vexed issue whether gender differentiation in the nonverbal sphere is innate or learned. It is however a profound difference, of perception and orientation to tasks. Studies show that, while girls and boys are equivalent in mathematical skills when young (Walden & Walkerdine, 1982), after puberty girls' quantitative skills are less developed than boys'. In particular, girls' spatial skills appear to be less developed — although the later the puberty, the better the spatial skills (Newcombe & Bandura, 1983). On the other hand, girls have more developed verbal capacities. These studies need to be assessed carefully, since they are often misrepresented as showing that women cannot do mathematics. This is a mistake, both statistically and conceptually. Women may be competent at higher mathematics, even if their spatial skills differ from men's (Slade, 1993). Nevertheless, whether the different spatial abilities of women are a result of different education or are innate, women do rely on verbal codes heavily. The telephone plays a greater social role for women than men, in part for this reason. Of course, telephones are also useful to women who are tied to the house and young children, and cannot go out to socialise. There is an interplay between social factors and gender based dispositions to behaviour.

Gender differentiation is not, in our society, a differentiation among equals. There is a clear divide of power. Nowhere is this so clear as in the question of body image. The images of women are primarily set by men. The media and the advertising industry present as the ideal body types those that are highly dimorphic: that is, with exaggerated gender differences. Thin, short women and tall strong men still pervade our media. Women are thus encouraged to appear weaker, less powerful than and subservient to men. So intense is the differentiation, that it has come to dominate how we perceive our own body types. Women set ideals for themselves which are not only thinner than is medically advisable: according to some surveys, it is thinner than men find desirable (Jackson, 1992). The prevalence of eating disorders such as anorexia and, on the other hand, of obesity is witness to the power of social structures which dominate our nonverbal codes.

Exercise 3.4 Breaking nonverbal conventions

One of the most illuminating ways to recognise the rules governing the various nonverbal codes is to behave in a fashion that will violate those rules. In groups of four (two active participants, two observers, then reverse roles) set about violating codes. Be extremely wary of offending. Some ideas for such observations include:

1. Select an office block or store and have the two observers enter a crowded lift and act normally. The two active participants should enter the lift and face towards the rest of the people.
2. One active participant joins an auto bank or bus queue and stands close to the person ahead.

Write up notes on your observations, using the following categories, allocating one to each student:

(a) Aims.
(b) Hypothesis — what you expect to happen. You should cite relevant research.
(c) Subjects — describe those you observe and the circumstances.
(d) Results.

Present the results to the class.

Semiotic accounts of visual codes

Visual codes are codes that use the arrangement of visual elements to communicate. They range from fashion and graphics to the use of space in architecture. A number of theories aim to explain visual communication. We will concentrate on certain recent developments in semiotic theory. Semiotic theory applies to the areas of interpersonal communication on which we have been concentrating, but has a far wider scope. Semiotic analysis applies to every feature of the culture: it includes painting, art, architecture. Indeed, it is fundamental to semiotic analysis that all components of a culture contribute to

visual codes
Codes that use the arrangement of visual elements to communicate.

communication, and that in order to understand any particular code, it is necessary to see its place in the culture.

Semiotic theory extends Saussure's account of language to the nonverbal domain. Recall the definitions of syntagmatic relations in language — the relations that bind elements of a sentence together — and paradigmatic relations, which are the relations between possible alternatives in the sentence. In **structuralist theories**, the meanings of signs in general are taken to derive from the contrasts within a paradigm or structure (Pettit, 1977; Hawkes, 1977). So, for instance, the meaning of kinship relations in a particular culture depends on what categories of kin were discerned. In certain Aboriginal tribes, for instance, sisters of a biological mother are categorised with mothers in contrast to others in the paradigm. The structuralist points out that different and apparently unrelated phenomena might be a consequence of an underlying structural pattern — such as the rules governing politeness and intermarriage within the tribe.

We can see how such a theory might apply to fashion. Each item of clothing would be a sign, with an associated concept: a particular belt, for instance. An outfit would correspond to a sentence, or utterance. We might say there are syntagmatic relations between the various components that make up an outfit: shirts, jackets, hats, belts and so on. The paradigmatic relations would hold between alternative types of shirt or T-shirts, and between alternatives such as trousers, skirts or shirts. That paradigmatic set would give the significance of the particular choice. The meaning of suit trousers can be recognised by setting them against jeans. We put together an outfit syntagmatically, choosing suitable elements within each paradigm, and linking them together when fully dressed. We even say, carrying on the parallel to language, that people 'make a statement' in the way they dress: the suit tells us of the man inside it. Of course, the comparison can only go so far: fashion does not have the syntactic and semantic structure of a language that makes it so unique and powerful a form of communication (see Chapter 2).

The analysis of fashion is still decompositional, in so far as it identifies and labels components of fashion. Further structuralist developments of semiotic theory have also been applied to fashion. Underlying structural similarities have been identified across a range of different codes. We might find, for instance, that at some level the meaning of a particular gesture, such as an aggressive hand sign, is also to be found in an aggressive style of dress.

In the application of semiotic theory to design, much use has been made of Barthes' (1972) notion of a 'second order signifier'. To take one example, the strict and literal meaning of an expression, such as 'AIDS', which refers to a physiological set of tendencies due to the autoimmune virus, has been overlaid with a cumbersome set of secondary meanings. AIDS is associated with certain practices, such as drug use, hence AIDS itself has been seen as a stigma, as a sign of evil. Indeed, it has been persuasively presented as the disease of the 'other', of the outsider. Its prevalence in Africa, and the theory that it originated there imports an overtone of the primitive, 'darkest Africa'. As Susan Sontag (1989) argues, this same process occurred with syphilis, which was identified as the French disease in England, the English disease in France. Syphilis had the role of the shameful disease until penicillin made cure possible and altered the second order meaning.

> **structuralist theories**
> Theories that consider that the meanings of signs derive from the contrasts within a paradigm or structure.

Such second order signification is inherent in visual codes. For instance, both the Australian and New Zealand flags are first order signifiers of a particular country. They represent far more than just the country, however. The Union Jack, the flag of Great Britain, stands in one corner of each flag: the Union Jack itself is a signifier of Britain. Australia and New Zealand, in using the Union Jack on their flags, make our flags a second order signifier of Britain. For many Australians and New Zealanders, in consequence, the flag represents an outmoded role as a member of an Empire. For them, the flag is a second order signifier of dependence. For monarchists, on the other hand, it signifies loyalty.

In the case of Australia, second order image of Australia is implicit in many representations of the Australian accent and of its culture: it is an image of Australians as overwhelmingly male pioneers of Anglo-Saxon origin, living in the bush. In fact, Australia is one of the most urbanised societies of the world, with a multicultural population and more women than men. As Barthes explains, the level of second order signification is the level of myth. The Australian myth is a product of the accretions of meanings to the signifiers representing Australia. An analysis of the signs can make us aware of the higher order meanings of our words and images. However, there is a difficulty with such analyses. A claim that such and such a signifier has a second order meaning is difficult to deny, since if even one person reads the signifier that way, the mythic meaning must be there. This is a difficulty of which semiotic theorists are well aware. The semiotician Umberto Eco (1989), in his novel, *Foucault's Pendulum,* tells of a world gone mad, with signifiers taking on meanings in an unsystematic way. Sustained critiques of semiotic theory question this and other features of the analysis (Sless, 1986). Nevertheless, such analyses have become a powerful tool.

The analysis of advertisements has been a particularly rich field for semiotic analysis. Williamson (1978) pioneered such analyses. Consider a soap powder advertisement, for a product such as Surf. In a series of very successful television advertisements in the early 1990s, Maggie Fitzgibbon, a middle-aged reassuring figure, is set against a basket of washing. As she folds it, she looks up and gives her message: *'In these days of inflation, one thing keeps its value: Surf'.*

Her style is far removed from the buzz of the 1990s — she is no elegant power dresser. Instead, she takes us back to the safer days of the 1950s, when mothers called up their mothers for advice on the washing. The product is identified with her presence — Surf becomes as reassuring as she is. Surf, that is, takes on a second order meaning of reassuring economy, in virtue of being associated with a woman, and her words, which themselves portray reassuring economy as a first order meaning. One of the executives in charge of the Surf soap powder account in Australia in 1990 talked of their television campaign in a style influenced by semiotic theory. He said: 'The ad has very good cut through. Viewers associate Maggie Fitzgibbon with reliability. She's been with Surf for years. They stay with Surf too.' The advertising campaign was developed with semiotic theory in mind.

Notice that here the product, which takes on an image of reassurance, is already a second — or much higher order — signifier. In the 1950s, soap powders first took on their image of gentle cleanliness. Barthes (1972) explored in a famous article 'Soap powders and detergents' what many users of soap powders had forgotten, that soap is an abrasive chemical substance, whose image of gentleness and softness is a creation of the advertising industry. In the 1990s we have had to discover again this simple but much disguised truth. Environmentalists have urged us to reduce our use of chemical cleansers because of the dangers of the effluent; doctors tell us that fabric softeners should not be used on nappies because they can burn a baby's skin — yet it is difficult even to entertain their claims, so convinced are we that soaps are gentle, fabric softeners even gentler and that all good mothers scrub and clean.

Just this issue together with Barthes' article became the topic of a dance by Mark Morris' Seattle-based dance group in Belgium in 1989. The dance represented the frantic efforts of the American housewife to banish dirt. Morris had taken on Barthes' article both as a theoretical claim about the way that second order signifiers dominate our lives in the manner of myth and as a critique of the cleanliness myth itself. The dance then serves as a third order signifier, in so far as it treats Barthes' notion of a second order signifier as itself a signifier. The levels of meaning can continue to proliferate.

One way to appreciate the force of semiotic theory as a means of analysing cultural objects is with reference to the practitioners who see their work as informed by post-structuralism. Mandy Martin's painting 'Red Ochre Cove' was commissioned for the Main Committee Room of the Australian Parliament House in Canberra. At one level it is a postindustrial landscape: one sees the Australian landscape littered with disused factories. However, there is a significant echo in the shape of the lake to a classic early Australian landscape by Eugene von Guerard, and the shaft of sunlight running diagonally across the painting is a direct reference to the sunlight in Tom Roberts' painting of the opening of the first Australian Parliament which hangs nearby. While it may be impossible fully to spell out the force of the cross-referencing of the symbols, there is a significance.

Red Ochre Cove, *Mandy Martin, commissioned 1987, Parliament House Art Collection, Canberra. Used with permission.*

Considering Martin's painting in the context of the collection of paintings of Parliament is one way to spell out its meaning. Australia is overwhelmingly an urban culture, with a higher proportion of city dwellers than any other country in the world. Yet the Australian myth concentrates on the bush. Over 90 per cent of the paintings in the Parliament House collection are landscapes, with little evidence of the impact of man. Martin's postindustrial landscape must be read in that context, and her reference to von Guerard's painting of the landscape before man's intervention seems pointed.

The Parliament House building itself has been the target of widespread criticism (Kleinert, 1989; Weirick, 1989). The symbolism of the building is made quite explicit: it is partly buried in a hill to represent 'small government'; the immense forecourt is set with an Aboriginal design to represent pre-colonial times, while the entrance foyer's marble columns are meant to be forest. Critics point out that the immense spaces of Parliament House dwarf people, whether demonstrators or members, and hence signify not small government but the overweening power of government. The Australian myth of the dominance of the landscape cuts through the rhetoric of the dominance of the will of the people. Parliament House shows how a building can dismiss the importance of people. The scale of the building is reminiscent of the great monuments of Ancient Rome and the immense structures of modern Moscow. Perhaps that throws light on why the building appears undemocratic.

Parliament House, Canberra.
(Photo: *Xu Bai-ming*)

Semiotic theory enables us to tap insights about the way meaning in one code can influence meaning in a quite separate code. The nonverbal codes which mediate and construct our vision of the world are everywhere. Not only do they betray our inner thoughts, as Freud said in the quotation at the beginning of the chapter, they also create our images of the world. When we conceive of ourselves as of a certain nationality, a certain body type, as sporty or elegant or down to earth, we already refer to images that belong to our society. The more critical we are about those images, the better we are able to construct them to suit ourselves.

Exercise 3.5 Analysing a cartoon

Analyse the following cartoon, showing Paul Keating. Work in groups of four. Your analysis should include an explanation of the role of Keating's remark in the cartoon, the force of the flag as a symbol and the context of the cartoon, both political and cultural. In writing up a brief report of the analysis, be sure to define relevant terms (signifier, myth, etc.), to give references and to structure your report clearly, with an introduction, an explanation of the theoretical background of your analysis, an account of the analysis and a conclusion.

Chapter 3

Keating's identity.
Source: *W. Mitchell,
The Australian,
29 April 1992.
Used with permission.*

Exercise 3.6 Smiling

This exercise is an investigation of smiling. There are a number of different models for such an investigation. You might take an approach based on any of the models discussed in the chapter. However, it is essential that you are not too ambitious and that you circumscribe your project, selecting one aspect only to investigate. In all cases you must be wary of offending those you observe.

If you wish to adopt perspectives from social psychology, you might look at literature such as Deutsch, LeBaron & Fryer (1987) and references therein. In this article, the differences between the smiling expected of women and men is discussed, together with the other behaviours that accompany smiling. You might adapt this material for an observation study. Your observation should concentrate on one factor. You might observe gender differences in smiling in the library, or coffee shop; or cultural differences as seen between students of different cultural backgrounds in one limited context, or differences due to age or subgroup.

Alternatively, you might follow the model offered by Kendon (1981a), and investigate (and possibly film) a brief segment of smiling between two people in a particular context, say for two minutes.

You might prefer to analyse just one advertisement on television and the smiling behaviour in it, and attempt to give a semiotic analysis of the role of the smile within the Australian advertising culture.

You should prepare the report of this observation exercise, using the conventions appropriate to your approach. You should look carefully at the readings you have done for an appropriate model. If you wish to take the semiotic approach, you should adopt general essay writing techniques (see, e.g. the revision exercise at the end of Chapter 2 for guidelines).

If you prefer an observation study you may use the following labelled sections, reminiscent of the report described in Table 2.1.

(a) Abstract (or executive summary): a brief summary, on a separate page, before the body of the essay.

(b) Aim.
(c) Hypothesis — what you suppose to be the case: say, that women smile more frequently than men when shopping at the chemist. Cite relevant research and theoretical background and define terms.
(d) Subjects — describe those you observe and the circumstances.
(e) Methods — describe how your observation was conducted.
(f) Results — describe your results.
(g) Discussion/conclusion — state your conclusions and, in particular, any difficulties or reservations you have about your results.

Summary

1. There is a range of nonverbal codes, from body language to advertisements and architecture. Nonverbal codes are defined as codes that are independent from spoken languages, that are conventional and culturally specific.
2. Body language is the range of nonverbal codes used in bodily communication. Kinesics is the study of gesture, and proxemics of the use of space in communication. Nonverbal signals can be used to modify and regulate spoken messages by matching or cancelling the spoken words.
3. There is also a range of nonverbal behaviours we may use with greater or lesser degrees of self-awareness. These are emblems, illustrators, affect displays, regulators and adaptors.
4. Nonverbal codes have a further feature: the meaning of nonverbal interaction is always specified in context. We should not isolate nonverbal acts and attempt to explain their significance independently of the context in which those actions occur.
5. Nonverbal communication is culture bound and the interpretation of the nonverbal codes of a culture must be relative to particular cultures and subgroups. There are major differences in the nonverbal communication practices of people from different cultures. There are also major gender differences within cultures in the ways men and women communicate nonverbally.
6. Both media messages and the design of public buildings and spaces may be interpreted using semiotic theory. A better understanding of the way those messages and spaces are designed, through semiotic analysis, can throw light on how nonverbal communication alters the way we conceive the world.

Discussion questions

1. Describe a situation in which verbal and nonverbal cues conflict.
2. How would you describe the conventions of greeting in your culture?
3. Is there a gender difference in greeting behaviours in your culture?
4. What are the major functional roles of nonverbal communication? Give examples from your own experience.
5. Describe the use of eyes as indicators of turn-taking in casual conversation.

6. What is open body language? Can one person manifest both open and closed body language at one time?
7. Define Hall's intimate, personal, social and formal distances. Do you think your culture follows the same rule?
8. He met William, and when he learned who he was, he looked at him with polite hostility: not because his face betrayed his secret, I was sure of that, but because he certainly wanted William to feel he was hostile.   (Umberto Eco, 1983: 301)
Explain what account of the nature of nonverbal communication is implicit in this quotation.
9. Explain the difference between syntagmatic and paradigmatic relations. Does it apply to nonverbal codes?
10. Describe the architectural structure of the library or refectory at your university. Are the structures designed to encourage interaction between students?

Further reading

Barthes, R. (1972) *Mythologies* London: Paladin.
Jackson, L. (1992) *Physical Appearance and Gender* Albany: State University of New York Press.
Kendon, A. (ed.) (1981) *Nonverbal Communication, Interaction and Gesture: Selections from Semiotica* The Hague: Mouton.
Kendon, A., Harris, R. & Mitcheley, M. (eds) (1975) *Organisation of Behaviour in Face-to-Face Interaction* The Hague: Mouton.
Knapp, M. (1990) 'Nonverbal Communication', pp. 50–70 in G. Dahnke, C. Fernandez-Collado, & G. Clatterbuck, (eds) *Human Communication: Theory and Research* Belmont, CA: Wadsworth.

References

Ardrey, R. (1966) *The Territorial Imperative* New York: Atheneum.
Argyle, M., Ingham, R., Alkema, F. & McCallin, M. (1981) 'The Different Functions of Gaze', pp. 283–96 in A. Kendon *op. cit.*
Baker, E. & Shaw M. (1980) 'Reactions to Interpersonal Distance and Topic Intimacy', *Journal of Nonverbal Behaviour* 5: 80–91.
Deutsch, F., LeBaron, D. & Fryer, M. (1987) 'What is in a Smile?' *Psychology of Women Quarterly* 11: 341–52.
Duranti, A. & Goodwin, C. (eds) (1992) *Rethinking Context: Language as an Interactive Phenomenon* Cambridge: Cambridge University Press.
Eco, U. (1983) *The Name of the Rose* London: Martin Secker & Warburg.
Eco, U. (1989) *Foucault's Pendulum* London: Martin Secker & Warburg.
Ekman, P. (1988) 'Lying and Nonverbal Behaviour', *Journal of Nonverbal Behaviour* 12 (3): 170.
Ekman, P. & Friesen, W. (1969) 'The Repertoire of Nonverbal Behaviour', *Semiotica* 1: 49–98.

Exline, R., Ellyson, S. & Long, B. (1975) 'Visual behaviour as an aspect of power role relationships', in P. Pilner, L. Krames & T. Alloway, (eds) *Advances in the Study of Communication and Affect* New York: Plenum.

Goffman, E. (1974) *Frame Analysis: An Essay in the Organisation of Experience* New York: Harper & Row.

Grice, H. (1957) 'Meaning', *Philosophical Review* 66: 377–88.

Hall, E. (1966) *The Hidden Dimension* Illinois: Free Press.

Hawkes, T. (1977) *Structuralism and Semiotics* London: Methuen.

Hochschild, A. (1983) *The Managed Heart* University of California Press.

Kendon, A. (1981a) 'Some functions of the face in a kissing round', pp. 321–56 in A. Kendon (ed.) (1981) *op. cit.*

Kendon, A. (1992) 'The Negotiation of Context in Face-to-face Interaction', pp. 323–34 in A. Duranti & C. Goodwin, *op. cit.*

Kleinert, S. (1989) 'Myths for the Future: The Art of Parliament House', *Transitions* 27 & 28: 9–18.

Mayle, P. (1980) *A Year in Provence* London: Pan.

Newcome, N. & Bandura, M. (1983) 'The effect of age of puberty on spatial ability in girls', *Developmental Psychology* 19: 215–24.

Nomura, M. (1990) 'Remodelling the Japanese Body', *Senri Ethnological Studies* 27: 259–74.

Pettit, P. (1977) *The Concept of Structuralism: A Critical Analysis* Berkeley: University of California Press.

Ramsey, S. (1985) 'To Hear One and Understand Ten: Nonverbal Behaviour in Japan', pp. 307-21 in L. Samovar & R. Porter, (eds) *Intercultural Communication: A Reader* Belmont CA: Wadsworth.

Rose, D. B. (1992) *Dingo Makes Us Human* Cambridge: CUP.

Rudder, J. (unpublished) 'Yolngu time', Australian Institute of Aboriginal and Torres Strait Islander Studies.

Scheflen, A. (1981) 'Micro-Territories in Human Interaction', pp. 159-73 in A. Kendon *op. cit.*

Slade, C. (1993) 'Logic in the Classroom', pp. 645–53 in M. Lipman, (ed.) *Thinking Children and Education* Dubuque, Iowa: Kendall Hunt.

Sless, D. (1986) *In Search of Semiotics* Sydney: Croom Helm.

Sontag, S. (1989) *AIDS and its Metaphors* London: Penguin.

Stanner, H. (1979) *White Man Got No Dreaming* Canberra: ANU Press.

Swain, T. (1988) 'The Ghost of Space', pp. 452–69 in T. Swain & D.B. Rose, (eds) *Aboriginal Australians and Christian Missions* Adelaide: The Australian Association for the Study of Religion.

Walden, R. & Walkerdine, V. (1982) *Girls and Mathematics: The Early Years* London: Institute of Education, University of London.

Watson, O. (1970) *Proxemic Behaviour: A Cross-cultural Study* The Hague: Mouton.

Weirick, J. (1989) 'Partial Visions', *Transitions* 27 & 28: 18–58.

Williamson, J. (1978) *Decoding Advertisements: Ideology and Meaning in Advertising* London: Marion Boyars.

Critical thinking

Objectives

After completing this chapter you should be able to:

- describe critical thinking skills and the roles they have in communication;
- understand the factors influencing clarity in communication, both at the level of thought and of language;
- define the notions of argument and validity;
- identify common fallacies;
- recognise that reasoning may require imagination and sympathy.

He had at first been in considerable fear of his straight loud north country friend, who showed signs of cultivating logic and criticism to a degree that was hostile to fine loose talk; but he discovered in him later a man to whom one could say anything in the world if one didn't think it of more importance to be sympathised with than to be understood.

The Princess Casamassima, *Henry James*

The hero of Henry James' novel is nervous of 'logic and criticism', fearful that it is incompatible with 'fine loose talk', or just ordinary chat. We too are nervous of criticism and logic. Very often, we communicate precisely because we wish to be sympathised with, not because we wish to be understood.

Moreover, we have grown aware of just how irrational, instinctive and unpremeditated much of communicative activity is. Think of the immense force of body language in communication; of the impact of communication in advertising, of the role of prejudices in understanding others — especially those of another race. Communication is largely unreflective, unmediated by conscious reasoning.

'Criticism' and its cognates are pejorative expressions in modern English as, indeed, they were for Henry James one hundred years ago. In part this is a result of the belief that criticism is incompatible with creativity. This is a mistake. Critical thought should not be contrasted with creative thought, but with mundane, uncritical thought. Every good musician or artist or creative thinker is self-critical to an intense degree. Conversely, good analytical critical thought can be very creative — think of physics. There has been a false assimilation between critical thought and sterile, unproductive analytic thought. The aim should be creative critical thought, not one or the other exclusively.

Henry James' hero does, however, point out one concern: his logical critical friend is unsympathetic. It is true that criticism often seems unsympathetic. However, the appearance of cruelty can be a result of another mistake: that of regarding criticism of one's ideas as criticism of oneself. People can cope with an objective criticism of their ideas, as long as they learn to separate criticism of their ideas from criticism of themselves. It is a skill fundamental to developing rigorous thinking procedures.

So critical thought need not be destructive. It directs itself to the truth, and examines the quality of reasons. In this sense, critical thinking involves taking an analytic view of one's own and others' ideas. This does not mean that critical thinking is purely objective. Language and meaning are developed intersubjectively — between people. So too are canons or criteria of good thinking. They are social constructs, just like meaning. But the criteria or the features whereby one judges good thinking are utterly fundamental to human intercourse. Unless we were basically agreed on what counted as sense, as good common sense, we could not even get about the world.

The importance of reason

The very process of communication involves an elaborate structure of reasoning: in so far as we understand another's words or gestures, we must grasp that they intend us to understand something in particular, by using a certain sort of expression or movements. This use of convention is predicated on communicators' abilities to recognise regularities in behaviour and look for an explanation — all a part of reasoning skills.

Moreover, reasoning and critical thinking skills underlie all human activity. Critical thinking skills are broad and essential to human activity. They include all the skills involved in connecting and organising ideas. We shall classify them as analysis, inference and evaluation.

Analysis involves
- identifying what is being said;
- distinguishing what is relevant from what is not;
- seeing connections between different strands of thought;
- recognising vagueness and ambiguity, then clarifying terms if necessary;
- identifying members of a class, in terms of likenesses;
- identifying counterinstances, as different in some respect;
- identifying analogies.

Inference involves
- drawing out the consequences of what is said;
- identifying underlying assumptions;
- generalising from particular instances, i.e. abstracting;
- applying analogies to reach new conclusions;
- recognising cause/effect relationships.

Evaluation involves
- giving reasons for beliefs and decisions and then choosing how to act;
- criticising ideas constructively;
- modifying ideas in response to criticism.
    (Lipman, 1985, 1988; Schlect, 1983; McPeck, 1990; Weinstein, 1990)

Most reasoning involves all components simultaneously.

The skills are extremely broad-ranging and utterly fundamental. No child learns to walk and talk without acquiring the ability to recognise cause/effect relationships, to classify and identify likenesses and to grasp what follows from actions or utterances. In doing so they are using reasoning skills. The enormous and very effective use we all make of our critical thinking skills all the time is often not recognised. Psychologists often remark that people do not reason logically, for instance (Sternberg & Smith, 1988). Of course, mistakes get made, but most of us do an extraordinary amount of critical thinking extremely well.

In this chapter, the focus is on critical thinking in communication. We will look at the analysis of reasoning in order to improve our communication skills, both in formulating our ideas and in understanding what is communicated to us. Very often, advertising campaigns, political leaders, even university lecturers, gloss over what would be accurate and logical. A clearer understanding of reasoning skills can help us identify those mistakes in reasoning, fallacies, and thereby get closer to the truth.

It is useful to use the notion of **presupposition**. A statement (question . . .) p presupposes a statement q if, whether p is true or false (whether yes or no is the correct answer), q must be true.

presupposition
A statement (question . . .) p presupposes a statement q if, whether p is true or false (whether yes or no is the correct answer), q must be true.

So, for instance, the sentence *The King of France is bald,* has a presupposition: *There is a King of France,* and *Have you stopped beating your wife?* presupposes *You beat your wife,* since both positive and negative replies make the presupposition *I used to beat her* true, as in *Yes, I have (I used to beat her)* and *No, I haven't (I still beat her).*

Consider, for example, the Mars ice-cream advertisement, in which a claim is made that Mars ice-cream contains real milk. There is nothing irrational in the claim that Mars ice-cream contains real milk, although it is very difficult to say what food is *not* real. But the intention of the advertisement was undoubtedly to elicit the irrational conclusion one child was heard to come up with: 'This is good for you, Mum. It's *real.*' The child's conclusion presupposed that everything that's real is good for you. This is clearly not a valid presupposition since sugar is real, fat is real and, for that matter, cancer is real, one hundred per cent natural (in the sense of not synthetic).

Another example concerns the Russian press, in the years before liberalisation. According to Valeriy Maximenkov of the then Soviet embassy in 1990, it was often impossible to say things directly. The press was very often extremely unclear and apparently irrational. In order to understand the press, it was necessary to 'read between the lines', rather than assume that what was said was truthful. The example he gave was of readers who inferred that a Minister had been deposed because a Deputy was quoted in the paper. The presupposition held by readers and the journalist was that *if* the Minister were still in power, then it would be he, not the Deputy who would be quoted. Readers were able to reason, on this basis, that the Minister had been deposed.

In order to discuss rationality in communication, we need a rather deeper conception of critical thinking. We begin with an account of clarity in communication, then give an account of informal logic. Finally, we turn to common fallacies and the issue of whether reasoning is incompatible with sympathy and persuasion.

Exercise 4.1 Presuppositions

Consider the following excerpts from a letter to the *Canberra Times,* 29/4/91. What are the presuppositions the writer is making about the beliefs of the reader? What are the assumptions and presuppositions you as reader make? Are your assumptions justified? Be prepared to discuss these questions in class.

Law reform for prostitution a good idea

I am a prostitute happily living and working in the ACT and I consider myself an expert on this subject. While I cannot claim that prostitution is emotionally fulfilling I certainly never feel degraded by what I do . . . Something must be done about the present archaic law which does demean me . . .

Many other occupations have far more stringent regulations than mine. Consider the books of rules that must be adhered to by electricians . . . People of my grandfather's era shouted in indignation when driving licences were made compulsory. I remember the protests about compulsory seat belts. But they all had to knuckle under, for the common good . . .

Prostitution is neither a good nor a bad thing. In an ideal world it would not need to exist. However, I live in this one and if I live to be 100 years old I doubt I'll see it even remotely approach 'ideal'.

Clarity in communication

> ... *the equivocation of the fiend*
> *That lies like truth*
>
> Macbeth, *Shakespeare*

There is no act of communication which is entirely clear, and few acts of communication which could not be clear in certain circumstances to certain people. Macbeth, in Shakespeare's play, was misled by witches who told him truths, intending him to misunderstand them. So, for instance, he was told he would never be defeated 'till Birnham wood do come to Dunsinane' nor killed by 'one of woman born' and was dismayed when troops came up camouflaged by branches from Dunsinane wood, and when he was then challenged by a man who had been born by Caesarean section.

If Macbeth had cross questioned the witches further, he may not have been misled. As he says, they **equivocated** — used one form of words that was ambiguous and had two interpretations. Since he did not, he mistook the meaning and was misled by ambiguities. In other cases, the most ambiguous utterances can make perfect sense.

equivocation
The intentional use of a form of words that is ambiguous.

The moral here is that clarity in communication is both relative and intersubjective: it is not an absolute notion. Any utterance or piece of writing could be clarified further. It is impossible to be clear for everyone, but it is possible to be clear for a particular audience. To use the classification of Bernstein (see Chapter 2), a restricted code used in the home may be clear enough for the family and possibly appropriate even in public forms such as poetry or humorous writing, whereas for scholarly purposes an elaborated scholarly code is necessary. Given that this is so, to ask for clarification is not necessarily to criticise the original statement, but may merely be a request to explain the context.

'Clarity' in communication is itself an ambiguous notion. It might mean clarity of thought, or clarity of expression. A representative of the Mars company was extremely clear about the aim of his campaign — to make an announcement, and to establish that the ingredients were real (what else could the ingredients be?). At no stage would the product be advertised as healthy, which would be misleading advertising. The intention of the ad was merely to tell people that Mars ice-cream existed, and to say what was in it. The advertisement is deliberately unclear.

A similar point holds for newspapers in the former USSR and China. Where information is constrained, the clearest way of expressing an idea may be indirectly, via a deliberately unclear presentation. Newspapers often exploit a certain ambiguity or lack of clarity in order to grab attention. Unclarity may serve clear purposes. Furthermore, what counts as a clear presentation in our society may look doubtful, at best, in another.

Words, or terms, may be unclear. Some are ambiguous, with more than one interpretation, as is 'present' in the phrase: 'Wait here for the present'. Such ambiguity is troublesome only if misinterpreted, but if said to a child meaning, 'Wait for a short while', the ambiguity might cause real distress. Ambiguity of this sort is a surface feature of language, not of the corresponding concepts. We have one term, but two concepts to which it may refer.

At times concepts themselves are vague. Consider again the Mars ice-cream. At the level of words we have 'real Mars chocolate'. There's nothing unclear about the expression 'real Mars chocolate'. However, at the corresponding level of thought — concepts — there is a lack of clarity. What is real is itself a notoriously difficult concept. There is a persisting question of whether beauty or love or numbers are real, which does not reflect a difficulty of language, but one of the concepts themselves.

Vagueness may be a feature of both language and thought, or just of language. To say 'come over next week' is vague: often intentionally so. Still, if the invitee comes it will be on a specific day — there is no such thing as a vague time. On the other hand, the vagueness of 'bald' or 'a heap of sand' is a feature not just of language but of the concept involved. Both are essentially vague concepts. It would not be true to our concept of baldness to say that there is an exact point at which one hair less will mean you are bald. Equally, a heap of sand is fuzzy: how many grains you take away to stop a heap being a heap is itself vague. Vagueness in this sense, where it is a consequence of essentially vague concepts, is not objectionable. Indeed, we can construct perfectly good logics for vague terms — the so called 'fuzzy logics'. Vagueness may be objectionable, however, when it leads to confusion. The utterance *Most people don't like the government* calls out for clarification — what is meant by most?

Sentences or statements are complete utterances, capable of being true or false. Sentences can be ambiguous by virtue of their syntactic structure: in *He killed the woman with the gun,* for instance, it is unclear who is holding the gun — the man or the woman? That is called structural ambiguity. Corresponding to the statement or sentence at the level of the thought, there are propositions. In this context, the term 'proposition' has a meaning different from that it might have when used in a bar or in a business context. A **proposition** is a statement abstracted from a particular language: it is whatever can be asserted, maintained or denied. English, French and Spanish statements which are translations of each other express the same proposition, which at the level of thought is sometimes called a judgment. Statements, propositions and judgments are all things that can be true or false. They describe or refer to facts. Clarity in the proposition depends on clarity of the language used, and clarity of the thought expressed.

Propositions may lack clarity, just as concepts do. The proposition corresponding to OMO *washes whiter* (if there is a fully specifiable proposition) is unclear, since it does not specify whiter than what? Lack of clarity in propositions may be a result of the complexity of the concepts involved. A report in a Mexican newspaper, for instance, in 1991, gave the results of a survey in Australia: *Men do more work in the house.* The conclusion was that this state of affairs is unjust. In this case there is a move from a true statement about the world of fact to one of moral evaluation, or value. Whether we can reason from facts to values is a matter of dispute, but the inferences should not be presupposed. For instance, the judgment above involves moral issues that are extremely complex, such as 'What makes for a just society?'; 'Should men and women share work in the house?'. These are not easy questions to answer, and their difficulty is reflected in actual clarity of thought. It may, for instance, be an assumption in Latin America that children are more effectively cared for by women. A judgment that society is most effectively organised when women care

proposition
A statement abstracted from a particular language; it is whatever can be asserted, maintained or denied.

for children would rest on justifying that presupposition. Very often, questions of values are very complex and deeply held. Indeed, there are those who believe that facts and values are always to be kept separate and that no accumulation of facts can determine what is right or wrong.

There may also be a lack of clarity of argument. We define arguments formally in the next section. For our purposes here we need only to remark that an argument is not a disagreement, but a sequence of utterances, or propositions, designed to support a conclusion. The most common feature of arguments as they are presented in language, is that the contents are not all there — most of the argument is simply left out, assumed, presupposed or gestured at. Such arguments are strictly called enthymematic arguments. An **enthymematic argument** is one in which premises are suppressed, or evidence or grounds not mentioned. Enthymemes may be a cause of confusion. For instance, the argument 'We are close to Asia, so we should be part of Asia' is enthymematic, and unpacking its content may, or may not, show it to be justified. On the other hand, it is impossible, even in principle, to be absolutely explicit about all premises. Ellipsis is most useful among like-minded people.

A less defensible but very common fault in argument is irrelevance, being beside the point. Again, what counts as relevant is intersubjective and relative to the interests of the group. We can all go off at a tangent when we are talking. Indeed, tangents are the essence of good conversation. But irrelevance may impede the development of the argument. While it may be difficult strictly to define what is and what is not relevant without first delimiting the subject, and thereby possibly limiting the scope of the argument, there is a good common-sense notion that we all use, of sticking to the point.

Facts and inferences

The much used and extremely vexed distinction between fact and inference is difficult to state. Indeed, the distinction as normally conceived might better be labelled as one between facts and interpretation (Rasool et al., 1993, ch 3). However, interpretation is included with inference since we defined inference very broadly in the first section of the chapter. Inference includes drawing out the consequences of what is said, identifying underlying assumptions, generalising from particular instances (such as abstracting), applying analogies to reach new conclusions and recognising cause/effect relationships.

The definition of fact used here relativises the notion of a fact to a state of information. In any state of information, **facts** with respect to that state of information are propositions held true in that state of information. In that state of information, other statements will require argumentation to be ascertained: in that state of information, those statements are **inferences**. Inferences are conclusions or arguments and may be just as true, and as well justified, as facts, even within the state of information in which they are inferences; but they may involve an element of supposition.

For instance, when I am told by a reliable source that the temperature in Sydney on 14 January was 34°C, that statement counts as a fact in that state of information. Some statements may not have a determinate truth value in a state of information: that is, they may be neither definitely true nor definitely false. I may suppose, or infer, that since it was 34°, it was fine. That supposition, or inference, may well be true, but it may not be: there may have been rain. The

enthymematic argument
One in which the premises are suppressed, or evidence or grounds not mentioned.

facts
In any state of information, some statements will count as facts; they are the propositions held true in that state of information.

inferences
In any state of information, other statements will require argumentation to be ascertained; those statements are inferences.

state of information that gives us the fact of the temperature does not guarantee the truth of 'It was fine on 14 January'. So, in that state of information, the inference is not a fact.

Of course, there is some fact to the matter about whether it was fine on 14 January in Sydney, which could be checked in an old newspaper. But that information was not accessible within the state of information. I inferred it — in this case using a probabilistic argument for the premise: if it's hot in Sydney in summer, it's probably fine. This inference does not guarantee the truth of the conclusion.

We often go beyond the facts in our judgments, and often we are not justified. Sometimes, we go beyond the facts using invalid reasoning and the resulting inference (i.e. conclusion) is not true. Psychological overgeneralisation is one example. When someone says, 'He's Mexican, he's violent', the inference is not a fact in the state of information we generally have access to. In order for that overgeneralisation to be a fact, there would need to be a state of information saying that 'All Mexicans are violent', and that does not exist. Notice, however, that if the inference is the conclusion of a good argument from good premises, then it will be as true as any fact could be.

The distinction between facts and inferences has common currency. It is used, for instance, in the courts. When a lawyer asks a witness: 'Is your claim about the accused being drugged a fact or just an inference?' she is asking: 'Did you see the drug being taken, or did you simply assume from the behaviour of the accused that drugs had been taken?' The distinction is based on the evidence available. We cannot define facts, as is sometimes done, as observables, and contrast them with inferences, based on theories. That is too simple a definition, for many observations involve inferences. Even to say you've seen a star is to make enormous demands on theory and inference: how do you know that a flash of light is a star, let alone what a star is, without inference?

Lack of clarity in inference, and the criteria for good inference form the topic of the next section.

Exercise 4.2 Fact or inference
Label the following statements True (T) or False (F) or Unknown (?), given the state of information described in the following story. Which are facts and which inferences?

A well-liked university lecturer had just completed making up the examination paper and had turned off the lights. Just then a short, dark figure appeared and demanded the examination papers. The lecturer opened the drawer. Everything in the drawer was picked up and the individual ran down the corridor. The Dean was notified immediately.

1.	The thief was tall, dark and broad.	T	F	?
2.	The lecturer turned off the lights.	T	F	?
3.	A short figure demanded the examination papers.	T	F	?
4.	The examination papers were picked up by someone.	T	F	?
5.	The examination papers were picked up by the lecturer.	T	F	?
6.	A short, dark figure appeared after the lecturer turned off the lights.	T	F	?
7.	The man who opened the drawer was the lecturer.	T	F	?
8.	The lecturer ran down the corridor.	T	F	?
9.	The drawer was never actually opened.	T	F	?
10.	In this report three persons are referred to .	T	F	?

(Based on DeVito (1974, p. 55), modelled on exercises of William Haney)

Logic

Logic is like the sword: those who live by it will die by it.
Samuel Butler

Logic is the study of the formal and informal rules governing argument and reasoning. It has been a separate area of study since Aristotle introduced a calculus of reasoning. Aristotle was the first to formalise a calculus of validity: of forms of argument. While formal logic has moved very much further than the Aristotelian logic, and is now a branch of pure mathematics, the basic notions can be introduced through the simpler examples Aristotle used.

The notion of validity is an extremely important one for critical thinking. In order to introduce the notion, we need first to define an argument. An **argument** is a logically interwoven set of statements, one of which, the **conclusion**, rests on or follows from the others. An argument is not a series of disagreements, as in common parlance. For instance:

$$\frac{\text{Women are irrational}}{\text{Sue is a woman}}$$
$$\text{Sue is irrational}$$

is an argument. A **premise** or set of premises are the grounds or statements assumed or presupposed as true, which are used as the basis of an inference to the conclusion. One convention draws premises above and conclusions below a line.

The premises may be true or false, and the argument may or may not necessitate the conclusion. In the argument above, the premises necessitate the conclusion if the premises are true. The first premise is not true, but the argument from the premises to conclusion is good. We say that the argument form is valid, since the premises necessitate the conclusion in a precise sense defined below.

Another example is:

$$\frac{\text{All ME sufferers have symptoms of fatigue and depression.}}{\text{I have symptoms of fatigue and depression}}$$
$$\text{So, I am an ME sufferer}$$

(Here ME refers to myalgic encephalitis, but that is not necessary for the structure of the argument)

Note that this argument structure is not good. We can see why by using **analogy** — an argument with the same structure but different premises.

All ME sufferers have a heart	Premise
I have a heart	Premise
So I have ME	Conclusion

Clearly, the conclusion does not follow, although the premises are true. Again:

All men have a heart	Premise
I have a heart	Premise
I am a man	Conclusion

Depending on who is speaking, this conclusion may be true or false. Therefore, the argument structure is *not* valid. We can now establish the definitions:

---

argument
A logically interwoven set of statements, one of which, the conclusion, rests on or follows from the others (the premises).

conclusion
The logical outcome of an argument.

premise
The grounds or statements assumed to be true that are used as the basis of an inference to the conclusion.

analogy
Argument by analogy infers from the basis of a similarity in some respect a similarity in other respects.

Chapter 4

valid argument
One in which, if the premises are true, the conclusion must be true. It is impossible for the premises to be true and the conclusion not to be.

invalid argument
An argument in which the premises can be true and the conclusion false.

A **valid argument** is one in which, if the premises are true, the conclusion must be true. An **invalid argument** is one in which the premises can be true and the conclusion false. Validity is a matter of form, not of truth of premises. This form is valid:

All women are irrational
<u>Sue is a woman</u>
Sue is irrational

However, the first premise is false, and the conclusion may well be. In a valid argument, the conclusion *must* be true *if* the premises are.

An invalid form is one in which the premises may be true, without the conclusion being true. It is possible for an invalid argument to have true premises and conclusions:

All sharks are fish
<u>All sharks have gills</u>
All fish have gills

We can establish invalidity by analogy, or by a counterexample of the same form:

All men are animals
<u>All men are mammals</u>
All animals are mammals

Here true premises arrayed in the same way as above yield a false conclusion.

Identifying an argument in ordinary discourse may be very complicated. Note that often arguments are elliptical: they are not fully spelt out in ordinary language. However, we do have clues in certain key words used:

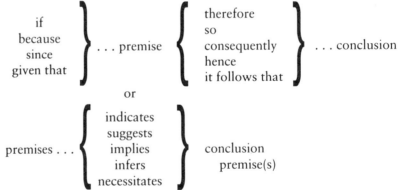

All these key words, and their variants (e.g. the nominal forms like 'The implication is') may be missing and an argument may still be present. Just imagine the following discussion:

'I'm so worried when she's late home. I always think there's been an accident.'
'Tennis practice.'

Fully spelt out, one side of the argument is the claim:

'If she is late, she had an accident,' to which the reply is:
'That is not true. If she has tennis practice she is late home. So she may be late and not have had an accident.'

Many advertisements make their impact by relying on implicit arguments, especially lifestyle ads: the Coke ads, for instance, rely on the implicit — and invalid — argument:

> They drink Coke
> They have a lifestyle I would like
> ―――――――――――――――――――
> If I drink Coke I will have that lifestyle

Normal Australians. Source: *G. Pryor,* The Canberra Times, *13 June 1991. Used with permission.*

Arguments may even be found in pictures and cartoons. Here the joke turns on the inference:

> All politicians are people who should be treated like other people
> Other people are losing their jobs
> ―――――――――――――――――――
> So politicians can lose their job

The intention of the remark was:

> All politicians are people who should be treated like other people
> The Government's actions are fair to most people, say on traffic offences
> ―――――――――――――――――――
> So politicians should be given traffic summonses

Deductive and inductive arguments

It is useful to distinguish two types of arguments. Those presented above are deductive arguments. A **deductive argument** leads from the premises (either particular or general) to a conclusion (either particular or general) by necessitation. It would be impossible to assert the premises and deny the conclusion without contradicting oneself. For instance, in

> All students work hard
> Those who work hard deserve a break
> ―――――――――――――――――――
> So all students deserve a break

it is impossible to claim that the premises are true but that the conclusion is not.

deductive argument
An argument that purports to lead from the premises (either particular or general) to a conclusion (either particular or general) by necessity.

inductive argument
An argument in which a generalisation is based on observed particular instances.

(It is irrelevant here that one or both of the premises may be false).

An **inductive argument** is one in which a generalisation is based on observed particular instances. So, for instance, we might argue:

> Many kookaburras have been observed with grey-brown plumage
> ───
> So all kookaburras have grey-brown plumage

Induction leads from observed cases in the past, and extrapolates to the future. It is not impossible that the premise may be true and the conclusion false. That would be the case if, for instance, a new race of pure white kookaburras were discovered. The discovery of black swans in Australia was precisely this sort of counter-example to what had previously been thought to be a true inductive conclusion. Nevertheless, inductive reasoning is one of the most used and reliable forms of reasoning (Girle et al., 1978).

In the first deductive argument, the generalisation *All students — always — are hardworking* is a premise, whereas in the inductive argument, the premise is *The kookaburras so far observed have grey-brown plumage.*

Exercise 4.3 Deductive or inductive

Label premises and conclusions in the following arguments. Which are inductive and which deductive?

(a)
> No degree can guarantee a job
> Unless a degree can guarantee a job it's worthless
> ───
> All degrees are worthless

(b) The galaxies we've observed so far exhibit a red shift. The most likely explanation is that it is a Doppler shift brought about by their movement away from us. So, the universe is expanding (i.e. all galaxies are moving away from us).

(c) We've been travelling now for 30 years. If we travel 185 million kilometres a year that means we've done 5550 million kilometres. Our sensor reveals the presence of intelligent life on a new planet we've named 'Plato'. On beaming down, we met a group of seven Platonians who proved friendly, but of unusual appearance. Their shape was humanoid, but their skin was coloured purple. In the distance, I can just make out another Platonian humanoid coming toward us. He'll be purple too, I guess.

(d) I have trouble getting to this class on time because I can't get away from work until half an hour before and when I get here the parking area is usually full.

(e)
> Some people who stayed on the dole for over
> nine months in the past were dole bludgers
> ───
> All people who stay on the dole after nine months are bludgers

sufficient condition
A proposition is sufficient for another when, if the former holds, the latter must.

conditional statement
One which has the form 'if ... then'; the antecedent follows the 'if', and the consequent follows the 'then'.

Necessary and sufficient conditions

Another useful distinction is that between necessary and sufficient conditions. A **sufficient condition** for an event is one that guarantees its occurrence. So, for instance, successfully swatting a fly is sufficient for its death — it is squashed. Successful swatting is not necessary for the demise of a fly: you could use Mortein. The sufficient condition can be expressed as a true **conditional** — a sentence containing 'if ... then': *If you swat a fly successfully then it dies.* Notice that the conditional has two parts — the antecedent which follows the 'if' and the consequent which follows the 'then'. A sufficient condition is the antecedent of a true conditional; if it holds, it guarantees that the consequent will. Indeed, if the fly had not died it could not have been successfully swatted.

The antecedent and consequent of a true 'if . . . then' sentence cannot be turned around, without altering the meaning and generally making the sentence untrue. It certainly does not follow that *If a fly dies it has been successfully swatted* since flies die of many causes. The very common mistake of reversing the conditional in this way is called affirming the consequent. What has happened, to use another term, is that in reversing the conditional, a condition which is just sufficient for the death of a fly is taken to be necessary for the death of a fly. There's no one necessary way to kill a fly.

A **necessary condition** is one without which another cannot hold. It is necessary to be female to bear a child. To use a conditional form, we say: *If someone bears a child then they must be female*, which is equivalent to *Only females bear children*, and expresses a necessary condition. The necessary condition is the consequent of a true conditional. It follows that if someone is not female then they cannot bear children — but it does not follow that if they don't bear children, they are not female. Turning the conditional this way is called denying the antecedent. We could put the point equally well that it is not sufficient to be female to bear a child; many females have not had children.

Some conditions are both necessary and sufficient. Having at least $1 000 000 is necessary and sufficient for being a millionaire. If you are a millionaire you have at least $1 000 000 and vice versa. Both of the following conditionals are true: If you have at least $1 000 000, you are a millionaire/If you are a millionaire, you have at least $1 000 000.

necessary condition
A proposition is necessary for another when, if the latter holds, the former must.

'Only students in need of cash and a holiday should read this brochure'. This advertisement strictly implies not (a) 'If you are a student in need of cash and a holiday read this' but (b) 'If you (should) read this brochure, you are a student in need of cash and a holiday'. However, since all students are in need of cash and a holiday, (a) follows. These are thus necessary and sufficient conditions. Although students are one of STA's main interests, STA also caters for the general public. *Used with permission.*

Chapter 4

Exercise 4.4 Facts/inferences Induction/deduction Necessary/sufficient

Is Sherlock Holmes in the following passage correct in saying that his conclusions are 'obvious facts' or are they in fact inferences? Are his conclusions derived by induction or deduction? Does the evidence provide necessary or sufficient ground for the conclusions? Define the terms you use during your discussion.

Our visitor bore every mark of being an average commonplace British tradesman, obese, pompous and slow. He wore rather baggy grey shepherds check trousers, a not over-clean black frock-coat, unbuttoned in the front, and a drab waistcoat with a heavy brassy Albert chain, and a square pierced bit of metal dangling down as an ornament. A frayed top hat and a faded brown overcoat with a wrinkled velvet collar lay upon a chair besides him. Altogether, look as I would, there was nothing remarkable about the man save his blazing red hair and the expression of extreme chagrin and discontent upon his features.

Sherlock Holmes's quick eye took in my occupation, and he shook his head with a smile as he notice my questioning glances. 'Beyond the obvious facts that he has at some time done manual labour, that he has been to China, and that he has done a considerable amount of writing lately, I can deduce nothing else.'

Mr Jabez Wilson started up in his chair, with his forefinger upon the paper, but his eyes upon my companion.

'How, in the name of good-fortune, did you know all that, Mr Holmes?' he asked. 'How did you know, for example, that I did manual labour, it's as true as gospel, for I began as a ship's carpenter.'

'Your hands, my dear sir. Your right hand is quite a size larger than your left. You have worked with it, and the muscles are more developed.'

'Ah, of course. But the writing?'

'What else can be indicated by that right cuff so very shiny for five inches, and the left one with the smooth patch near the elbow where you rest upon the desk?'

'Well, but China?'

'The fish which you have tattooed immediately above your right wrist could only have been done in China. I have made a small study of tattoo marks, and have even contributed to the literature of the subject. That trick of staining the fishes' scales of a delicate pink is quite peculiar to China. When, in addition, I see a Chinese coin hanging from your watch-chain, the matter becomes even more simple.'

(Sir A. Conan Doyle, 'The Red-Headed League', in *Adventures of Sherlock Holmes*)

Fallacies

'Got one,' Algie Wyatt underlined a phrase on the page before him.
'What?' asked Lidia Korabetski, looking up from the passage she was translating.
'Contradiction in terms.' Algie was collecting contradictions in terms: to a nucleus of 'nuclear intelligence' and 'competent authorities' he had added such discoveries as the soul of efficiency, easy virtue, enlightened self-interest, Bankers' Trust and Christian Scientist.
'What?' Lidia asked again.
'Cultural mission,' replied Algie, turning the page and looking encouraged, as if he studied the document solely for such rewards as this.

People in Glass Houses, *Shirley Hazzard*

Fallacies are errors of argument, whether inductive or deductive, which may be the result of invalid argument forms or of misguided strategies. Much ordinary talk appears fallacious, although, when the arguments are fully spelt out, they

Critical thinking

In this cartoon, the cartoonist identifies an inconsistency in the remarks of Bob Hawke, in advocating withdrawal of troops from Vietnam in 1971 and as Prime Minister in sending troops to the Gulf War in 1991. Notice that the PM might well have replied that there was no inconsistency, since it was not the same war the troops were being sent to, and hence there were different circumstances driving his difference in view. We do, however, expect people to be prima facie (have the first appearance of) consistent in their views on similar issues over time.
Source: G. Pryor,
The Canberra Times,
22 February 1991.
Used with permission.

may be justifiable. Algie Wyatt's special love is evidently fallacies that are generally accepted. Algie had identified contradictions in terms.

A **contradiction** is a simultaneous assertion and denial of one and the same proposition. The claim:
1. All men in hats are awful drivers.
   can be disagreed with in two ways:
2. No men in hats are awful drivers.
3. Some men in hats are not awful drivers.

The contradiction of (1) is (3). If the first is true then the contradiction cannot be true and vice versa. (2) is inconsistent with (1) — they cannot be true together but they are not contradictories.
Consider the following statement:

Some computers cost less than $2 000.

In order to deny this statement, we need to claim that no computers cost less than $2 000, not that some computers do not cost less. The claims that some computers do and others do not cost less than $2 000 are consistent, they can be jointly true. We cannot take both a proposition and its contradiction to be true. Of course it is possible to say: 'It's cold and it's not cold', meaning there's a cold wind, but it's warm in the sun, but in this case the two statements are true in different respects. Contradicting oneself is always an error.

Exercise 4.5 Contradictions
Write the contradiction of each sentence:
1. Every dog has its day.
2. Only aerobic exercise keeps you fit.
3. Possums are a pest in New Zealand.
4. Rain is rare in the Western Plains.
5. Most immigrants to Australia are of European origin.
6. Never will the dead speak.

fallacies
Errors of argument, whether inductive or deductive, which may be the result of invalid argument forms or misguided strategies.

contradiction
The contradiction of a proposition is such that if the proposition is true then the contradiction cannot be true and vice versa.

7. All the king's horsemen couldn't put Humpty together again.
8. Only the unemployed are lazy.
9. Few men are happy.
10. Squinks are sometimes ginks.

Other fallacies are less obvious than self-contradiction. Consider the following remark: 'Lady Di watches *Neighbours* so it must be good.' This is called an **appeal to authority** since the evaluation is based not on content but on a recommendation of a supposed authority. Unless Lady Di is an expert, the fact that she watches a television program is no recommendation: we are merely swayed by her high profile. On the other hand, when someone has relevant expertise, there is good reason for accepting their views. It would be foolish to disregard the medico's prescriptions on the grounds that doing so is an appeal to authority. An **appeal to tradition** is an argument which suggests that it is worth behaving in a certain way because you have always done so. The conclusion of the following argument, 'This university has always had a 20% failure rate, so it should go on doing so.' might be justified on other grounds, but the fact that something has always been done in a particular way is not in itself a good reason for continuing.

Ad hominem arguments are arguments which are directed not at ideas but at the identity of the speaker. Politicians are experts at ad hominem debate. To ask 'Can you believe that gay/black/ woman?' is to suggest that the person's identity determines the truth of their claims. The argument is clearly invalid, if psychologically compelling. We prefer to believe those who are as we wish to be and to distrust those who are unlike us. Of course *ad hominem* arguments may be justified. The local councillor who is arguing in favour of rezoning a nature reserve as residential and who, we discover, owns the land in question, is likely to be influenced by his own financial gain. Facts about the councillor are then relevant to the assessment of his argument.

Causal fallacies are fallacies in which an event that is prior to another is wrongly supposed to cause it. Imagine the following:

It was terribly hot yesterday, so I had a few beers, and got a shocking headache
Last time it was very hot I had a few beers and got a headache
―――
Hot weather really gives me a headache

The mistake here is to believe that just because one event regularly followed another, the first event caused the second one. This is to parody the fallacy known as *post hoc ergo propter hoc*, a Latin tag meaning roughly: 'It follows, so it is caused'. Causal fallacies are very widespread. For instance, an advertisement for a weight loss program makes a claim that 'If you weigh 170 pounds (68 kg) you could weigh 140 (63)'. That claim is probably necessarily true: almost anybody could weigh less. The implicit claim — the implication — is that the weight loss program will achieve the feat of reducing weight, that it will cause the weight loss so desired. In fact, the advertisement is very careful to equivocate at this point, so as not to make false claims.

A less commonly recognised fallacy is that of **moderation or compromise**. It is the fallacy of arguing that extremes are necessarily wrong, and the mid point, or compromise most likely to be true. It is indeed the case that a compromise solution may be the best solution in negotiation. It does not follow that a compromise is correct. One way of demonstrating this is to show that any

---

appeal to authority
An argument where the evaluation is based not on logical content but on the recommendation of a supposed authority.

appeal to tradition
An argument that suggests that it is worth behaving in a certain way because it is traditional to do so.

ad hominem argument
One that is directed not at ideas but at the identity of the speaker.

causal fallacy
Where an event that is prior to another is wrongly supposed to cause it.

fallacy of moderation or compromise
Where it is argued that extremes are necessarily wrong.

position whatever can be described as a compromise. In Australian politics, we could say that the Democrats are a compromise between the right (Liberals) and the Left (Labor), that the Liberals are a compromise between the right (National Party) and the left (Labor Party); that the Labor Party is a compromise between the right (Liberal) and the far left (Communist) and so on. The exercise can be done in any political system. However, the strategy of presenting the extremes of argument and then choosing the middle way is very persuasive. Implicitly, the reader or listener is invited to think that the compromise is reasonable. *Time* magazine has exalted this strategy to a formula: most of its articles take two extremes and plump for the middle. It is important to remember when using the technique or evaluating it that it does not follow that the compromise view is correct.

It is easy to list fallacies. It is far less easy to identify accurately when reasoning is fallacious. We have explained that each of the so called fallacies above could be justified. Lists of fallacies serve only to alert us to the possibilities of error, not as a foolproof guide to truth.

Exercise 4.6 Valid arguments
Are the following valid arguments? If not, why not?
(a) Only if she finds a better paying job will she leave. She's found a better paying job, so she must be leaving.
(b) The mass has always been in Latin, so why change it now?
(c) The Head of the Reserve Bank believes that we should lower interest rates. Therefore, we really ought to lower interest rates.
(d) People who go to health farms are generally overweight. Going to health farms must cause obesity.
(e) If everyone lived within their means, everyone would be able to afford an annual holiday abroad. Last year a record number of Australians went overseas for their annual holidays. Therefore, more people are living within their means.
(f) I tried the new Turkish restaurant in Weston last week. I won't go back, because they overcook the kebabs.
(g) All babies are illogical.
No one is despised who can manage a crocodile.
Illogical persons are despised.
Therefore, no babies can manage a crocodile. (*Lewis Carroll*)

Reasoning with others

So I chose lesser arguments, more petty, more acceptable, which reassured him in a way. But one who reasons more, loves less.

Salt on Our Skin, *Benoîte Groult*

Reasoning and being critical have often been thought inimical to the good life, to loving and getting on well with friends and colleagues. As Groult puts it 'One who reason more, loves less.' Yet is this so? Is it possible to be clear and critical yet imaginative and sympathetic, reasonable and persuasive?

If we conceive of critical thinking skills and reason in terms of a formal mathematical system, then, indeed, no amount of battering with formal

Chapter 4

conclusions is likely to be sympathetic, nor may it persuade. However, our model of reason is not disembodied. Reasoning, we said at the beginning of the chapter, is intersubjective: good clear thinking is a result of fitting the reasons to the audience. Moreover, critical thinking skills are used in dialogue. Only rarely do we construct arguments or analyse them as a solitary activity. Thinking is not something we do in isolation.

Rodin's statue of the thinker embodies the myth of the individual thinker. A man is seated, elbow on knee, hand on a forehead furrowed in concentration. The process of thinking well is represented as a task to be done alone. This is a view many of us share. Our image of genius is of lonely giants — men like Einstein or Beethoven. But we do not need to think of reasoning like this.

Argument often appears unsympathetic.
(Photo: *Helene Walsh*)
Used with permission.

Argument is embedded in a social and dialogical context. Reasoning is not a given set of formal rules and fallacies defined by a text book. Indeed, many of the fallacies we have mentioned in this chapter are heard frequently. It would be absurd to jump on a person and say *'Ha, appeal to authority!'* when they cite the remarks of a person they regard highly. It is not surprising that we tend to believe people we regard as attractive, competent and charismatic figures and those whose attitudes and style resembles our own. Such people are credible, that is, believable, for good reason. For instance, if a politician sounds uncertain, however good her arguments are, we tend to doubt the message, yet if someone who is admired for, say, their sporting ability recommends a breakfast cereal, we tend to believe them, even though the arguments might be weak, and the sporting figure no expert on diet. There are reasons for the snap judgments. Few of us have time to examine all our beliefs all the time. If we find someone who shares our basic beliefs recommending that we vote in a certain way, or even drink a certain drink, it may be very efficient just to take their advice and not repeat the argument. A good athlete, we might argue, must eat well — so why not try what they have for breakfast? Of course, they probably don't eat the cereal they advertise, so perhaps it is absurd, but there is a reasonable chain of inferences supporting the appeal to authority. Even the nervous politician should not too quickly be given the benefit of the doubt. A nervous politician will not put her case as well as a brazen one, so a vote for her might be wasted.

Human beings do often behave inconsistently or make inconsistent claims. The will is weak in certain cases; for instance, *'I know I should exercise, but I don't really want to'* is quite comprehensible said at 6 a.m. There is no doubt that much human activity may appear irrational or difficult to understand. People are frequently convinced by views that appear incomprehensible to others. Nevertheless, such disagreement is possible only in the context of massive agreement. If someone acted totally illogically, they would be regarded as mad. If someone were to claim to believe a view that is, from our perspective, totally unreasonable and inexplicable, we would have to assume that they had misunderstood the claim or, as Wittgenstein (1969) says in a discussion of these cases, 'we should regard him as demented'.

Classical accounts of logic, like Aristotelian syllogistic, represent arguments as if prepared for a written document, not for the everyday hurly-burly of discourse and decision making. The extent to which the model of reason is appropriate depends on the conventions governing that context. A formal academic essay has strict conventions governing the presentations of ideas: the presuppositions must be made explicit, the logical structure of an argument must be made clear, and conclusions must be drawn out. A public relations exercise for a manufacturer of, say, children's clothes, would sound ridiculous in an academic style. Even in conversation, arguments are alluded to, brushed over.

Are conversations reasonable? Is there a logic of conversation? Many theorists believe that there is. In Chapter 2, we discussed the structures of discourse or dialogue. One genre among the many forms of talk we use is the rational conversation, a conversation governed by logical criteria. In such a conversation, it is appropriate to ask for reasons, to question presuppositions, to inquire critically into the arguments used, the apparent fallacies, the irrelevancies. Such a form of conversation may or may not be used to persuade: it certainly does not appeal to the so called ' hidden persuaders', the implicit and unspelt out inferences that drive us to do as advertisements or propaganda suggest.

It is true that most conversations are not strictly governed by logical criteria. Indeed, as we described the characteristic discourse structures of women in Chapter 2, their supportive uncompetitive forms of discourse do not appear to conform to the model of rational conversations. One of the concerns of feminists has been that rationality, as presented in the formal logical models, excludes women and defines the rational as non-female (Lloyd, 1984; Slade, 1994). Certainly, there is a long tradition of defining men as rational, women as irrational. One can imagine that the female forms of conversation may have contributed to this stereotyping. This is a mistake. There is no reason why being reasonable should require competitive modes of talking. To say *I wonder what you would make of this? It doesn't seem to fit.* can be a very effective way to introduce a counter-example, more effective than *Ha got you! What do you make of this?*

Being reasonable and being critical need not and should not involve blind adherence to rules of logic, or a sniping and carping insistence on narrowly defined terms. It may require imagination and a suspension of disbelief to understand another's point of view, to enter into their way of conceiving the world. It might require encouragement to extract the presuppositions and justify them, to spell out apparent fallacies and find they are acceptable. It may take time and persistence.

Schopenhauer said:

> Instead of working on your opponent's intellect by argument, work on his will by motive; and he will at once be won over to your opinion, even though you got it out of a lunatic asylum.

Schopenhauer thought of argument as no more than the dry and disembodied arguments of Aristotelian logic. Those logical forms are only one part of reasoning and argument, useful to draw distinctions and form a basis on which criticisms can be begun. Understanding other people's reasons, what Schopenhauer calls 'working on their will by motive' has an equal role in thinking critically.

Exercise 4.7 Critical appraisal
Choose an issue of interest to the members of a group of four. You might wish to debate the issue or let students present their views on separate issues such as multiculturalism, green issues or whether students should be banned from having cars . . .

Muster the evidence you have available, and attempt to put a brief case to members of the group. The group then debates the content of presentations looking for fallacies, holes, interesting new ideas or lines of thought and particularly effective strategies of persuasion. The discussion will be chaired informally.

This activity must not be regarded as a point-scoring exercise. The process of reasoning and debating reasons should be a mutually supportive, not denigrating, affair.

Now write two submissions as a group. One is for a government or decision-making body and the other for a student newspaper, canvassing the issues and arguing your case. In the first you should keep rhetorical flourishes to a minimum, and present your own case and criticisms of other views concisely and compellingly. You may wish to write up your submission using dots to mark major points and dashes to mark subpoints, to highlight your arguments and conclusions with phrases such as 'so' or 'in conclusion' and to end with recommendations.

The newspaper piece may be as polemical as you choose.

Summary

1. Critical and creative thinking skills are interwoven in our communicative practices and essential to them. We define critical thinking skills as analysis, inference and evaluation. Reasoning should not be conceived as a formal device but as intersubjective and relative to context.
2. In order to communicate effectively, it is important to be clear and logical and to avoid fallacies, to the degree appropriate to the context. We identified a number of different forms of unclarity — equivocation, vagueness, fact/value and fact/inference ambiguity and ellipsis.

3. An argument is a logically connected set of premises that give grounds for a conclusion. Certain forms of argument are valid: i.e., if the premises are true, the conclusion must also be true. We use arguments all the time, although we often conceal or do not make explicit each step.
4. Fallacies are often accepted but misguided modes of reasoning. A range of classical fallacies are identified, such as statistical and causal fallacies.
5. Reasoning and critical thinking are not dry disembodied skills. They involve imagination, sympathy and the ability to persuade.

Discussion questions

1. To what extent is critical thinking incompatible with creativity?
2. Do different styles of writing have different levels of clarity? Give examples.
3. Identify the premises and conclusions in the following argument. Is the argument inductive or deductive?

    Capitalism requires continuing and limitless exploitation of natural resources to make possible a constantly expanding market and rising productivity. Without this, it must break down. Now greenies tell us that 'space ship earth' as they call it, is a closed system, whose natural resources are finite and limited. It has been shown often enough that capitalism is the one true form of economic organisation. Events in the Soviet bloc have confirmed that view. So the greenies must be wrong.

4. Identify the premises and conclusions in the following argument. Is the argument inductive or deductive?

    The Mayan Empire, an advanced complex American civilisation, collapsed about six centuries before the Spanish invader came across the Atlantic. Why it collapsed has long been a mystery. Dr Nick Schmuck, a professor of bioengineering, conducted an examination on bones from 90 skeletons unearthed by a university expedition to Guatemala. He identified numerous lesions due to syphilis and vitamin deficiencies. He found other disorders, including parasitic infestations and childhood infections. He concluded that the decline of the Mayan civilisation was to be explained by the ravages of malnutrition and disease.

5. In the following extract, are Edith's conclusions facts or inferences? Does she use induction or deduction in deriving her conclusions? Does she have sufficient conditions for her conclusions? Define your terms.

    Everything about her seemed exaggerated: her height, the length of her extraordinary fingers, her carrying voice, her huge oyster-coloured eyes, today slightly bloodshot, Edith could see, behind her dark glasses. A breakdown, she decided. A bereavement. Tread carefully.
    Monica nodded towards the cigarette. 'Forbidden, of course. Strict instructions. To hell with it.' She inhaled deeply, as if about to submerge in several fathoms of water. After a few seconds, two plumes of smoke emerged from perfect nostrils. A patch on a lung, perhaps, thought Edith, revising. And how beautiful she is. I had not thought so before.
    Hôtel du Lac, *Anita Brookner*

6. Watch a segment of a current affairs program. What fallacies can you identify?
7. Identify fallacies in a major current debate, such as discussion of the environment.

8. Should we expect our politicians and public figures to speak logically?
9. Do women argue differently from men?
10. To what extent is being reasonable persuasive?

Further reading

Fisher, A. (1988) *The Logic of Real Arguments* Cambridge: Cambridge University Press.
Flew, A. (ed.) (1979) *A Dictionary of Philosophy* London: Macmillan.
Fogelin, R.J. (1978) *Understanding Arguments: An Introduction to Informal Logic* New York: Harcourt Brace Jovanovich.
Mellor, H. (ed.) (1990) *Ways of Communicating* Cambridge: Cambridge University Press.
Scriven, M. (1976) *Reasoning* New York: McGraw-Hill.
Toulmin, S., Rieke, R. & Janik, A. (1984) *An Introduction to Reasoning* New York: Macmillan.

References

Board of Studies NSW (1993) *Philosophy Distinction Course: Reasoning Workshop*.
DeVito, J.A. (1974) *General Semantics: Guide and Workbook* Deland, Fla: Everett Edwards.
Doyle, A. (1968) 'The Adventures of Sherlock Holmes' in *The Annotated Sherlock Holmes* London: John Murray.
Girle, R., Halpin, T., Miller, C. & Williams, G. (1978) *Inductive and Practical Reason* Brisbane: Rotecoge Press.
James, H. (1948) *Princess Casamassima* New York: Macmillan.
Lipman, M. (1985) 'Philosophy and the Cultivation of Reasoning' in *Thinking* 5: 33–41.
Lipman, M. (1988) 'Critical Thinking: What Can it Be?' *Educational Leadership* 46: 38–43.
Lloyd, G. (1993) *The Man of Reason; 'Male' and 'Female' in Western Philosophy* London: Routledge, 2nd edn.
McPeck, J. (ed.) (1990) *Teaching Critical Thinking: Dialogue and Dialectic* New York: Routledge.
Rasool, J., Banks, C. & McCarthy, M. (1993) *Critical Thinking, Reading and Writing in A Diverse World* Belmont, CA: Wadsworth.
Schlect, I. (1983) 'Critical Thinking Courses: Their Values and Limits', *Teaching Philosophy*, pp. 131–40.
Slade, C. (1994) 'Harryspeak and the Conversation of Girls' in D. Camhy, (ed.) *Proceedings of the Fifth International Conference of Philosophy for Children* Hamburg: Academia Verlag, pp. 220-229.
Sternberg, R.J. & Smith, E.E. (eds) (1988) *The Psychology of Human Thought* New York: Cambridge University Press.
Weinstein, M. (1990) 'Towards a Research Agenda for Informal Logic and Critical Thinking', *Informal Logic* 12: 121–43.
Wittgenstein, L. (1969) *On Certainty,* (eds) G.E.M. Anscombe & M. Black, Oxford: Blackwell.

Interpersonal communication

5

Objectives

After completing this chapter you should be able to:

- define intrapersonal and interpersonal communication;
- understand the relationship of self-image and self-esteem to self-concept;
- distinguish between self-disclosure, self-presentation and self-monitoring;
- explain interpersonal communication in terms of communication apprehension and social involvement;
- discuss different views of social relationship development.

Chapter 5

Her name was Rose Jenkins. She was a talker, and she invited me back to her kitchen, where she made tea I didn't drink. She gave it to me in great detail: she managed the boarding house in which there were fourteen rooms. Leon she let sleep in a lean-to out back for a nominal rent . . . I was beginning to get a rounded-out picture of Leon.

The Empty Beach, *Peter Corris*

Peter Corris' character Cliff Hardy needs time to find out what other people are like, as do most of us, though we don't often hire a private detective. Adults usually have considerable skills in interpersonal perception and other areas, but their understandings of the processes themselves are likely to be common-sense ones. To have achieved an adequate level of interpersonal communication competence, however, they will need to have a relatively positive level of self-esteem to be able to act assertively towards others. They also need to have reasonable clarity about their own goals and motives, a capacity for forming accurate interpersonal perceptions, and some skills in explaining and predicting their own and others' interpersonal actions.

To explain these behaviours an initial distinction needs to be made between intrapersonal and interpersonal communication. Intrapersonal communication concerns individuals' communication with themselves, while interpersonal communication involves others. There are also two degrees of intrapersonal and interpersonal communication. One is the routine monitoring of your own thoughts and feelings; sometimes this is referred to as 'self-talk' and is mostly done preconsciously (Goffman, 1959). This kind of routine intrapersonal communication has its counterpart in many of the interpersonal dealings we have with others. Buying groceries at the supermarket, or dealing with any of the numerous chores of daily life, involves interpersonal communication, but usually of a low order of intensity and social significance.

So there are routine communication practices at one end of this scale of significance and matters of greater personal importance at the other end. At the important end of this imaginary scale we are dealing with matters of value, social significance and personal worth. Thought of in this way, **intrapersonal communication** is the process of creating a sense of meaning for yourself. Correspondingly, **interpersonal communication** is the process of engaging in meaningful face-to-face interactions with others.

intrapersonal communication
Creating a sense of meaning for yourself.

interpersonal communication
Engaging in meaningful face-to-face interactions with others.

Dimensions of the self in communication

There are some two hundred entries in the *Collins Dictionary* for hyphenated combinations beginning with 'self'. We will return to the implications of this obsessive western concern for 'the self' as a locus of interpersonal communication study at the end of this chapter. Yet how we perceive ourselves is a major factor in determining the quality of our interpersonal relationships. If we feel 'comfortable' with ourselves we are likely to feel comfortable with others and vice versa.

One 1950s US study of the answers people gave to the question 'Who am I?' found that they described themselves first in terms of their social roles — their age, sex, social status and occupation — and second in terms of their personality traits, such as 'happy' or 'intelligent'. A third dimension of answers concerned their own evaluations of their personal worth, such as 'trustworthy' or 'competent' (Argyle, 1978: 187). A more recent study of children's self-descriptions also found that they were more likely to mention some particular feature about themselves, such as their birthplace, if this set them apart from their classmates (Michener et al., 1986).

Self-concept, self-image and self-esteem

A good starting point in exploring how our sense of self is socially constructed is to distinguish between the ideas of self-image and self-concept. If you look back through your family photo album, for example, you will find pictures of yourself taken at different ages when some feature of your physical appearance, probably your clothes and hairstyle, varied from what it is now. The pictures are snapshots of your image at that time, not of your self-concept. So we can distinguish the ideas of self-concept and self-image by defining **self-image** as how a person perceives themselves at a particular time, whereas an individual's **self-concept** is the set of relatively stable perceptions they hold of themself.

self-image
How you perceive yourself at a particular time.

self-concept
The relatively stable set of perceptions you hold of yourself.

Self-image in family photos — the image changes but the person is the same.
(Photos: *Glen Lewis*)

Exercise 5.1 Defining your self-concept — who are you?
1. Spend five minutes writing two or three brief statements about:
   (a) Your social roles (e.g. student/parent/eldest child).
   (b) A self-description of your personal qualities (e.g. happy/tall/loves dancing).
   (c) A self-evaluation of your personal strengths and weaknesses (e.g. hard working/creative/confused).
2. Exchange these self-descriptions with a classmate, then discuss whether they would have chosen these terms to describe you.
3. Next rewrite the same set of self-descriptions but refer to how you saw yourself three years ago. Also rewrite (a) in terms of how you hope to see yourself five years from now.
4. Exchange these self-descriptions with your classmate and discuss how your self-image has changed and how it could change in future.

As our self-concept is made up of a shifting mix of our various role identities, our personality traits, and our own judgments about our personal worth, it is the qualifier 'relatively stable' in the preceding definition of self-concept that is one of its most important features. That is, we need to be stable and confident enough to be sure of our own decisions and judgments and yet also to be

self-esteem
The extent to which you approve of and accept yourself.

sufficiently realistic to recognise that we sometimes make mistakes. The key element in our self-concept that regulates this perennial balancing act between psychological certainty and doubt is the level of our self-esteem.

Self-esteem is the extent to which we approve of and accept ourselves. More technically, self-esteem can be thought of as the evaluative part of the self-concept — how we make positive and sometimes negative judgments about our self. Our level of self-esteem expresses our sense of personal efficacy, that is, of our competence to deal with other people and to be in charge of our own lives. At different stages of our life-cycles, notably during adolescence and later during mid-life, many people experience periods of extreme self-doubt and sometimes suffer from feelings of inadequacy and insecurity. All being well, however, the majority come through these normal crisis times and manage to readjust themselves.

The extent to which people develop levels of confidence and self-esteem is usually explained in terms of their family and social experiences in their infant, childhood and teenage years. Two complementary theories that account for the development of the self-concept this way are reflected appraisal theory and social comparison theory. Reflected appraisal theory argues that we form our self-concepts as a result of receiving both approving and critical feedback about ourselves from the 'significant others' with whom we grow up. These significant others are, first, our immediate family, then later our friends, peers, teachers and workmates. Children who have parents with positive self-concepts and who are raised in loving and secure environments are likely to develop positive self-concepts themselves. Conversely, children raised by parents with poor self-concepts are likely to develop low levels of self-esteem (Adler et al., 1989: 33).

As we get older the importance of these appraisals we get from others in forming our self-concept changes. We become increasingly more selective about whom we consider 'significant others'. In deciding whether we will accept or reject appraisals of ourself from others several factors are relevant. First, the appraisal needs to come from someone we see as being sufficiently competent to offer it. As students, for instance, we are more likely to accept criticism of our work from our lecturer than from a fellow student. Second, the evaluation must be seen as highly personal. We are more likely to accept judgments about our conduct from close friends than from acquaintances. Last, the appraisal needs to be seen as reasonable in the light of what we already believe about ourself. If we are usually hard-working, then we are unlikely to be too upset by criticism about our behaviour as lazy, whoever makes that criticism.

Where reflected appraisal theory emphasises the development of our self-concept in terms of the messages we get from others, social comparison theory reverses the process and maintains that we shape our own self-concepts by choosing particular reference groups to compare our performance against. To illustrate, we may like to think we are very fast runners, or great long jumpers, but this can be objectively determined by trying ourselves out against others. The outcome will either confirm this initial expectation or you may have to modify your previous evaluations of your sporting abilities. Again, you may think of yourself as a brilliant conversationalist, but this may only be true when you are with a particular group of friends.

All individuals have to deal with failures of this kind when they move outside their family environments. The extent to which they develop the capacity to cope, adjust, and eventually succeed in social and occupational life, however, varies greatly according to their backgrounds, their level of self-confidence and their social and intellectual skills. Some US research suggests that 10 per cent of children are born with predispositions towards shyness, while another 10 per cent are unusually sociable (McCroskey et al., 1986). This leaves most of us somewhere in between, so usually we become more selective in making social comparisons. It is one thing trying to match the performance of your classmates in school athletics, but another to go on to international contests. Normally we learn to balance the accumulated reflected appraisals from others about our social and occupational performance against increasingly appropriate comparisons with others.

People with positive self-esteem are likely to think well of others, while those with poor self-esteem will be likely to evaluate others negatively. One effect of this is that the expectations they hold about the outcomes of interpersonal interactions are likely to influence them for better or worse. This effect is referred to as the self-fulfilling prophecy — when your expectations of an interpersonal event are likely to influence its outcome. For example, if you go to a party expecting to have a good time you are likely to do so. Conversely, if you go to a job interview expecting to perform badly, then that is likely to happen. Further, people with positive self-esteem are more likely to evaluate their own performance favourably, to work harder for authority figures who demand higher levels of performance, and are also more inclined not to feel threatened by others who hold superior social positions.

Self-disclosure, self-presentation and self-monitoring

Imagine you are meeting two strangers. You spend equal time talking to them and both seem friendly, but afterwards you feel that you have a good sense of one person's personality, while the other made less of an impression. There is a variety of possible explanations for this but one is that the person who made the strongest impression on you may have had a higher level of self-esteem and therefore behaved more openly towards you. The fact that people behave with varying degrees of interpersonal openness can be explained in terms of two related factors: people's different levels of self-awareness and their readiness to engage in interpersonal self-disclosure.

People with positive self-concepts are likely to behave in relatively open ways in dealing with others. They are also more likely to engage in appropriate levels of personal self-disclosure. This is the process that takes place when people are getting to know each other. **Self-disclosure** is when you intentionally disclose personal information about yourself to someone else, usually in a one-to-one situation. The appropriateness of self-disclosure depends on the social context and the degree of intimacy in the relationship. Genuine self-disclosure, however, requires you to reveal relatively private information about yourself which otherwise would not be available. Just making 'small talk' is not engaging in self-disclosure. Telling someone about a particular ambition of yours may be. The aim of communicating this kind of personal information is usually to encourage the development of a relationship with the other person. The higher the degree of trust in the relationship, the more likely it is that self-disclosing behaviour will be considered appropriate.

self-disclosure
The intentional disclosure of personal information about yourself to someone else, usually in a one-to-one situation.

There is a considerably greater normative bias (i.e. saying this is what you should do) towards treating self-disclosure as one of the golden rules of interpersonal communication in American textbooks. It follows that some US research on self-disclosure may not accurately reflect non-American interpersonal norms. Their findings in some areas, such as gender differences in self-disclosure, however, may be applicable in other Western societies. For instance Jourard (1971) found that women self-disclose more about themselves than men, yet men are likely to disclose more about their family relationships and personal interests than women do. Further, women who perceive themselves as attractive disclose less than do other women, whereas that pattern of behaviour is reversed for men. Both men and women prefer to self-disclose personal information to members of the opposite sex, but overall men are less intimate in their approaches to interpersonal communication than women (Adler et al., 1989: 242).

Exercise 5.2 Self-disclosure — taking the plunge
Are you prepared to share personal information about yourself with another classmate about the following topics? Mark each, 1 for 'would disclose', 2 for 'not sure', and 3 for 'unwilling to disclose'.

1. My goals and ambitions.
2. My biggest weakness.
3. My physical attractiveness.
4. My bank balance.
5. My relations with my parents.
6. My religion.
7. My relations with my girlfriend or boyfriend.

Then discuss which areas you scored similarly.

Just as people with a positive self-concept are more likely to be interpersonally open and participate appropriately in self-disclosing behaviour with another person in one-to-one settings, they are also more likely to be capable of engaging in effective modes of self-presentation in small groups and in public situations. The way you selectively present aspects of yourself to others in this way, however, derives primarily from the set of role identities you have. Role identities are behaviour patterns, or plans for action, you have for yourself. They are concepts of yourself in specific social roles. Now, unless you are a professional actor, the range of role identities you will have access to will depend on the social position you already hold in society.

Goffman (1959) argued that waiters, salespeople and other service workers regularly engage in selective self-presentation, or impression management, to others as part of their jobs. Even if the restaurant kitchen is in a mess, for example, the waiters are expected to perform their role for their customers in a calm, friendly and organised way. In these terms Goffman distinguishes between 'back stage' (behind the scenes) and 'front stage' (in the presence of the customer) behaviours, and concludes that one perennial cause of social embarrassment is when any person's 'back stage' behaviour becomes visible to 'front stage' clients. **Self-presentation**, then, is the way you choose to present yourself for the purposes of interpersonal communication in a specific social context.

self-presentation
The way you choose to present yourself in a specific social context.

Interpersonal communication

Self-presentation is something we do not do randomly but by making a selective commitment to the various social identities we may have. The choices we make here depend mainly on, first, the involvement of time and effort we have already put into the development of a particular identity and, second, the salience of that identity in our own unique network of social relationships. So, for instance, if your education has prepared you for a career in advertising you are most likely to seek employment in that area, instead of applying for a job as a social worker. Similarly, the importance you ascribe to your various identities (student, friend, dating partner, or parent) depends on the importance of the particular social relationship each involves. The choices we make about self-presentation are also linked to the preservation and the enhancement of our self-esteem.

Enhancing our self-esteem.
Source: *G. Pryor,
The Canberra Times,
20 November 1993.
Used with permission.*

Another dimension to self-presentation is the extent to which we enact various role identities to others in a conscious way. One way some social psychologists explain this is in terms of the degree of self-monitoring undertaken in interpersonal behaviour. **Self-monitoring** is the extent to which you are aware of consciously attempting to project a particular image of yourself. Snyder (1987) argues that self-monitoring can be thought of as a continuum with two extremes: at one end are people who are high self-monitors, and at the other end are low self-monitors. When high self-monitors encounter a new social situation they will ask themselves: 'Who does this situation want me to be, and how can I be that person?' Low self-monitors will ask themselves: 'Who am I and how can I be me in this situation?' (A simple version of Snyder's self-monitoring test occurs in DeVito, 1988: 229).

Obviously these are ideal-type responses. In reality we may behave in much less clear-cut ways. Nevertheless, it is likely that because of particular personality orientations we will be predisposed to regularly act more in one way than another. According to self-monitoring theory, people who are high self-monitors are striving to present themselves best according to the situational cues available in the social context. In contrast, low self-monitors are more

self-monitoring
The extent to which you are aware of consciously projecting a particular image of yourself.

inclined to display their true dispositions and attitudes in every situation possible.

One example of this is a party. Imagine you arrive and the guests are in two separate groups on different sides of the room. As you exchange greetings with the host you can overhear some of the different conversations in the two groups. Now, self-monitoring theory predicts that if you are a high self-monitor you are more likely to join the group which has the highest clarity of conversational subject matter regardless of the topic. In contrast, if you are more of a low self-monitor you are likely to be drawn to the conversational group which has a topic that appeals to you or if you hear someone talking whose viewpoint you are sympathetic with, even though the clarity of the conversation in that group may be quite divergent.

These different approaches to self-monitoring arise from different conceptions of the self. Snyder distinguishes the high self-monitor as having primarily a pragmatic sense of self, whereas low self-monitors have more of a principled sense of self. It follows that high self-monitors are likely to describe themselves in terms of their external roles, where low self-monitors are more likely to define themselves in terms of their stable inner traits. Yet both have their advantages and disadvantages. In terms of friendship behaviours, for example, high self-monitors are likely to have a wider circle of friends than low self-monitors, but it is likely that these friendships will not be so intimate as those favoured by low self-monitors. Though low self-monitors may have more intimate friendships, they are also likely to be more vulnerable to friendship losses than high self-monitors, considering the smaller size of their circle of friends. Lastly, there are no clear gender differences in self-monitoring.

Interpersonal perception

interpersonal perception
How we see other people.

Interpersonal perception is how we see other people. The first stage is selecting information about the other person. We tend to notice some people more than others. Perhaps this is because they may be wearing an article of clothing similar to one of ours, or because they are behaving in an unusual way. Cultural differences are central here in forming our expectations about what we should consider 'normal' or 'abnormal' about others, or what we consider attractive about someone else. Similarly, if you are among a university class of mostly young Anglo women then you are more likely to notice either a man in the group or a non-Anglo.

The second stage in interpersonal perception is organising information about other people. One way of explaining this process is by introducing the idea of interpersonal constructs. Constructs are schemata of opposites we use to categorise the appearances and behaviours of others in interpersonal settings. There are basically four kinds of constructs used in organising this kind of information. We use physical constructs in terms of classifying people as good looking or plain. Second, we can use role constructs to classify others as fellow students or lecturers. Third, we may apply interaction constructs to class other people as friendly or hostile. Last, we might classify others on first meeting in terms of particular sets of psychological constructs — whether we see them as nervous or relaxed.

Exercise 5.3 Person perception — how do you see Freddie?

Freddie is a final year high school student in a well-to-do private boys' school. He has a reputation for being honest, though some people see him as pig-headed. Freddie is big for his age and sometimes this intimidates people. Freddie's father told him when he was young that he had to stand up for his rights, because if he didn't then others might take advantage of him. Sometimes when Freddie meets people for the first time he speaks quite bluntly about what he thinks, as he believes it's better to get to the point rather than waste time on idle chit-chat. Some people don't like his manner, but quite a few girls find him attractive. Freddie is inclined to think they are right and that people who don't appreciate his direct manner are too concerned with the appearance of people. Some of his teachers see him as a bit of a dreamer.

List as many physical, role, interaction, and psychological constructs about Freddie that you can.

The third stage of interpersonal perception is when we make some kind of interpretation of the behaviours of other people. To an extent this is done rationally in terms of the attribution processes we go through in describing their behaviours so as to explain their motives, either to ourself or to others. In these terms, social attribution is the process by which we make sense of the behaviours of other people. In reality many of the judgments we make about others may not be primarily based on reasoning, as much as on our own concerns, our past experiences, and our particular personal goals, all of which may colour our perception of the other person.

Our age, our cultural background, our psychological sex role, our occupational role and our particular personality traits may all act as sets of filters which we will use in processing new information in evaluating others. These factors are all rich potential sources of inaccuracy and bias in interpersonal perception. In each case the danger is that we are likely to project our own individual interests onto the other person in such a way that we make unreasonably negative (or positive) judgments about them and their actions. Despite the risks of prematurely labelling people in this way, we often use a variety of these psychological short cuts in evaluating other people.

Implicit personality theory and stereotyping

Some of these short cuts are implicit personality assumptions, the application of self-fulfilling prophecies to others, and interpersonal stereotyping. We have treated the self-fulfilling prophecy already in the context of discussing the self. The same principle applies when we treat others that way — if teachers expect some of their students to do badly, the students are in fact likely to do badly. What these three psychological short cuts have in common is that they are all unreliable ways of coming to a considered judgment about another person.

Implicit personality assumptions are based on the development of an implicit personal set of rules about what we think people are like, based on our own experience. They can be seen as a special kind of **stereotyping**. Interpersonal stereotyping is when we judge people by their labels or roles. Just as we may assume that Japanese people have particular traits (e.g. 'All Japanese work hard'), we also tend to assume that 'happy' or 'unhappy' people have particular attributes. So if we think that Joe or Juanita have certain positive qualities, then

stereotyping
Judging others by their labels or roles.

we are likely to go on to attribute certain further good qualities to them in the absence of definite information. Therefore we tend to judge people who have some good traits we know of as generally good and vice versa. This tendency to evaluate other people's personalities as clusters of either good or bad qualities is referred to as the 'halo' effect. So when we describe Juanita to a friend as vivacious and sharp it is likely that the friend may conclude that Juanita is also likeable, though this may not be so.

Exercise 5.4 Making judgments about other people
Read the following description of this person, Olga.

Olga has lived in an affluent North Shore suburb in Sydney for most of her life, though she was born of poor but honest Italian parents in Melbourne. She completed her school-leaving exam recently at an exclusive private girls' school and is now enrolled at the University of Canberra in a communications course.

Olga is very popular and has many friends of both sexes. She also has several gay friends. Till now she has got her way by smiling frequently and basically doing what she thought others wanted her to do. She is very conscious of her appearance and how she is seen by others. She likes to be liked by everyone. Not wanting to seem uninformed she often seeks help from a group of friends who did the same course. Sometimes they help her with assignments and let her use their last year's work. Among her male friends Olga has the reputation of being a bit of a rager after a few drinks.

How do you see Olga? First, using the following list of adjectives, choose the ones that most suit her. Second, choose the particular word in that pair that best describes her. Select five or six.

Adjective descriptors:

1. Generous/ungenerous
2. Shrewd/gullible
3. Sociable/unsociable
4. Popular/unpopular
5. Goodlooking/unattractive
6. Self-centred/altruistic
7. Frivolous/serious
8. Strong/weak
9. Moral/immoral
10. Dishonest/honest.

After doing so, compare your choice with your neighbour's and discuss any differences.

> **interpersonal stereotypes**
> Rigid perceptions of members of one group that are widely shared by others in a different group.

The other main kind of a psychological short cut we may fall back on is stereotyping. **Interpersonal stereotypes** are rigid perceptions of members of one group that are widely shared by others in a different group. They set up an often artificially exaggerated division between an 'in-group' and an 'out-group' (Tajfel, 1978). We may hold stereotypes about people's national, religious, ethnic, age or gender identifications. Generally, interpersonal stereotypes are one of the greatest obstacles to interpersonal communication. They are likely to stop us from seeing a person as an individual and to treat them instead only as a member of a group. When negative stereotypes are widespread in a society this may lead to extreme forms of prejudice and discrimination, which in turn may cause social division and possibly violence.

Prejudice is holding a strong dislike for people who are seen as members of a particular out-group. When people with prejudiced attitudes towards out-groups act harmfully towards them, this is termed discrimination. A person may hold prejudiced attitudes towards, say, homosexuals, yet do nothing about it. But if that person decides to join in the persecution of a member of that out-group, either passively by denying them employment, or aggressively by going 'poofter bashing', then they are actively discriminating against gay people.

Here it is more useful to consider the implications of interpersonal stereotyping in terms of sex role differences between men and women. Stereotypes about sex roles are among the most pervasive in society, yet as a consequence of the postwar increased participation of women in the workforce and also due to the activities of the women's liberation movement, many of the traditional gender stereotypes have been critically reappraised (e.g. Bem, 1974). Men's roles as well were re-examined both in America (Pleck, 1976) and in Australia (Connell & Dowsett, 1992; Russell, 1984).

This attempted revision of traditional gender stereotypes centred around the idea that masculinity and femininity — defined in terms of psychological gender orientation rather than biological difference — were not two ends of the one continuum, but rather two independent sets of behaviour. This means that someone's ability to identify psychologically with the opposite sex is not necessarily limited by that person's own sex. Whereas, traditionally, male roles were expected to be primarily instrumental (i.e. task-oriented) and female roles were supposed to be mainly expressive (i.e. nurturant), Bem suggested it was possible that men and women could share some of the traditional personality traits ascribed to the opposite sex. Though researchers are still debating this view, it has at least the egalitarian implication that people should not be psychologically limited by rigid, traditional sex roles.

There are still some significant gender differences between men and women. First, after about age ten girls display greater verbal abilities than boys. Second,

prejudice
Holding a strong dislike for people who are seen as members of a particular out-group.

Boys get bigger toys — an artist's comment on masculinity. (Mixed media and photo: *Guy Pascoe*)

Chapter 5

Growing up female.
(Photo: *Robert Hamilton*)

after that age boys tend to develop greater spatial and mathematical skills than girls. Last, boys and men do show more aggressive behaviours than girls, both verbal and physical, through their life-cycles. Females, however, when directly provoked are no less aggressive (Callan et al., 1986: 85). In some other areas where tradition decreed there were stereotypical sex role differences, recent research either disagrees or is inconclusive. There is little or no evidence that women are more fearful than men. Similarly, when face-to-face pressure is not present, and when they are both knowledgeable about a subject in dispute, neither men nor women are more readily persuaded. Finally, though the quality of men and women's friendships may differ, neither regularly seeks more social contact (Michener et al., 1986).

Despite this new research a range of older stereotypes still continues to influence interpersonal perception. When men and women do choose to go into occupations that go against the prevailing norms for their sex roles, this may involve considerable personal role conflicts for them. One Adelaide study, however, found that successful women in traditionally male jobs were rated more highly than their male counterparts (Callan et al., 1986: 93).

Exercise 5.5 Gender differences or gender stereotypes?
Go through the following list on your own and mark each description according to whether you think it is masculine, feminine, or neutral.

1. Loves children
2. Absent-minded
3. Aggressive
4. Forceful
5. Dependent
6. Tense
7. Childlike
8. Ambitious
9. Patient
10. Interesting
11. Sensitive to needs of others
12. Affectionate
13. Analytical
14. Self-reliant

- Which of these adjectives best describes traditional Western gender roles about men and women?
- Which adjectives are neutral, even in traditional gender roles?
- How many of them are now neutral or inapplicable?

Because of this range of potential misunderstandings, accurate interpersonal perception is obviously difficult. Yet despite these difficulties, taking an empathic approach to others is the best way of forming reliable impressions. Empathic behaviour has both cognitive (thought) and affective (feeling) dimensions. Cognitively, **empathy** is the ability to take another person's viewpoint. Empathy, however, should not be confused with sympathy. Sympathising with someone means you feel sorry for them. Empathic behaviour is a means of imagining their attitudes and feelings, rather than merely observing in a detached way how that person is reacting. Finally, you need to signal your understanding of the other person through your own verbal and nonverbal behaviours.

empathy
The ability to take another person's viewpoint.

Communication apprehension and social involvement

Two of the most pervasive barriers to interpersonal communication are shyness and loneliness. McCroskey (1986) interprets shyness as a form of '**communication apprehension**', which is a sense of fear or anxiety associated with either real or anticipated communication with others. He defines high talkers as non-shy people and low talkers as shy people. There are several causes of communication apprehension: they may be hereditary, or due to childhood reinforcement, to a personal trait of social introversion, to feelings of social alienation, or to ethnic or cultural differences. (For the 'Personal Report of Communication Apprehension Scale' and instructions for interpretation, see McCroskey et al., 1986: 40).

McCroskey also distinguishes between communication apprehension as a generalised personality trait and as due to situational factors. If people consistently experience anxiety about going out on a date, for example, they may have developed strong negative expectations about it. Situational communication apprehension, on the other hand, is more likely to arise when the person is getting an unusual amount of attention from others, for instance in making a public speech, or in dealing with another person of superior social or occupational status.

Communication apprehension is likely to have several negative outcomes. These may be interpersonal communication avoidance, when we avoid others, or communication withdrawal, when we do not respond to others, or there may be various forms of communicative disruption, such as stuttering, being stuck for words, or even talking too much. Goffman identified similarly inappropriate behaviours from another perspective when he argued that people who engaged successfully in 'face work' (where people gave each other 'face', or recognition and respect) were primarily interaction conscious. Conversely, when communication breakdowns occurred, this was where one or both parties became too self-conscious or too other-conscious (Goffman, 1972).

communication apprehension
A sense of anxiety associated with either real or anticipated communication with others.

Loneliness is a condition related to shyness. Bell (1987) distinguishes short term loneliness, due to life-cycle factors — such as occupational mobility or divorce — and chronic loneliness, which is likely to be associated with depression and anxiety. The conditions of modern living, with an increasing number of people living in single-person households, promote social isolation. Bell found there was a relationship between low self-disclosure and loneliness and that lonely people self-disclosed more to same-sex friends. Loneliness also appeared to be related to a tendency to judge others negatively. In one US study lonely men were rated more negatively than non-lonely men, though women were not rated differently whether they were lonely or not.

If communication apprehension is one of the main barriers to interpersonal communication, then the ability to be socially involved with others is perhaps the most fundamental social skill. Various models of interpersonal competence have been developed at both advanced and introductory levels, mostly by North Americans, though there are also some useful British models (Argyle, 1988; Guirdham, 1990; Duck, 1986), and a few Australian ones (Kotzman, 1989; Nelson-Jones, 1990). A model that incorporates elements of these approaches and also makes more explicit the factor of gender differences is that of Wheeless and Lashbrook (1987).

Their model incorporates a variety of interpersonal behaviours along the dimensions of responsiveness and assertiveness. **Responsiveness** is the capacity to be sensitive to the communication behaviours of others. In terms of conversations, it is the ability to find appropriate ways to extend the other person's comments. Responsive interpersonal behaviour is also empathic. Nonverbally this means we attend to the other person carefully and make encouraging responses. The other key dimension of interpersonal behaviour represented is assertiveness. **Assertiveness** is the capacity to stand up for your own rights while respecting the rights of others. This is the ability to communicate your attitudes, opinions and feelings, verbally and nonverbally. Just as interpersonal responsiveness should not be confused with submissiveness, assertive behaviour should not be equated with aggressive behaviour. In terms of Berne's 1960s transactional analysis theory, which divided people's consciousness into child, adult, and parent ego states, assertive behaviour should work on an adult-to-adult level, from an 'I'm OK, You're OK' position (Berne, 1966).

According to Wheeless and Lashbrook, then, there are four ideal-types in relation to psychological gender roles: competent androgynous, aggressive masculine, submissive feminine, and noncompetent undifferentiated. Effective interpersonal communication behaviours are most likely to be displayed by people who are capable of being both responsive and assertive. Those who are highly sex-typed, either male or female, are considered to be less flexible in their behavioural ranges, as one is primarily assertive and the other responsive. The fourth role, noncompetent undifferentiated, is the least satisfactory, as such people are likely to be withdrawn and uncommunicative. The competent androgynous role, in contrast, combines behaviours that traditionally have been considered masculine (e.g. confidence and interaction management) and feminine (e.g., empathy and openness).

One model of interpersonal communication which synthesises most of these interpersonal skills is Bell's work on social involvement. This suggests that

---

responsiveness
The capacity to be sensitive to the communication behaviours of others.

assertiveness
The capacity to stand up for your own rights while respecting the rights of others.

people who display high levels of social involvement are likely to be seen as sociable and outgoing. He discusses the role of social involvement in interpersonal communication in terms of empathy, self-disclosure, self-monitoring, and other factors. Bell argues that three behaviours are specially important in communicating social involvement, namely perceptiveness, attentiveness and responsiveness (Bell, 1987: 201).

First, **perceptiveness** involves the integration of meanings of self in relation to another in the course of interpersonal communication. Second, after a person behaves perceptively, they need to follow up their behaviour by behaving attentively. **Attentiveness** is the selective directing of one's senses towards information relevant to the ongoing interaction. Third, the socially involved person displays *responsiveness* (i.e. the ability to act appropriately with awareness of his or her interpersonal role). The last factor that needs to be added to Bell's model is *assertiveness*. You need to have sufficient behavioural flexibility to choose whether to act perceptively, attentively, responsively or assertively, as the situation requires. An important part of interpersonal communication competence, therefore, is the ability to pursue interpersonal goals by adapting your behaviour to the needs of the particular situation.

perceptiveness
The integration of meanings of self in relation to another in the course of interpersonal communication.

attentiveness
The selective directing of attention towards information relevant to the ongoing interaction.

Communication in social relationships

Most of what has been said so far has assumed that one of our main goals in interpersonal communication is to be involved in mutually satisfying social relationships. Interpersonal competence, that is, should not be thought of primarily as the instrumental pursuit of personal goals. Rather, we should consider our communication behaviours competent when we have the ability to interact regularly on social terms with family and friends, and professionally with colleagues and co-workers. The real point of displaying the interpersonal skills needed for **social involvement** — responsiveness, assertiveness, perceptiveness and attentiveness — is to maintain a positive level of social relationships with other people.

The term 'social relationships' may refer to either personal or professional relationships. Areas concerning friendship traditionally have been studied by social psychologists, while developmental psychologists concentrated on parents and children, and sociologists examined marriage and family relationships. In these disciplines a greater current emphasis is being placed on studying the role of communication in those relationships (Wiemann & Giles, 1988).

One of the most widely cited theories of the role of communication in relationships is Knapp's (1984). He argues there are a series of stages in most opposite-sex dyadic relationships that hinge around relationship development and relationship decline — a 'coming together' and a 'coming apart' cycle. He identifies five stages of relationship development. In the 'initiating' stage, one person meets another for the first time and makes contact. Next, in the 'experimenting' stage, the two start to identify common interests and perhaps mutual friends. As the relationship develops the 'intensifying' stage begins and greater mutual self-disclosure takes place. At the 'integrating' stage, the two begin to treat each other specially and to present themselves to others as 'a

social involvement
Maintaining a positive level of social relationships with other people.

couple'. Last, in the 'bonding' stage, the couple may make serious commitments — either by living together or marrying.

What are the factors that make some people affiliate with others in this way? Social affiliation is a broader process than romantic love. We may seek friendships in the workplace or in other social settings. Non-romantic friendships may also go broadly through stages of building and decline, but they will not follow the same stages of development that romantic relationships do. Three of the most important factors psychologists have found to influence friendship development are interpersonal attraction, physical proximity and attitude similarity.

In most friendships, even in same-sex friendships, there is usually some element of shared physical attractiveness between the people concerned, though this is likely to be a much stronger factor in opposite-sex friendships. Physical proximity is also an important element in influencing friendship development. If you regularly run across a person in the course of your day some kind of interpersonal affiliation is easier to establish. Last, of course, we have to like the other person to want to make friends, and similarity of attitudes — likes and dislikes, or beliefs and opinions — is an important part of many friendships. Mostly we tend to choose friends who are the same age and of a similar social background, though they may well have different personalities (Argyle, 1988).

Friendship, like many marriages and love affairs, often comes to an end. The reasons for this may be geographical separation, when friends have to move away from one another. Or the friendship may end either because one breaks the communication rules of the friendship, or because there has been a gradual 'growing apart' as their interests or values change over time. Just as people have a range of communication behaviours for establishing relationships, they also have ways of ending them. Older people tend to withdraw gradually from declining relationships, while people who are younger are more likely to end them with direct confrontation.

As well as generational differences in relationship behaviours there are also likely to be significant gender differences in friendship. Rawlins' study of the role of communication in young North American adults (aged 20 to 30), for example, found some interesting differences in the way young men and women saw friendship (1989). He studied the way friends communicated across four different dimensions, namely the degree of affection and instrumentality (caring for a friend or as means-to-an-end), of judgment and acceptance, of expressiveness and protectiveness (i.e. open self-disclosure vs emotionally withdrawing behaviour), and of independence and dependence. His conclusions were, first, that women placed more emphasis on the caring nature of their friendships, while men saw friendship more instrumentally (e.g. 'doing things together'). Secondly, women tended to be more judgmental than men in their friendships. Thirdly, women placed more value on expressiveness (e.g. showing and expecting emotional concern) than did men. And, lastly, men valued independence more in their friendships.

There are major differences too in the ways that people from diverse cultural backgrounds see interpersonal relationships. Some North American theories of relationship development have been based on the idea that a 'social exchange' process takes place as relationships form, and that people to an extent calculate the costs and benefits of entering into a relationship (Altman & Taylor, 1973).

There is also a characteristically North American approach to communication which tends to assume that more communication is always better and that relationships can be 'worked on'. However, these assumptions may be quite foreign to people from other cultures. Neither British, European nor Australian people, for example, may readily accept the assumptions made about the desirability of interpersonal openness and self-disclosure, which are so strongly emphasised in many American textbooks. Some new trends in US interpersonal communication studies are also querying the discipline's traditional focus on the individual and arguing that more attention to the social nature of communication is desirable (Lannamann, 1992).

Similarly, it has been argued by Chang and Holt (1991) that Taiwanese Chinese people think about their relationships in a less instrumental and rationalistic way. They consider that their ideas about *yuan fen* (good relationships between two people) are based on Buddhist as well as Confucian philosophical traditions that de-emphasise the element of conscious choice in relationship development. One Chinese saying, for example, is *tian shi, di li, ren he* (to be successful in relationships requires the timing, the place and the human factors). So relationships, in their view, are something that cannot be forced. The concept of *yuan* focuses on contextual, not just individual, factors, unlike American approaches. Relationships are not always something that can be 'worked on', just as communication is not something that can always be strategically seen as a means to an end.

Yuan fen: very good relationship.
(Photo: *Xu Bai-ming*)

Although most of the connotations of *yuan fen* for Taiwanese Chinese concern romantic relationships, the concept of *ren yuan* ('human *yuan*') has more of an individual–group reference. People who, in general, are liked by many others are said to have *ren yuan*. However, for Chinese people, popularity of this kind means that the person is sociable, in the sense of having social skills, but this is seldom considered a virtue. Such people may be seen as more naive than those around them. For this reason the term *ren yuan* is more often used to describe children than adults. As Chang and Holt suggest, the standardised measures of Anglo-American psychology are often not sensitive enough to capture different cultural meanings. In future, more culturally sensitive and social approaches to interpersonal communication study are likely to become important.

Exercise 5.6   Evaluating student friendships
1. Using Rawlins' four dimensions of friendship listed previously, and any standard text on psychological survey method, design a questionnaire to apply to student friendships, either for students in your own year, or in a year above or below you.
2. As well as posing questions related to Rawlins' categories, also distinguish between same and opposite-sex friendships and size of friendship networks.
3. You may also add other variables to make the questionnaire more specific, e.g. usual place of residence, number of close friends, ethnic origin, Australian or overseas born, etc.
4. Pilot the questionnaire with a small number of subjects then discuss your results in class with the aim of further improving the instrument.

Social approaches to communication and subjectivity

So far this chapter has moved from discussing several dimensions of the self in communication, to interpersonal perception, then to communication apprehension and social involvement, and lastly communication in social relationships. This final section will draw attention to some of the limitations of these perspectives with reference to the most recent theorising about the field. Interpersonal communication studies is a hybrid area which draws from psychology, social psychology, and symbolic interactionist sociology. Traditionally as a field it has been sharply separated from mass communication studies, and many of its concepts have been drawn from studies which have been decontextualised and reductive (see Chapter 1) and used mainly quantitative methods. The recent strong influence of postmodernism on social theory, however, has encouraged some interpersonal researchers to query some of the orthodoxies of their field. More qualitative and contextualised approaches are being introduced.

Leeds-Hurwitz (1992), for example, argues that the field should pursue what she describes as social approaches to interpersonal communication. She identifies three main assumptions that connect these new approaches. First, that reality is a social construction created through human interaction. This assumption questions the value of traditional psychological experimental methods, which often relied on artificial, controlled conditions, and used undergraduate college students as their main subjects. Secondly, there needs to be a greater recognition of the need for reflexivity in interpersonal research. This requires that research should be placed in a particular social context, rather than be seen as something claiming universal validity. In communication research, **reflexivity** is the understanding that research is a social process that involves the researcher as much as the subjects and is influenced by the researcher's own intentions and motivations. The third assumption she sees in recent social approaches to communication research is that it should have a sociocultural, rather than an individual, focus. Although organisational and

reflexivity
Understanding that research involves the researcher as much as the subjects.

mass communication studies have been strongly influenced by cultural analysis approaches, interpersonal communication studies so far have been remarkably resistant to this trend.

What are the specific implications of these constructionist, reflexivist and culturally oriented perspectives for interpersonal communication studies? In terms of what this chapter has discussed, it means that a meta-critique can be made of most of the key concepts already advanced. For instance, the idea of self-presentation should be seen contextually as an activity that individuals engage in as a means of exerting social influence over others to maintain and extend their own self-esteem (Tedeschi, 1990). Similarly, even recent views of gender typing that emphasise androgyny are also seriously limited, in that they reproduce a traditional model of self-contained individuality, even if it is a gender-neutral one (Kitzinger, 1992).

Thirdly, the idea of communication competence is also over-individualistically focused. This is implicitly recognised in a popular US text which suggests there are three models of interpersonal competence — a pragmatic one, a humanistic one and a social exchange model (DeVito, 1988). These are explained without any criteria of selection which might be used to choose between them. Lastly, the notion of relationship development, either humanistically in Knapp or instrumentally in Altman and Taylor, also leads to the celebration of individual rationality and reflects US consumerist conceptions of relationships as a search for individual satisfaction (Lannamann, 1992).

At the centre of postmodern concerns for a revision of orthodoxies in social theory, one particular theme most directly threatens the traditional approach of interpersonal communication studies. This is the idea of the 'de-centred subject'. That is, just as literary critics such as Barthes declared the 'death of the author' in favour of asserting the autonomy of the text, the notion of the self-contained individual that much of US psychology and social psychology assumes is now challenged as unrealistic. The self in postmodern terms is more a shifting mix of de-centred selves with no necessary point of constancy.

To some extent these postmodern ideas about the unavoidability of subjectivity were anticipated by such social theorists as Goffman. His idea of 'role distance' and his concept of the self as a crossover point between different communication networks that is constantly being renegotiated has some similarities with postmodern views of subjectivity (Battershill, 1990). Similarly, European social psychology, more than North American, via scholars such as Tajfel, has also traditionally placed greater emphasis on the socially situated nature of the self (Deaux, 1992). This more socially oriented approach to interpersonal communication has been restated recently by Harre (1993), who suggests that a range of non-experimental methods, such as conceptual analysis, repertory grid analysis, and discourse analysis, are viable alternatives to the use of experimental methods in social psychological research.

One final, good, example of these proposed new approaches is a study by Ellis and Bochner (1992) on abortion. Based on their own personal experience, they have written a narrative of their discussions about the event. This presents the twin voices of the man and woman concerned discussing the pregnancy test, making the decision to have the abortion, through to the aftermath. They presented their account at a conference on personal relationships as a performance (in performance art terms), with the aim of dealing with the issues of reflexivity, subjectivity and narration. They describe their approach as 'radical empiricism' that has the aim of opening up discussion about areas of emotion in interpersonal communication that traditionally have been overlooked. This case of how the researchers made themselves their own experimental subjects is not entirely new, as participant observation in ethnographic studies has long been practised. Nevertheless, it is a striking current example of how the field of interpersonal communication may change to take account of postmodernist themes and develop a more genuinely social approach.

Summary

1. The most important factor influencing your interpersonal dealings is the extent to which you have a positive self-concept based on self-acceptance. While your self-image may vary with circumstances, it is essential your self-concept is stable enough to withstand criticism, yet flexible enough to accept it when justified.
2. To engage others in interpersonal communication you need to be motivated to do so and you also need to be open to others. A central dimension of this is your willingness to engage in appropriate self-disclosure. Some social situations may also require you to present different sides of yourself. Your own style of self-presentation will be influenced by whether you are a high or low self-monitor.
3. When we first meet others we need to form accurate impressions of them. Yet we may fall back on a range of psychological short cuts in doing so. These include the use of the self-fulfilling prophecy, implicit personality theory, the halo effect, and various stereotypes. Gender and ethnic stereotypes are enduring barriers to accurate interpersonal perception.
4. Communication apprehension and loneliness are both potential barriers to interpersonal communication. Their causes can be either situational or dispositional, and they may be of either short or long-term duration.
5. Interpersonal communication competence is the ability to act appropriately in a responsive or assertive way towards others. We also need to be able to be attentive to others via our listening and nonverbal behaviour, and perceptive in terms of the spoken and physical responses we make.
6. Social relationships, either personal or professional, are the context in which interpersonal communication takes place. We engage in communication behaviours suited to different kinds of relationships and friendships, though these vary according to our age, gender and cultural background.
7. Differences in language, philosophy, values and religion are so great between some societies that it is unlikely that Anglo-American theories, which concentrate heavily on the individual rather than the group, will be accurate in explaining the nuances of interpersonal communication in other cultures.
8. The impact of postmodernism on social theory has had less influence so far in interpersonal communication studies than in mass and

organisational communication. New social approaches to the field, however, use more contextual and qualitative methods which are more sensitive to subjective experience.

Discussion questions

1. What is the difference between intrapersonal and interpersonal communication at both routine and non-routine levels?
2. What are the three dimensions of the self-concept people usually refer to in defining themselves?
3. Give several examples of possible ways children may develop a positive sense of self-esteem, using both reflected appraisal and social comparison theories.
4. Discuss examples of when interpersonal self-disclosure may be appropriate and when it may not.
5. What kinds of different preferences will people with high and low self-monitoring tendencies have in choosing a circle of friends?
6. What are some of the main sources of inaccuracy in interpersonal perception?
7. How has recent research challenged some of the traditional stereotypes held in Australia about the social roles of men and women?
8. What is meant by perceptiveness, attentiveness, responsiveness and assertiveness?
9. How may cultural and gender differences cause people to evaluate differently the role of communication in friendship?
10. What are some of the postmodern objections to the traditional themes of interpersonal communication research?

Further reading

Argyle, M. (1988) 'Social Relationships', pp. 220–43 in M. Hewstone (ed.) *Introduction to Social Psychology* Oxford: Basil Blackwell.

Bell, R. (1987) 'Social Involvement', pp. 195–243 in J. McCroskey & J. Daly, (eds) *Personality and Interpersonal Communication* Beverly Hills, CA: Sage.

Callan, V., Gallois, C. & Noller, P. (1986) *Social Psychology* Sydney: Harcourt Brace Jovanovich.

Chang, H. & Holt, R. (1991) 'The Concept of *Yuan* and Chinese Interpersonal Relationships', pp. 29–57 in S. Ting-Toomey & F. Korzenny, (eds) *Cross-Cultural Interpersonal Communication* Newbury Park, CA: Sage.

Connell, R. & Dowsett, G. (eds) (1992) *Rethinking Sex* Melbourne: Melbourne University Press.

Guirdham, M. (1990) *Interpersonal Skills at Work* Hertfordshire, UK: Prentice Hall.

Knapp, M. (1984) *Interpersonal Communication and Human Relationships* Boston: Allyn & Bacon.

Leeds-Hurwitz, W. (1992) 'Social Approaches to Interpersonal Communication', *Communication Theory* 2 (2): 131–8.

Snyder, G. (1987) *Public Appearances, Private Relations* New York: Freeman and Coy.

References

Adler, R., Rosenfeld, L., & Towne, R. (1989) *Interplay* New York: Holt, Rinehart & Winston, 4th edn.

Altman, I. & Taylor, D. (1973) *Social Penetration* New York: Holt, Rinehart & Winston.

Argyle, M. (1978) *The Psychology of Interpersonal Behaviour* Harmondsworth, UK: Penguin, 3rd edn.

Battershill, C. (1990) 'Erving Goffman as a Precursor to Postmodern Sociology', pp. 163–83 in S. Riggins, (ed.) *Beyond Goffman* Berlin: Mouton de Gruyter.

Bem, S. (1974) 'The Measurement of Psychological Androgyny', *Journal of Consulting and Clinical Psychology* 44: 155–62.

Berne, E. (1966) *Games People Play* Harmondsworth, UK: Penguin.

Corris, P. (1983) *The Empty Beach* Sydney: Allen & Unwin.

Deaux, K. (1992) 'Personalizing Identity and Socializing Self', pp. 9–35 in G. Breakwell, (ed.) *Social Psychology of Identity and the Self Concept* London: Surrey University Press.

DeVito, J. (1988) *Human Communication* New York: Harper & Row, 4th edn.

Duck, S. (1986) *Human Relationships* Beverly Hills, CA: Sage.

Ellis, C. & Bochner, A. (1992) 'Telling and Performing Personal Stories', pp. 79–102 in C. Ellis & M. Flaherty, (eds) *Investigating Subjectivity* Newbury Park, CA: Sage.

Goffman, E. (1959) *The Presentation of Self in Everyday Life* Harmondsworth, UK: Penguin.

Goffman, E. (1972) 'Alienation from Interaction', pp. 347–64 in J. Laver & S. Hutcheson, (eds) *Communication in Face to Face Interaction* Harmondsworth, UK: Penguin. First published 1957.

Harre, R. (1993) *Social Being* Oxford: Basil Blackwell, 2nd edn.

Jourard, S. (1971) *The Transparent Self* New Jersey: Van Nostrand, 2nd edn.

Kitzinger, C. (1992) 'The Individuated Self Concept', pp. 221–51 in G. Breakwell, (ed.) *Social Psychology of Identity and the Self Concept* London: Surrey University Press

Kotzman, A. (1989) *Listen to Me, Listen to You* Ringwood, Vic: Penguin.

Lannamann, J. (1992) 'Deconstructing the Person and Changing the Subject of Interpersonal Studies', *Communication Theory* 2 (2): 139–47.

McCroskey, J., Richmond, V. & Stewart, J. (1986) *One on One* New Jersey: Prentice Hall.

Michener, H., DeLemater, J. & Schwartz, S. (1986) *Social Psychology* New York: Harcourt Brace Jovanovich.

Nelson-Jones, R. (1990) *Human Relationship Skills* Belmont, CA: Brooks-Cole, 2nd edn.

Pleck, J. (1976) 'The Male Sex Role', *Journal of Social Issues* 32: 155–64.

Rawlins, W. (1989) 'Communication in Young Adult Friendships', pp. 157–89 in J. Anderson, (ed.) *Communication Yearbook 12* Newbury Park, CA: Sage.

Russell, G. (1984) *The Changing Role of Fathers* Brisbane: University of Queensland Press.

Tajfel, H. (1978) *Differentiation Between Social Groups* London: Academic Press.

Tedeschi, J. (1990) 'Self-Presentation and Social Influence', pp. 301–24 in M. Cody & M. McLaughlin, (eds) *The Psychology of Tactical Communication* Clevedon, PA: Multilingual Matters.

Wheeless, V. & Lashbrook W. (1987) 'Style', pp. 243–75 in J. McCroskey & J. Daly, (eds) *Personality and Interpersonal Communication* Beverly Hills, CA: Sage

Wiemann, J. & Giles, H. (1988) 'Interpersonal Communication', pp. 195–219 in Hewstone *op. cit.*

Intercultural communication

6

Objectives

After completing this chapter you should be able to:

- define intercultural communication, intracultural communication, host and minority cultures, subculture, multiculturalism and cross-cultural communication;
- discuss the relationship between social distance and ethnocentrism;
- differentiate between stereotypes, role models, discrimination and prejudice;
- understand acculturation as a cultural learning process and be able to identify personal and social variables in acculturation.

Chapter 6

> *'Your picture please, Desposini?'. . .*
> *'She's a peasant girl,' he thought.*
> *'Very pretty,' he said, closing one eye and raising the camera.*
> *'Italian?'*
> *'Cyprus.'*
> *'Speak English, then?'*
> *'Little.'*
> *The shutter clicked. 'Won't take too long to learn. Your name, Desposini?'*
> *Desperately she wondered whether to give her own family name or that of Yannis. But he was not her husband yet, and perhaps he never would be; maybe he had thought better of it and was not waiting for her down there.*
>
> The Young Wife, *David Martin*

The kind of nervousness this young Greek bride-to-be felt was doubtless shared by many of the postwar arrivals to Australia, even if they were not coming to meet a new marriage partner. If anything, the influence of immigrants in Australia has increased since then. This chapter will introduce the field of intercultural communication by adapting North American and European theories of intercultural communication to the Australian multicultural scene. The following chapter will provide more depth about the main ethnic subcultures in 1990s Australia.

Several recent writers have seen the cross-border shifts of emigrants and refugees as one of the main characteristics of the end of the twentieth century. Some have also developed theories about how the circulation of a new media and communications based global consumer culture has diminished the importance of traditional national identities. Postmodern global culture is creating new psychological landscapes in which there is a movement away from fixed standards and identities and a fragmentation of traditional cultural meanings (Milner, 1990). Though the main emphasis of what follows will be the construction of ethnic group identity, it is important to remember that these identities are comprised of the experience of individuals. Some scholars have discussed their own personal experience of ethnic dislocation in ways that are sensitive and illuminating (e.g. Ang, 1993), but the approach in this chapter will necessarily be more of a broad-brush picture.

Definitions of intercultural communication

> **intercultural communication**
> Face-to-face communication between people from differing cultural backgrounds.

Intercultural communication is about how people from different cultures communicate. More specifically, **intercultural communication** is concerned with unmediated communication between people from differing cultural backgrounds. This particular definition has the advantage of foregrounding the importance of interpersonal communication in intercultural exchanges. Differences in interpersonal perception and attitudes to social involvement are also important factors in intercultural communication.

However, although we are mostly concerned with the interpersonal dimensions of intercultural communication, what needs stressing about the distinctiveness of intercultural face-to-face exchanges is group identity as a decisive contextual factor. Immigrants tend to form strong inter-ethnic group networks to act as social support systems when they come to a new country. These may endure for some time and be more essential to their social life than such ties are to members of the host culture. In this light, one challenge of intercultural communication study is to distinguish the interaction of the twin elements of social and personal identity in interpersonal exchange.

It should not be assumed that members of any one ethnic subgroup are necessarily like-minded. So, for example, if a Greek-American and a Greek-Australian meet each other as strangers they will have an important common element in their social identity — both being from native Greek parentage — but they may well have strong differences based on their personalities. To emphasise the importance of group experience, Asuncion-Lande has suggested a more complex definition of intercultural communication. She sees it as the process of symbolic interaction between groups of people with recognised cultural differences (1990: 213).

Previously the distinction was made between *inter*-personal and *intra*-personal communication. A parallel distinction can be made between *inter*-cultural and *intra*-cultural communication, though only a few writers, such as Folb (1988), have stressed this. We will define **intracultural communication** as the extent to which there is shared interpersonal communication between members of the same culture — whether this is in the majority culture, or within minority cultures. There may be small but important differences, for example, between members of the same majority culture. So in Australia, Anglo-Australians share a common culture, but still have different geographical and family origins. Similarly, Italian immigrants to Australia came mostly from southern Italy, but they can have significant differences among themselves based on their own regional traditions.

intracultural communication
Shared interpersonal communication between members of the same culture.

Host and minority cultures

The **host culture** is the mainstream culture of any one particular country. By contrast **minority cultures** are those that are smaller in numerical terms in relation to the host culture. So, for example, seasonal workers from Turkey and Greece living in Germany are called 'guest workers' and form minority subcultures while they live there, even though this may be for years, while German citizens, German culture and the German language make up the mainstream culture. It may be more accurate at times to describe the host culture as the dominant culture. In the case of Australia, for example, Aboriginals were here first historically, yet it is white Anglo-Australian culture which is now the dominant culture while Aboriginals are a minority subculture.

Countries like Japan and the US are almost polar opposites regarding the relation between their host and minority cultures. Japan has very few minority subcultural ethnic groups that live and work there — mainly Chinese, Korean and Filipino workers and students — and the Japanese sometimes claim their sense of national uniqueness is due to their ethnic homogeneity. The US, in contrast, has long been 'the melting pot'. It has a very large minority of Hispanic people, who often retain Spanish as their preferred language, as well as black Americans whose subcultural values and speech patterns may vary radically from those of white Anglo-Saxon Protestant (WASP) Americans.

host culture
The mainstream culture in any one particular country.

minority cultures
Cultural groups that are smaller in numerical terms in relation to the host culture.

Chapter 6

Subcultures

Black Americans — who used to be referred to as Negroes before the civil rights movements of the 1960s — are an example of an American subcultural group. Another numerically smaller group are American Indians, who now prefer to be called Native Americans. Some subcultures, like black Americans, are more socially visible because of their skin colour and their speech differences. Black American spoken English has a number of features that diverge from 'standard American' speech. 'Standard American' speech is a neutrally accented form of spoken English, most characteristic of mid-Western whites, whereas black American English is likely to be heavily accented and have a special rhythm and vocabulary of its own. The term 'rappin' actually dates back to the early 1970s, when it was used to describe a particular freewheeling style of black talk, before it became the basis of black pop music in the 1990s.

Other US subcultures may also be highly distinctive in terms of their language differences, as with Hispanic-Americans (Latinos), or in terms of unusual religious beliefs or dress codes, such as the Amish people shown in Peter Weir's film *Witness*. These are a small fundamentalist Protestant sect in the North-East who prefer to avoid the use of modern technology. Some US subcultures such as German-Americans, Jewish-Americans and Italian-Americans, though they have a distinct subcultural style of their own, may be much less socially visible. As individuals, member of those subcultures can if they choose be indistinguishable for most purposes from the mainstream.

One important complication in defining a subculture is that it may be based on lifestyle differences expressed in distinctive codes of dress and speech, and not necessarily on ethnic or religious differences. There has been extensive discussion about these kinds of subcultures in British society, where different groups — usually young people — have chosen to diverge quite radically from the mainstream culture by adopting nonconformist styles and values. There have been the Teddy Boys (and Girls) in the 1950s, the Mods and Rockers and the Hippies in the 1960s, as well as the Punks (Brake, 1980). The element of

A subcultural crossover: Chinese self-defence traditions adopted in Australia. (Photo: *Xu Bai-ming*)

124

generational change in the identity of these subgroups is linked with strong fashion statements, from long hair and beads for the Hippies, to shaven skulls and nose-rings for the Punks. There may also be crossovers between subcultures based on lifestyles and ethnic differences, such as gangs of Maori bikies or Australian tae-kwan-do clubs.

So **subcultures** are smaller, often nonconformist subgroups within the majority culture. They may be based on racial or ethnic difference, but they can be based on religious difference (e.g. the pairs of North American Mormons who diligently bicycle around Australian suburban homes spreading God's word) or on occupation, such as members of the armed forces or the police. They may also be based on a geographical location which, in a metropolitan context, often signals their status differences, such as Sydney 'Westies', beachside 'Surfies', or Blacktown 'Home Boys'. Lastly, subcultures can also be based on nonconventional sexual preferences. Gay lifestyles are often concealed where they do exist in small towns and in suburban areas, but in parts of the big cities, such as New York's Christopher Street or Sydney's Oxford Street, they are openly displayed.

subculture
A smaller, possibly non-conformist, subgroup within the host culture.

Exercise 6.1   Recognising subcultures

Divide the class into subgroups according to age.

First, each subgroup should identify subcultures in their own age group, and in the younger and older generations in terms of dress codes, slang terms, musical tastes and leisure activities.

Second, discuss these questions:

- Is there a subculture at your university according to different courses?
- How important are subcultures in the city you live in, or others you have visited?
- How are subcultures shown on television?
- Are vegetarians members of a subculture?
- Are boys or girls more influenced by subcultural norms?

Multiculturalism

Whereas subcultural identity positions people as members of a particular subgroup in relation to the majority culture, **multiculturalism** is the official recognition of Australia's cultural and ethnic diversity (Hollway, 1992). This concept of multiculturalism is linked with social and educational policies assisting the integration of minority subcultures, yet preserving a sense of their ethnic uniqueness. If this sounds like a rather delicate balancing act, it sometimes is. There were major, and occasionally nasty, public debates about multiculturalism during the last decade, centred on academic Geoffrey Blainey and Liberal politician John Howard in relation to immigration policies.

Australian multiculturalism is relatively recent. Traditionally, in its short post-1788 history Australians pursued restrictive and racially selective immigration practices — known as the 'White Australia' policy — which lasted until the 1960s. Since then, with the large postwar influx of non-British migrants to Australia, governments have bipartisanly endorsed multicultural policies. Ethnic radio began in 1975 and was soon broadcasting in an astonishing variety of languages. Ethnic TV, SBS-0/28, began in 1980 but, unlike ethnic radio, used English as its main language. Programs not in English

multiculturalism
The official recognition of Australia's cultural and ethnic diversity.

Chapter 6

Community policing for social harmony: a Jogjakarta billboard in Indonesian.
(Photo: *Glen Lewis*)

were still featured, but dubbed by a special subtitling unit in the hope this would help immigrant viewers to learn or improve their English (Jakubowicz, 1987). In addition to the ethnic media, there has since developed a complex set of welfare, health, employment and antidiscrimination policies aimed at facilitating the settlement of Australia's diverse immigrant groups. Jayasuriya (1990) has argued, however, that many of those policies are outdated and based on an earlier model of multiculturalism as cultural pluralism. Instead, multicultural policies need to be more concerned with the principles of equity and justice, rather than access and cultural pluralism.

The idea of multiculturalism as a national social policy is also employed in other countries, notably in Canada, Indonesia, Malaysia, Singapore, and what was the Soviet Union until 1991. The particular meanings given to multiculturalism, however, are very different in each. In Indonesia, for example, the policy is termed *Pancasila* (the Five Principles). These five principles, meant to preserve social harmony among a large and diverse population with an Islamic majority, are (1) Belief in One God, (2) Humanity, (3) National Unity, (4) Democracy and (5) Social Justice. Similarly, Malaysia, ethnically composed of a Malay majority, and Chinese and Tamil minorities, pursues a policy of national unity via its media and public communication programs to promote racial harmony and religious toleration. Both Indonesian and Malaysian multiculturalism, however, are often more symbolic than real, at least by Australian standards (see Chapter 12).

Exercise 6.2 Intercultural awareness roleplay

Divide the class into three groups and randomly designate them as the Lilliputians, the Brobdignanians, and the Antalians. Each subgroup should also have an observer to report finally on elements of stereotyping that may emerge and whether this influenced the group outcomes.

The Lils and the Brobs are members of refugee groups who have settled in Antalia in the last decade. They have been invited by the government to participate in a meeting to plan a new community centre for their city. The centre is planned to provide health services, a lending library, a job placement agency, child care facilities, a sports hall, and a young people's leisure centre. The three groups, all local residents of the area, have to decide on the funding priorities of these services, conditions of access to the facilities, and to determine any additional services. There are, however, severe budget restraints on the project. The total funds available are $100 000.

Each subgroup should aim to get the best deal for themselves, without jeopardising the future of the whole project. There should be three separate group meetings — first in the original subgroups, then one for mixed groups with members from the three ethnic backgrounds, and lastly a whole class meeting where subgroup members present their case, before the whole meeting votes on the best options.

Table 6.1 *Subcultural differences between the three groups*

	Ants	Brobs	Lils
Tactile	Touch often	As little as possible	Touch occasionally
Eye contact	Direct	Rarely	Only when speaking
Gender	Women rule	Men rule	Equality
Decisions	Group consensus	Individuals decide	Compromise
Priorities	Education first	Sport first	Jobs first

Table 6.1 outlines the main subcultural differences between the three groups in terms of five behavioural dimensions. Each subgroup should display these behaviours in the meetings, while the observer should record major instances of those behaviours.

Cross-cultural communication

Cross-cultural communication takes place at a number of different levels. Where intercultural communication involves interpersonal exchange between people from different cultural backgrounds in the same nation, **cross-cultural communication** is international unmediated communication between representatives of business, government and professional groups. Diplomacy is one of the oldest forms of cross-cultural communication. Whereas diplomats normally represent their countries and arrange political and legal agreements with a range of different nation states, consular officials aim at facilitating international trade agreements and setting up cultural awareness and exchange programs. Austrade, for example, fosters external foreign trade by arranging introductions between managers of Australian and foreign firms.

Travel and tourism is a second form of cross-cultural communication which has mushroomed in the postwar years and tourism is now seen as a vital leisure industry in earning foreign exchange. Before the twentieth century only a small elite of world populations travelled abroad. Most of the migrants who came to Australia in the last century saw it as a one-way trip and at best returned 'home' infrequently for family and sentimental reasons. Probably because of their geographical isolation, however, Australians have always been inveterate travellers. In 1894, for instance, the journalist George Morrison trekked 5000 kilometres from Shanghai to Rangoon. More recently, Kay Cottee became Australia's first woman to sail solo round the world.

A third form of cross-cultural communication unique to this century has been

cross-cultural communication
Face-to-face communication between representatives of business, government and professional groups from different nations.

the growth of the mass media. From the early 1920s world audiences began watching Hollywood stars. In the interwar years *Time* and *Newsweek* became global news-magazines, and in the 1950s US television shows such as *I Love Lucy* and *Bonanza* exported US family values all over the world. In non-modern and non-English-speaking states like Indonesia those same US programs were sometimes seen as subversive of traditional folk values. Current media research suggests, however, that different national audiences prefer to watch their own home-made programs. Also, some programs are not culturally transferable. *Dallas*, the No. 1 US television serial of the 1970s, was as popular in Britain as it was in North America, yet made no impact in Japan.

Most recently, cross-cultural communication has been accelerated by cross-border information flows brought about by computerisation. Communication satellites and computers know no national boundaries and are replacing the older sea cable and wireless and telegraphy communication systems that nations previously relied on for international communication. Where in the 1960s the US was seen by the Communist bloc as the villain of the piece with its globally-present television and movies, in the 1990s it is more often Japan that is depicted as the most 'informationised' society in the world — Japan as a *Johoka Shakai* (information society) — and sometimes seen as a threat to less powerful nations. The 1990 decision to build a Multi Function Polis, a high-tech, high-touch model science city, in Adelaide, for instance, was hindered by traditional Australian fears of Japan (James, 1990).

Exercise 6.3 Distinguishing cross-cultural communication
A fourth and more specialised meaning of cross-cultural communication may be distinguished in terms of some of the techniques of comparative social research. Cross-cultural studies are those which compare the same phenomena across two or more different countries. If researchers compare organisational communication patterns in Japan and Australia, that is an example of cross-cultural study. On the other hand, if they consider the introduction of Japanese management methods, e.g. quality circle methods, into Australian manufacturing industries, that is not a cross-cultural but an intercultural study.

Questions
1. Using the example of intermarriage between Filipina women and Australian men, suggest two examples of social research which could examine this subject from an intercultural and a cross-cultural perspective respectively.
2. In the late 1980s the Japanese Ministry of Education sent out representatives to Australia with a view to learning from Australian educational practices. What do you think they might have learnt?
3. When countries import new methods and ideas from other countries, does the process of cross-cultural communication then become intercultural communication?

Principles of intercultural communication

It is often complicated enough communicating with someone with whom we have a shared cultural background. But when it comes to communicating with someone from a quite different cultural background, especially if it is important, then the chances of misunderstandings multiply. Intercultural communication may be intergovernmental or interpersonal, but in either case the people involved have a previous membership in their own cultural groups, which have a history of their own. Condon has highlighted three areas as most problematic in intercultural exchanges: language barriers, differerent values and different cultural patterns of behaviour (Condon & Saito, 1974).

The problem of language barriers is a real one but, as Condon argues, they may be less of a barrier in the long term than other obstacles. Language can be learned and taught. The difficulty for Australians and New Zealanders is that their British heritage and US influences have all been transmitted in English and the languages of their Asian neighbours have little or no linguistic similarity to English. Japanese is a particularly difficult written language to learn as it has three sets of written characters, while other Asian scripts, such as Thai, Vietnamese and Chinese, seem equally incomprehensible to those raised on the English roman alphabet. Though Bahasa Malay and Indonesian are relatively straightforward, they have not been taught in Australian schools until recently.

And yet language obstacles are not impassable. For immigrants, their degrees of competence in a new language will vary, but in time can be improved. One legacy of 1990, which was the International Year of Literacy, was the movement in Australia towards more workplace training in English language programs for immigrant workers. A disturbing feature of the research conducted nationally in that year, however, was that it found a significant percentage of native born Australians did not have a satisfactory level of language skills, as defined in their ability to read official documents and basic prose (Wickert, 1990).

A second source of intercultural misunderstanding is different standards of nonverbal communication. Perhaps one of the central examples here is different cultural attitudes to the presentation of the body in public between Australians and New Zealanders on the one hand, and their South Pacific and Asian neighbours. Though there is some historical tradition of public nudity in some Asian societies — such as Japanese bath-house practices, as well as in traditional native life in the South Pacific — the only bare breasts you are likely to see on Balinese beaches will belong to Westerners. Most Asian societies observe extremely modest standards in terms of body displays.

Value differences are likely to be just as serious a cause of misunderstandings. Imagine a Chinese overseas student comes to dinner at his Australian teacher's house and brings a watermelon as a gift to thank the host. There is plenty of food and at the end of the meal the host casually suggests that the student should take the melon home. Though this is well intended it may cause offence to the student, as the rejection of a gift in Chinese culture can cause the giver to lose 'face' (self-respect). Another option the host might choose instead would be to present a gift to the student. Different rules for gift-giving vary considerably between cultures. Westerners often open gifts as soon as they receive them, whereas Chinese people are expected to wait till the gift-giver leaves before opening the present.

Misunderstandings can be much more serious than this when religious or political values are concerned. For instance, Sikh-Australians in Woolgoolga — a small northern New South Wales town where they make up 35 per cent of the population — until 1993 were refused admission to the local RSL club so long as they wore turbans. It was against their religion not to, while it was a breach of the club's by-laws for anyone to wear a hat or head covering in the club (Gilhotra, 1984). Similarly, in 1990 the attempt by a Muslim group in western Sydney to have their own mosque built was angrily challenged by other local residents; while during the 1991 Gulf War some critics saw the media as promoting racist anti-Arab views (Hage, 1991). Several important controversies about the tendency of foreign-language media to bring country-of-origin feuds into the new host culture have also arisen. SBS-TV was threatened several times for screening Serbian and Croatian movies even before the Yugoslavian civil war. Public broadcasting radio stations have frequently experienced bitter conflict among rival ethnic groups for air time. Similarly, some Sydney Cabramatta Vietnamese language papers have provoked community conflict by conducting outspoken anti-Communist campaigns.

The third main source of intercultural misunderstanding that Condon mentions is the use of different culturally based patterns of behaviour. White Australian settlers could make no sense at first of many Aboriginal customs, such as that of the 'walkabout', when Aboriginals left one tribal area to move to another. Prejudiced whites took this as a sign of Aboriginal shiftlessness, not appreciating the different customs of a traditionally nomadic people. Similar conflicts continue between Aboriginals and whites over the application of tribal and white laws.

Differences in language — including nonverbal behaviour — in values, and in patterns of behaviour, are some of the most common sources of breakdown in intercultural communication. To examine the principles of effective intercultural communication more closely, what follows will consider some of the principal inhibitors and facilitators in intercultural exchange. The main inhibitors include ethnocentrism and social distance preservation, and of stereotyping, discrimination and prejudice. The main facilitators are intercultural acculturation and the development of skills in intercultural communication effectiveness.

Exercise 6.4   The problems of a foreign student with a host family
A foreign student experienced some problems of adjustment with the host Australian family she was staying with. The student felt the whole family was demanding too much time and attention. She was expected to spend time with the young children, and to accompany the family regularly on social outings. In turn, the family felt the student was being discourteous for wanting to spend time away from the family. The friction became so oppressive it was affecting the student's grades.
Put yourself in the student's place — what should you do?
1. Make some excuse, leave the family and find another place to live.
2. Confront the family and insist you be allowed more time to study.
3. Continue to socialise with the family but study more at university.
4. Do nothing. Make the best of things.
5. Or what else?

Social distance and ethnocentrism

Every society has a tacit scale of **social distance,** used to express relationships of social hierarchy. Writing in the late 1940s, Muzafer Sherif, a Turkish-American social psychologist, argued that there was a North American scale of social distance which informally but carefully ranked American, Canadian, and English people at the top, then in a descending order of preferred association were the French, Germans, Swiss and Northern Europeans, followed by Southern Europeans. At the bottom were black Americans, Turks, Chinese and Hindus. Sherif considered the hierarchy of prejudice in any society flowed from the socially and economically strongest groups at the top of the social scale down to the low end. He believed each ethnic group had a social distance scale that was built on the prevailing values on society, not on the basis of experiences that individuals themselves had with other groups (Sherif, 1948).

A degree of preference for members of one's own social network is quite normal. Research on interpersonal relationship development suggests that people have a natural tendency to form friendships and belong to social networks with others who have a certain degree of social similarity (Duck, 1986). However, to the extent that people may exclusively evaluate the beliefs, values and attitudes of their own network as superior to others, this form of social behaviour may be ethnocentric. **Ethnocentrism** is the tendency for people to consider their own social groups as 'normal' and to judge others as abnormal or inferior. There are certain traditional conceptions of superiority that different nations and tribal societies have held. The Chinese term for China is *Zhang guo*, meaning the Middle Kingdom, and traditionally China's Imperial rulers saw themselves as civilised people and foreigners as barbarians, or *Gweilos* (foreign devils). A degree of social distance and ethnocentrism is usual in social life, but when exaggerated it can lead to serious social conflict and interpersonal discrimination on racial or ethnic grounds.

Stereotyping, discrimination and prejudice

Ethnic stereotypes are relatively fixed conceptions of an ethnic group. When we stereotype someone on the basis of their ethnic identity, we are identifying them first as a group member and only secondarily as an individual. We are communicating with them in terms of their ethnic identity and being indifferent about their personal identity. A classic example of this is the cliché that Westerners and Asians are unable to describe each other as individuals because 'they all look the same'. More harmful are stereotypes that stigmatise groups on the basis of their supposedly inferior traits — such as Jews as avaricious money-grubbers, or Maoris as violent and dangerous. Australian talkback radio is a fairly rich ground for these forms of prejudice.

However, there is a more positive side to the use of stereotypes in intercultural communication. Whenever children learn approved ways of social behaviour one standard way of teaching them is by the use of role models. Role models are positive examples of desirable behaviour, whether teachers are using examples of sports performance or interpersonal competence. Police, defence personnel and doctors are also usually expected to wear uniforms: these are clear nonverbal signals about their particular job. Positive role models, therefore, are both necessary and desirable in social life. In intercultural terms, the importance of role models for minority groups is the example of personal success that individuals from those groups can be for others. Evonne Goolagong-Cawley's Wimbledon victory, the election of Neville Bonner as the

social distance
Every society has a tacit scale that is used to rank other ethnic groups in a social hierarchy.

ethnocentrism
Considering one's own social groups as 'normal' and judging others' as abnormal or inferior.

ethnic stereotypes
Relatively fixed negative conceptions of an ethnic group.

Chapter 6

But they all look the same . . .
Source: *G. Pryor,* The Canberra Times, *9 December 1993. Used with permission.*

first Aboriginal Senator, and the appointment of Pat O'Shane as the first Aboriginal woman magistrate, for example, were inspirational for Aboriginal people, while the success of the late Sydney heart surgeon Dr Victor Chang was a source of pride for the Australian Chinese community.

The greater problem in intercultural communication is when people from different ethnic subgroups focus destructively on the negative stereotypes they may hold about each other. The perception of these stereotypes may be relatively dormant, in which case these attitudes can be termed prejudice. Prejudice can take either mild forms — such as beliefs that women are bad drivers — or be quite extreme, as in considering that all Hare Krishna are dangerous. The difference between discrimination and prejudice is that **prejudice** is a negative attitude towards ethnic or minority groups. It is the social psychological basis of discrimination and does not necessarily lead to discriminatory action. **Discrimination** is when people take some harmful action against individuals on the basis of their different religious or political beliefs, ethnic origins, or their gender or sexual preference. The most routine form of discrimination in contemporary Australia is discrimination in the workplace, where people may not be hired, or be passed over for promotion, because of their ethnic origin, their gender or their religious beliefs.

prejudice
A negative attitude towards ethnic or minority groups.

discrimination
Taking harmful action against individuals on the basis of their different religious or political beliefs, ethnic origins, or their gender or sexual preference.

Exercise 6.5 Humour and prejudice

One of the most common forms of prejudice is when racist stereotypes are used in telling jokes to denigrate people from other cultures. Perhaps some of these at times can be very funny. There is also the possible reversal of prejudice that can take place when ethnic group members choose to make fun of themselves, such as Greek-Australians did in the immensely popular early 1990s stageplays 'Wogs out of Work' and 'Wogarama' and their TV show 'Acropolis Now'.

Prior to that, in the late 1960s, US comedian Lenny Bruce — who was Jewish himself — had a series of comedy routines poking fun at Jewish people and Jewish culture.

In the 1960s best-selling Aussie novel *They're a Weird Mob* the author Nino Culotta (really John O'Grady) confronted a newly arrived Italian immigrant with Australian blue collar culture and found plenty to laugh about. ('Itsa your shout, mite,' he said to me in the pub, so I shouted, etc.)

See if you can tell your class members any jokes that are ethnically or racially based but that are neither sexist nor racist.

Acculturation

Prejudice, discrimination and stereotyping, as well as ethnocentrism and fixed ideas about social distance, are all factors likely to inhibit intercultural communication. A more positive approach, however, is possible when we consider intercultural communication facilitators. The most important are the process of acculturation and the development of interpersonal skills in intercultural communication effectiveness.

Acculturation is a cultural learning process (Kim, 1988). It is the means by which immigrants learn to acquire a set of competencies — interpersonal, social and vocational — which enable them to function effectively in their new cultural environment. More formally in the context of intercultural communication, **acculturation** is the process by which immigrants learn to identify, then internalise, the significant symbols of the host culture through communication. This learning process is an interactive and continuous one which may extend over many years. Some immigrants blend easily into a new culture like chameleons, while others experience terrible difficulties.

The first stage of acculturation for the immigrant is to experience the initial shock of actually existing in the new culture — this is often referred to as 'culture shock'. Culture shock, though, does not happen just to immigrants. It may be experienced by anyone travelling for the first time in another country, or by a new recruit to an organisation. 'Culture shock' is the psychological reaction people experience when they find themselves in a culture very different from the one they are used to. It is usually temporary, but it may be frustrating and last for a long time. It can be extremely worrying not to know how to make a public phone call, or read street directions, let alone haggle with dishonest shopkeepers or apply for a job in a new country. There is often a honeymoon phase, when the immigrant is fascinated with the novelty of the new culture, followed by a crisis period when feelings of personal inadequacy surface. There will then usually be a readjustment period in which the traveller learns to cope. When the immigrant or sojourner (e.g. a student) returns home after a long absence, there is also the possibility of experiencing reverse culture shock. They may find it difficult to readjust to being back in their own culture.

The time that new immigrants take to become acculturated depends on a range of personal and social variables. Their age, their level of education, and personality will all have a bearing on their rate of acculturation. Generally, younger people are more adaptable in new situations, and immigrants with higher levels of education are less likely to be confused by a new environment. If they are also personally inclined to be outgoing and open-minded, then they are more likely to initiate and respond to social interaction with members of the host culture.

Another way of thinking of these personal factors that influence the rate of an immigrant's acculturation is in terms of the complexity of their cognitive maps in perceiving the new environment. These are likely to be relatively stark

acculturation
How immigrants learn to identify, then internalise, the significant symbols of the host culture through communication.

and simple for immigrants at first, but as they learn more about the sense-making processes of the host culture — the formal and informal rules of social and public interaction — their understanding should richen and diversify.

There is also a range of social variables that determine new immigrants' degree of acculturation. These are primarily the degree of similarity of the immigrants' culture to the new host culture, the extent to which the immigrants remain in their own ethnic social networks, and the amount of use they make of their own ethnic media. An example of the degree of cultural similarity facilitating acculturation is the ready acceptance that immigrants from England, New Zealand, Canada or the US usually enjoy in Australia. Though each of these groups speaks a different brand of English from Australians, it is relatively easy for them to become acculturated. At the opposite end of the scale come immigrants from radically different societies, such as the Vietnamese. In Sarbaugh's terms (1979), the degree of intercultural difference between these immigrants and the host culture is very great.

The more new immigrants stay exclusively within their own ethnic networks the longer the acculturation process will take. The availability of these ethnic social networks, and their degree of cohesiveness, depends on the particular origin of the immigrants and where they are in Australia. Different eating and drinking habits and different leisure preferences may discourage immigrants from confidently socialising with new acquaintances in the host culture. Foreign students are more likely to mix this way via student associations and social activities that are interculturally oriented. Immigrants who have come to stay, however, may find it very difficult at first to step outside their own ethnic social networks.

The real element of social dislocation in immigrant experience has often tended to be ignored or overlooked by Anglo-Australians, who have a cultural norm about 'minding your own business'. It was not unusual among first generation Italian, Greek, Turkish or Lebanese migrants to Australia to have a family structure where the father acquired some competence in English, because his job took him out of the house, but where the mother stayed home and did not learn English. Their own children then would become acculturated to a much greater degree. This process, however, was often one of intergenerational conflict and considerable personal difficulty. Many of the Italians who migrated to Australia have preferred to return home. It is also not unusual now to meet Australian-born Chinese (ABCs) who do not speak or write the native language of their parents.

The role of the media in acculturating new immigrants is broadly similar to the influence of ethnic social networks. Recent arrivals prefer to read their own language papers, and use their own language radio and TV programs. The normal trend, however, as they become more fluent in English, is to consume the same kind of media entertainment and information as their social counterparts in the host culture (Bednall, 1988). One complication here is the availability of various forms of ethnic media. The representativeness of SBS-TV programming, for example, has at times been queried. In 1992 the main ethnic language backgrounds SBS programs came from did not correspond very well to the size of those groups in the real population. The figures, taken from the SBS Annual Report of 1992 and 1991 ABS Census figures, are shown in Table 6.2.

Intercultural communication

Relocating culture:
Chinese New Year in Canberra.
(Photo: *Xu Bai-ming*)

Table 6.2 *Main ethnic language SBS-TV programs and real size of ethnic group*

Ethnic group	TV programs %	Population %
Italian	6.2	2.6
Greek	4.0	1.8
German	3.7	7.0
Polish	1.2	0.4
Chinese	0.8	1.6
Vietnamese	0.2	0.7

Intercultural communication accommodation theory

The systematic study of intercultural communication has been relatively recent. For this reason, theoretical perspectives on the field are not as well developed as those in interpersonal, organisational or mass communication studies. There tends instead to be a variety of competing theories. A simplified version of Kim's acculturation theory (1988) has already been presented in the previous section. Other approaches include theories that focus on information sharing with the aim of reducing uncertainty in communication, such as Gudykunst (1988) and Kincaid (1988), and Yum's (1988) theory of strong and weak intercultural communication networks.

One theory that has considerable merit is intercultural accommodation theory. The current title of this theory is **communication accommodation theory (CAT)**. It derives from sociolinguistics and cognitive social psychology, as in the work of Giles, Street, Gallois and others. The special focus of CAT originated with research attention to the speech interaction patterns of individuals. The earlier version of this theory was labelled by its authors as Speech

communication accommodation theory (CAT)
People may adjust their speech styles with respect to others as a way of expressing their values, attitudes and intentions.

Accommodation Theory (SAT). The basic argument of SAT was that people will adjust their speech styles with respect to each other as a means of expressing their values, attitudes and intentions. SAT predicted that speakers would choose one of three conversational strategies — speech convergence, speech maintenance or speech divergence.

If speakers adopted a convergent speech approach this indicated the speaker's desire for social integration with the other person, either in seeking or showing approval or identification. Research indicated, for example, that high-status speakers could converge with low-status others by slowing down their speech or using non-standard accents. Conversely, low-status speakers could seek communication convergence by quickening their own speech rates or standardising their accents. Though SAT research in the 1970s and early 1980s considered individual speech behaviour one of its main concerns, it was also applied to intergroup speech behaviour between peoples of different cultural and ethnic backgrounds.

In one US study it was found that, when Chicano (Spanish-American) and Anglo-American children were asked to explain how to play a game they had just learned to two other children of their own age but with different ethnic backgrounds, the great majority of the Chicano children tended to converge by adapting their language to the English-speaking child listener. In contrast, only a small proportion of the Anglo-American children chose to accommodate their explanations to the Spanish-speaking child listener (Street & Giles, 1982: 206).

As opposed to making a speech convergence choice, speakers could either diverge or maintain their speech patterns with others from differing social or ethnic backgrounds. This could be done by emphasising rates of speech, turn-taking, length of speech pauses, speech topic content, or other paralinguistic features of their speech. The aim of speakers adopting speech maintenance or divergence strategies was usually to maintain or increase the sense of social distance between themselves and the other person. Whereas listeners' perceptions of speech convergence were likely to be taken positively as expressing warmth, affection or cooperation, their perceptions of speech maintenance or divergence were likely to be seen as colder, less friendly and uncooperative.

This approach to intercultural communication theory was revised and retitled Communication Accommodation Theory (Gallois et. al., 1988). Though previous SAT research included an emphasis on intercultural group differences, CAT went one step further by foregrounding the issue of intercultural differences in interpersonal and intergroup speech behaviour. Drawing on earlier work by Henri Tjafel, CAT researchers argued that the salience (importance) of the interpersonal or intergroup features of intercultural communication exchanges should not be viewed as a simple linear continuum. This was the distinction made earlier in this chapter, when the different experiences of a Greek-Australian and a Greek-American were contrasted.

Instead, CAT researchers suggested that the possible ways individuals might react conversationally in any intercultural exchange could be thought of in four interrelated ideal-type dimensions. These represented four possible combinations of alternative speech behaviours which varied according to the salience of group or interpersonal elements in the exchange. A situation where communication is taking place between husband and wife, for example, is a case of High Intergroup (sex difference) and High Interpersonal (close relationship). In contrast, an example of High Intergroup/Low Interpersonal, is a meeting between strangers from two rival ethnic groups. Where behaviour is Low Intergroup/High Interpersonal, an example is a meeting between friends of the same age, sex and ethnic group. Lastly, Low Intergroup and Low Interpersonal could be a simple routine encounter, say between customer and checkout person at a supermarket.

CAT has implications for understanding how different ethnic groups may adjust in a particular host culture. It implies that members of subordinate groups (subordinate in terms of numbers, length of stay in the host country, and relative status) will tend to arrive at a level of accommodation to the dominant group's speech style. Australian research tends to bear out this prediction. First, studies of Italian and British speakers' reactions to Australian nonverbal behaviours after a number of years residence in the country tended to converge, at least in public places. Second, Italo-Australians did not evaluate the social prestige of Italian and English language use very differently, in contrast to Greek-Australians who tended to perceive Greek as more important than English. The reason for this difference was that Italo-Australians as a group were relatively well assimilated into the host society, but still showed strong solidarity with the Italian community (Gallois et al., 1988: 179).

Exercise 6.6 Language accommodation — multicultural trick or treat?
Kalantzis, Cope and Slade (1989: 9–14) have questioned what they see as 'simple pluralist multiculturalism'. Their objections are:

1. It is a trivialised view of what culture is to think that a variety of languages and cultures can be preserved.
2. A simple pluralist view may be unselfconsciously conservative or even racist. Peoples cannot be 'preserved as museum pieces'.
3. Behind most pluralism there is a hidden agenda of assimilation.
4. Simple pluralist multiculturalism implies that culture is little more than the traditional or the exotic.

Discuss their views with reference to the question of communication accommodation theory. Does it mean, in practice, that ethnic cultures in Australia will lose their languages?

Intercultural communication competence

Cultural exchange is a two-way street. Whereas acculturation is the learning process immigrants need to go through to become competent citizens, cultural adaptation is what members of the majority Australian culture need to do to appreciate their multicultural fellow citizens. Previously, in Chapter 5, interpersonal communication competence was defined in terms of selecting and enacting interpersonal behaviours that are appropriate and effective in particular contexts. This definition was derived from meaning-centred theories of communication, as discussed in Chapter 1. We can extend that definition here to intercultural communication.

Though a number of reservations need to be made about this, intercultural communication competence is the ability to negotiate shared interpersonal meanings in an intercultural context. This is necessarily constrained by the abilities of the participants to recognise the contextual demands of the logic of the situation. Such a precondition is considerably more demanding in scenes involving intercultural communication. Usually there will be some kind of comprehension gap between the people concerned because of their limited knowledge of the other person's cultural background or their language.

In other words, unless we have sufficient understanding of the different norms, values and attitudes that shape the world view of people from a different culture, then even our best efforts at interpersonal communication may be inadequate. This is not to say that the same principles of interpersonal communication competence previously defined should not be practised. What it does require is greater sensitivity to their limitations. When we engage in interpersonal perception and attribution processes in an intercultural setting, we need to do more perception checking than usual, to provide clear and accurate feedback more frequently, and be prepared to have a high tolerance of ambiguity. It may be specially difficult, for example, to recognise different verbal and nonverbal cues in the expression of emotions (Gallois, 1993).

This chapter will end by considering several examples of possible misunderstandings to highlight the difficulty of engaging in intercultural communication. First, Barnlund's 1975 study of differences in Japanese and North American communication styles concluded that the two peoples had quite different conceptions of 'the public self' and 'the private self'. This means that Americans are prepared to talk spontaneously and at length about a wide range of topics, as well as to engage in fairly intimate forms of self-disclosure, e.g. the Phil Donahue TV show. Verbal articulateness is valued highly in American society: most US communication textbooks, for example, place great emphasis on methods of effective speaking.

In contrast, Japanese culture is relatively sceptical of the value of being verbally articulate (Barnlund, 1975). One striking Japanese proverb is 'By your mouth you shall perish'. By North American standards Japanese people engage in little private self-disclosure, but this is because they do not regard speech as the most important form of communication. In both Japanese architecture and music, for instance, there are quite different cultural emphases given to the importance of spaces between objects and silences between musical notes. Barnlund's argument has been restated more recently by Ito (1991), who argues that the collectivistic/individualistic dichotomy often used to contrast American and Japanese society is misleading and that both societies are now converging towards each other. Barnlund and Ito are therefore suggesting that explanations of cultural differences between Japanese and North Americans should be made as non-reductive, holistic accounts.

We end with three examples closer to home. First, similar intercultural communication difficulties arise when we consider the speech behaviour of tribal Aboriginals and white Australians. Walsh's 1991 study suggests wide gaps in social conventions about appropriate speech behaviour between these groups. For white Australians the conventions of effective conversational behaviour include clear turn-taking and direct eye contact. However, for tribal Aboriginals, conversation is more of a continuous activity in contrast with white speech habits. That is, white Australians leave their homes, their studies, or their offices, to engage in relatively directed speech interactions with others;

tribal Aboriginals do not live in privatised environments of the same kind, therefore their speech behaviours are not regulated in the same way. They do not necessarily have to face each other, or look each other in the eye, when speaking. In tribal Aboriginal culture speech is controlled by the listener — on whom there is not as strong an obligation to respond — where in white culture speech is controlled primarily by the speaker.

Second, Irwin (1992) has argued that the recent concern of Australian management to become more involved with Asia has led to a sometimes simplistic approach in intercultural training courses aimed at giving business people a 'quick fix'. He points out that research into communication competency has long since abandoned the search for lists of 'communication skills' and instead now seeks to identify broad 'domains' of competence. Questioning the usefulness of culture 'training', which aims to produce lists of tips of 'what every manager should know' in Thailand, Irwin argues that Furnham and Bochner's (1989) idea of 'culture learning' is more appropriate. Culture learning is an ongoing experience that should be seen as a form of lifelong learning. Business executives need to learn the salient characteristics of foreign cultures as well as their basic business and social skills (see Hofstede, 1991: 207–34).

Last, it is likely that the long-term effects of multiculturalism will have significant modifying effects on Australian culture that go beyond simple changes in eating habits or clothing styles. The 1960s generation paid fashionable attention to Eastern mysticism, meditation, drugs and Maharishi guru figures. In the 1990s, with Asian cultures and languages being taken much more seriously, various non-Anglo and non-Western conceptions of the self and society may substantially influence younger Australians. Anthropologists have long established that a number of world societies have conceptions of the self that have no notion of individuals as autonomous beings. Many Australians have been to Bali, which was where US anthropologist Clifford Geertz wrote a pioneering study that introduced the idea of human ecology into social research. More recently, he has observed:

> The Western conception of the person as a bounded, unique, more or less integrated ... cognitive universe, a dynamic centre of awareness, emotion, judgment, and action, organized into a distinctive whole and set contrastively against other such wholes and against a social and natural background is, however incorrigible it may seem to us, a rather peculiar idea within the context of the world's cultures (1984: 126).

Exercise 6.7 Reading the ethnic press

1. Delegate several class members to collect either a daily or weekly ethnic-language newspaper or magazine, which is either in English or has some English-language materials.
2. Bring these to class and discuss some topics in these sources, referring to Bell's (1993) analysis of the ethnic media.
3. As a follow-up exercise contact a journalist or an editor working in this area. See if they can talk to the class about the role of their publication in terms of how their paper may facilitate immigrant acculturation. Alternatively, interview that person about how the news values of the paper's readers are perceived by journalists and editors.

Chapter 6

4. Using APAIS or CD/AUSTROM, research and write an essay about ethnic press coverage either of the 1993 campaign for the Sydney Olympics or on another topic of your choice.

A Balinese temple: an early representation of Dutch colonisers. (Photo: *Robert Hamilton*)

Summary

1. Intercultural communication is about how people from different cultures communicate. It is concerned with face-to-face communication between individuals who belong to different host and minority cultures. The host is the mainstream, or dominant, culture while the minority cultures are made up of immigrant and sometimes native subcultures.
2. Both the host and minority cultures will have subcultures of their own. Subcultures are smaller subgroups within either the host or the minority culture, though mostly in the former. They can be based on ethnic, religious or lifestyle differences. Whereas subcultural differences mark off social boundaries between differing groups, multiculturalism aims to reconcile these subgroups to the majority culture.
3. The main inhibitors to intercultural communication are differences in language, values and reasoning. These are expressed in social life by people's tendency to keep a certain social distance between themselves and others, and to behave ethnocentrically. Ethnocentric behaviour is when people consider their own social group as the 'in' group and judge other groups unfavourably as 'out' groups. The interpersonal mechanisms of social distance and ethnocentrism are stereotyping, discrimination and prejudice.
4. The main facilitator of intercultural communication is the social process of acculturation. This is the means by which immigrants learn to identify and

then to adopt the important symbols and meanings of the new host culture through communication. The extent of immigrant acculturation depends on a range of personal and social variables, such as an individual's age and their media use habits.
5. Intercultural communication accommodation may take place either on an individual or an intergroup intercultural level in terms of the way language is used. Speakers may use strategies of speech convergence to draw closer to their listeners, or diverge their speech patterns to increase social distance between them.
6. Lastly, intercultural communication competence is the ability to negotiate shared interpersonal meanings in an intercultural setting. Effective interpersonal contact in an intercultural or cross-cultural context between people from different cultures usually requires more patience, tolerance of ambiguity and regular perception checking.

Discussion questions

1. What is the difference between intercultural, intracultural, and cross-cultural communication?
2. Are subcultures good or bad? Or are some good and some bad? Why?
3. Discuss some of the alternative meanings given to multiculturalism in different countries.
4. In what ways is the phenomenon of social distance expressed in urban life?
5. What importance do successful role models have for minority groups?
6. What are the main stages of culture shock? When is it more and less likely?
7. What are the four main personal variables that affect the acculturation process?
8. What are the three main social variables that affect acculturation?
9. What kind of paralinguistic cues can be used to indicate speech convergence and speech divergence in intercultural exchanges?
10. How does intercultural communication competence differ from interpersonal communication competence?

Further reading

Asuncion-Lande, N. (1990) 'Intercultural Communication', pp. 208–27 in G. Dahnke, C. Fernandez-Collado & G. Clatterbuck, (eds) *Human Communication* Belmont, CA: Wadsworth.
Condon, J. & Saito, M. (eds) (1974) *Intercultural Encounters With Japan* Tokyo: Simul Press.
Gallois, C., Franklyn-Stolnes, A., Giles, H. & Coupland, N. (1988) 'Communication Accommodation in Intercultural Encounters', pp. 157–86 in Y. Kim & W. Gudykunst, (eds) *Theories in Intercultural Communication* Newbury Park, CA: Sage.
Irwin, H. (1992) 'Cultural Sensitivity and Management Communication Competence', *Australian Journal of Communication* 19 (2): 126–39.

Jayasuriya, L. (1990) 'Rethinking Australian Multiculturalism', *Australian Quarterly* 62 (1): 50–64.
Kim, Y. (1988) 'Communication and Acculturation', pp. 344–55 in L. Samovar & R. Porter, (eds) *Intercultural Communication: A Reader* Belmont, CA: Wadsworth, 5th edn.
Walsh, M. (1991) 'Conversational Styles and Intercultural Communication', *Australian Journal of Communication* 18 (1): 1–13.

References

Ang, I. (1993) 'The Differential Politics of Chineseness', pp. 17–27 in G. Hage & L. Johnson, (eds) *Identity/Community/Change* University of Western Sydney: Centre for Intercommunal Studies.
Barnlund, D. (1975) *Public and Private Self in Japan and the U.S.* Tokyo: Simul Press.
Bednall, D. (1988) 'Television Use by Melbourne's Greek Community', *Media Information Australia* 47: 44–9.
Bell, P. (1993) *Multicultural Australia in the Media*, Canberra: AGPS
Berger, C. & Roloff, M., (eds) (1982) *Social Cognition and Communication* Beverly Hills, CA: Sage.
Brake, M. (1980) *Youth Culture and Youth Subcultures* London: Routledge.
Duck, S. (1986) *Human Relationships* London: Sage.
Folb, E. (1988) 'Intracultural Communication', pp. 121–30 in L. Samovar & R. Porter, (eds) *Intercultural Communication: A Reader* Belmont, CA: Wadsworth, 5th edn.
Furnham, A. & Bochner, S. (1989) *Culture Shock* London: Routledge.
Gallois, C. (1993) 'The Language and Communication of Emotion', *American Behavioural Scientist* 36 (3): 309–38.
Geertz, C. (1984) 'From the Native's Point of View: On the Nature of Anthropological Understanding', in R. Schweder & R. Levine, (eds) *Culture Theory* Cambridge: Cambridge University Press.
Gilhotra, M. (1984) 'Language Maintenance among the Sikhs of Woolgoolga', *Ethnic Studies* 1: 33–55.
Gudykunst, W. (1988) 'Uncertainty and Anxiety', pp. 123–57 in Y. Kim & W. Gudykunst, (eds) *Theories in Intercultural Communication* Newbury Park, CA: Sage.
Hage, G. (1991) 'Racism, Militarism, and the Gulf War', *Arena* 96: 8–13.
Hofstede, G. (1991) *Cultures and Organizations* London: McGraw-Hill.
Hollway, S. (1992) 'Multiculturalism as Public Administration', *Australian Journal of Public Administration* 51 (2): 248–55.
Ito, Y. (1991) 'Theories on Interpersonal Communication Styles from a Japanese Perspective', pp. 238–67 in K. Rosengren, W. Gudykunst & J. Blumler, (eds) *Comparatively Speaking* Newbury Park, CA: Sage.
Jakubowicz, A. (1987) 'Multiculturalism, Mainstreaming and 'Special' Broadcasting', *Media Information Australia* 45: 18–32.
James, P. (ed.) (1990) *Technocratic Dreaming: Of Very Fast Trains and Japanese Designer Cities* Melbourne: Left Book Club.

Kalantzis, M., Cope, B. & Slade, D. (1989) *Minority Languages and Dominant Culture* London: The Falmer Press.

Kincaid, D. (1988) 'Convergence Theory and Intercultural Communication', pp. 280–99 in Y. Kim & W. Gudykunst, (eds) *Theories in Intercultural Communication* Newbury Park, CA: Sage.

Martin, D. (1962) *The Young Wife* Melbourne: Macmillan.

Milner, A. (1990) 'Postmodernism and Popular Culture', pp. 46–57 in S. Alomes & D. den Hartog, (eds) *Post Pop* Melbourne: V.U.T.

Sarbaugh, L. (1979) *Intercultural Communication* New Jersey: Hayden.

Sherif, M. (1948) *An Outline of Social Psychology* New York: Harper.

Street, R. & Giles, H. (1982) 'Speech Accommodation Theory', pp. 193–227 in C. Berger & M. Roloff, *op.cit.*

Wickert, R. (1990) *No Single Measure* Canberra: AGPS.

Yum, J. (1988) 'Network Theory in Intercultural Communication', pp. 239–59 in Y. Kim & W. Gudykunst, (eds) *Theories in Intercultural Communication* Newbury Park, CA: Sage.

Communicating in multicultural Australia

7

Objectives

After completing this chapter you should be able to:

- distinguish between the concepts of culture and communication;
- explain some of the key ingredients of Anglo-Australian culture;
- discuss some of the key elements of Aboriginality;
- appreciate some of the cultural norms of Southern European, Middle Eastern and Asian immigrants.

Chapter 7

> *A huge painting masked one whole wall. Was it a Whiteley? A Pollock?*
> *'No stupid,' she said. It was an original Nolan. The painting made me perspire. Australia had always made me perspire. Some people said it was the most beautiful climate in the world. Others were actually looking forward to the Greenhouse Effect.*
>
> Pomeroy, *Brian Castro*

Brian Castro's novels are clever kaleidoscopes with a multi-racial cast of characters juxtaposing their Asian, European and Anglo-Australian cultural experiences. But what is Anglo-Australian culture? The question is simple enough but there is no easy answer. There are no generally agreed on definitions of 'culture' to begin with. Additionally, there is no agreement on what being 'Australian' means. When one recent ABC-TV program asked young people what Australians were like, many answered that Australians were 'tall and blonde with blue eyes'. More than that there was no agreement.

The real Australia? (Photo: *Glen Lewis*)

It is important not to confuse the concepts of 'culture' and 'communication'. They are closely related, yet they are distinguishable. Culture precedes communication and makes it possible. In Chapter 1 culture was defined, following Williams, as a way of life. Another definition of culture more relevant to considering an intercultural context is: 'the understandings that have been generated among individuals and groups about the role of human relationships . . . [it] describes a history of experience that has been shared by a people in the context of a nation' (Edelstein, 1989). It follows that the way individuals learn and enact their culture is through communication. In this sense, communication is culturally engendered behaviour. **Culture** is the distinctive national pattern of social behaviours that develop over time.

culture
Distinctive national pattern of social behaviours that develops over time.

Anglo-Australian culture

Anglo-Australian culture is the culture white Anglo immigrants have established in Australia in the time since settlement. That culture was predominantly Anglo (strictly speaking, Anglo-Celtic) in the sense that the immigrants were British — English, Irish, Scottish, and Welsh — and there were relatively small numbers from non-Anglo backgrounds. There was some early immigration by Germans, Italians and Chinese, but with the adoption of the White Australia Policy in 1901 Asian immigration was stopped and non-British migration was sharply limited (Jupp, 1992). By the 1950s it was a common boast that Australians were 'more British than Britons'. When we try to decode the main features of Anglo-Australian culture, however, we quickly enter an ambiguous area where the historical record is shrouded in myths, rituals and legends of origins. This is the so-called 'Myths of Oz' territory, as referred to by Fiske, Turner and Hartley (1990) in their book of the same name. They made an iconoclastic reading of Australian popular culture which was subsequently disputed by both feminists and nationalists.

Anglo-Australian culture
The culture that white Anglo immigrants have established in Australia since settlement.

History, language and values

Australians do have a national identity of their own, nevertheless, which derives from their cultural heritage. A nation's **cultural heritage** is its distinctive history and language. Novelists, journalists, historians and painters have attempted to define 'the' Australian identity. They seized on distinctive features of white settlement, such as the convict years and life in the bush, as well as the unique geography of Australia to construct their stories and images. Ward's *The Australian Legend*, for instance, argued that mateship was built on the experience of the convicts, gold-diggers, bushmen and unionists to create a distinctive working class ethos. Subsequently, however, this too was challenged by feminists, radicals and liberals who maintained his story left out women, Aboriginals and the middle class. It has been suggested by one historian that attempts to construct images of a 'real' Australia are subjective and chimerical (White, 1981).

Another way of gauging what is important in Anglo-Australian culture is to look at some of the most prominent national secular rituals (Alomes, 1988). Like Europeans, Australians traditionally observe Christmas, New Year and Easter as holidays. Whether they spend these in church or on the beach depends on their own preferences. The Australian calendar, however, also includes more distinctive days for ritual observance, notably sporting events such as Melbourne Cup Day and football Grand Finals. Our one military ritual day is Anzac Day, which was used as a symbolic means of exploring changing generational values by Alan Seymour in his 1950s play *The One Day of the Year*. Lastly, the ritual day which has signalled the most recent changes in cultural values is Australia Day itself. This now seems to be as much a day for Aboriginal Australians to remember as 'Invasion Day', and for ethnic groups to celebrate a culturally pluralistic Australia, as to commemorate traditional British allegiances to God, Queen, and Country.

There were significant religious and class differences between the British who came to Australia. The most culturally visible different group was the Irish who, if they were Southern Irish, usually retained their Catholic faith and strong resentment against English rule. With the exception of the Northern Protestant Irish, many Irish-Australians tended to become the 'poor whites' in nineteenth and even early twentieth century Australia. Pascoe has suggested that the Irish were not formally and finally assimilated into Australian life until the 1950s (Pascoe, 1992).

cultural heritage
Any group's own distinctive history and language.

The Scots, on the other hand, usually had higher socioeconomic origins and educational levels. They mixed comfortably into the mainstream of Australian commercial and cultural life in areas such as banking, grazing, publishing and university teaching. Like the Welsh — who were not as well educated and who tended to settle in mining areas — the Scots were usually Methodists, Presbyterians or Congregationalists. The English, in contrast, were the dominant British group, and expatriate English culture, with its Anglican religion and sense of then-Imperial loyalty, was the main basis on which Anglo-Australian cultural identity grew. Since the 1950s the differences between these original Anglo-Australian white settlers have decreased with the passage of time and the influx of a new strata of non-British immigrants.

Another real Australia?
(Photo: *Xu Bai-ming*)

One of the most distinctive features of Anglo-Australian culture is that of language difference. In 1945 the Minister for Immigration, Arthur Calwell, on the eve of the first great postwar wave of non-British immigration, said all newcomers would have to learn to speak Australian. That attitude has changed but it remains true that while Australian written English is similar to British and American English, spoken Australian English is different from both. Foreign students who learn English overseas on British or American models have to go through an acclimatisation period before understanding spoken Australian English.

Australian spoken English is remarkably homogeneous throughout the country. In the US and Britain there are substantial regional variations in daily speech, but in Australia there is relatively little variation. If there is any one single important regional variation in spoken Australian English it is between city and country. The more leisurely and colourful speech styles, which are sometimes considered typically Australian, are most likely to be found among bush or country-town dwellers. Status and educational differences are mostly the causes of genuine variations in Australian spoken English. Postwar research, referred to previously in Chapter 2, suggested there were three categories of spoken English used by Australians — broad, standard and cultivated.

The second distinctive feature of Anglo-Australian culture is its **core values**. These are the social values and attitudes that the mainstream culture sees as normal. Australia has modelled itself on Britain and the US. Like Americans and the British, Australians share common social values, though their particular cultural expression often differs. These are essentially those of individualism, competitiveness and materialism. Australians expect the right to work, to have a house, a car and a family. To achieve these aims they also expect to have to compete for them and meet the basic citizenship obligations that these rights entail. So a certain level of material security is essential to acquiring the kind of interpersonal rewards most Australians desire, as well as some degree of community involvement and responsibility.

Anglo-Australian values can be identified readily enough in this common-sense way, but theorists have also investigated them using social research methods. The US, which pioneered applied psychological research, has conducted national opinion polls on beliefs and values for many years. Social research techniques are less readily used in Australia, yet some studies have looked at the question of individual values, such as Connell's 1956 study of Sydney teenagers, and more recent examinations of student values by Feather (1986) and Forgas (1988).

Connell's mid-1950s examination of Sydney teenagers aged 13–18 gave a detailed profile of what teenagers valued in their peers. In the choice of a friend the same qualities were identified by both boys and girls — an attractive personality, good character, sociability and the capacity to mix in with the group. One extra trait that boys mentioned was their admiration for sporting ability. In their choices of conversational topics boys listed sport, mechanical things, sex and current affairs, while girls nominated films, art and literature, sex and interpersonal relationships. This research did not inquire into the question of ethnic differences, although Connell did say that Sydney teenagers attached little importance to this issue (Connell, 1957: 133).

More recent values studies by cross-cultural psychologists have produced different findings. Examining the values of university students in New Guinea, China and Australia, Feather found that Australian students rated love, accomplishment, friendship and being cheerful most highly. In contrast, students from New Guinea nominated equality, salvation, national security and obedience, while Chinese students preferred competence, scholarship, respect, hard work and national security (Feather, 1986: 221). These findings were similar to those of Forgas, whose survey found that Australians most valued competition, self-confidence, freedom, and hedonism. Hong Kong Chinese students, in contrast, valued communality, collectivism and social usefulness (Forgas, 1988: 205).

One of the most widely cited social psychological cross-cultural values studies of this kind was Hofstede's (1980). He identified four primary cultural dimensions: power distance, uncertainty avoidance, individualism vs. collectivism, and masculinity/femininity. Australian culture was characterised by small power distance and had a low tolerance of inequality and authority. Australians also scored very highly on individualism and mid-range on uncertainty avoidance and masculinity. Overall, Australian culture appeared to have a loose-knit social framework and a relatively weak sense of communal obligations. Hofstede's study, however, had several limitations. First, his data

core values and behaviours
The social values and sense-making practices that the mainstream culture sees as normal.

were collected almost entirely from the world-wide staff of the IBM organisation, hardly a representative sample. Secondly, in the updated version of his earlier work he made it plain that his notions of culture were essentially behaviourist: he defined culture as 'mental programming' or as 'software of the mind' (1991: 4).

Exercise 7.1 Anglo-Australian values clarification
Divide into subgroups of three or four. Select one person to speak as an Anglo-Australian, a second to be British, and a third to be American. Then go through the following checklist of core Anglo-Australian values and cultural assumptions and discuss how the people concerned may see these differently.
1. How do you approach daily life?
    (a) a concern with 'doing', progress and change
    (b) a concern with external achievement
    (c) in a generally optimistic, striving way
    (d) taking things as they come
2. What are the important goals in your life?
    (a) material wealth
    (b) comfort and security
    (c) having a good time
    (d) helping others
3. Who are the most important people in your life?
    (a) your friends
    (b) your family
    (c) your marriage partner or boyfriend or girlfriend
    (d) the people you work with

Anglo-Australians and multiculturalism

Perhaps the biggest social change to take place in Australia in the last generation has been the move towards a policy of multiculturalism. The White Australia Policy was abandoned in the 1960s, then there was an influx of numbers of Vietnamese refugees in the late 1970s which signalled a bigger wave of Asian immigration. In the meantime other longer-established ethnic groups became more politically active, SBS ethnic radio was established in 1975, and the 1978 Galbally Report set an agenda for a multicultural approach to welfare and education (Seneviratne, 1993). Debate continues over the extent to which Australia is becoming genuinely multicultural (Goot, 1993).

One relevant study here is Ho's 1990 survey of community attitudes to multiculturalism in Darwin. This tested how respondents felt about the question 'Would Australian multiculturalism lead to social cohesion or intragroup conflict?' It was concluded that there was considerable confusion about multicultural policies. Darwin residents had favourable attitudes to several of the principles underlying multiculturalism — e.g. that multicultural policies could be an effective social justice strategy — yet there was weak overall support. Ho considered that many respondents saw multiculturalism as socially divisive, and that 'a paradox exists in the proposed national agenda for social cohesion which is based on the promotion of cultural differences' (Ho, 1990: 271). In the New Zealand setting, Fitzgerald (1992: 130) has also indicated some of the ambiguities in the cultural identity of Cook Islanders, who see

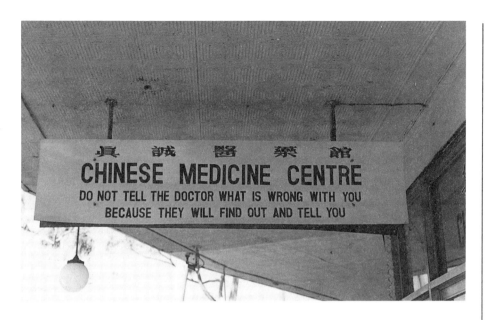

Multicultural medicine in Sydney.
(Photo: *Glen Lewis*)

themselves as different from both Maoris and Pakehas, but concludes that multiculturalism as an official policy is working.

These findings are in line with the views of James Jupp (1991: 51), who argues that 'the ethnic situation in Australia [is] fairly benign ... despite an undercurrent of hostility to mass Asian immigration'. The debate is certain to continue (Vasta, 1993). Australia's experience here is part of a world-wide dilemma. The post-1945 period has seen a huge movement of peoples across national boundaries. Currently in the US, blacks and Hispanics make up 17 per cent of the population and approximately one in four people in New York and Los Angeles have non-Anglo parents. In Britain 4 per cent of the population comes from New Commonwealth and Pakistani origins, but this does not include European or Irish immigrants. In New Zealand, Maoris and Polynesians constitute 12 per cent of the population. Today in Australia roughly some 25 per cent of people have non-English-speaking (NESB I or II) backgrounds (Jupp, 1991).

A recurrent issue in these countries is whether the process of immigrant acculturation should be of an assimilationist or a pluralist kind. Some writers argue that it is too crude a contrast to juxtapose these as alternatives, as in practice there is a variety of outcomes, including social segregation and ethnic conflict (Edwards, 1985: 104). Australian government policies prior to the adoption of multiculturalism, however, were strongly assimilationist. **Assimilationism** is the process whereby immigrants become more similar to the host population as a result of social interaction. Since then government policy has changed and now the emphasis is on cultural pluralism. **Pluralism** is where immigrants retain their original sense of cultural identity while supplementing it by the selective adaptation of the norms of the new host culture.

Jupp (1988) has identified three versions of assimilationism — conservative, rational and radical. The first is held by those critics of multicultural and immigration policies who fear the degradation of Anglo-Australian culture, such as RSL spokesperson Bruce Ruxton and academics such as Lauchlan

assimilationism
The process whereby immigrants become more similar to the host population as a result of social interaction.

pluralism
A situation where immigrants retain their original sense of cultural identity while supplementing it with selective adaptation from the norms of the new host culture.

Chipman. Secondly, there are 'rational' assimilationists who argue that the cultural baggage of the homeland is of no use in a new society. Thirdly, 'radical assimilationists' are left-wing critics who see multiculturalism as a policy that papers over the cracks in inadequacies in government services for migrants and reduces their sense of class consciousness in the workforce. One version of this approach is the book by Castles et al. (1988) *Mistaken Identity*, which argued that traditional Australian nationalism needed to be replaced by a new sense of community not based on irrelevant nationalist myths.

In the post-1945 years migrants who came from Britain, Scandinavia and Holland were seen as most desirable. With the exception of some strong anti-German feelings due to the war, Northern Europeans generally were seen as ideal settlers. This attitude also applied to New Zealanders. One subgroup of Kiwis that has sometimes been seen less favourably, however, is that of Maoris and Polynesians. A recent study of the inter-ethnic perceptions of New Zealand teenagers suggested that Pakeha (white) teenagers tended to see Maoris as 'happy, musical, easy-going, family-oriented generous and friendly, but also as uneducated, dirty and aggressive'. Pakeha teenagers saw Pacific Islanders and Maoris in similar terms, whereas those two groups saw sharper differences between themselves (Oliver & Vaughan, 1991: 19). Anglo-Australian perceptions of Maoris and Islanders probably resemble those of Pakehas.

Exercise 7.2   Locating immigrant communities in an urban context

Draw a map of an Australian city you know well. The map should explain the social geography of the city to a new arrival. On the map highlight two features — first, the areas where rich and poor live and, second, the areas where a particular migrant community lives. Add a few details about any of the city's tourist highlights that have an ethnic dimension.

Take ten minutes to draw your map, then discuss it with the person next to you. The class may pool these maps, if you are concentrating on the same city, to build up a group representation of the city's social and ethnic geography.

The first Australians

In 1993 the national debate over the Mabo case concentrated public attention on Aboriginal issues. For the last decade, however, there has been an increasing engagement by white writers and intellectuals with questions of white moral responsibility and the need for reconciliation with the original people of Australia (Rowse, 1993). A cultural renaissance has now taken place for some Aboriginal Australians. In painting, design, poetry and popular music, Aboriginal culture has achieved greater prominence in mainstream Australian life. Musicians such as the Warumpis, Yothu Yindi and Kev Carmody, and dance and theatre groups with successes like the Aboriginal-Chinese playwright Jimmy Chi's *Bran Nue Dae* 1992 musical, have added a rich new dimension to the place of Aboriginal life in Anglo-Australian culture (Muecke, 1992). Some, such as Sally Morgan, have been recognised both as novelists and painters, and film-makers like Tracey Moffatt have made award-winning films.

Similarly, Aboriginals have greater visibility in public life and in the media.

They have their own TV service Imparja in Alice Springs, while a number of Aboriginal programs are broadcast on public radio, such as Sydney's 'Radio Redfern'. The first exclusively Aboriginal radio station began in Alice Springs in 1985 (Browne, 1990; Bell, 1990). This is not to say that the media always present objective coverage of Aboriginal affairs (Langton, 1993), especially concerning Land Rights issues (Meadows, 1994), yet compared to media coverage a generation ago Aboriginals are now more often positively represented (Bennett, 1989).

Aboriginality and the land

Though the component parts of Aboriginality are complex and often ambiguous, the sense of Aboriginality itself is perhaps the most important cultural distinguishing feature of Aboriginal Australians. According to Coombs (1983) there are several dimensions of **Aboriginality**. These include Aboriginals' sense of their being the original inhabitants of the continent, their belief in the Dreamtime, and their distinctive beliefs about the land. It may also include their attitudes to and values about kinship and their ability to speak and understand more than one language. 'Aboriginality' is a very difficult idea for non-Aboriginals to grasp (Bell, 1993). Its complexity is similar to the diffuseness of the Indian and Chinese philosophical concepts of Dharma and the Tao, which have, by Western standards, elements that defy rational definition.

First, Aboriginal people have a strong sense of being the original inhabitants of Australia. Archaeological research proves they have been here for between 40 000 and 80 000 years. Pre-settlement Aboriginals had a highly efficient material culture as well as complex patterns of social organisation. Their customs and beliefs, however, were incomprehensible to most white settlers. The prevailing neo-Darwinist racial beliefs of the time disposed whites to believe that Aboriginals were close to the bottom of the ladder of racial types, while whites were at the top.

Second, Aboriginal society had a central set of beliefs linked to 'the Dreaming'. Aboriginal writer Kevin Gilbert said this referred not only to a heroic past, but was a means for Aboriginals to continue their spiritual life in the present (1981: 34). The Dreaming is a set of doctrines about the value of everything in life, which were determined irrevocably in the distant past. Anthropologist W. H. Stanner described it as a 'largely intuitive, visionary and poetic understanding of reality, truth, goodness and beauty', expressed in mythological terms. It also acts as a set of unwritten communication rules for the present, as Aboriginals are expected to live out Dreamtime precepts in the social customs of their daily life and in their rituals and expressive arts (Stanner, 1979: 30). Perhaps the most confusing thing about 'the Dreaming' for whites is that usually it is taught to initiates in terms of mythical stories that are not structured chronologically but have a circular character (Langton, 1981).

The third feature of Aboriginality is their distinctive beliefs about the importance of the land. Where whites saw land primarily in terms of legal property rights, Aboriginals had a complex sense of spiritual and material rights about land. A fourth feature of Aboriginality is their complex kinship relations. Coombs considers that it is the link of Aboriginal relations to the land with Aboriginal kinship practices — or interpersonal relations in our terms — which

Aboriginality
Aboriginals' sense of their being the original inhabitants of the continent, their belief in the Dreamtime, and their distinctive beliefs about the land.

Chapter 7

Painting an indoor Aboriginal mural. (Photo: *Cecilia Burke*)

is the essence of Aboriginality. Unlike Anglo-Australians, Aboriginals saw kinship as the basis for all social relations.

The special value that Aboriginals attach to the land can be illustrated from Rhys Jones' study (1985) of the Anbarra people. They were one of four Gidjingarli speaking subgroups resident at a river mouth in northern Arnhem Land at the time of first white settlement. They lived in a small speech community surrounded by lands belonging to other groups who spoke different languages. The Anbarra described themselves as people of the *djaranga* (beach). Their definition of their landscape labelled different ecological areas according to flora and fauna. The open woodlands, called *malpi*, were seen as inhospitable places lacking sufficient food. They would refer to a man seen as wild or unsophisticated as an *an-malpi*. After the woodlands were the open flood plains, termed *kapal*, with wide open vistas that the Anbarra liked. In contrast, the monsoon jungles, or *man-nga*, were seen as mysterious and potentially dangerous places. They thought of their land in terms of localities marked by a series of wells. It was believed that women became pregnant through the spirit of the land entering their bodies at particular sacred, or totemic, wells. This perceived relationship between totemic wells, birth and clan identity was mythologised in bark paintings and sacred song cycles. In this way, concepts of kin relationship and the land were inextricably interwoven.

Exercise 7.3 Aboriginal culture and conservation

Anderson (1989) considers it a naive assumption that Aboriginal interests necessarily coincide with modern conservationist principles. His study of a 1984 controversy in North Queensland found that some of the Kuku-Yalng people supported a proposed road through the Daintree Forest because they believed that no sacred sites were at risk. Some were also antipathetic to white conservationists and considered the Aboriginal members of the North Queensland Land Council had no relationship with their own area.

Examine press treatment of the Mabo issue after July 1993 to explore how, if at all, conservationist and Land Rights issues were presented. For background on the media and Aboriginals, see Bennett (1989).

Language and interpersonal relations

Aboriginal languages were oral. None had a written form until relatively recently. The 1984 *Report on a National Language Policy* found that some 30 000 Aborigines spoke a traditional language — such as Aranda or Pitjantjatjara — as their first language, another 30 000 used pidgin or creole English, and the remaining 50 000 spoke Standard Australian English (1984: 81). Even where Aboriginals have no fluency in their traditional languages, the way they use Australian English in different social contexts expresses distinctive Aboriginal standards (Eades, 1988). They have a variety of terms to describe themselves and whites. On Palm Island and in other parts of Queensland they refer to themselves as *Murries* and to whites as *Migaloos*. In south-east Australia an increasingly common Aboriginal self-description is *Kooris*, with *Gubbas* for whites.

One of the most helpful guides to understanding Aboriginal spoken English was written by John Von Sturmer (1981). Though Von Sturmer made a number of emphatic reservations about treating his findings as an inflexible set of rules, he advanced a set of five guidelines for talking with Aborigines. These were (1) Avoid personal names and references whenever possible, (2) Avoid direct criticisms of particular individuals, (3) Do not cause anyone to suffer loss of personal dignity, (4) Practise circumspection and the use of disclaimers, and (5) Do not 'knock people back', i.e. refuse requests.

The paramount communication rule that is involved here is the importance of indirection. In contrast to Western standards of frank and open conversational approaches, Von Sturmer emphasises that Aboriginal speech preferences are grounded in indirection. When Aboriginals meet each other or whites for the first time they are often reluctant or embarrassed to give their names. When they do exchange names they are likely to use their full names and do so more formally, rather than just casually swap names as Anglo-Australians generally do. Before this, their nonverbal means of approach to strangers is likely to be indirect. Strangers are expected not to surprise others, but approach tentatively, with careful avoidance of facial contact.

When the initial approach has been made and names have been exchanged, Aboriginal people will be most concerned to clarify their kinship relations with the new person by identifying mutually known others. In the case of a renewed meeting after a long absence, they will usually seek to establish which people they know, if any, have died. In the case of meetings after short absences, however, they may engage in a certain amount of small talk to establish what each has been doing. After these stylised greetings, when the conversation comes to a point when requests are made, disagreement is expressed, or when important matters are being discussed, the general guideline of circumspection and indirection will be followed.

In public meetings there will usually be a marked division of the sexes: women will keep a low public profile, though they may be the most forceful members of their own families. Second, when a meeting takes place with a group of visitors there is no certainty that those Aboriginals who speak are the most important. Powerful group members are more likely not to speak about their viewpoints until they have observed the positions of others. The prolonged silence of some individuals may be the best sign of their disapproval of proceedings. Aboriginal public meetings are usually used to ratify a group consensus, rather than to establish one.

Von Sturmer concludes that the primary consideration is to practise caution and circumspection. Where Anglo-Australians expect others to behave in certain culturally normative ways in discussions and negotiations, many Aboriginals do not share these norms. Traditional Aboriginals expect each other not to present themselves too forcefully and not to link themselves too closely with their own ideas. They are more likely to express their ideas indirectly by attributing them to what they say other groups of Aboriginals also believe. They do not consider it polite to interrupt others and they will often express their ideas conditionally. In other words, Anglo-Australians should not expect their own speech style to be privileged.

In contrast to white norms, Aboriginal kinship is seen as the basis for all social relations and is defined much more widely. The classificatory nature of traditional Aboriginal society was complex: children could belong to the country and spiritual group of their father, and to the totem groups of their mother. Aboriginals worked out the social relations of each person to everyone else on the basis of these classifications. The nature of their kinship systems regulated interpersonal relations to create an extended sense of social obligations, and set group rules for the avoidance of particular others. Aboriginals involve themselves in wide-ranging social networks of care and obligation with members of their own 'mob'. A range of communication rules regulates eating, living arrangements, the sharing of goods, marriage and child raising.

Traditional families were usually organised on a patrilineal basis — i.e. a man and his descendants in the male line — though in some regions family descent was determined via females. Currently, two features of Aboriginal urban families are, first, their relatively large family size and their extended nature and, second, the greater proportion of families with female heads. Mothers, grandmothers, aunts and other female relations act as the cultural centre for many urban Aboriginal families and the mother–child relation is the centrepiece of the family (Langton, 1981: 18). The importance of women in contemporary Aboriginal families was an adaptive cultural response by urban Aboriginals to their difficulties in dealing with whites. Aboriginal men were the prime victims of unemployment, violence, imprisonment and social security regulations, which discouraged them from retaining their family leadership roles (Merlan, 1988).

Exercise 7.4 Differences in white and Aboriginal group decision making
Marvin Watson, a business consultant to an Aboriginal pastoral company in Queensland, was required to negotiate for a leasehold with a local white community group, made up of pastoralists, dairy farmers and some environmentalists. A meeting of community leaders was called so Marvin could put his company's case. Marvin seemed a good choice for the job as he had a mixed-race background and an MBA. The community leaders appeared to Marvin to be the older men, though some of the

younger men had an active role in the negotiations, while some of the women gathered on the edge of the group to listen.

At the first meeting it was decided more time was needed, so Marvin agreed to return a week later. He met with the group periodically over the next few months and each time seemed to make some headway. He was told the company might be allowed to lease the land they wanted, provided access rights, compensation and several other conditions were agreed to. The meetings were usually followed with great interest by everyone except for one older lady environmentalist who regularly left early. After being told by Marvin they had permission to proceed the company support staff moved in two weeks later, but were dismayed when they were told by some of the community representatives that they would not be allowed.

How could Marvin explain the group's action to his employers? Why did the community group reject the agreement?

Discuss and prioritise the following alternatives:
1. Marvin was misled unintentionally or on purpose.
2. White people cannot make binding decisions.
3. Marvin had not obtained approval from the environmentalists.
4. The community group thought the compensation wasn't enough.
5. Marvin was not considered to be a representative of his people.
6. Or what else?

The new multicultural communities

Any analysis of the diverse ethnic make-up of contemporary Australia is bound to leave some groups out of the picture. Hungarians, black and white Africans, Afghans, Balts, Canadians, Czechs, Cook Islanders, Germans, Indians, Koreans and other European and Latin American peoples have migrated to Australia since World War II. The following overview, however, discusses only the largest ethnic communities, the Southern Europeans, the Middle Easterners, and the Chinese and Indochinese Asians. The two largest groups not considered are the Germans and Spanish, some 115 400 and 86 300 (ABS, 1993). The 1991 census suggests that Melbourne is a more European ethnic city, while Sydney now has a larger share of Asian and Arabic immigrants (*The Australian*, 10 November 1993: 1).

Three concepts are useful in discussing communication practices among the main Australian ethnic communities. These are the ideas of an 'ethnic pecking order', of 'chain migration', and 'intracultural communication networks'. The idea of an **ethnic pecking order** means that the majority of immigrants from any one ethnic group will have to stand in an unofficial queue before gaining acceptance from the host culture. Any ethnic group's place in this invisible queue is influenced by two main factors — their time of arrival in relation to other migrants, and the degree of cultural similarity their group has to the host culture.

For example, Southern Europeans preceded Arabs and Asians as postwar immigrants and this is one reason why many Greek and Italian-Australians have integrated more fully into mainstream Australian life. Though there was a relatively small number of Chinese in Australia before the 1970s, many

ethnic pecking order
How each ethnic group has to take its place in a queue while waiting for acceptance into the host culture.

Australian-born Chinese have lost their distinctive Chinese cultural identity and do not share the attitudes or beliefs that recent Chinese immigrants have. This loss of cultural identity for the Australian-born Chinese has led recently to a search for their roots, as poignantly expressed in William Yang's 1993 one-person stage play *Sadness*.

Southern Europeans: Italians and Greeks

It was particularly the social impact of Southern European immigrants from Italy and Greece that challenged the monocultural dominance of Anglo-Australian society in the immediate postwar years. There had already been substantial immigration to Australia by Italians in the 1920s, but between 1950 and the late 1960s there was an unprecedented increase. By 1983 there were some 555 000 Italian-Australians and 307 000 Greek-Australians (National Languages, 1984: 12). Not all of these were overseas-born. In 1986, 262 000 Italian-Australians were Italian-born, but there were 243 000 second generation and 58 000 third generation Italian-Australians (Cresciani, 1988: 244). The 1991 census identified 409 200 Italian language speakers, and some 275 000 speaking Greek (ABS, 1993).

Migrating mainly as unskilled labourers, Italians helped build railways in outback Western Australia, worked on the Snowy Mountains project, and on the North Queensland canefields. They spoke, dressed and ate differently from Anglo-Australians and their young men played soccer instead of the mainstream Australian football codes. Many encountered hostility or indifference from Anglo-Australians, who in the 1950s referred to them as 'New Australians', or more disparagingly as 'Wops' or 'Dagos'.

In the case of the Southern Europeans, their main phase of large-scale immigration was in the 1950s and 1960s. Only with the passage of time was the place of the Southern Europeans at the bottom of the ethnic-Australian social ladder taken by later arrivals from the Middle East and Asia. The 'ethnic pecking order' did not just affect the allocation of rewards between ethnic groups, it impacted on the success of immigrants within those groups. Greek and Italian settlers who arrived before World War II tended to become small business owners, where a much greater proportion of the postwar Southern Europeans became factory workers and labourers (Collins, 1992).

Whereas pre-war Italian immigrants came from Northern Italy, some 60 per cent of postwar arrivals came from the south, specifically Calabria, Sicily, Abruzzi and Campania. With Greeks, pre-war immigration was from coastal and island Greece, but the postwar settlers came from Cyprus, Crete, Lesbos, Macedonia and even Egypt. The other distinctive feature of the postwar migration experience for Southern Europeans was that they were concentrated overwhelmingly in big cities. By 1981, 40 per cent of the Italians born in Australia lived in Melbourne.

The strength of the intracultural communication networks that developed between Southern Europeans in Australia was one of the main factors that made them socially visible. For both Greeks and Italians the essence of these bonds was a shared locality of origin, and their cultural ties of language, religion (Catholicism for Italians, Greek Orthodoxy for Greeks) and extended family networks. Certain suburbs in the major Australian cities became known as 'Little Italys', such as Coburg and Fitzroy in Melbourne, and Haberfield and Leichhardt in Sydney.

The foundation of Italian and Greek language newspapers and magazines reinforced Southern Europeans' sense of belonging to an ethnic community. *La Fiamma* began in Sydney in 1947, and the political, welfare and social group FILEF began in Melbourne in 1974 with its own paper *Nuovo Paese* (Alcorso, 1992). Sometimes the new settlers were equally visible in country areas. The Trevisani Italians, for instance, moved into Griffith, NSW, in the 1920s. Through chain migration ties were formed between *paesani* (countrymen), workmates and neighbours, establishing a community within the local rural economy. After establishing themselves they formed clubs and associations that sometimes excluded even other Italians in the area. Finally, in the postwar years, the Trevisani social networks opened out through intermarriage (Huber, 1977).

Greek-Australians held strongly to the notion of a core culture, or *Ellenismos*, based on Greek family values. Traditional Greek family structures emphasise the importance of *kombourous*, where a special relation is established with wedding sponsors who subsequently baptise the children from the marriage. Godparents, or *noni*, also play a central part in traditional Greek families. By Anglo-Australian standards, Greek family life is relatively conservative and stable. Women are expected to be chaste and restrained and men are required to be assertive and courageous. Relatively less intimacy is expected of the husband and wife roles, whereas the mother and son relationship is privileged. Generally, Greek children are enjoyed and indulged. The Greek-Australian subculture tends to set the moral and social climate for Greek families, including the older tradition of arranged marriages (Storer, 1985: 133).

Though the cultural strength of the Southern European groups' intracultural communication networks has been central to retaining their own identity, the very strength of these ties sometimes worked against their integration. Isaacs' research on Greek children in inner-city Sydney in the early 1970s found some pupils were considered by their Anglo-Australian teachers to be difficult to control because they were given so much attention at home by their parents. The other side of this story was that some Greek pupils were dismayed by the apparent lack of respect pupils showed their teachers. Mutual misunderstandings also occurred between adult Greeks and Australians. Many Greek-Australians mixed only with Australians at work and their perceptions were ambivalent. Some saw Anglo-Australians as 'nice, kind and helpful', and others valued Australian neighbours because they minded their own business. On the other hand, they thought Australians drank too much and had an inadequate sense of family responsibilities. Most Greek parents disapproved of intermarriage with non-Greeks, with some insisting their children should only marry someone from their own birthplace (Isaacs, 1976).

Arabs: Lebanese and Turks

The cultural and religious differences between Lebanese and Turkish immigrants and Anglo-Australians are often even greater than with Southern Europeans. The major differences are religious, due to the importance of the Islamic religion for the Turks and for many Lebanese. Though a 1982 survey of

Melbourne's Lebanese migrants concluded that some 20 per cent were not attached to a church or a mosque, this does not necessarily mean they were not Islamic. Although a variety of sects of Christianty are important in Lebanon, the different moral and cultural codes of Islamic Lebanese and Turkish families tend to make their values and attitudes sharply different from those of Anglo-Australians. There is also a longstanding tradition of hostility between devout Christians and Muslims and the resurgence of fundamentalism in both religions in recent years has rekindled these old antagonisms.

Currently some 147 400 people in Australia come from a Lebanese or Arabic background, and 38 000 are from Turkey. About 70 per cent of Australia's Arabic-speaking population now live in Sydney (ABS, 1993), mainly in the western and south-western suburbs. The majority of the recent arrivals came between 1959 and 1979, when 48 000 arrived, and after the Israeli–Arab war of 1982. Most of the Lebanese settled in Sydney, Melbourne and Adelaide, as have the bulk of Turkish migrants. Though some Lebanese immigrants are highly educated and fluent in English, the majority of both the Turks and Lebanese frequently have limited literacy skills and have gone into blue-collar occupations — unemployment has been a problem for Lebanese migrants particularly.

Like the Southern Europeans, Arab immigrants to Australia followed a process of **chain migration.** This is the process whereby immigrants do not come at random, but follow established patterns, where the first settlers sponsor family members, relations, neighbours, and friends, usually from their own geographical place of origin. Lebanese society, because of its unsettled recent political history, is fragmented on social, political, and religious lines, with significant cleavages between different Islamic sects, such as the Sunni, the Shia and the Druze, and between the Christian Lebanese, such as the Maronites, and the Greek and Syrian Orthodox.

Similarly, although Turkish society is less fragmented, and secular marriage laws in modern Turkey have replaced the traditional Islamic family law (the *Shari'a*), Islam still remains the dominant faith of Turkish immigrants. For both migrant groups, therefore, the preservation of their own ways tends to depend on their observance of traditional marriage customs and the maintenance of certain attitudes to women and children. This sometimes produces significant conflict when their family and schooling practices come into contact with Anglo-Australian ways.

The traditional Lebanese family was based on extended kin structures and patrilineal descent. It functioned both as an economic unit and as a social welfare system. A key emphasis in Lebanese family organisation was a stress on honour (*ird*) and shame. Family honour was associated with the preservation of a family's good name, while families that broke religious conventions (for example, by intermarrying with a partner of lower social status) lost their honour and were shamed. Lebanese family values also strictly defined sex role standards — men were expected to be responsible for the welfare of women, children and the elderly, while the preservation of women's purity and chastity was essential to upholding the family honour (Storer, 1985: 182). The conflict between these traditional values for Muslim Lebanese in Australia with its *Family Law Act* is potentially great, as the *Shari'a* has no Australian legal status.

chain migration
Immigrants sponsor family members, relations, neighbours and friends, usually from their own geographical place of origin, for immigration.

Comparable moral and religious conflicts arose for Turks in Australia. Different attitudes to divorce, child-rearing practices and schooling were some of the problem areas. Divorce is rare in both traditional Lebanese and Turkish families, but the most frequent form of divorce under Islamic law was the practice of the *talaq*, the unilateral repudiation of a wife by her husband. This has no recognition under Australian law. Similarly, a study of Melbourne Turkish families in 1982 found that many were fearful of what they saw as permissiveness in the Australian educational system, especially the teaching of female children. Turkish parents did not want their children taught at school that they were legally entitled to leave home at age sixteen (Mackie, 1982: 62). Limited child-care facilities were another problem for Turkish parents and their dissatisfaction with after-care arrangements sometimes led them to send their children back to relations in Turkey to be raised.

A final source of misunderstanding concerns traditional Turkish ideas about the place of women. Turkish culture established a quite separate-but-equal set of rules governing interaction between the sexes. Women's place was sharply separated from men's in both public and private spheres via a set of dress, ritual and interaction rules. Though Western feminists at times have seen this as an archaic practice, others have concluded that, within the relatively socially secluded world occupied by traditional Turkish women, they have considerable personal autonomy and are in some ways less dependent on the approval of men than Western women (Storer, 1985: 158). The requirements of the workplace, however, have brought Turkish migrant women out from their traditionally cloistered life, and this has posed new problems for the maintenance of family values by challenging the man's traditional place as head of the household.

Exercise 7.5 Cultural differences in marital role perceptions

Discuss the following checklist of beliefs about proper marital behaviour in groups of three or four, with one person being an Anglo-Australian and the others selecting either a Southern European or Middle Eastern ethnic identity. What beliefs, if any, are distinctively different? Also consider any differences between your own and your parents' generation.

1. Elderly parents should live with their children.
2. It's okay for the wife to earn more than her husband.
3. If the wife wants children, the husband should agree.
4. Both partners should be prepared to look after their own parents.
5. If a husband runs around, so can his wife.
6. Children should be brought up to respect their father and love their mother.
7. Almost all money matters should be decided by the husband.
8. Disciplining the children is a man's job.
9. Both husbands and wives are entitled to have any friends they wish.
10. Children should be allowed to marry whoever they want to.

Asians: Chinese and Indochinese

Australians' experience with Asian migrants has been mostly with the Chinese and Indochinese (Vietnamese, Laos and Khmers). There are two main difficulties for Anglo-Australians in coping with these migrants. The first of these is the legacy of the past. There has been a strong current of anti-Asian

Chapter 7

An old stereotype with a new touch — Japanese tourists as 'the yellow peril'. Source: *G. Pryor,* The Canberra Times, *15 September 1992. Used with permission.*

feeling in the Australian historical experience and several anti-Asian stereotypes still persist (McConnochie, 1988). The second more recent problem for Anglo-Australians in understanding the experience of Chinese and Indochinese immigrants is the variety of different backgrounds they come from.

At the top of the social scale are immigrants from Malaysia and Singapore. These are usually fluent in English, well qualified educationally, often earn high incomes from professional jobs, and live in the more affluent suburbs. For example, in 1986 some 45 per cent of Malaysian-born immigrants worked in professional or technical occupations (Ho & Kee, 1988). In contrast, both the ethnic Vietnamese and the Chinese-born Vietnamese, having arrived more recently in Australia in the aftermath of the Viet Nam war, are relatively poorly off. The 1986 census showed that about one-third of Vietnamese and Khmer were unemployed, while employed Vietnamese were either in blue-collar jobs or in wholesale and retail trade.

This wide diversity of experience of the Chinese and Indochinese makes it difficult for Anglo-Australians to appreciate their problems. The Chinese who came from Hong Kong or Singapore on the now revised Business Migration Program, for instance, are usually affluent and commercially inclined. In contrast, the students who came as refugees after the Tiananmen Square crisis of 1989, though highly educated, are usually not as wealthy or as commercially experienced. The Hong Kong and southern mainland Chinese who came to Australia also speak Cantonese, where the majority of the Tiananmen student refugees speak Mandarin. In the late 1980s national concerns about the scale of Asian immigration resurfaced. In reality, however, the 1986 census showed there were some 536 000 Asian-born living in the country, and some 672 000 of Asian descent, which made up about 4 per cent of the total population (Coughlan, 1989).

Part of the reason for these concerns about the presence of the Chinese and Indochinese immigrants in the last decade has been their cultural visibility. The Asians have tended to live in close proximity to each other, mostly in Sydney and Melbourne, though the Malaysian and Singaporean Chinese have also settled in Perth. In Melbourne there are large numbers of Chinese-Australians living in middle class suburbs in Kew, Prahran, Hawthorn and Camberwell, as well as Malaysian-born Chinese students at Oakleigh who attend Monash University, and numbers of Chinese born of Russian ancestry in Dandenong. The Vietnamese-born Chinese, however, in Melbourne are located in relatively low-status suburbs such as Springvale and Footscray (Ho & Kee, 1988). About 60 per cent of Australia's Chinese-speaking population now live in Sydney, which has the contrast of some recently arrived Chinese living in poor conditions in central Chinatown in the inner city, while more affluent Hong Kong Chinese live in areas such as Chatswood. Some 55 per cent of New South Wales' Indochinese migrants are in Canterbury, Fairfield and Marrickville, with a strong Vietnamese presence in Cabramatta (Coughlan, 1989).

The Asian immigrants, like the Southern Europeans and the Arabs, have relied heavily on their own **intracultural communication networks** to establish themselves in Australia. These networks are the social and familial bonds that exist between members of the same ethnic group and act as channels of cultural interaction and communication (Yum, 1988). The natural tendency of Asian and other migrants to socialise and live close together has sometimes led to negative stereotypes, such as media scares about 'the Hong Kong triads' infecting Australia. The Chinese, in their own culture, place special emphasis on personal connections as a way of doing business, using the term *guanxi* to denote this.

The relatively lower levels of economic success of the Indochinese immigrants compared with those from Hong Kong, Malaysia and Singapore is a direct result of the catastrophic dislocation the former experienced during the Vietnam war. Between 1975 and 1983 some 62 000 Vietnamese came to Australia, along with 9500 Khmers from Kampuchea and 6000 Laotians. It was estimated in 1991 that there were 133 400 Vietnamese-born residents in Australia, 34 per cent of whom had Chinese ancestry (Thomas & Balnaves, 1993). The Laos and Khmers had greater proficiency in the English language and so far have had greater economic success. Viviani's research suggests that there were actually 200 000 Indochinese, 155 000 of whom were Vietnamese, 25 000 Cambodians, and 13 000 Laos. About 41 per cent of Australia's Vietnamese live in New South Wales (Viviani, 1993).

All these immigrants from the war period, however, experienced great personal stress from family separations and their experience in refugee camps. Their limited English skills and their unfamiliarity with Anglo-Australian norms were often sources of disadvantage. Vietnamese medical methods, for example, such as *Cao gio*, an indigenous therapy for headaches, created problems with Australian health officials and led to prosecutions. Some of the Indochinese experienced severe loneliness and psychological disturbances (Krupinski & Burrows, 1986: 241). There were also very large numbers of single young Vietnamese men in relation to smaller numbers of women which created social problems.

This kind of problem linked with immigration, however, has a reverse side as well. Traditionally, there has been some prejudice about the intermarriage of Asian women to Australian men, as with the postwar issue of Japanese war brides settling in Australia. More recently, a concern about Asian 'mail order brides' became a regular media topic in Australia in the 1980s. An ABC

> **intracultural communication networks**
> Social and familial bonds that exist between members of the same ethnic group and act as channels of cultural interaction.

Chapter 7

The first WWII Japanese war bride allowed to live in Australia and her husband. (Photo: *National Library of Australia*) Used with permission.

telemovie of that name painted an unpleasant picture of an attractive young Filipina married to an older, ugly, beer-swilling Australian in the outback. Press articles about 'Brides for Sale' and academic studies such as 'Filipina Brides: Slaves or Marriage Partners?' followed. In reality, by 1984 Filipina women in Australia were a very small proportion of the total female population, though many had come to Australia to be married. More sober studies concluded that such media attention was unwarranted, that their presence in Australia presented no major social problem, and that Filipina women were quite capable of looking after themselves (Wall, 1983; Chuah, 1987).

Despite a widespread public health communication program recently, little examination has been made of the differences between ethnic groups in their responses to the anti-AIDS campaign. One study found that Anglo-Australian teenagers were more sexually active and better informed about AIDS than teenagers from Greek, Italian or Chinese backgrounds. There were lower levels of knowledge and concern about AIDS issues in the latter groups. Greek and Italian-Australian teenage boys seemed to display a traditionally male 'macho' culture, with girls in those groups being less sexually active but also less well informed. Young Anglo-Australian women were the most AIDS-vulnerable group, while Chinese-Australian teenagers, in contrast, appeared to be the least at risk because of their relatively low levels of sexual activity (Rosenthal, 1990).

Exercise 7.6 Recognising generational differences in ethnic groups
Choose one of the three main ethnic community groups previously discussed and use some of the references listed below (e.g. NCVER, 1992) as well as the MAIS (Multicultural Affairs Information Service) database through OZLINE to research generational differences in one group. Especially see if you can identify differences in attitudes to intracultural communication networks (see Yum, 1988) among different generations of the same ethnic group. What kind of social networks, for instance, do young Chinese-Australians have compared to their parents?

A good starting point may be to actively seek out younger members of that group, either through your own personal or class contacts, or in public spaces such as shopping centres, or through local ethnic community associations. You can use this exercise either as material for class discussion or to write up as an essay or report.

Post-multiculturalism?

This chapter has schematically outlined several features of Anglo-Australian culture, such as its core values and alternative views about multiculturalism. It then considered ideas of Aboriginality and aspects of language and interpersonal behaviour in Aboriginal society. Lastly, a little of the background and current experience of Southern European, Middle Eastern and Asian migrants was sketched in. This final section will highlight some of the theoretical difficulties in developing a satisfactory communicative analysis of Australian multiculturalism.

The preceding account, which descriptively positions different ethnic and Aboriginal subgroups against the mainstream culture, runs the risk of celebrating the specificity of those groups, yet concealing the power relations that are the basis of significant internal divisions in society. This point has been made in the British context (Bhaba, 1988) and for Latin America (Canclini, 1992). That is, a liberal and well-intentioned celebration of cultural diversity in multi-ethnic societies may conceal cultural differences and itself contribute to social inequality. However, in situating these debates in the Australian context there have been few discussions of multiculturalism by communication scholars.

There are some Australian communication studies of multicultural and Aboriginal television (O'Regan, 1993), of ethnic perceptions of commercial and public television content (Coupe and Jakubowicz, 1992), and of the reporting of multiculturalism in the press (Putnis, 1989). Yet these are mainly empirical and offer few theoretical insights into how a communication model of multiculturalism might be constructed. This is not an exclusively Australian shortcoming. Despite a recent flood of European and US writing on the media (e.g. Skovmond & Schroder, 1992) and on postmodernism (e.g. Lash, 1990; McGuigan, 1992), there is little attention given in most communication and cultural studies writing to the issues of ethnicity and multiculturalism.

In North America, research on intercultural communication has been concerned with the training needs of US diplomats and businessmen (sic) in dealing with foreigners (Leeds-Hurwitz, 1990). This tradition remains dominant in US intercultural communication theory today. For instance, one of the leading writers in the area, William Gudykunst, is mainly concerned to develop effective communication strategies to bridge cultural differences (1991). A slightly more idealist version of this behaviourist model was advanced by Korean-American Young Kim (1985), who advocated the development of an 'intercultural personhood' that aimed at integrating Eastern and Western perspectives. These approaches are the 'strong' and 'weak' versions of the US intercultural skills-training model which relies on the quantitative and reductionist research methods discussed in Chapter 1.

On the other hand, US cultural studies writers, such as Grossberg (1989) and Carey (1993), who are concerned with mass communication instead of interpersonal contexts, derive their arguments from history, political economy, rhetoric and philosophy. Cultural studies has embraced postmodernism more fully than has social psychology, and both writers introduce perspectives about subjectivity and difference into their works in a way that Gudykunst and Kim do not. The paradox here is that, despite their more sensitive qualitative approaches, neither Grossberg nor Carey directly address issues of intercultural or ethnic difference.

This paradox has some parallels in the Australian research setting. The studies of SBS and Aboriginal TV by O'Regan (1993), and of the attitudes to commercial and public television by ethnic groups (Coupe & Jakubowicz, 1992) do consider ethnic difference in terms of its relevance to Australian television, yet they do not make their frame of analysis any wider than that of ethnic relations with the media. Recent Australian cultural studies work by Willis and During, however, comes closer to developing a theoretical framework to analyse multiculturalism with. Willis (1993), for instance, locates the current position of Aboriginal art in relation to earlier discussions about Primitivism as a stylistic influence in Australian painting. She goes on to criticise how much of the new prestige of Aboriginal art has been appropriated, commercially and nationalistically, by official culture (1993: 121).

During (1992) is equally iconoclastic in his critique of the emergence of **postcolonialism** as a field of academic study. The term itself refers to the cultural and political consequences of decolonisation. He sees several problems with postcolonial themes. First, the idea that it engenders 'a global popular', or a sense of universally-shared culture, e.g. with the 1985 'Live Aid' concert, is undercut by its marketing and consumer practices. Secondly, the idea of postcolonialism implies that the historical process has ended and that previously colonial societies are now liberated. Many of them actually remain significantly internally divided along the class and racial lines that their original colonial rulers exploited. Lastly, the idea of postcolonialism resembles postmodernism (see Chapter 12) in that it fragments reality and makes undecidable many current issues — such as multiculturalism. By postcolonial logic, for example, there is no real 'Aboriginality' which Kooris can identify with, except as mythology. In the light of this admittedly brief literature survey, it must be concluded that neither Australian, European nor US studies have contributed significantly to a communications analysis of multiculturalism. This appears to be a major lacuna in the field.

postcolonialism
The cultural and political consequences of decolonisation.

Summary

1. Culture precedes communication and makes it possible. Culture is the distinctive national pattern of social values and behaviours that develop over time. All communication is culturally based behaviour.
2. Anglo-Australian culture has its own distinctive history and certain national secular rituals such as Melbourne Cup Day. Anglo-Australian culture has its own original ethnic divisions between English, Irish, Scots and Welsh migrants, with the English as the once dominant group.
3. Anglo-Australian language has its own spoken form. It has few significant regional variations but has differences based on different status and levels

of education and includes a rich slang vernacular. Anglo-Australian culture has its own core values which are similar but different to the British and US equivalents.
4. Ideas about Aboriginality are one of the most distinctive features of Australian Aboriginal experience. These ideas and values are complex and ambiguous and include their beliefs about the importance of 'the Dreaming' to their culture and the special relationship they have with the land.
5. Aboriginal attitudes to the land help define their relation to their personal and group identity and are the basis of their sense of being the original inhabitants of Australia. Aboriginal conversational patterns are relatively indirect and have different norms of propriety. Aboriginal kinship rules are also more expansive and inclusive than Anglo-Australian practices.
6. Acculturation — the integration of migrant groups into the mainstream society — can be pursued either by policies of assimilation or pluralism. Until the 1960s Australian policies were essentially assimilationist, but since that time the gradual endorsement of multiculturalism has shifted community attitudes towards pluralism.
7. Southern Europeans, Italians, then Greeks were the first of several different ethnic groups to come to Australia as postwar immigrants and were first in line in the unofficial ethnic pecking order.
8. Middle Eastern immigrants, Lebanese and Turks were the next major non-Anglo group to settle in postwar Australia. Like the Southern Europeans, they came by a process of chain migration. Their distinctive, mostly Muslim, religious beliefs distinguished them from both Anglo-Australian culture and from the Southern Europeans.
9. Asians are the most recent immigrant group to arrive. There are major variations between them in terms of their educational and economic status and there are marked differences in their own intracultural communication networks.

Discussion questions

1. Explain the difference between culture and communication and what is meant by the idea of a country's 'cultural heritage'.
2. What were the main ethnic and religious differences between white Australian settlers?
3. What kinds of differences are there between Australians, Americans and British people in terms of their use of English, their ritual days and their core values?
4. How do current Australian debates about multiculturalism fit into international debates concerning the place of immigrants and refugees?
5. What are some of the main features of Aboriginality?
6. Should Aboriginals be seen in government policies as another ethnic group and therefore part of Australian multicultural society?
7. What were the main ethnic groups to come to Australia after 1945 and where did they fit into the ethnic pecking order?
8. Give examples of chain migration from the experience of Southern Europeans in Australia.

9. What features of traditional Lebanese and Turkish family life make them different from Anglo-Australian families?
10. Which parts of Asia do Australia's Chinese and Indochinese mainly come from and how might their intracultural communication networks benefit Australian exporters?

Further reading

Alcorso, C. et al. (1992) 'Community Networks and Institutions', pp. 106–25 in S. Castles (ed.) *Australia's Italians* Sydney: Allen & Unwin.
Alomes, S. (1988) *A Nation at Last?* Sydney: Angus & Robertson.
Bell, P. (1993) *Multicultural Australia in the Media* Canberra: AGPS.
Coupe, B. & Jakubowicz, A. (1992) *Nextdoor Neighbours* Canberra: OMA.
During, S. (1993) 'Postcolonialism and Globalization', *Meanjin* 51 (2): 339–53.
Ho, R. (1990) 'Multiculturalism in Australia: A Survey of Attitudes', *Human Relations* 43 (3): 259–72.
NCVER — National Centre for Vocational Education Research (1992) *Cross-Cultural Communication: A National Resource Guide* Canberra: DEET.
Oliver, P. & Vaughan, G. (1991) 'Interethnic Perceptions of New Zealand Teenagers', *Journal of Intercultural Studies* 12 (1): 17–39.
Storer, D. (ed.) (1985) *Ethnic Family Values in Australia.* Sydney: Prentice Hall.
Von Sturmer, J. (1981) 'Talking With Aborigines', *Australian Institute of Aboriginal Studies Newsletter* 15: 1–19.

References

ABS — Australian Bureau of Statistics (1993) *Basic Community Profile* Canberra: ABS.
Anderson, C. (1989) 'Aborigines and Conservationism', *Australian Journal of Social Issues* 24 (3): 214–27.
Bell, D. (1993) *Daughters of the Dreaming* Sydney: Allen & Unwin, 2nd edn.
Bell, S. (1990) 'Filming Radio Redfern', *Media Information Australia* 56: 35–7.
Bennett, S. (1989) 'Aborigines and the Media', pp. 133–50 in his *Aborigines and Political Power* Sydney: Allen & Unwin.
Bhaba, H. (1988) 'The Commitment to Theory', *New Formations* 5: 5–25.
Browne, D. (1990) 'Aboriginal Radio in Australia', *Journal of Communication* 40 (1): 111–120.
Canclini, N. (1992) 'Culture and Power', pp. 17–48 in P. Scannell, P. Schlesinger & C. Sparks, (eds) *Culture and Power* London: Sage.
Carey, J. (1993) 'May You Live in Interesting Times', *Australian Journal of Communication* 20 (3): 1–13.
Castles, S. Kalantzis, M., Cape, B., & Morrissey, M. (1988) *Mistaken Identity* Sydney: Pluto Press.
Castro, B. (1990) *Pomeroy* Sydney: Allen & Unwin.
Chuah, F., Chuah, L., Reid-Smith, L., Rice, A. & Rowley, K. (1987) 'Does Australia Have a Filipina Brides Problem?' *Australian Journal of Social Issues* 22 (4): 573–84.

Collins, J. (1992) 'Cappucino Capitalism: Italian Immigrants and Australian Business', pp. 73–85 in S. Castles, (ed.) *Australia's Italians* Sydney: Allen & Unwin.
Connell, W., Francis, E. & Skilbeck, E. (1957) *Growing Up in an Australian City* Melbourne: ACER.
Coombs, H. Brandl, M. & Snowdon, W. (1983) *A Certain Heritage* Canberra: ANU.
Coughlan, J. (1989) 'A Comparative Study of Indochinese Migrants in Australia'. Asian Studies Association of Australia Conference paper. National University of Singapore.
Cresciani, G. (1988) *Migrants or Mates: Italian Life in Australia* Sydney: Knockmore Enterprises.
Eades, D. (1988) 'They Don't Speak an Aboriginal Language, Do They?' pp. 97–117 in I. Keen, (ed.) *Being Black* Canberra: AIAS.
Edelstein, A., Ito, Y. & Kepplinger, H. (1989) *Communication and Culture* New York: Longman.
Edwards, J. (1985) *Language, Society and Identity* Oxford: Basil Blackwell.
Feather, N. (1986) 'Cross-cultural Studies with the Rokeach Value Survey', *Australian Journal of Psychology* 30: 21–40.
Fiske, J., Turner, G. & Hartley, J. (1990) *Myths of Oz* Sydney: Allen & Unwin.
Fitzgerald, T. (1992) 'Media, Ethnicity and Identity', pp. 112–33 in P. Scannell, P. Schlesinger & C. Sparks, (eds) *Culture and Power* London: Sage.
Forgas, J. (1988) 'Episode Representations in Intercultural Encounters', pp. 186–213, in Y. Kim and W. Gudykunst, (eds) *Theories in Intercultural Communication* Newbury Park, CA: Sage.
Gilbert, K. (1981) *Because a White Man Will Never Do It* Sydney: Angus & Robertson.
Goot, M. (1993) 'Multiculturalists, Monoculturalists, and the Many in between', *Australian and New Zealand Journal of Sociology* 29 (20): 226–54.
Grossberg, L. (1989) 'The Context of Audiences and the Politics of Difference', *Australian Journal of Communication* 16: 13-37.
Gudykunst, W. (1991) *Bridging Differences* Newbury Park, CA: Sage.
Ho, C. & Kee, P. (1988) 'A Profile of the Chinese in Australia', *Journal of Intercultural Studies* 9 (2): 1-17.
Hofstede, G. (1980) *Culture's Consequences* Beverly Hills, CA: Sage.
Hofstede, G. (1991) *Cultures and Organizations* London: McGraw-Hill.
Huber, R. (1977) *From Pasta to Pavlova* Brisbane: University of Queensland Press.
Isaacs, E. (1976) *Greek Children in Sydney* Canberra: ANU Press.
Jones, R. (1985) 'Ordering the Landscape', pp. 181–210 in I. Donaldson, (ed.) *Seeing the First Australians* Sydney: Allen & Unwin.
Jupp, J. (1988) 'Immigration and Ethnicity' pp. 62–82 in J. Najman & J. Western, (eds.) *A Sociology of Australian Society* Melbourne: Macmillan.
Jupp, J. (1991) 'Managing Ethnic Diversity', pp. 38–55 in F. Castles, (ed.) *Australia Compared* Sydney: Allen and Unwin.
Jupp, J. (1992) *Immigration* Melbourne: Oxford University Press.
Kim, Y. (1985) 'Intercultural Personhood', pp. 400–410 in L. Samovar & R. Porter, (eds) *Intercultural Communication* Belmont, CA: Wadsworth, 5th edn.
Krupinski, J. & Burrows, G., (eds.) (1986) *The Price of Freedom: Young Indochinese Refugees in Australia* Sydney: Pergamon Press.

Langton, M. (1981) 'Urbanising Aborigines', *Social Alternatives* 2 (2): 16–22.
Langton, M. (1993) *'Well, I heard it on the radio and I saw it on the television'* Sydney: AFC.
Lash, S. (1990) *The Sociology of Postmodernism* London: Routledge.
Leeds-Hurwitz, W. (1990) 'Notes on the History of Intercultural Communication', *Quarterly Journal of Speech* 76: 262–81.
McConnochie, K., Hollinsworth, D. & Pettman, J. (1988) *Race and Racism in Australia* Sydney: Social Science Press.
McGuigan, J. (1992) *Cultural Populism* London: Routledge.
Mackie, F. (1982) *Structure, Culture and Religion in the Welfare of Muslim Families* Canberra: AGPS, DIEA.
Meadows, M. (1994) 'The Media, Land Rights and Mabo', *Media Information Australia* 71: 100–109.
Merlan, F. (1988) 'Gender in Aboriginal Life', pp. 17–76 in R. Berndt & R. Tonkinson, (eds) *Social Anthropology and Australian Aboriginal Studies* Canberra: AIAS.
Muecke, S. (1992) *Textual Spaces: Aboriginality and Cultural Studies* Sydney: NSW University Press.
O'Regan, T. (1993) *Australian Television Culture* Sydney: Allen & Unwin.
Pascoe, R. (1992) 'The Construction of an Italo-Australian Space', pp. 85–98 in S. Castles, (ed.) *Australia's Italians* Sydney: Allen & Unwin.
Putnis, P. (1989) 'Constructing Multiculturalism', *Australian Journal of Communication* 16: 155–66.
Report on a National Language Policy (1984) Senate Standing Committee on Education and the Arts, Canberra: AGPS.
Rosenthal, D., Moore, S. & Brumen, I. (1990) 'Ethnic Group Differences in Adolescents' Responses to AIDS', *Australian Journal of Social Issues* 25 (3): 220–40.
Rowse, T. (1993) 'Mabo and Moral Anxiety' *Meanjin* 52 (2): 229–53.
Seneviratne, K. (1993) 'Community Radio in Australia', *Media Asia* 20 (2): 66–75.
Skovmond, M. & Schroder, K. (1992) *Media Cultures* London: Routledge.
Stanner, W. (1979) *White Man Got No Dreaming* Canberra: ANU Press.
Thomas, T. & Balnaves, M. (1993) *The Vietnamese Elderly and the Family Migration Program* Canberra: Bureau of Immigration and Population Research.
Vasta, E. (1993) 'Multiculturalism and Ethnic Identity', *Australian and New Zealand Journal of Sociology* 29 (2): 209–26.
Viviani, N., Coughlan, J. & Rowland, T. (1993) *Indochinese in Australia* Canberra: AGPS.
Wall, D. (1983) 'Filipina Brides: Slaves or Marriage Partners?' *Australian Journal of Social Issues* 18 (1): 217–22.
Ward, R. (1958) *The Australian Legend* Melbourne: Melbourne University Press.
White, R. (1981) *Inventing Australia* Sydney: Allen & Unwin.
Willis, A. (1993) *Illusions of Identity* Sydney: Hale & Iremonger.
Yum, J. (1988) 'Network Theory in Intercultural Communication', pp. 239–59 in Y. Kim & W. Gudykunst, (eds) *Theories in Intercultural Communication* Newbury Park, CA: Sage.

Small group communication

Objectives

After completing this chapter you should be able to:

- explain the main factors shaping group effectiveness;
- distinguish several models of small group stages of development;
- explain the categories of Interaction Process Analysis and distinguish positive from negative group membership roles;
- discuss the relationship between task and team leadership in small groups;
- understand the advantages of agendas in group problem solving and be aware of three methods of group decision making;
- discuss five interpersonal conflict styles group members may employ.

Chapter 8

The importance of groups for humans has led a number of social scientists to perceive groups as the salvation or the bane of our species. To some, groups are the basis for everything that is good in our lives. For others, groups are destructive influences on our lives. Both views are oversimplified: Groups can have constructive or destructive effects depending on how they are used.

Joining Together, *David and Frank Johnson*

We grow up in family groups, go through school and higher education in learning groups, then, hopefully, we enter and remain in the workforce in a variety of occupational groups. We can also choose to belong to a wide range of social, cultural, professional, sporting, and community groups. At different times of life we all have some overlapping membership in a variety of groups that will have different salience for us as our needs and interests change. The previous chapter discussed group experience in terms of subcultures and ethnic group identities. This chapter considers group communication in a different context by narrowing the focus of the analysis to concentrate on the social psychology of intra-group task behaviours.

The nature of small group communication

What exactly is a small group? The answer depends on the social context in which the group is situated. There are educational groups, social groups and task, or work, groups. It is primarily the task, or work-oriented, groups, which are mainly concerned with problem solving and decision making, that will be considered here. It is important to make this distinction because, when we consider what is meant by the effectiveness of small group communication, the criteria for evaluating effectiveness of that group depends on the group's purpose. The most important aim of family groups, for example, is to support each other emotionally and financially, whereas the goal of pop music or theatrical groups — such as the Sydney Post-Arrivalists shown in action here — is to put on a good performance. Work task groups, in contrast, usually have more specific and impersonal performance standards to meet.

small group
A collection of individuals in contact who act interdependently as they work towards a common goal.

A **small group** is a collection of individuals in contact who act interdependently as they work towards some common goal. This definition foregrounds the element of interdependence among individual group members in seeking to achieve a particular outcome. Group interdependence means the degree to which individual members must rely on each other to reach the group's goal. In undergraduate educational groups, for example, if an assignment is set that requires students to work together to complete it, then this is a case of enforced interdependence. The students who manage to work together most cooperatively are likely to complete the best assignment, whereas if they have group members who are unwilling to do their share of the work, then the chances of their group completing a good assignment are much less.

Group assignments of this kind are probably one of the least favoured kinds of assignment for many students, as they require a high degree of individual responsibility and commitment. This type of work, however, often does accurately reflect the way that task groups in the 'real world' are actually required to perform. That is, in most workplaces you are likely to find yourself

Small group communication

The Post-Arrivalists at work.
(Photo: *Jayne Waterford*)

a member of various small work-teams where the group is required to perform particular tasks (Marchington, 1992). Perhaps the greatest interpersonal skill needed in that context is the ability to work compatibly with others, regardless of whether or not you like them personally. There is now extensive evidence that Australian employers are increasingly valuing the ability to work in groups (NBEET, 1992). As a result, group learning techniques are receiving much attention (see Slaven et al., 1984).

Before proceeding to examine the interpersonal dimensions of small group communication, note that our previous definition of a small group described it as 'a collection of individuals in contact'. The implication of this definition is that group members do not necessarily have to be in face-to-face contact. With recent advances in communications technology, people at work can interact through mediated electronic systems, such as electronic mail or local area computer networks (Irwin & More, 1994: 120–38). Some of these questions, especially the role of communication networks, will be taken up in Chapters 9 and 10. Understanding the interpersonal dynamics of face-to-face communication in groups, however, is the primary aim of this chapter.

Exercise 8.1 Current awareness of group membership
1. Write down any work-related task groups you are a member of, either at university or off-campus.
2. Write down which family, social, recreational, religious, cultural or other groups you are presently in, or have been a member of in the past three years.
3. Identify the kind of task groups you expect in future to be involved in when you leave university.
4. Do you think men or women perform differently in task groups? If so, how and why?

Factors shaping group effectiveness

The extent to which small groups are likely to be **effective** can be analysed in terms of the attitudes of individual group members to each other and to the group as a whole. Four factors are central here — group interdependence, group cohesiveness, group attractiveness, and group satisfaction. Let us consider each of these. First, **group interdependence** is the extent to which individual members in the group need each other to achieve the group's goals. This factor is specially important as it highlights the link between perceived individual interdependence and the group goal outcome (Johnson & Johnson, 1987: 6). A precondition of group effectiveness is that group members feel psychologically committed to their membership of the group. The nature of the group's goals is also a key factor. The more clarity a group has in the goals it has been set, the more likely the group will perceive the importance of acting interdependently.

The other three main factors defining individual members' involvement in a group build on this precondition of perceived goal interdependence. Second, there will be a certain degree of perceived **cohesiveness** in the group. This is the extent to which members perceive external forces that influence them to choose to remain in the group. Like group interdependence, group cohesiveness may be high or low, but groups with higher levels of cohesiveness and interdependence are likely to be more effective. For instance, if students are required to complete a particular group project as an important part of their course, then their group cohesiveness is likely to be high.

The third main criterion of member involvement in a group is **group attractiveness**. This refers more to the internal relationships within the group, whereas cohesiveness is more a result of external constraints. The degree of the group's attractiveness to individual members is affected by individual members' attraction to others and to the whole group. The larger the group, the less likely it will be that individual members will feel attracted to all other members. This suggests that there is a maximum size for group effectiveness, and this will be considered presently.

The final important dimension influencing member involvement in a group is the sense of **group satisfaction**. This is the overall evaluation that members make of the worth of their membership in the group and their evaluation of the group's overall effectiveness. The main factors likely to influence members' perceptions of group satisfaction include their degree of satisfaction with the way tasks have been allocated in the group, and the methods of decision making and problem solving the group chooses to employ. Perceived group satisfaction will depend on the members' opinions about the group's task outcome, in terms of how members have worked interdependently to achieve their goals, as well as about the quality of the group process, i.e. the way in which the group has retained its cohesiveness and attractiveness for its members.

Exercise 8.2 The effects of goal clarity on group performance

1. The class should divide into two groups, which are separated physically as far as possible from each other. An observer for each group should be appointed.
2. The instructor will allot a tasks to each group to complete. The tasks are related, but different. Both tasks have the same purpose, but one will be specific and the other will be left in general terms. The groups have 10–15 minutes to generate ideas about the task.

---

group effectiveness
The extent to which the group's interaction patterns results in a positive outcome.

group interdependence
The extent to which individual group members need each other to achieve group goals.

group cohesiveness
The extent to which members perceive external forces as influencing them to remain in the group.

group attractiveness
The degree of individual members' attraction to other members and the whole group.

group satisfaction
The evaluation that members make of the worth of their membership in the group and of the group's overall effectiveness.

3. The observers are informed of both groups' directions and asked to record their impressions of their group's performance in terms of their interdependence (degree of cooperativeness) and their apparent satisfaction with the process and the outcome. Observers will be fully briefed.
4. At the end of the time period one subgroup representative should report to the class on the group's solution to the task and also on how satisfied the group felt with the outcome.
5. Each group may then respond to the observer's comments.

Group size and stages of group development

There is really no optimum size for a small task group. It depends on the task. Small groups are sometimes defined as consisting of two or more people. In practice, however, a group of between three and twelve people is probably an optimum size. The exact number that is appropriate can only be defined in relation to the particular task and the skills of the people concerned. The more complex and specialised the task, the more likely a larger group will be needed.

On the other hand, the larger the group the more difficult group cohesiveness, attractiveness, and communication will be. Five or six is often seen as an optimum size for the creation of a sense of team values. It is likely that once the group includes more than eight people communication problems will emerge, and that when there are more than twelve members it may no longer be possible to function effectively. Also, the larger the group, the longer it is likely to take to go through the necessary stages of group development.

There has been a large amount of research about the desirable stages of development that small groups should go through in completing tasks. First, it is important for group members to have as accurate a picture as possible of the stage of development their group is in. Otherwise they may come to premature conclusions about the best solution, or it may take too long to work through the preliminary stages. Second, the main external factors affecting the stage of a particular group's development are the complexity of the task the group has to complete and the time constraints it is facing. Projects that are not too complex may see groups go quickly through some of the usual stages of development, and even bypass some of them, without any negative consequences.

Third, the main internal factors influencing the rate of a group's development will be the degree to which members already know each other and the levels of interpersonal trust that have been established. Educational groups of first year students meeting for the first time, for example, are likely to take longer in the orientation stage, compared to groups comprised of members who are already well-known to each other. Finally, the group's progress through those stages will not be smooth or continuous. It is more likely that it will move through various stages in a spiralling or even a cyclical manner. Sometimes group members have to go back to an earlier stage to rework some of the issues they have already dealt with.

The three models of group development that will now be summarised are from US social psychologists Schutz (1966), Bales (1970) and Tuckman (1965). Schutz argued that groups developed in a circular or spiral fashion, with the group repeating its processes sometimes by falling back on grounds it had covered earlier. His schema identified three main phases of group integration —

an inclusion phase, a control phase and an affection phase. In the first phase members are mainly concerned to establish and communicate their own identity to others in the group. People are sizing each other up and deciding how much to disclose about themselves in their statements about how the task should be completed and how the group should operate.

In the second, or control phase, of group development, Schutz considered the group had resolved most of its inclusion problems and that members could move on to more task-related issues. Here they become more concerned with questions about sharing responsibility, of leadership, and matters of power and control. This is the stage in which group rules of procedure are likely to be set. Third and last, the group moves into an affection phase. Here members could go on to achieve an optimum level of individual member participation in the group's task resolution. At this point members are close to achieving a balance between their own social–emotional needs and the task responsibilities of the group.

Another model of group development that resembles Schutz's but is more detailed in terms of its analysis of individual role requirements is that of Bales. He developed a set of categories that observers of group process could use to measure and analyse the individual performance of group members. The method and categories are called Interaction Process Analysis and this will be discussed presently. His model, however, basically saw three main phases that groups went through — an orientation phase, an evaluation phase and a control phase.

In the orientation phase, essentially members are asking questions and seeking and giving information about the purposes of the group and the nature of the task. For example: 'What is it we have to do?', 'Why do we have to do it?', 'How do we do it?' and 'How do we get it done best?'. There will be a good deal of repetition and confirmation about group task requirements at this stage. After the completion of this initial stage, orientation-type questions and answers should decrease as group members move into the evaluation stage. Here there will be more questions and answers about the task and about members' individual roles. There will be more expression of opinions and feelings about the issues concerned, and more analyses made.

Finally, in the third or control phase, the group will become more concerned with getting the task done. More statements will be made where members seek and give directions to and from each other. Both positive and negative statements from group members will increase substantially. That is, there should be more creative controversy among the group as it moves to complete its task. There is also likely to be more joking as members express their increased solidarity and seek tension release from the task as its end draws near.

The third and last model of group development, Tuckman's stages theory, consists of four stages — *forming*, *storming*, *norming* and *performing*. The **forming** stage is the orientation period when group members are 'testing the water' with each other and trying to decide who they can best depend on in the group. The **storming** stage comes second. This is a conflict phase when there is a necessary polarisation around ideas and people. There is likely to be some individual resistance to group task demands, and this may be expressed by the display of some interpersonal animosity between members. This stage is perhaps the most difficult one. If a group does not go through it, it may mean

forming
The orientation stage of group development.

storming
The conflict stage of group development.

Small group communication

A group working positively.
Stage one: initiation.
Stage two: discussion.
Stage three: agreement.
(Photos: *Xu Bai-ming*)

that the group is undermotivated to achieve its task and is indifferent to a quality outcome. Alternatively, if individual group members become too personally identified with their own solutions to what they see as the group's needs, this may result in disruptive interpersonal conflict.

Assuming the storming stage is satisfactorily worked through, then the third and second-last stage the group goes through is the **norming** stage. Here group feeling and cohesiveness increase and members will feel more comfortable in expressing their opinions and feelings about the task and each other. A set of norms or standards of task performance will emerge which are seen to be necessary and appropriate for the effective completion of the group task. Finally, there will be a **performing** stage. Group energy will be concentrated on the completion of the task and members will work effectively and efficiently as a collective unit. Tuckman also considers that the group will finally go through an 'adjourning' or 'mourning' stage, when group members emotionally disengage from each other after the job is done.

> **norming**
> The stage of group development when feeling and cohesiveness increase.
>
> **performing**
> The stage of group development when the group concentrates on the completion of the task.

Exercise 8.3 Stages of group development and group size

1. Two groups should be formed. One should be a group of three and the other should be much larger. The groups should be physically separated and one observer appointed for the small group and two or more for the larger group.
2. Before the task is explained, the two groups should leave the room while the purpose of the exercise and the observation procedure is explained to the observers.
3. When the groups return the instructor briefly explains that they will both be asked to do the same task — namely to make up as many words as possible in a specified period of time using certain information, with the aim of making as much money as possible. The more words that are made in the shortest time, the greater the profit will be. The instructor then places an instruction sheet and a sealed envelope in front of the groups and tells them they have 25 minutes — a 15 minute planning period, and a maximum of 10 minutes to actually do the task.
4. At the end of the exercise, check that the group has reached its nominated goal. The observers should then report back to the group in terms of the categories they have been told to observe. The whole class may then discuss the process.

Membership and leadership roles in groups

> **task leadership**
> A leadership style concerned with getting the job done.
>
> **team leadership**
> A leadership style concerned with how well group members are working together; sometimes referred to as social-emotional or climate leadership.

Effective group leaders will have to be concerned with two main features of communication: first, the achievement of group goals and, second, the maintenance of interpersonal morale within the group. These two functions are **task leadership** and **team leadership**. Sometimes the team leadership function is also referred to as social–emotional or climate leadership. The task leader is concerned with getting the job done, while the team leader is equally concerned with how well the group members are working together. Effective groups need *both* kinds of leadership (Eunson, 1994). If there is too much of an emphasis on the task then interpersonal relations between group members may be put at risk. Conversely, if the group leader is overly concerned with members' individual needs then the group may not be disciplined enough to get its task done.

Task and team leadership functions may actually be performed by the one person, or they may be shared between different leaders within the group. First, there is the task leader, who is best at getting the group job done, who initiates structure in the group, and who specialises in giving ideas, making suggestions and offering opinions about how the group task might best be done. Second, there is the team leader, who initiates cohesiveness in the group, and who specialises in promoting solidarity and contributes to tension release in the group. An effective leader needs to balance the group's concern for the task with the concerns of members for each other. The leader will be able to coordinate the social functions of the group with procedural functions (e.g. setting rules for contributions), so that the group can evolve methods of decision making, problem solving and conflict resolution best suited to the task requirements.

Three task leadership actions, for example, are goal setting, planning and guiding. First, when helping the group set its goals, the leader may propose goals, seek clarification and agreement on those goals, or determine the priorities concerning the different objectives that the group has set to achieve its goals. Second, when exhibiting planning behaviours, a leader will assess group needs, set agendas for the group, and make physical and material arrangements for group meetings. Third, the leader may give the group task guidance by keeping the group to its agenda and seeing that any necessary records of decisions are kept.

In performing team-building leadership roles, the leader may enact encouraging, mediating or opening communication roles. As encourager, the leader can support individual group members and work towards building the status and confidence of members. As mediator, the leader can seek to establish a middle ground on issues that the group may have become divided on and also maintain the group's emphasis on issues rather than on personalities. Third, the leader can seek to keep communication open in the group by maintaining a permissive atmosphere and preventing dominance by any of the group's more outspoken members.

When we turn to consider research studies of the individual roles that members, as contrasted with leaders, play in groups, the work of Bales (1970) and Benne and Sheats (1948) is valuable. Bales developed Interaction Process Analysis, an observational instrument for studying communication within small groups that identified their **positive membership roles**. These are roles that facilitate group cohesion and group task completion. His categories aimed to distinguish members' task behaviours from their social–emotional behaviours. He assumed that when a group had a task to complete its members engaged in task-related actions on an unequal basis. It is usually the case that not every group member has an equal degree of motivation or commitment to the group task. He theorised that members who were high on task behaviours would tend to create some tension and hostility in the group for other members who were less committed to the task. It follows, given this potential for intra-group conflict, that there was a need for positive actions (social–emotional behaviours, such as joking and agreeing) that would maintain cohesiveness within the group. Accordingly, his observational instrument sought to categorise these different role behaviours between group members, as shown in Table 8.1.

positive membership roles
Roles that facilitate group cohesion and group task completion.

Table 8.1 *Bales' group observation categories*

Social–Emotional: Positive
1. Shows solidarity
2. Shows tension release
3. Agrees

Task Area: Neutral
4. Gives suggestions
5. Gives opinions
6. Gives orientation
7. Asks for orientation
8. Asks for opinions
9. Asks for suggestions

Social–Emotional: Negative
10. Disagrees
11. Shows tension
12. Shows antagonism

Benne and Sheats (1948) made a similar division between task roles and social–emotional roles as Bales, except that they termed the latter 'maintenance' roles. Task roles were communication roles that helped groups to accomplish tasks, while maintenance roles were communication roles that promoted social support among group members. In addition, they identified a number of self-centred roles, which were seen as potentially negative for the group. These **negative membership roles** are roles that suit the particular interests or needs of individual members but which are not necessarily compatible with the group's overall needs. Some of these individual negative roles were defined as:

- *Blocker* (a person who constantly says that nothing can be done);
- *Attacker* (a member who acts aggressively by expressing disapproval of others in the group);
- *Dominator* (a person who controls by talking too much, by constantly interrupting, or by acting in a superior or patronising way);
- *Clown* (a member who refuses to take anything seriously and sidetracks the group with the use of inappropriate humour).

In contrast, the list of task and maintenance roles that Benne and Sheats identified (shown below) can generally be considered productive for group interaction. The accompanying dialogue illustrates the roles based on a meeting among advertising executives who are discussing how a new campaign should be run.

Group task roles

1. *Initiator.* 'Why don't we try a new approach to this year's campaign?'
2. *Information seeker.* 'Can we find out what our competitors are planning this time?'
3. *Information giver.* 'We picked up three new accounts as a result of last year's campaign. On the other hand, we went considerably over-budget.'
4. *Procedure facilitator.* 'I'll write all this down to keep track of it while you argue out the pros and cons.'

> **negative membership roles**
> Roles that suit the particular needs of individual group members, but which are not necessarily compatible with the group's overall needs.

5. *Opinion seeker*. 'Don't you think last year's campaign was a great success?'
6. *Opinion giver*. 'I think we ought to stick with what we know best. Let's not branch out into areas that we have no experience of.'
7. *Clarifier*. 'I think we need to do a more detailed analysis of exactly why we picked up those new accounts after last year's campaign.'
8. *Summariser*. 'It seems that there's some disagreement whether we got those new accounts because of last year's campaign. While some of us are enthusiastic about trying something new, we need to check what the competition is doing before we make a binding decision.'

Group maintenance roles

1. *Social supporter*. 'Whatever option we go with we can be proud of the job we've done already.'
2. *Harmoniser*. 'Carlos and Ki-sung have valid points of view, even if they don't match up exactly. Let's see how we can get the best of both worlds.'
3. *Tension reliever*. 'We don't need to get uptight about this, whatever option we go with. We're doing just great and when you think about some of the idiots our competition have got working for them we all look good.'
4. *Energiser*. 'I can't wait to get my teeth into this next campaign. Whatever we decide, let's get in there and give it everything we've got.'
5. *Compromiser*. 'I'm sure there are two sides to this issue and that both of you have got valid viewpoints. I think we need to split your differences right down the middle.'
6. *Gatekeeper*. 'I'd really like to hear what Charmaine has to say about this. You know she's got a unique insight into this kind of issue; let's listen to her.'

Exercise 8.4 Recognising individual member roles
1. Divide the class into two groups of 3–6 with two observers for each group. Give the observers their observation sheets and asks them to monitor particular member's roles in those terms.
2. The task for each group is to select a new capital city for Australia. It is the year 2001 and the new United States of Australia has agreed to replace Canberra as the traditional capital. A new capital is to be chosen from existing state capitals.
3. Some individual members in each group will be nominated particular preferences to argue for. The others are free to support them or make their own choices. The groups have 5 minutes to prepare, then 10–15 minutes to debate the issue.
4. At the conclusion the observers report back to the group in terms of their identification of individual member roles. The members concerned should then comment on the accuracy of the observers' reports.

Bales found that group members were more likely to volunteer opinions and information (46 per cent of the time) than to ask for them (7 per cent). He also found that positive emotions were expressed about twice as often as negative ones. However, exactly how these roles will be enacted in a group depends on a range of contextual factors, such as group size and the characteristics of group members. Very small groups showed less tension, and more agreement and asking for opinion, whereas larger groups gave more suggestions and information and showed more tension. It seemed that in larger groups interpersonal compatibility was not considered so important. Groups with even numbers also had more difficulty in agreeing on a task because of the greater problems they had in coming to a majority decision.

Other factors affecting individual role performance in groups are members' personality traits, their age and their sex. Informal leaders, for example, are likely to be higher in dominance, assertiveness and empathy. They may also possess specialised task-relevant abilities. Additionally, conformity to group norms is more likely when members are younger. Some research also suggests that women are likely to be more conformist than men in groups, though this needs qualification. A literature review of gender differences of women's and men's behaviour in task groups by Bartol and Martin (1986) suggested that one variable was whether the groups were leaderless and informal, or designated-leader groups. This is an important practical distinction, as most groups in organisations usually have some predetermined hierarchy in their composition. Bartol and Martin's main findings were:

1. In mixed-sex leaderless groups, women frequently took a more passive role towards leadership.
2. Women were more active in engaging in leadership in same-sex groups than in mixed-sex leaderless groups.
3. Men tended to resist leadership by women in leaderless groups and to a lesser degree in designated-leader group situations.

They also found that the behaviours of both men and women were influenced by the gender ratios in task groups, and that both sexes behaved similarly in designated leadership situations (1986: 291–2). In other words, when women were actually in designated leadership positions in groups they were equally effective as leaders as men. The constraining factors on women acting as effective group leaders were more the structural and cultural obstacles hindering women from becoming designated leaders in the first place. Some of these factors have been discussed previously in Chapter 2.

Group problem solving

Are groups really better than individuals at making decisions and solving problems? The answer is a qualified 'yes'. Overall, the more complex a task and the greater the number of people affected, the better it is that groups should make the decision. Groups have several advantages. First, they have a greater pool of knowledge and information available and can add multiple perspectives to the way a problem is thought about. Group discussion may lead to solutions to problems which individual members had not previously thought of. Second, people working in groups tend to be more motivated to make higher-quality decisions than if they work alone. Third, participation in group problem solving is likely to increase acceptance of the final solution both by group members themselves and others external to the group.

Nevertheless there are many potential problems with groups when they have to make decisions and solve problems. One common difficulty is that group members may have conflicting goals. Another may be inappropriate group size — it may be too small and therefore lack sufficient resources, or it may be too large and leave some members underutilised. Also, if groups are too similar in their member composition they may not be especially productive. Further, if the group lacks sufficient time to deal properly with a task it may be better left to individuals. In short, groups are potentially advantageous in making decisions and solving problems, but there is nothing that guarantees their automatic success.

Problem solving is the process a group has to work through in recognising, exploring, and solving a problem. **Decision making** is what the group finally decides to do about the problem. In practice, these two processes are closely interrelated. For the problem-solving process to proceed, the group has to make decisions at the start and along the way, as well as at the end of the exercise. There is an important difference, though. Before groups can come to an informed decision in choosing from a set of alternative actions, the alternatives first need to be clarified. In this sense, effective group decision making requires the group initially to go through a problem solving process (Guirdham, 1991: 340).

The most widely used problem solving method that groups employ, especially in organisational or formal public contexts, is an agenda. Agendas are provisional plans or procedures for groups to follow on the way to arriving at a problem solution. The more formal the meeting, the more tightly organised the agenda is likely to be and vice versa. The advantages of agendas for groups are, first, they can clarify group goals and procedures in guiding the use of discussion time allocated for topics. Second, they are a way of coping with hidden purposes that individual group members may have. Third, they may help the group to avoid coming to hasty conclusions. There is no guarantee that the use of an agenda will achieve these things, but it is a useful starting point.

The invention of the **standard problem-solving agenda** is often credited to the US pragmatist philosopher John Dewey. This agenda identified six steps for groups to work through. One version of it is:

1. *Problem recognition.* This is where the group clarifies its task and sets its agenda.
2. *Problem description.* Here the group decides on the current nature of the problem by collecting information about it.
3. *Problem analysis.* This is where the group seeks to determine the cause of the problem and sets criteria for evaluating solutions to it.
4. *Problem solution proposal.* The group suggests as many solutions as possible.
5. *Problem solution selection.* Now the group chooses the best possible solution by matching possible alternative actions against the previously selected criteria.
6. *Implementation.* Finally the group decides what should be done and specifies who in the group is responsible for the particular actions considered necessary to put the solution into practice.

The stages in the group's application of the problem-solving agenda may not always be linear or clear-cut. Groups may sometimes go back, for example, to analysing the problem if their original preferences for a certain solution appear to have overlooked some contingencies. Generally, the more complex the problem, the more the group will need to work methodically through the

group problem solving
The process a group has to work through in recognising, exploring and solving a problem.

group decision making
What the group finally decides to do about the problem.

standard problem-solving agenda
This identifies six steps for groups to work through: problem recognition, problem description, problem analysis, problem solution proposal, problem solution selection, and implementation.

standard agenda. If the task is less complex, or the skills of group members are highly developed, then some of these stages may be by-passed.

An alternative way of summarising the standard agenda problem-solving method is to say that groups engaged in problem solving will go through a diagnostic phase, a solution phase, and an action planning phase. In the diagnostic phase members engage in fact-finding, clarifying the problem and setting possible criteria for solutions. Second, in the solution phase, members concentrate on the feasibility of solutions to decide which course of action best suits the problem. Last, in the action planning phase, there needs to be a decision about who is going to do exactly what.

Though the standard problem-solving agenda in either of the above versions is a good model for problem solving, in practice one of the most difficult things for groups to do is to engage in positive controversy. The drawback of the problem-solving agenda is that it is overly rational in its expectations of how group members will behave. In practice, when groups attempt to engage in productive controversy with the aim of generating as many possible solutions to a problem as possible, two things can go wrong. First, group members may be insufficiently motivated to care about the task and so will not engage in real controversy. Second, some group members may be so emotionally involved in the group task that their strong advocacy of their own definitions of the problem may lead to interpersonal conflict within the group.

Controversy in a group may arise when one member's ideas or opinions are not compatible with those of another, and disagreement results. Positive controversy is a necessary preliminary to the efforts of members to reach an agreed-on solution to the group task. Negative or unproductive controversy, on the other hand, is when disagreement among group members gets out of control and becomes a problem in itself. Controversy is a good and necessary thing in group problem solving. It may take place at any stage of the standard problem-solving agenda. According to the stages of group development model discussed earlier, controversy is seen as the group's 'storming', or second phase of development. In practice, some degree of controversy may actually occur when a group is defining a problem, selecting criteria for its solution, or in finally deciding how to implement its decisions.

The steps that group members need to follow to engage in **constructive controversy** have been summarised by Johnson and Johnson (1987: 241). First, members need to be clear about their own positions and realise that other group members have different views. Second, they need to step back from their preferred views and question their own solutions. Third, there needs to be a reconceptualisation of the issues to take into account the valid parts of other members' arguments, as well as adhering to a revised version of one's own views. To achieve constructive controversy this way requires an overall group commitment to cooperative rather than competitive outcomes. This does not preclude individual members from strongly advocating their own views, but it does limit the extent to which they may do so.

Constructive group controversy also requires members to have certain interpersonal skills in presenting their own views and in responding to others. First, they need to have a capacity for *skilled disagreement*. That is, they need to be able to deal with both the feelings and ideas of other members they disagree with. This requires acknowledging the personal worth of others, even when

constructive controversy
A positive approach to dealing with group disagreement.

disagreeing with them. Second, they have to engage in *perspective taking*. This may mean paraphrasing the other person's ideas or attitudes differently to encourage accurate recognition of them. Third, there is a cycle of *conceptual differentiation and integration* necessary for group members to work through. Differentiation is needed to clarify differences among members' ideas. Lastly, integration is when members can pool their new information and ideas so that a more complex set of problem definitions and solutions can be arrived at.

In encouraging groups to engage in constructive controversy, US small group trainers have evolved a number of specialised techniques that aim to facilitate effective group processes, such as the use of the Delphi and Nominal Group Techniques (Mitchell, 1988: 367). One of the more straightforward techniques is called **brainstorming**, and is likely to be specially useful in the initial stages of a group's problem solving. The steps required are:

- All criticism or evaluation of ideas is ruled out.
- The aim is to generate and collect as many ideas as possible. It is the quantity of ideas collected that is important at this stage, not their quality. It is crucial that all members of the group contribute ideas.
- After this collection stage, ideas should be shared out among the group and built on. Improvements and additions to ideas first suggested are sought.
- All ideas should finally be recorded in writing.
- The final step is to evaluate the ideas generated by the group. The real point of the exercise, however, is to encourage all members of the group to be non-critical at the idea-generation stage and to collect as wide a range of ideas as possible.

brainstorming
A method of group problem solving that aims at initially generating as many ideas as possible.

Dealing with group conflict

The experience of working in an unproductive or personally divided group is likely to happen to everyone at some stage. In some voluntary groups, for example, members may simply leave. This is not a positive outcome for the group, but for the individual member it may be the best option. Though what follows concentrates on group conflict, it is also important to realise that individuals tend to have their own styles of dealing with conflict (Sillars & Weisberg, 1987).

Exercise 8.5 Individual styles of conflict resolution
Sally and Jack have been friends for several years, ever since they came to work for the same organisation. They have gradually come to exchange work and personal favours in a cooperative way, but lately Sally has been depending more and more on Jack. She asks him to take care of routine work matters too often because she says she's busy doing other things. She has also borrowed money from Jack and talks to him at great length about her personal life. Until recently Jack hasn't minded too much, as before Sally had always been supportive, efficient and friendly. But now he has become tired of her behaviour.
   What should Jack do?
   Rank the following options in order of their likely effectiveness with your preferred choice as number one.

(a) Do what she wants, but hint to her about the trouble she's causing him.
(b) Tell her he's had enough and that her continued impositions will end their friendship.
(c) Tell Sally how her requests make him feel, then ask her to cooperate in finding a way to solve her problems without alienating him.
(d) Avoid Sally as much as possible.
(e) Do what she wants and hope she'll stop imposing soon.
(f) Tell her about his growing resentment, but say he's still willing to do favours for her.

The instructor then leads a class discussion about the choices.

Two recurrent sources of conflict in groups are, first, individual members may have conflicting goals which cannot be resolved and, second, a climate of conformity or 'group-think' may result in low-quality decision making. The first scenario can occur when members are pursuing agendas of their own which they intentionally do not disclose to the group (hence the term **hidden agendas**), or if a severe personality clash has developed between any group members. When a group experiences conflicts of the first kind, other members need to try to persuade the dissatisfied members to say what their own plans for the group are. This may require patient restatement of positions by the cooperative members to encourage others to disclose their own goals.

> **hidden agendas**
> When members pursue aims of their own which they do not disclose to the group.

Alternatively, if a group is being disrupted by repeated personal clashes between some members, the rest of the group needs to attempt to short-circuit the problem by redirecting the conversation of those members away from their personal antagonism and back towards the group task. If the argumentative ones can be persuaded that there is a superordinate task that the group has to deal with, which needs the cooperation of all members, then they may find it easier to limit their personal quarrels.

An opposite kind of problem may emerge when the group is either so anxious to avoid controversy, or so poorly motivated to achieve its task, that it limits discussion to avoid disagreement. In this situation the leader, or other group members, may choose to present themselves as devil's advocates — i.e. taking the contrary position to the majority view on purpose — as a means of provoking more active discussion. A slightly different version of this problem is sometimes referred to as 'group-think'. This is a pattern of defensive avoidance that is most likely to happen when a group has too many like-minded people in it, when the leader is too directive, or when the group is insulated from outside criticism. The result is a strong unspoken pressure for members to conform that stifles productive controversy. Members may be unreasonably optimistic about the task they have to do and the time they will take to do it, or they may go to the other extreme and take excessive risks in the solutions they come up with.

There are two possible ways of dealing with groups experiencing group-think problems. First, a member external to the group might be brought into the group to encourage the development of new perspectives. A second option, which can only be done with a group leader's direction, is for the group to engage in a process of structured advocacy. With this method the group is divided in two, with one subgroup being directed to take an opposite position to the other concerning the task. The aim is to generate new perspectives on the problem (Mann & Janis, 1983).

Another way of recognising signs of conflict in a group is to think of **group**

Small group communication

A group breaking down.
Stage one: conflict.
Stage two: standstill.
Stage three: withdrawal.
(Photo: *Xu Bai-ming*)

group conflict episodes
Latent conflict, emergent conflict, explicit conflict, and a conflict aftermath period.

conflict as a series of episodes. The main conflict episodes a group can go through are latent conflict, emergent conflict, explicit conflict and a conflict aftermath period. In the *latent conflict* stage it may not be clear to members that they will be likely to disagree about their procedures or how they will deal with conflicting members' needs. Members may not be listening carefully enough to each other to appreciate the potential differences that may emerge between them, or they may be too optimistic about what they have to do.

In the *emergent conflict* stage, genuine conflict does begin to appear when members realise there are significant frustrating differences between them. These may be personal, procedural, or based on different opinions about the best course of action that the group should pursue. In the *explicit conflict* stage, disagreement between members comes out into the open. This is likely to be a very difficult emotional stage as some group members clash sharply, while others may withdraw from the group, either by leaving it entirely or by remaining there physically but withdrawing psychologically. The danger here is that some members will be discounted by the rest of the group and their future contributions may be dismissed.

Finally there will be a *conflict aftermath* stage. If the group has dealt satisfactorily with its conflicts and arrived at either a compromise or a consensus outcome, this is likely to be a positive time when some reference, often jokingly, will be made back to the earlier disagreements in the group. Conversely, if the group has dealt poorly with its explicit conflict stage, then grudges between members may linger on. This can create a legacy of distrust that will severely handicap any further task interaction between members and make any further social contact unlikely.

A last technique members may use to limit destructive conflict in the group is to suspend the group's task operations while they explicitly discuss the group's process, referring to their perceptions of the interpersonal conflict styles of individual members. This may require the introduction of an external facilitator. Research into **interpersonal conflict styles** has shown that usually individuals have their own orientations towards group conflict that are expressed in one of five ways — namely, avoiding, competing, compromising, accommodating or collaborating. Individuals may shift between these styles depending on the situation, but overall their behaviours are likely to show a consistent disposition to react in one or two ways.

interpersonal conflict styles
Individuals have their own orientations towards group conflict that can be expressed in avoiding involvement, competing, compromising, accommodating others, or collaborating.

The worst individual conflict style is avoidance, while the most productive is collaborating. Individuals who avoid interpersonal conflict in a group situation are likely to be seen as both uncooperative and unassertive. Conflict is likely to make these group members uncomfortable and even fearful. They are unlikely either to pursue their own goals actively, or to support others effectively in the pursuit of their goals. In contrast, group members who have a collaborative interpersonal conflict style are likely to be seen by other group members as being both cooperative and assertive.

Though this approach is the most desirable of the five types of different interpersonal conflict styles, it is also the most difficult. It requires the most interpersonal skill, is time-consuming, and can only work properly when other members behave collaboratively. If this cannot be achieved, the remaining options are to fall back on being competitive (dominating others in the group), accommodating (appeasing others), or by compromising. In practice, compromise is one of the most frequent outcomes for groups caught up in conflicts. Here members negotiate with the aim of minimising losses. The limitation of compromise is that it may only be a short-term solution to a problem that can re-emerge. It may also lead to decisions that are difficult to implement because the whole group is not committed to them.

Exercise 8.6   Alternatives in group conflict resolution
Read the following examples and discuss the best choices in sub-groups. Rank order all the options from best to worst.
1. One group member insists on making remarks that only she thinks are funny. Should you:
    (a)   Laugh along with her.
    (b)   Question her about what she means.
    (c)   Go out and buy her a comic book.
    (d)   Consider whether the joke is relevant.
    (e)   Get the discussion back to the point right away.

2. One group member has become too personally involved in one of the many issues the group is discussing. He rejects everything anyone says about the entire range of issues, unless it agrees with his views on his pet issue. Should you:
    (a)   Ask the person for some facts about his pet issue.
    (b)   Cancel or postpone the meeting.
    (c)   Insist on discussing the main issue.
    (d)   Make your disagreement with the person clear so that discussion can return to the other issues.
    (e)   Suggest the person leave the group.

3. The group is not treating ideas critically but seems to be going along happily with anything that the leader is suggesting. You think you are watching a bad case of 'group-think'! Should you:
    (a)   Attempt to make the 'yes' men and women in the group feel isolated.
    (b)   Suggest a new leader.
    (c)   Try changing the way people are seated in the room.
    (d)   Argue for the introduction of a 'devil's advocate' to the group.
    (e)   Ask for a special outside consultant to help the group look critically at its own process.

Group decision making

Group decision making requires both problem solving and constructive controversy. There are three main ways a group can come to decisions. The first is by the leader deciding what final course of action will be taken. This is group decision making by **leader mandate**. In structured groups when a designated leader is already in place during the group discussion, this is a fairly routine method. Depending on the importance of the decision, this method has the advantage of speed and of clearly allocating the responsibility for the decision to the leader. Assuming the leader has allowed the group to discuss the issue fully, this method has the additional advantage of being able to resolve divisions in the group. Its main drawback is that group members who disagree with the

leader mandate
Where a final decision is made by the group leader.

majority vote
Where a final decision is made by a formal or informal vote of all group members.

result may not support it and could make its implementation difficult (Guirdham, 1991: 317).

A second way that groups can reach decisions is by the use of the **majority vote** method. This can be done formally or informally. This method is modelled on the the electoral process in most democracies and is a regular feature of the more formal meetings in many organisations. It has the advantage of counting every group member's opinion as important and registering their decision. In some meetings members may choose to abstain from voting and have this registered. They may do this either because they have a personal stake in the group outcome that might bias their vote, or they do not agree with any course of action being proposed.

The majority vote method is widely used but it has two drawbacks. It may be used as a superficial ritual and foreclose on the problem before all options are properly considered. The method may also override minority interests in the group who might remain dissatisfied with the outcome. This can lead to a 'winners vs losers' approach and reduce the quality of the decision made.

group consensus
A method of reaching a decision, in which all group members have the opportunity to express their views, to challenge and re-define the views of others, and work towards a reformulation of the problem.

The third main way that groups can make a decision is by reaching a **group consensus**. This is the best method when the decision is about a major issue that will have long-term effects on the group. It is the most time-consuming method of the three and so is less often used in dealing with routine or low-importance decisions. Arriving at a genuine consensus requires all group members to have the opportunity to express their own views, to challenge and possibly redefine the views of others, and to work towards a reformulation of the problem which incorporates revised versions of their own and other members' proposals.

The advantages of arriving at important group decisions by the consensus method are that all members will be committed to implementing the decision and that the process of criticism and discussion pursued by the group to reach consensus will make the optimum use of the resources of all group members. Another advantage is that if the group has to meet again to solve other complex problems, then the satisfaction of already having made a high-quality decision will increase the future decision-making capacity of the group. Last, though extra time is necessary to reach a consensus decision, this is likely to reduce the time necessary to put it into practice.

Exercise 8.7 Group problem solving and decision making

1. The instructor presents the following memo to the class and explains the various interest groups involved — the student newspaper, the Union Treasurer, the travel agency director, the cafeteria manager, and the sports association secretary.

   Memo to: All Communication Students
   From: Your University Student Union President
   Date: Week 7, 1999
   Subject: Are student union fees to be raised?

   There needs to be an extraordinary meeting of the University Students Association to decide whether student fees should be increased and if so by how much.

   The annual $50 fee presently covers sports union dues, the production of the student newspaper, membership of the Student Travel Association, and cafeteria concessions. The Union has a membership of 2000 and revenue of $145 000 pa, but outgoing expenses of $160 000. An increase of $7.50 has been suggested by

the Union Treasurer, but some committee members suggest that reduction in support for the student newspaper is desirable. The extraordinary meeting will be attended by the Union President, the Secretary, the Treasurer, Committee and ordinary student members to discuss alternatives and come to a decision.

2. Roles for the meeting are decided either by allocation or direction. The main role players will be briefed. As many as twenty students can take part and there should be at least three observers.

3. The agenda for the meeting is to be developed by the Union President and the Secretary. This should include minutes of the previous meeting, and verbal reports by representatives of the interest groups concerned. Other class members will be considered as ordinary student representatives and have voting rights.

    The time allocated for the meeting is 30 minutes or more. A preliminary in-class consultation time of 30 minutes is needed for parties to negotiate their interests. This should take place as follows:
    (a) First 10 minutes — Agenda drawn up by President and Secretary. Meeting of Committee (representitives of Travel Association, newspaper, Sports Association, cafeteria). Meeting of students and Treasurer.
    (b) Second 10 minutes — lobbying meetings between first half of students, who do not have executive roles, and sports and newspaper representatives and Treasurer, and between second half of students and Student Travel Association and cafeteria representitives and President and Secretary.
    (c) Third 10 minutes — second round of lobbying meetings with different student groups.

4. At the conclusion of the meeting the observers should report back to the group on the problem-solving and decision-making features of group process that were evident.

The model of group interaction presented in this chapter is derived from US social psychology. One limitation of this approach is that most studies in this tradition ignore the content of group discussions and instead focus on interpersonal processes. Such studies rarely identify what is a crucial feature of small group interaction, namely the fashion in which groups may use rational procedures in arriving at a consensus. Some recent studies, however (e.g. Slade, 1994), show that small group interactions may be better understood in terms of a discourse aiming to come to the truth of a matter. Another dimension that has been intentionally avoided in this chapter is that of intercultural differences. Some discussions of Japanese organisational communication, for example, consider their unique use of small group training methods in the workplace, as in Quality Circles, or in consensus-style decision making by *nemawashi* (inter-group negotiation) practices (Goldhaber, 1993: 102–10). Both these innovations have had some impact on Australian organisations, although such practices cannot simply be transferred to the local situation (Bamber et al., 1992).

However, the treatment here has intentionally been limited to the analysis of interaction patterns in Western task groups. As the quotation from Johnson and Johnson at the beginning of the chapter pointed out, groups can be seen either positively or negatively, depending on the experience individuals have in particular groups. The next two chapters will show that groups are central to the communication practices of organisations, and that the development of interpersonal skills in group work is essential for people to act effectively in those settings.

Summary

1. Small groups may be educational, social or task groups. In a task context, groups are collections of individuals who need to act interdependently to reach a common goal. Four factors determine group effectiveness — member interdependence, cohesion, attractiveness and satisfaction.
2. The appropriate size of a task group varies with the task it has to deal with, the time available, and the skills of its members. Effective groups are usually composed of five or six people.
3. There are several models of small group development. Schutz's inclusion, control and affection phases, Bales' orientation, evaluation and control phases, and Tuckman's four stages — forming, storming, norming and performing.
4. Effective groups need both task and team leadership. Task leadership concerns activities bearing directly on the job, such as goal setting, planning, and organising. Team leadership is concerned with maintaining positive interpersonal relations among group members.
5. Positive and negative roles are played by members in groups. Positive task roles are: initiating, information requesting and giving, procedure facilitating, opinion requesting and giving, clarifying and summarising. Positive maintenance roles are: social support, harmonising, tension release, energising, compromising and gatekeeping. Negative roles include blocking and aggressing.
6. Group problem solving usually needs to precede decision making. The use of agendas is intended to help groups organise their discussion time and to aid the solution of the problem.
7. Groups may become ineffective by being too conformist or too confrontational. Conformity problems may be resolved by the use of structured advocacy discussion methods. Group conflict may be redirected by an awareness of the interpersonal conflict styles of group members.
8. After groups have developed alternative courses of action by problem solving, they need to make a decision. This can be done either by leader mandate, by majority vote or by consensus.
9. Consensus decision making and constructive controversy are both forms of positive group behaviour and are likely to lead groups to make high-quality decisions.

Discussion questions

1. What makes task groups different from social and family groups? How are their goals and the interdependence of their members different?
2. How does the size of effective task groups compare with the size of some sporting teams? How do some sports teams work in subgroups?

3. What is the relation between group size, the complexity of the task, and stages of group development?
4. Do men or women make better leaders in small task groups? Are they likely to be better at task or team group leadership behaviours?
5. What are some of the positive and negative membership roles that people play in groups? Can you identify any of these, either in groups you are familiar with, or in group-centred TV shows, in politics, or in sport?
6. Why is constructive controversy in a problem-solving group more likely to lead to a consensus decision?
7. What can you do to redirect a group where severe interpersonal conflict has developed between two or more group members?
8. What can you do to liven up a group that is too apathetic or conformist?
9. What are some advantages and disadvantages of decision making by leader mandate and by majority vote?

Further reading

Barker, L. & Barker, D. (1993) *Communicating* New York: Prentice Hall, 6th edn.
Bartol, K. & Martin, D. (1986) 'Women and Men in Task Groups', pp. 259–301 in R. Ashmore & F. Del Boca, (eds) *The Social Psychology of Female–Male Relations* New York: Academic Press.
Eunson, B. (1994) *Communicating for Team Building* Brisbane: Wiley.
Goodall, L. (1990) *Small Group Communication in Organizations* Dubuque, IA: Wm. C. Brown, 2nd edn.
Guirdham, M. (1991) *Interpersonal Skills at Work* London: Prentice Hall.
Gulley, H. & Leathers, D. (1977) *Communication and Group Process* New York: Holt, Rinehart & Winston, 3rd edn.
Johnson, D. & Johnson, F. (1987) *Joining Together: Group Theory and Group Skills* New Jersey: Prentice Hall.
Luft, J. (1984) *Group Processes* Palo Alto, CA: Mayfield, 3rd edn.

References

Bales, R. (1970) *Personality and Interpersonal Behaviour* New York: Holt, Rinehart & Winston.
Bamber, G., Shadur, M. & Howell, M. (1992) 'The International Transferability of Japanese Management Strategies', *Employee Relations* 14 (3): 3–19.
Benne, K. & Sheats, P. (1948) 'Functional Roles of Group Membership', *Journal of Social Issues* 4: 41–9.
Goldhaber, G. (1993) *Organizational Communication* Dubuque, IA: Wm. C. Brown, 6th edn.
Irwin, H. & More, E. (1994) *Managing Corporate Communication* Sydney: Allen & Unwin.
Mann, L. & Janis, I. (1983) 'Decisional Conflict in Organizations', in D. Tjosvold & D. Johnson, (eds) *Preventive Conflict Management* New York: Irvington.

Marchington, M. (1992) *Managing the Team* Oxford: Blackwell.
Mitchell, T. (1988) *People in Organizations* Sydney: McGraw-Hill.
NBEET — National Board of Employment, Education and Training (1992) *Skills Sought by Employers of Graduates* Canberra: AGPS.
Reddy, W. (ed.) (1988) *Team Building* San Diego, CA: University Associates.
Schutz, W. (1966) *The Interpersonal Underworld* Palo Alto, CA: Science and Behaviour Books.
Sillars, A. & Weisberg, J. (1987) 'Conflict as a Social Skill', pp. 140–72 in M. Roloff & G. Miller, (eds) *Interpersonal Processes* Newbury Park, CA: Sage.
Slade, C. (1994) 'Reasoning in Groups', pp. 15–31 in P. Casey, (ed.) *On Different Premises: Proceedings of the Third National Reasoning Conference* Wagga Wagga: Charles Sturt University.
Slaven, R. (1984) *Learning to Cooperate, Cooperating to Learn* New York: Plenum.
Tuckman, B. (1965) 'Developmental Sequence in Small Groups', *Psychological Bulletin* 63: 384–99.

Organisational communication (1) Structure and culture

9

Objectives

After completing this chapter you should be able to:

- understand how individuals follow a career path through organisations and in doing so play both personal and positional roles;
- define organisations as open systems in terms of their environments, goals and resources, technologies and structure;
- explain the relation between organisational structure and formal and informal communication via the direction of message flows;
- compare the notions of organisational communication climate and organisational culture;
- recognise three different levels of organisational culture analysis.

Nominees for promotion at all levels were considered twice a year by a Promotions and Probations Board, and a printed list of the successful candidates was subsequently circulated throughout the Organization. Since those directly concerned were told in advance of the verdict, the main interest of the list lay in keeping abreast of the fortunes of one's fellows. It is a rare heart that truly rejoices in a friend's prosperity, and it must be confessed that the offices and corridors of the Organization were swept, every six months, by gasps of indignation, of disgust and incredulity, at the revelation of the latest promotions — and by correspondingly magnified sighs of solicitude on behalf of those rejected.

People in Glass Houses, *Shirley Hazzard*

Hazzard's story, reputedly based on the United Nations, gives many humorous insights into what it feels like to be in a big, powerful organisation. Organisations are a central part of our modern urban environment. You will not find major organisations in countries which are not modernised. Organisations are very much a twentieth century cultural hallmark and yet their internal workings are often a mystery to those outside them, especially to young graduates. This chapter will introduce some of the main areas of organisational communication by emphasising the way people first join companies as new employees.

Australian organisational communication contexts

We take organisations for granted, often without knowing much about them. Whereas the news media give us a running record of political life, organisational affairs normally do not make headlines. This is partly because organisations do not have the excitement of politics, and partly because organisational affairs are frequently confidential. Business organisations, for example, are often reluctant to open up their practices for fear of revealing information that might disadvantage them with their competitors. Conversely, public organisations, such as the Tax Department, cannot reveal information about their clients without risking charges of invading citizen rights to privacy.

Another reason why public knowledge of organisational affairs is limited is that organisations are highly specialised. In the private sector this specialisation is related to the industry group the organisation belongs to. People working in particular organisations are likely to know most about other organisations in the same industry. So BHP, which is one of our biggest ('the Big Australian') and best known companies, is linked with the iron and steel industry, Woolworths is a grocery retailer, and so on. Reconsider these organisations, however, in terms of the potential career paths they offer for people who work in them. People who are working in an organisation in a particular industry will be most familiar with other people and companies in the same industry. So if they change jobs they will change companies, but usually not move from the industry or business they know.

A similar pattern of organisational specialisation characterises the Australian public sector. The very biggest agencies are huge Federal government departments, such as Defence or the Department of Administrative Services (DAS). DAS acts as a construction agency for all other Federal departments. Next comes state organisations, such as the various state railways, or those more profitable ones that have recently been privatised, such as the Government Insurance Office (GIO) in New South Wales. A third, smaller tier of public sector organisations exists at the local government level, with agencies such as shire and council electricity and water boards.

This is a broad picture of the wide variety of organisations that exist in 1990s Australia. There are actually many more, ranging from giant multinational organisations with Australian branches — such as IBM, Rank-Xerox and Sony (American, British and Japanese based respectively) — big public sector communication utilities such as Telecom and the newer private company Optus, down to quasi-government agencies such as CSIRO (Commonwealth Scientific and Industrial Research Organisation), the ABC (Australian Broadcasting Corporation) and SBS (Special Broadcasting Service), and quasi-corporate organisations such as car owners' associations like the NRMA (New South Wales), the RACQ (Queensland) and the RACV (Victoria).

There is also a spectrum of smaller business organisations in Australia, from franchised versions of existing licensees (Angus & Robertson bookstores or McDonald's restaurants), down to small family owned and operated business, such as corner stores or management consultancies. There is too also a variety of non-profit organisations, including environmental groups like Greenpeace and the Australian Conservation Foundation, as well as religious and charitable organisations, such as St Vincent de Paul. Because of this diversity in the range of organisations, some adaptation of the prevailing theories of organisational communication, which are based on the experience of North American, big business organisations, needs to be made. For more information, there are several useful case studies of the communication practices in Australian organisations in Irwin and More (1994).

Exercise 9.1 Presentational speaking

In organisational settings you are always on stage. You may be required to speak informally, semi-formally or formally, but in any case your performance is usually being evaluated by others. The basic rules for making presentations are:

1. Know your material. Presentation skills are no substitute for substance.
2. Rehearse your presentation if you have the chance to do so.
3. When speaking always aim to establish rapport with your listeners and respond to their reactions.

To practise, choose one or more of the following topics and in next week's meeting speak to the class for five minutes. Make up or research your own information, but speak to the main point. Do not use overheads, notes or palm cards when speaking.

- Make an election speech for your university students union Presidency, explaining how you would improve the quality of university life.
- Make a testimonial speech for a colleague who is leaving your department after five years.
- Deliver a goodwill talk to your employees, congratulating them on a good year's work but warning them of tough times to come.
- Make a welcoming speech to a party of Japanese visitors who are considering investing in your company.

- Give a farewell talk to staff who have been unavoidably laid off by your organisation due to the recession.
- Make a welcoming speech at the opening of a conference on small business which your government department has arranged.

Functional and meaning-centred theories of organisations

Theories about the development and functions of organisations, and of the nature of organisational communication, have been alternately functional or meaning-centred. By **functional** we mean theories that stress 'bottom line' factors in organisations, such as profitability and productivity. Normally, these 'bottom line' factors have been measured, as far as possible, in quantitative terms based on performance indicators. Such results are used to evaluate the overall effectiveness of the organisation. In contrast, **meaning-centred** theories of organisations consider the workplace as a human environment where people work most effectively via a shared sense of meaning and purpose about their goals. People working in these organisations will be sensibly concerned about 'bottom line' indicators, but they will also define their motivations in terms of the pursuit of appropriate professional standards (Shockley-Zalaback, 1991).

Both functionalist and meaning-centred approaches to understanding organisational communication are necessary. For example, in summarising the development of the main organisational theories during this century, an alternation between functionalist and interpretivist (i.e. meaning-centred) positions can be seen. The original emphasis of classical organisation theory on organisational design largely neglected the place of people, while the human relations school that followed tended to go to a 'warm and fuzzy' extreme by minimising organisation structure issues. The same 'hard/soft' cycle repeated itself with the systems and contingency theories of organisations in the 1960s, giving way to culture-based theories after the 1970s.

Classical organisation theory is associated with the work of Taylor, Fayol and Weber before World War I. It emphasised the division of labour in organisations and the way a formal chain of command is required to communicate and enforce organisational rules. Taylor, an American engineer, was concerned with time and motion studies of work procedures. He wanted precise job descriptions to avoid worker 'soldiering' (wasting time), and thought organisations ran best when channels of formal authority were used and informal communication channels avoided. Fayol and Weber added other elements, such as Fayol's stress on horizontal communication and Weber's discussion of how authority was legitimised, but it was Taylor's views that aroused most union antagonism because his model advocated strict controls on how work should be done.

This over-reliance on formal authority structures in organisations was challenged by human relations theorists, such as Mayo (an Australian who migrated to the US) in the 1940s, and later McGregor and Likert in the 1960s. The latter two stressed the value of participative management in organisations via the activities of groups of workers. The assumption here was that happier and more committed workers would develop group norms and this would boost organisational productivity. Their attention to the nature of the small work group as the basic unit of organisations, and Likert's idea of 'link pin' members

> **functional theories of organisations**
> Theories that stress 'bottom line' factors in organisations, measured in quantitative terms based on performance indicators, e.g. productivity, profit or staff turnover.
>
> **meaning-centred theories of organisations**
> These theories consider that people work most effectively through a shared sense of meaning and purpose about their goals.

connecting different groups in the organisation, was an enduring legacy of their research.

With the postwar effects of computerisation a number of information processing based models of organisational behaviour developed. These drew on elements of both classical and human resources theory and added features of their own. Some important British–Australian research was done by Trist and Emery with their idea of organisations as sociotechnical systems. Most of these newer approaches, however, were American, as in Lawrence and Lorsch's contingency theory, or Katz and Kahn's systems theory. These approaches agreed there was no single best way of managing either organisational design or organisational communication. They favoured 'open system' models that highlighted the complex interrelations between an organisation, its environment, technology and people.

Most recently a range of cultural theories of organisations have emerged, ranging from popular models of company excellence (Peters & Waterman, 1982), to cross-cultural comparisons of why Japanese companies are out performing American ones (Ouichi, 1981), and more complex theories about the role of imagery and ideology in shaping the language and rituals of organisations (Morgan, 1986). This approach is partly a move away from the ethnocentrism of earlier studies, which often assumed that only American experience counted. Further, it may also reflect the facts that for the first time there are substantial numbers of women in organisations, that gender factors were overlooked by earlier theorists, and that women scholars are making major contributions to the field (e.g. Putnam & Pacanowsky, 1983).

Career paths: organisational entry and assimilation

When new employees first join an organisation they go through a period of orientation, which can be easy, tough or somewhere in between. The outcome all depends on the organisation itself — its size, if it has a regular induction progam, etc. — and also on how motivated and skilled the new employee is. Jablin has termed this process 'organisational entry, assimilation and exit' (1987). The 'exit' stage refers to the individual leaving the organisation. We will concentrate here instead on the 'entry' and 'assimilation' stages as a useful way of considering how individuals cope with their earliest organisational experiences. The process of organisational entry and assimilation can also be constructively examined from functionalist as well as interpretivist perspectives.

One of the key requirements for the new employee is to learn to make appropriate distinctions between *personal* and *positional roles* in dealing with others at work. Organisations are necessarily formal in their structure: they have policies and procedures, rules and regulations. Therefore the organisation members the new employee meets on Day One need to be seen as occupying specific positional roles, such as 'line' or 'staff' positions. Line positions are those involving workers who are directly concerned with the organisation's main business. Staff positions, in contrast, are supporting roles that are important, but not directly involved with the company's main business. So in a university, for instance, academic staff are line staff, whereas administrative, cafeteria and library staff are support staff.

Chapter 9

Support staff in an organisation.
(Photo: *Cecilia Burke*)

Exercise 9.2 Distinguishing line and staff positions

Go through the following examples, first individually, then as a group. Decide and discuss which positions are line and which staff.

Position title	Organisation	Line or staff?
Librarian	Company research library	
	University library	
Accountant	Public accounting company	
	Manufacturing co. accounts dept.	
Journalist	Metropolitan newspaper	
	Mining company PR dept.	
TV producer	Metropolitan TV station	
	Company Corporate Video dept.	
Market research director	Marketing consultancy co.	
	Retail marketing dept.	
Tax lawyer	Investment banking co.	
	Law firm	

The most important co-workers for new employees, in positional terms, will be their immediate superior or supervisor and their peers. Supervisors are specially important for new employees. US studies suggest that supervisors spend between one-third and two-thirds of their time communicating with subordinates, usually about work-related issues, and usually face-to-face. It was also found that subordinates are likely to distort information they send upward to superiors so as to present their job performances in a favourable light. This finding needs the qualification, though, that such behaviour depends on the subordinate's perception of the supervisor: if the supervisor is trusted, then it is less likely that information passed on upwards will be distorted, or withheld altogether.

Another finding about superior–subordinate communication relevant to organisational entry is that some large gaps in understanding about job duties and performance expectations may exist between new workers and their supervisors. An example of this is the difference between American employees and supervisors in their perceptions of what motivates workers. In 1946 employees rated 'full appreciation of work done' as Number 1, and rated 'good wages' as 5; in contrast, supervisors rated the first factor as 5, and the second as 1, and a similar disparity still existed in these perceptions in 1979 (Pace & Faules, 1989: 187).

In analysing how new employees establish their career paths, we must also consider how new workers 'learn the ropes'. There are several stages in organisational socialisation. First, there is an anticipatory phase, when the potential employees are forming their expectations about the organisation (e.g. 'So you've worked here for three years? Tell me about it . . .'). Second, there is the encounter phase when the ideal meets the actual. For instance, Jablin (1987) studied how a new intake of trainee nurses initially overestimated how positive they would feel about their new jobs. Last, there is a metamorphosis stage. This is when the new recruits successfully adapt to the cultural norms of other organisation members. They then negotiate their own role within the constraints of the organisation's rules.

As new employees become more familiar with other organisational members, contacts with their co-workers will increase, while their degree of reliance on their immediate superior for job-related information will decrease. To the extent that new workers find themselves in an environment where their co-workers express positive feelings about the job, they will feel relatively satisfied themselves and begin to feel 'part of the team'. However, this is only the start of new employees' long march through the organisation. So far they have only established themselves as junior members. For them to go further they will have to learn to compete and cooperate with their co-workers, and deal successfully with clients or customers.

New employees need to become skilled at identifying alternative career paths for themselves, both in their own and potentially other organisations. A **career path** is the normal route an individual employee will travel through an organisation in a particular vocational role. Note, however, that this is looking at what a career path is through the eyes of the new employee. For the purposes of senior managers already in the organisation, and for personnel managers, the idea of a career path may be thought of quite differently. For them, it may be how the structure and availability of career paths need to be changed to plan future staffing for the organisation.

> **career path**
> The normal route an employee travels through an organisation in a particular vocational role.

Exercise 9.3 Writing a job application

Select a job advertisement for a recent graduate in a communications-related area from the positions vacant section of any major newspaper. Make sure the position identifies the selection criteria for the job, either formally or informally. Then write a one-page résumé and a one-page covering letter.

Your résumé should include:

1. Your full name, address and phone number.
2. Your educational record, specifying dates of study and your major areas of study. (Some employers may require you to include an official university transcript.)

3. Your work experience. Give dates and specific examples. (Note: Both 2 and 3 should list your experiences from the most recent to the earliest.)
4. Your special skills, training, or abilities relevant to the position you are applying for. These could include technical skills, such as desk-top publishing abilities, or interpersonal skills, such as team work experience.
5. Membership or associate membership of any professional associations, participation in any university or community activities, and any awards for personal achievements.

You should aim to highlight the features of your résumé most directly relevant to the job. There are three basic principles to follow:

1. Be concise and clear. It is inappropriate to write a long letter for most junior positions. Keep it short and simple. Specify the position you are applying for and how you found out about it (see Dwyer, 1993: 199).
2. Be complete and correct. Strike a balance between excessive formality and inappropriate informality. Address all the job's selection criteria and wherever possible cross-refer to the relevant parts of your résumé. Do not make claims your résumé does not bear out. The names and positions of referees usually go with the letter, rather than the résumé.
3. Take a 'you' attitude. That is, try to see the job requirements from the employer's perspective as well as your own. Also, do not start too many paragraphs or sentences with the word 'I'.

Organisational structure

The word 'organisation' has two potentially different meanings. As a verb, 'organising' means the process of putting things into order; as a noun, the term 'the organisation' means something relatively static and established. When we think of the organisation as a pre-established structure, this is somewhat misleading, as organisations are rarely static. However, it is helpful initially to conceive of the organisation as relatively static, as this emphasises the importance of formal structure considered as a collection of practices that new employees have to learn to deal with. Organisational structure is the formal design of the prescribed chain-of-command in the organisation.

Figure 9.1 presents a model of an organisation as an open system. Defining it like this is intended to stress the importance of the organisation's external and internal environments. The aim here is to highlight the functional and structural dimensions of organisations. In these terms, an organisation is an **open system** which has an external and an internal environment. It is a work unit with a structure that includes goals, resources and technologies that are used to achieve planned outcomes.

Let us unpack this rather dense definition to explain the idea of organisations as being open systems by referring to different parts of Figure 9.1. Like any model, this diagram is basically static and two-dimensional, but it should be seen as a simplification of something which is actually dynamic and complex. Different parts of the model have been numbered to indicate the way in which the organisation actually works, though this too is a simplification as some of the processes overlap. However, to explain the model's component parts, let's start with the external environment.

open system
A theoretical perspective that considers that organisations have an external and an internal environment.

Organisational communication (1)

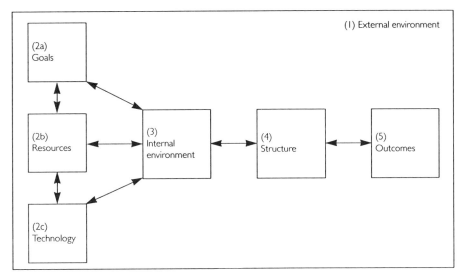

Figure 9.1 *The organisation as an open system*

The external environment

The **external environment** (1) is the set of contextual factors outside the organisation that it is vitally concerned with. These factors make organisational activity possible but they also constrain it. For a private sector organisation its primary external environment will be its markets and its customers; for a public sector organisation it will be its relations with its various clients or its publics. The external environment may also include suppliers of goods or services to the organisation, other industry competitors, government or industry regulatory agencies, and other community groups that may have a stake in the organisation's product or output.

Relationships between an organisation and its external environment are rarely constant. In times of peace and quiet, this relation can be relatively *static*; in times of greater change or disorder, it can be *turbulent*. Generally, larger organisations have more control over their external environments and may influence their environment, at least up to a point. If a major grocery retailer, such as Coles, decides to extend its shopping hours to seven days a week, this is more likely to have an effect on other traders than if the corner store did so.

Organisational goals, resources and outcomes

The way an organisation deals with its external environment is, to an extent, determined by its goals. **Organisational goals** (2a) are the shared aims that the members of an organisation have developed over time. **Organisational outcomes** (5) are the endproducts of the organisation, while its goals are the starting point. These organisational outcomes may be defined in terms of profits, services, or products. They can be thought of, in business terms, as share of the market or percentage growth rates; or they can be defined in terms of type of service provision — for instance, the number of patients treated by a hospital, or the number of students graduated from a college. One useful distinction in discussing organisational goals is between official and operational goals.

external environment
The set of contextual factors outside the organisation that it is vitally concerned with.

organisational goals
The shared aims that the members of an organisation develop over time.

organisational outcomes
Outcomes that are defined in terms of profits, services or products.

official goals
The mission statements of the organisation.

operational goals
Targets that are specific, functional and measurable; different departments may be given goals they have to reach in a set time period.

organisational resources
The factors an organisation uses as its raw materials.

Official goals are the mission statements of the organisation. These are comprehensive, ideal-type statements made about how the organisation will serve the community or the public by producing products or services of a high quality. Sometimes they are referred to as 'motherhood' statements — a sexist term for anything bland and non-controversial. In fact, they should be genuine manifestos of social purpose for organisations, whether they are public or private. The difference with **operational goals** is that they are specific, functional and measurable. So, for example, different departments may be given target goals they have to reach in a set time period. In short, official goals relate to organisational policies, whereas operational goals relate to company procedures.

Organisational resources (2b) are what the organisation uses as its raw materials. These are its inputs, which can be physical or social. Its resources may be raw materials and machines if it is a mining company, or salespeople if it is an insurance agency. So resources can be thought of as people, material or capital, and can include inputs such as information and energy. It is one of management's key functions to ensure an adequate supply of resources for the organisation, then to ensure that these resources are used economically to meet organisational goals and to produce the planned outcomes.

Technology and the internal environment

If the organisation's external environment provides both opportunities and limits, its goals produce a sense of purpose, and its resources provide the physical means for the organisation to produce, then the organisation's technology gives it the power to do so. In converting organisational inputs into outcomes, all organisations make use of technology (2c), whether they are manufacturing or service organisations. Naturally, organisations that are concentrated on materials processing, such as mining companies, will use more costly production technologies than those which have a service orientation, such as insurance companies. Even in insurance companies, however, the technical expertise of their personnel is vital to organisational success.

Technologies used in different organisations can range from capital-intensive machinery, such as machine tools in car plants, to smaller, but still powerful management information systems, which computerise and automate organisational accounting processes. In either case, **organisational technologies** are how information, equipment, and techniques are used to transform organisational inputs into outputs. Technologies related directly to the organisation's business are classified as core technologies, while those used in support of the company's main business are termed peripheral technologies (Kriegler, 1988: 12).

organisational technologies
The information, equipment and techniques that are used to transform organisational inputs into outputs.

internal environment
An organisation's climate and culture.

The way in which technology is applied to organisational resources to pursue organisational goals will be influenced most directly by the organisation's internal environment (3). The organisation's **internal environment** is the organisation's climate and culture. It is determined by the way in which the organisation's formal structure interacts with its informal networks. This sets the tone of the climate and culture. Thus, individual organisational members work together in informal but interdependent communication networks with the aim of meeting their own personal goals and the organisation's formal goals.

While organisational technology is mainly concerned with information and production systems, the internal environment is more concerned with the operation of its personnel system.

Three dimensions of organisational structure

The structure (4) is the centrepiece of the organisation (Mintzberg, 1979). Communication may be the organisation's lifeblood, but its bones are the organisational structure. **Organisational structure** is the formal design of the prescribed chain-of-command in the organisation. The chain-of-command is the officially approved hierarchy of authority and decision making that is represented in the formal organisation chart. The organisational structure is crucial because it specifies the division of tasks in an organisation: who should do what jobs and make what decisions, in terms of members' positional roles in the organisation. Certain duties will be allocated to certain positions and these can be changed only after a formal restructuring of the authority hierarchy. The organisational structure, therefore, spells out superior and subordinate relationships through the organisation's formal decision-making networks.

> **organisational structure**
> The formal design of the prescribed chain-of-command in the organisation.

The terms *'organic'* or *'mechanistic'* are used to distinguish different ideal types of organisational structure. This dichotomy assumes that organic organisations are less bureaucratic and more flexible than mechanistic ones. Control in an organically structured organisation is more diverse, while it is highly centralised in a mechanistic one. Similarly, communication flows in organic organisations are more often lateral, where in mechanistic organisations they are more vertical. These are ideal types of organisational structure that define two ends of a continuum. Mechanistic organisations are more likely to be suited to stable external environmental conditions, while organisations with organic structures may be better suited to turbulent environments.

Exercise 9.4 Quiz on organisational structure

Re-match the first part of the following statements with their correct second parts.

1. If an organisation is thought of as an open system it has
2. The external environment of an organisation is
3. The internal environment of an organisation is
4. Organisational goals are
5. External environments can be

A. general mission statements and specific operational goals.
B. the interaction of its formal structure with its informal networks.
C. static or turbulent.
D. its markets, clients, suppliers, competitors, and others.
E. an internal and external environment.

There are three main dimensions of organisational structure — complexity, formalisation and centralisation. **Complexity** is the degree of specialisation that is reflected in the organisational hierarchy. Complexity arises out of the need for specialisation, one of the central advantages of organisations. As the size of an organisation increases so will its complexity. Organisational specialisation can take place at any one of three levels: horizontally, vertically or geographically. Horizontal specialisation is indicated by the degree of departmentalisation that

> **complexity**
> The degree of specialisation in an organisation's hierarchy.

takes place. Departments can be constructed on the basis of their function (e.g. manufacturing, marketing or personnel) or of different products.

Vertical specialisation, the second feature of organisational complexity, is the depth of the organisation's hierarchy. This is also referred to as the *span of control*, meaning the number of subordinates that managers have under their direct supervision. The wider the span of control, the more subordinates a manager must supervise. The smaller it is, the 'taller' the organisation is likely to be (i.e. it will have more levels in its vertical hierarchy). Conversely, the 'flatter' an organisation, the wider the span of control is likely to be. Flatter organisational structures sound more democratic, but the larger the organisation the less effective flat structures are. They may be better for work that is loosely supervised and technically simple, such as in some sales and service organisations.

Formalisation is the second main dimension of organisational structure and it too increases with the size of the organisation. **Formalisation** refers to the extent to which work roles are closely defined by the organisation. The more formal the organisation is, the more standardised workers' jobs will be. Highly formalised organisations will have carefully worked-out rules, procedures and policies. Rules are the tightest operational constraints on employees, policies are more guidelines to action, while procedures lay down a series of steps that should be followed in performing a particular task. One reliable sign that you are dealing with a highly formalised organisation is when you're told: 'Put it in writing!'.

The third dimension of organisational structure is **centralisation**. This is the extent to which decision making is concentrated in the organisation. If the decision-making processes are mostly located in the upper echelons of the chain-of-command then the structure can be described as vertically centralised at the top. Conversely, if greater decision-making powers belong to lower level members in the organisation, it may be described as decentralised. Whereas an increase in organisational size increases the other two dimensions of structure, it should decrease centralisation.

Organisational structure and communication

One of the traditional ways of studying the interrelation between organisational structure and communication is by observing the written and spoken **message flows** in organisations. These can be classified into three kinds: downwards, from superior to subordinates; upwards, from subordinates to superiors; and, laterally, between workers on the same level of the organisational hierarchy. Considered in these terms, the organisation's hierarchy is the conduit for information flows, and informal communication — sometimes described as 'the grapevine' — is the only other avenue for communication in the organisation.

Goldhaber takes a pro-managerial stance about how information flows should be studied by suggesting that downward information is most important in an organisation. The types of information of greatest value have been found, in North American research, to be about:

1. Job instructions — how to do the job
2. Job rationale — why you should do the job that way

---

formalisation
The extent to which work roles are closely defined by the organisation.

centralisation
The extent to which decision making is concentrated in an organisation.

message flows
The ways in which written, oral and electronic messages move through the organisation. There are three kinds: downwards, from superior to subordinates; upwards, from subordinates to superiors; and laterally, between workers on the same level of the organisational hierarchy.

3. Company procedures and policies — organisational rules, penalties, and benefits
4. Managerial feedback to subordinates — information about how you're doing
5. Information about the organisation's mission — motivational messages.

Such information is most effectively conveyed by a combination of oral and written methods, depending on the particular message. Goldhaber believes that most employees want information about personal, job-related matters first, and about organisational decision making only second (1993: 146).

Upward message flows are still important for management planning, motivation and decision making. Such information needs to cover (a) what workers are doing, (b) what unsolved work problems they have, and (c) any suggestions they can make about work improvements. Third, horizontal communication needs to take place across the organisational hierarchy between people on the same level of authority for purposes of task coordination, as well as for problem solving and information sharing.

This suggests that organisations are often biased towards favouring a bureaucratic, top-down model of how they should work. However, Goldhaber's normative model need not be seen as inevitable. Rather, we need to be careful of accepting the conduit metaphor of communication (see Chapter 1), which the message flow approach implies uncritically (Pace & Faules, 1989: 117). Not all organisations are centralised bureaucracies. Interpersonal, informal and small group communication are likely to be more important in many workplaces than the orderly transmission of messages from top management.

Most organisations will strike a balance between centralisation and decentralisation. There is likely to be an inverse relation between formal and informal communication channels. The less formal the structure is, the greater will be the development of informal communication. Just as there are dangers of excessively formal top-down communication practices in a bureaucratic system, there are also potential problems with too many decentralised channels. Problems of multiple management authority and role conflict may emerge. A balance needs to be sought between an organisation's emphasis on formal structure and its ability to be adaptable. Unless communication channels are free enough to gather honest feedback from workers across all ranges of the organisation, then management decisions are unlikely to be well informed or widely supported.

Exercise 9.5 Prioritising organisational information flows

You are a new editorial member of your insurance company's newsletter, which is currently being upgraded to suit the company's changing needs. Recently it has moved to a two-divisional interstate structure, with the Queensland branch being a complex, formal department, while Victoria has a relatively informal and decentralised structure.

You have been asked to produce two versions of the newsletter with the same content, but with a different editorial emphasis to suit each division. The class should form two groups, one for Queensland and one for Victoria, and discuss how best to prioritise the following kinds of information to suit the communication needs of that division.

1. Previous month's sales record.
2. New computing equipment being installed.
3. Suggestions for direct mail selling of policies.
4. The activities of regional sales representatives.
5. Why certain legal procedures must be followed in writing policies.
6. The company's new policy on employing disabled staff.
7. Each department's involvement in community affairs.
8. Ways for office clerical staff to express their opinions on departmental clerical needs.
9. Information about a proposed revision of the company's mission statement.
10. Unsolved problems that sales staff and middle managers are experiencing.
11. Company awards for new client contacts.
12. Ways for new recruits to know each other in the two departments and share information.
13. Changes in company procedures arising from enterprise bargaining.

Organisational culture

When we consider the formal allocation of tasks in an organisation by discussing organisational structure, we are approaching organisations in functional terms. However, if we consider an organisation's climate and culture, then we are moving into the territory of meaning-centred theories. The notions of organisational communication climate and culture are related but different. Climate is a snapshot of what it feels like in the organisation at any one time, while culture is more enduring. Climate is usually described in terms of perceptions of the degree of trust in supervisor–subordinate relations, whereas culture can be studied as the organisation's language, its artifacts, its symbols, and its rites and rituals.

Organisational communication climate

Though an organisation's communication climate is frequently subjective (i.e. it looks different depending on the point of view of the observer within the hierarchy), it can also be measured in a variety of quantitative ways. The **organisational communication climate** comprises the current feelings that organisation members have about how satisfying it is to communicate with others in the organisation. In these terms, the organisational communication climate is made up of organisational members' perception of communication events.

The choice of the metaphor 'climate' to describe this process is instructive. Not all of us have the same perceptions of the weather — a good day to a drought-stricken farmer is likely to be a wet one. Similarly, some organisational members may feel relatively satisfied with what they perceive to be responsible and competent communication practices by their superiors, while others may feel dissatisfied. The perception of an organisation's climate, then, is intersubjective. How employees feel about communication practices will depend upon the quality of their interpersonal relations with their superiors.

Two points about both the subjective and dynamic nature of an organisational communication climate need emphasis. First, the climate will broadly be

> **organisational communication climate**
> The current feelings that organisation members have about how satisfying it is to communicate with others in the organisation.

perceived as good, neutral or bad. It will be interpreted either as supportive or unsupportive. Other factors associated with perceptions of the organisational climate are:

- the level of participative decision making practised;
- perceptions of trust and credibility between colleagues and supervisors–subordinates;
- the degree of open communication;
- the extent to which members feel there is clear identification of job performance goals.

The more positive organisation members are about these matters, the more likely they are to be satisfied with the information they receive. Organisations with a positive communication climate are likely to have high levels of morale, and employees in those organisations are likely to have greater levels of job satisfaction (Pace & Faules, 1989: 123–6).

Second, the organisational communication climate is only a current perception of organisational communication practices. A new manager may introduce different performance standards that could radically change the organisational communication climate for better or worse. This point about its short-term nature is also central in distinguishing organisational climate from culture. Climate is essentially a collection of beliefs held in the organisation concerning the here and now: in contrast, organisational culture is something more long-term. It is the unique sense of the place and how the organisation defines itself. Organisational culture reflects perceptions about the organisation's past, its present and its likely future, whereas beliefs about climate concern right now. Culture influences the development over time of organisational climate, not vice versa.

Some Australian attempts to measure organisational communication climate have been made, such as Muhki's 1982 study (Bordow & More, 1991: 52). Ticehurst and Ross-Smith (1992) also have considered the relation between communication satisfaction, job satisfaction, and organisational commitment in Australia.

A range of instruments have been developed to measure organisational climate. These often concentrate on the quality and reliability of information available in an organisation and the degree of trust in superior-subordinate relationships. Most of them are rather lengthy and some require computer-based analysis because of the amount of data they generate. To illustrate the method the above climate measure is a simplified version. Detailed surveys of organisational communication measurement instruments are in Downs (1988; 1991).

Exercise 9.6 Measuring organisational communication climate

For this exercise, think either of an organisation you have worked in or are working in. Alternatively, think of your present university — in that case, substitute 'fellow-students' for 'subordinates'.

Go through the following eight dimensions and place a (1) above the number that represents your opinion of current practices in the organisation. Then reconsider how you think the organisation should be ideally performing on that dimension and place an (A) above that number. If you are satisfied with any one particular dimension then place (I) and (A) above the same number. The numbers 1–10 represent a continuum.

1. The information I get from my
co-workers is reliable   The information I get from my co-workers is not always reliable
   10   9   8   7   6   5   4   3   2   1

2. Management provides me with
the kind of information I want   Management is not providing me with the kind of information I want
   10   9   8   7   6   5   4   3   2   1

3. I can say what I really think
to my superior   I cannot say what I really think to my superior
   10   9   8   7   6   5   4   3   2   1

4. My superior gives me a fair go when
we disagree   My superior does not give me a fair go when we disagree
   10   9   8   7   6   5   4   3   2   1

5. I really understand my subordinates'
work problems   I do not always understand my subordinates' work problems
   10   9   8   7   6   5   4   3   2   1

6. I believe my subordinates are
open and honest with me   I believe my subordinates are not always open and honest with me
   10   9   8   7   6   5   4   3   2   1

7. My work group can establish their
own goals and objectives   My work group cannot establish their own goals and objectives
   10   9   8   7   6   5   4   3   2   1

8. My views have a definite influence
on this organisation   My views do not have much influence on this organisation
   10   9   8   7   6   5   4   3   2   1

After completing the instrument, calculate the overall difference between your real (current) and ideal (as you would like it to be) scores.

Also calculate four separate scores for the sum of questions 1 and 2, 3 and 4, 5 and 6, and 7 and 8. These paired scores refer to four dimensions of climate — quality and reliability of information, superior/subordinate communication, superior openness and upward communication.

For both the aggregate and paired scores, the higher the result, the less supportive is the climate.

The origins and uses of organisational culture studies

Through the 1970s organisations were becoming more globally interlinked. The growth of the European Common Market, the economic recovery of previously war-devastated Japan, and the spread of mostly US-based multinationals, such as IBM, exemplified the new trend towards globalisation. With the changing mission of large organisations, a range of new theories were developed that moved away from the relatively mechanistic approaches implicit in the prevailing systems and contingency models of organisational behaviour. This was signalled by the publication of a number of popular business books that introduced the idea of organisational culture to a wider audience.

The book that did this first was William Ouichi's *Theory Z* (1981). It argued that American and Japanese organisations differed sharply on the basis of longstanding cultural value differences. US companies, for instance, had a preference for individualism, so employees were rewarded on the basis of their personal merit, rather than for their years of membership in the organisation. In contrast, Japanese organisations rewarded employee loyalty to the company, by lifelong employment and promotion by seniority. Ouichi saw these different practices as deriving from a different spirit of loyalty to the organisation, one that expressed the group-orientation of Japanese society. He argued that US and Japanese organisations were converging.

This fashionable new emphasis on organisational culture as a key factor in business success was highlighted with the publication in 1982 of three more best-sellers that also saw organisational culture as a vital ingredient. These were Pascale and Athos' *The Art of Japanese Management*, Deal and Kennedy's *Corporate Cultures*, and Peters and Waterman's *In Search of Excellence*. Overall, they emphasised the role of organisational culture as a unique factor.

The key term here is 'unique'. That is, all organisations — even if they are in the same industry — are plainly not the same. Though Australian universities are almost all publicly funded, for instance, there is still a strong sense of competitive difference between them. And even those relatively elite universities, such as Sydney and Melbourne, still have significant differences between them. The same generalisation could also be made about Australian companies engaged in car manufacturing, or about banks, or various newspaper groups. So, in this light, **organisational culture** refers to the values and interpretive frameworks used to construct a unique sense of shared meaning in an organisation.

Organisational culture is a pattern of shared meanings held, to a greater or lesser degree, by all organisational members. Many organisational processes — and especially communication — should be thought of in terms of how organisation members understand and act on their interpretation of what the organisation is, what it has been previously, and what it may yet become. This set of shared understandings of the organisational culture can be thought of as the interpretive framework — or sense-making habits — of the organisation's members. If you understand enough of the company's organisational culture, then in many situations you can figure out what you need to do and say.

That is, employees need to have adequate cognitive maps to understand the various ways in which information is processed by the organisation, both formally and informally. This approach was elaborated in Weick's theory of organisation (1969). He saw organisations as constantly changing through the interdependent and interlocking communication behaviours of organisation members.

Another important emphasis in the definition of organisational culture is its reference to the importance of the symbolic and emotional components of organisational experience. Organisations are not just rational, information-processing machines; rather, as Weick satirises them, they can be 'garrulous, clumsy, superstitious, hypocritical, monstrous and grouchy'. In other words, they are made up of human beings. Deal and Kennedy (1982) outline the importance of values in organisations, of the importance of having organisational heroes, of the need for rites and rituals in organisations, and of the centrality of cultural communication networks.

organisational culture
The values and interpretive frameworks used to construct a unique sense of shared meaning in an organisation.

Chapter 9

organisational values
Shared beliefs about organisational activities that members use to make judgments about events in organisational life.

organisational heroes
Dominant people who imprint their vigorous personalities on the company culture.

organisational rites and rituals
In-house ceremonies by which the organisation validates its own cultural meanings.

Organisational values are the shared beliefs about organisational activities that members use to make judgments about events in organisational life. These values can sometimes be summed up as company slogans, some of which endure ('IBM Means Service') and some of which end up on the scrap heap of company history (the now bankrupt New South Wales car-dealer Tony Packard's 'Let me do it right for you'). Further, **organisational heroes** are those dominant people, usually the founding fathers (or, more rarely, mothers), who imprint their vigorous personalities on the company culture. This is what Henry Ford did in the US in the 1910s, or as ex-Australian Rupert Murdoch does with his media companies.

Organisational rites and rituals are those in-house ceremonies by which the organisation validates its own cultural meanings. This might be by regular award-giving ceremonies for best annual sales performance, or it might be indicated by the nature of company induction programs for new staff. It could be demonstrated by traditional retirement practices for older staff, ranging from a gold-watch presentation and a bonus in Western organisations, to singing special songs in Japan. Or it could be shown by the company's enthusiastic participation in national Best Practice awards. As part of these organisational rites and rituals a body of folklore, company stories and jokes may develop about well-known organisational members, which will circulate through informal communication networks.

However, the point of these various cultural practices, according to Deal and Kennedy, is to promote business success. That is, the fostering of the cultural features of organisational life is meant to promote the development of a 'strong' organisational culture. Organisations with 'weak' cultures, they maintain, can learn how to change their cultures into 'strong' ones. Here there is a rather sharp divergence in the organisational culture literature between approaches that seem to be promising simple and simplistic formulas for organisational change, and other analyses which are more cautious about changing organisations by tinkering with their cultures.

Symbolising organisational culture. Governor-General Bill Hayden announces prizewinners in the University of Canberra short story competition. (Photo: *John Holdsworth*)

Smircich & Callas (1987), for example, argue that organisational culture cannot be treated instrumentally. They maintain that it should be studied only with a view to understanding it. Organisational culture does not belong exclusively to management nor to shareholders: it should belong to every member of the organisation. 'Quick-fix' approaches to changing organisational culture may also underestimate the task. Schein (1985) argues that any significant degree of organisational change is difficult. It may take from four to five years or longer. Whether culture can be managed or not depends on a number of factors. These include the size of the organisation, the strength of the current culture, the particular stage of the organisational life-cycle the company is at, and the effectiveness of organisational leadership (Robbins & Barnwell, 1989: 311).

Exercise 9.7 Surveying organisational culture
Below is a draft interview schedule you could use to inquire into the culture of any organisation.

1. *Introductory*
(a) How long have you been with this company?
(b) How did your career in this organisation start?

2. *The organisation's mission*
(a) What is the basic business or purpose of this organisation?

3. *Rites, rituals, and ceremonies*
(a) How do you make decisions here?
(b) What special company events are celebrated?
(c) If you compared your organisation to an animal, which one would you choose?

4. *Language and power*
(a) What are the ways that employee or job positions are described here?
(b) Do you think this company speaks the same language as its competitors? What kind of language is it?
(c) Can anyone talk to anyone else in this business?

5. *Past and future*
(a) How did this company get started?
(b) Does your organisation have any particular heroes?
(c) What have been the most important events in the life of the company?
(d) What do you think it will be like here in five years time?

The class should form into groups and consider how this questionnaire could be adapted for different kinds of organisations, e.g. video rental stores, public service departments, computer companies, management consultancies, public relations firms, hospitals or retail stores.

Levels of analysis in organisational culture studies

One problem with organisational culture analyses is that some studies do not make it clear which level of analysis they are working on. Some confusion may arise because the concept of culture is such a broad one, so the three **levels of organisational culture analysis** need to be distinguished. First, the national culture in which the individual organisation is located; second, the particular

levels of organisational culture analysis
The different levels at which organisational culture can be studied: the level of the national culture; the particular industry context; and the subcultural variations within an organisation.

industry context in which the organisation is operating; and, third, the degree of subcultural variations within an organisation's dominant culture.

Beck and Moore's (1985) examination of the Canadian banking industry is a good example of research that does clearly identify elements of the national culture, and then shows how these relate to the organisation's culture. Their research on a selection of local branches of Canadian national banks relied on a literature study plus a critical incident series of interviews with local managers. They were asked to respond to a variety of hypothetical situations found in a local branch, both positive (the promotion of a good teller) and negative (offensive odours). Beck and Moore distinguished between the societal, organisational and branch levels of culture, with the aim of developing an ideal-type profile of what the 'typical' branch bank manager was like.

Their main conclusions were that the local managers had to deal with the problem of split loyalties, in that they were responsible to head office for enforcing central branch bank policies, but that they also had a personal loyalty to their own local branch workers. Beck and Moore argue that the banking industry culture was seeking to progress via gradual, orderly developments. However, this was threatened, first, by the role strain local managers experienced arising from their organisational positions and, second, by central branch pressures to shed staff due to rapid computerisation. In attempting to deal with these problems the best branch managers were described as playing the role of 'coach', which reflected Canadian national culture's respect for this role in sports like baseball and ice hockey.

The second level of analysis of organisational culture studies concerns the industry or sectoral service level. One of the best examples here is Evered's (1983) study of language in the US Navy as an indicator of corporate culture. His article relies on sociolinguistics and symbolic interactionist sociology to interpret the Navy's organisational culture from a detailed examination of its language. Evered discusses the confusion new recruits to the USN frequently undergo due to the highly specialised language and other complex communication systems used in the Navy, such as its signalling codes, its dress codes, and its detailed rules and regulations.

Evered analyses the way in which Navy language is used to induct new officers via Navy training programs, ceremonies and the use of historical models in education sessions. He then details the rich vocabulary of seafaring and the USN's extensive use of acronyms and abbreviations (e.g. CVN-65 = the USS Enterprise). His account concludes that specialised language is used in most organisations, including the Navy, to differentiate that group from others, and that organisational change requires a language change in the organisation. A comparable Australian study is More and Ross-Smith's (1990). Their research on a religious order with declining membership employed interviews, document analysis and a questionnaire to diagnose the association's problems.

The final level of organisational culture analysis concerns larger organisations where notable subcultures have developed within the organisation. This can take place either in departmental terms or geographically. In his study of the New Zealand Insurance Company in the 1980s, Hill (1991) drew a rather dismal picture of an organisation wracked by an intense period of change. The introduction of a major mainframe computing installation centralised decision making in the organisation and deskilled many work practices for lower level

This new sign at the University of Canberra, displaying the university logo and colours, was satirised by local student pranksters to represent petrol pumps.
(Photo: *Melinda Bromley*)

employees. Managers insisted the new technology was essential for the company, but few had terminals on their own desks.

These changes, which came after a difficult merger with another company and radical changes in senior management, led to a wave of staff retrenchments. The outcome was a 'split culture', or a kind of adversarial subculture. The new management culture was imbued with ideals of instrumental efficiency, but this coexisted uncomfortably alongside the lower-level culture where workers were relatively unattached to management's organisational goals. Hill's account of the divisive uses of new information technology is a salutary one. Whereas the NZI new managers saw the computer system as a symbol of company progress, many workers had negative or mixed feelings. The new, divided 'split culture' situation that resulted left management with more centralised power, but less flexibility to move in the future.

Communication and organisational culture

Analysing companies in terms of their organisational communication climate and their culture are important ways of understanding how well the organisation is working. Considering the horizontal, downwards and lateral flows of communication is essential in evaluating how the company's organisational structure is influencing communication, but attending to climate and culture gives us the possibility of more specific knowledge about communication factors affecting the company's performance. Organisations that have strong cultures and supportive communication climates will treat employees as their primary resource and have built-in feedback measures for ensuring communication channels are open and effective.

The main problem with climate measures is that they are static. They are based on subjective self-report measures and they have an individual bias, whereas much organisational work is done in groups. Considering an organisation's culture as a means of analysing how the organisation is communicating is potentially more useful, as culture analyses are neither individualistically biased nor static. On the other hand, there are no agreed methods of carrying out organisational culture studies. They are also likely to be time-consuming and their findings can be ambiguous. Climate studies are examples of quantitative research as described in Chapter 1, whereas culture studies are based on qualitative methods. In practice, there is a good case for using both approaches in researching organisational communication, as neither may be reliable or informative enough if used solely in its own right.

Summary

1. Organisations may be large or small, but it is important to distinguish between private and public sector organisations. Theories of organisations that are applicable to large companies may not apply to small business.
2. Organisational theories can be classified as either functionalist or meaning-centred. Classical, human relations, systems and culture theories have been the main approaches.
3. When employees first join an organisation they need to identify a career path. In doing so they should appropriately distinguish their personal and positional roles.
4. Organisations can be considered as open systems with internal and external environments, with goals, resources, technologies and outcomes. Organisational structure is the formal design of authority in the organisation.
5. Three main kinds of communication flows take place in organisations — downwards, upwards and laterally. The more formalised an organisation, the more emphasis will be placed on downwards communication.
6. The organisation's internal environment is its climate and culture. The organisational communication climate comprises the current feelings that members have about the levels of trust and openness there are in the communication process.
7. Organisational culture is a long-term set of values and sense-making practices that members use to explain organisational decisions and their own personal experience in the organisation. Organisational rites and rituals and organisational heroes are also part of organisational culture.
8. Organisational culture has three possible levels of analysis: first, the national culture: second, the industry the organisation is in: third, subcultures within the same organisation.

Discussion questions

1. Identify and discuss examples of large, medium and small private and public sector organisations. Which are the most effective?

2. Who are some of the theorists associated with functional and meaning-centred theories of organisations? What are their main differences?
3. In a large organisation, how are junior employees' relations with their supervisors likely to change through their first year in the job?
4. What are the main component parts of an organisation considered as an open system?
5. Discuss the interrelation between complexity, formalisation and centralisation in an organisation's structure.
6. What kinds of information will be communicated upwards, downwards and horizontally in organisations?
7. How can you define organisational communication climate? Is it different from organisational culture? How can it be measured?
8. What is meant by 'organisational culture'. How did it become to be considered important?
9. Distinguish between organisational values, artifacts, heroes, and organisational rites and rituals. What are some examples of these?
10. What are the four different levels at which organisational culture analysis can take place? How are they related?

Further reading

Bordow, A. & More, E. (1991) *Managing Organisational Communication* Melbourne: Longman Cheshire.

Evered, R. (1983) 'The Language of Organizations', pp. 125–144, in L. Pondy, (ed.) *Organizational Symbolism* Greenwich, CT: JAI Press.

Goldhaber, G. (1993) *Organizational Communication* Iowa: Wm. C. Brown. 6th edn.

Hill, S. (1991) 'White Collar Factory', pp. 114–49 in S. Aungles, (ed.) *Information Technologies in Australia* Sydney: UNSW Press.

Jablin, F. (1987) 'Organizational Entry, Assimilation and Exit', pp. 679–740 in F. Jablin, L. Putnam, K. Roberts & L. Porter, (eds) *Handbook of Organizational Communication* Newbury Park, CA: Sage.

More, E. & Ross-Smith, A. (1990) 'Organisational Communication — the Culture Approach', *Australian Journal of Communication* 17 (1): 98–113.

Pace, W. & Faules, D. (1989) *Organizational Communication* New Jersey: Prentice Hall, 2nd edn.

References

Beck, B. & Moore, L. (1985) 'Linking the Host Culture to Organizational Variables', pp. 335–54 in P. Frost, L. Moore, M. Louis, C. Lundberg & J. Martin, (eds) *Organizational Culture* Beverly Hills, CA: Sage.

Deal, T. & Kennedy, A. (1982) *Corporate Cultures* Reading, MA: Addison-Wesley.

Downs, C. (1988) *Communication Audits* New York: Scott, Foresman.

Downs, C. (1991) 'Audit Instrumentation in Organisational Communication', *Australian Communication Review* 12 (1): 45–70.
Dwyer, J. (1993) *The Business Communication Handbook* Sydney: Prentice Hall, 3rd edn.
Hazzard, S. (1967) *People in Glass Houses* Melbourne: Macmillan.
Irwin, H. & More, E. (1994) *Managing Corporate Communication* Sydney: Allen & Unwin.
Kriegler, R., Dawkins, P., Ryan, J. & Wooden, M. (1988) *Achieving Organizational Effectiveness* Melbourne: Oxford University Press.
Mintzberg, H. (1979) *The Structuring of Organizations* New Jersey: Prentice Hall.
Morgan, G. (1986) *Images of Organization* Beverly Hills, CA: Sage.
Ouichi, W. (1981) *Theory Z* New York: Avon Books.
Pascale, R. & Athos, A. (1982) *The Art of Japanese Management* London: Penguin.
Peters, T. & Waterman, R. (1982) *In Search of Excellence* New York: Harper & Row.
Putnam, L. & Pacanowsky, M. (eds) (1983) *Communication and Organizations* Beverly Hills, CA: Sage.
Robbins, S. & Barnwell, N. (1989) *Organisation Theory in Australia* Sydney: Prentice Hall.
Schein, E. (1985) *Organizational Culture and Leadership* San Francisco: Jossey-Bass.
Shockley-Zalaback, P. (1991) *Fundamentals of Organizational Communication* New York: Longman.
Smircich, L. & Callas, M. (1987) 'Organizational culture: A critical assessment', pp. 228–57 in F. Jablin, L. Putnam, K. Roberts & L. Porter, (eds) *Handbook of Organizational Communication* Newbury Park, CA: Sage.
Ticehurst, B. & Ross-Smith, A. (1992) 'Communication Satisfaction, Commitment, and Job Satisfaction in Australian Organisations', *Australian Journal of Communication* 19 (1): 130–45.
Weick, K. (1969) *The Social Psychology of Organizing* Reading, MA: Addison-Wesley.

Organisational communication (2) Networks, gender and power

10

Objectives

After completing this chapter you should be able to:

- explain the composition of organisational communication networks;
- distinguish between several different uses of networking in and across organisations;
- understand the concepts of gender-typed organisations and gender-based managerial stereotypes;
- discuss the use of personal influence strategies to deal with the problem of organisational resource dependency;
- be familiar with the communication implications of Industrial Democracy programs.

Before coming to the City of Women Ella had been in industry, one of those converted who had internalised the goals and methods of a large organisation. Her surrender of herself had been voluntary and complete.

'I considered that, in general, the goals of the organisation were superior to mine,' she told me. Something I could never have said about any organisation.

City of Women, *David Ireland*

This kind of scepticism about organisations is often widespread among young Australians, who fear their personal independence is likely to be limited by the rules and regulations endemic in organisations. Organisations, however, are the principal employers of most Australians, and learning to cope with their demands may be a prerequisite for having a job. This chapter will build on the previous one by considering the role of communication networks, gender and power in organisational life.

Organisational communication networks

Australians are all part of various social networks, regardless of their ethnic origin, their age or sex, and whether or not they have professional jobs. In the first instance, the one they are primarily embedded in is the intimate circle of their immediate family and close friends. Wrapped round that circle is usually another group of relations and good, but not so close, friends. Outside that there is usually a variety of links with others, who may be distant relations, acquaintances, work colleagues, neighbours, or members of various social, sporting, religious or community groups.

Although network studies agree that wherever they live people are part of their community via these interlocking networks, some students react with surprise when asked to identify their own. Possibly this is due to the high premium Australians place on social informality, or to the natural reluctance of young adults to acknowledge that they may have relatively fixed social identities. In any case, one feature of social networks which is of obvious importance to that age group is their own position in the social networks that form part of the labour market. Their success in negotiating those networks will influence their chances of gaining employment.

Social networks and job searching

Labour market networks have been discussed by Carson (1989) with reference to Australia, US and the UK. He analysed the way people use their social networks to look for work. Formal methods include responding to job advertisements and using public or private employment services, such as the CES. Informal methods are where job-seekers use their family, friends and acquaintances to find work. Often the most significant information may come from acquaintances seen infrequently, rather than close friends or relations. Though friends are likely to 'put in a good word' for job-seekers and thus play an advocacy part that acquaintances may not, the people with whom the unemployed person has relatively weak social ties are more likely to move in different social circles. They are therefore likely to be sources of newer information about jobs.

In contrast, if job-seekers rely on their own immediate personal contacts for job information they might find work more quickly, but it may be short-term and relatively insecure. This intepretation of job-search patterns and social networks implies that blue-collar workers — who rely more on personal and informal means of information acquisition about job possibilities — have more immediate advantages over white-collar workers, who take longer to find jobs. The reliance of white-collar workers on formal job-search networks, however, is likely to result in longer periods of unemployment, but positions finally obtained this way may be more secure. Women, according to Carson, rely less than men on extensive work-centred networks and more on intensive local networks of friends and family, and therefore are likely to be relatively disadvantaged in the labour market.

Exercise 10.1 Analysing your communication networks

This is a simple example of how you could go about gathering data on communication network relationships in an organisation.

Draw up a table like the one shown below. Write your name and degree specialisation (eg., public relations) in 001. Write the name of a fellow student you see regularly in 002. Write the name of your specialisation coordinator in 003.

Then give a rating score for how you communicate with your fellow student, with your specialisation coordinator, and with the university administration respectively about the following subjects:

coursework; personal matters; university enrolment matters.

Score your answers using this scale.

Communication frequency:
  1 = once a semester
  2 = once a month
  3 = several times a month
  4 = once a week
  5 = several times weekly

Communcation importance: 1 (low) to 10 (high)
Communication satisfaction: 1 (low) to 10 (high)

For example, with coursework:

	Frequency	Importance	Satisfaction
001 Chloe Wang Public Relations	—	—	—
002 Jack Kesteven	5	8	8
003 Petra Gravy	3	7	7
004 Administration	—	—	—

Then repeat the process for 'personal matters' and 'university enrolment matters'. When complete, discuss:
- which section of the university body (students, staff or administration) do you have most contact with for each matter

- which of these contacts gives you the most satisfaction
- how you could make the instrument more comprehensive and accurate

Organisational communication network properties

When you first join an organisation it is a relatively easy matter to get some sense of the organisation's formal structure. You can do this by examining the company's organisation chart and the official procedures manual, or by receiving training about organisational procedures in an induction session. However, there is a more vital dimension to how communication actually works in the organisation — the existence of informal networks.

organisational communication networks Regular patterns of interaction and interdependence among organisational members.

Organisational communication networks are the regular patterns of interaction and interdependence among organisational members. These link the communication behaviours of organisation members in terms of both their formal positional and informal personal roles. They are used by organisation members to exchange information and ideas, to express interpersonal liking or dislike, to attempt to exert influence in the organisation, and sometimes to exchange goods and services. Tichy (1979) defines these four kinds of communication network functions as meeting cognitive, affective, power and instrumental needs respectively.

One way to grasp the principle of what organisational communication networks are quickly is by considering them diagrammatically. For instance, Figure 10.1 shows a cross-section of organisational communication networks and individual member roles. Note that this diagram is not the result of a communication network analysis, but only a model of preliminary findings representing who communicates with whom. The most common individual roles are those of clique members, bridges, liaisons and isolates. Before defining these, however, let us consider the diagram from an overall perspective.

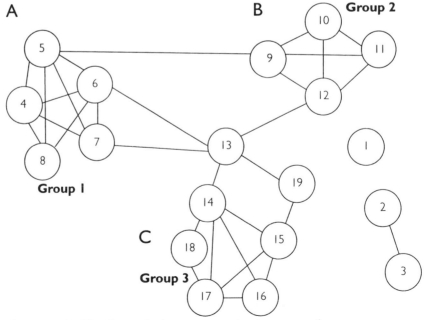

Figure 10.1 *Member roles in a communication network*

What the figure suggests is that in this work group there are nineteen people. There are three main 'clusters', i.e. points where communication is most reciprocal between members of a subgroup. The three clusters are Groups A, B and C, with A and C being five-person clusters and B a four-person cluster. It also suggests there is a high degree of density in the work group. That is, the number of actual links in the network as a ratio of the number of total possible links is quite high. So 'density' in a communication network means the degree of potential member inter-connectedness. The diagram also suggests that fourteen members of the three clusters A, B and C are all members of interlocking personal networks, or cliques. Members 13, 19, 1, 2 and 3, however, are not members of any of these three clusters.

The five individual roles played by the various network members are labelled cliques, bridges, liaisons, isolates and stars. A clique, or subgroup, is the heart of the network system. A **clique** is a subgroup in the department, composed of members who have at least half their contacts with each other. Clique members are also linked to all other members in the subgroup and each clique must consist of at least three members. So, in Figure 10.1, there are three cliques — A, B and C. Note, however, that some clique members have overlapping roles — i.e. some will also act as bridges, but not as liaisons.

The difference between these two roles is that a **bridge** (5 or 9) is a clique member, with most of their communication links within the subgroup, but who has one or more links with a member of another clique. In contrast, a **liaison** (13) is not a member of one of the original cliques. Instead a liaison is the person who links two or more cliques within the work unit. The importance of distinguishing liaisons from bridges is that message distortion is more likely when subgroup links are provided by bridges rather than liaisons (Farace, 1977). People who become liaisons in organisations are also likely to act as informal leaders. They are likely to have been organisational members for some time and to have higher formal organisational status. They will convey a sense of 'knowing the ropes'.

Two more individual roles are important — isolates and stars. First, there are **isolates**. This may be a person with few communication links in the organisation. In technical terms this person is described as a 'true isolate'(1). There may also be two individuals in that role (an 'isolated dyad': 2 or 3) or there may be an 'isolated group'. For instance, in a three-division organisation, one division may see itself 'on the outer' from the other two. In daily organisational life drawing this distinction is not so clear-cut. Some participants might be network members, but may not be influential with other groups; this could be true, for instance, of members in the A, B and C groups who do not have bridging roles.

There is less ambiguity about who an organisation's **stars** are. These are people, usually in leadership and or liaison positions, who receive the highest number of nominations as a communication link by other organisational members. One of the greatest means of influence organisational leaders may have is their 'network centrality'. That is, the organisational star, or effective organisational leader, ensures a position central to organisational activity. In Figure 10.2 this is member 13. This person is in a position of information and communication richness, where important information about organisational decisions and plans is both given out and received.

network clique
A subgroup in the network, composed of members who have at least half their contacts with each other; a clique must have at least three members.

network bridge
A clique member, most of whose communication links are within his or her subgroup, but with one or more links to a member of another clique.

network liaison
A person who links two or more cliques within the work unit.

network isolate
A person with few communication links in the organisation.

network star
The person who receives the highest number of nominations as a communication link by other organisational members.

Chapter 10

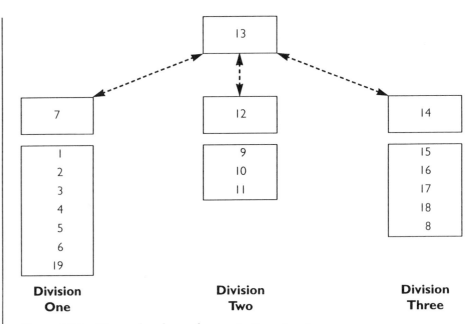

Figure 10.2 *Network roles and organisation structure*

Here it is helpful to reconsider the relation between communication networks and organisational structure. Figure 10.2 shows this particular organisation's hierarchy divided up vertically in terms of the chain-of-command, and horizontally in terms of its divisional structure. What is important is how the organisation's existing communication networks 'fit' the organisational hierarchy. **Organisational communication fit** is the extent to which the organisation's informal communication networks adequately match the organisation's official hierarchy. If there is a good 'fit', there will be a high degree of overlap between the communication network and the organisation chart. There will be reasonable congruence between formal and informal communication and decision-making channels. The smaller the organisation, the more likely this 'fit' will be achieved (Monge & Eisenberg, 1987).

Though our example shows an organisation where there is a relatively good 'fit', it still indicates several points where communication breakdowns might happen. Taking Figures 10.1 and 10.2 together, the good news is that the organisation leader, member 13, has a high degree of network centrality. Further, the three divisional managers (members 7, 12 and 14) are well-placed in their own cliques as they are already acting as secondary bridges for their cliques via member 13. Yet there are several potential trouble-spots. Division One, for example, has eight members, as opposed to Division Two's four members, and Division Three's six members, and three of Division One's members have been identified in the network diagram as organisational isolates. Can you identify more potential troublespots?

A central role is also played in the organisation's external dealings with its environment through its gatekeepers. **Gatekeepers** are those organisation members who are positioned in networks where they can control information flows into or across the organisation. Senior 'stars' in the organisation are likely to have important gatekeeper roles in keeping their own organisation members

organisational communication fit
The extent to which an organisation's informal communication networks match its official hierarchy.

gatekeepers
Organisation members who are positioned in networks so that they can control information flows into, out of, or across the organisation.

224

in touch with what is happening in the organisation's external environment. There is also likely to be a range of significant gatekeeper roles played by other liaisons in the organisation (Tichy, 1979).

Exercise 10.2 Quiz on communication networks
Re-match the first part of the following statements with their correct second parts.
1. Gatekeepers
2. Liaisons have
3. Isolates have
4. A bridge is
5. A clique is
6. Stars

A. have the highest number of communication links.
B. few communication links in the organisation.
C. links with two or more cliques.
D. a sub-group whose members have at least half their links with each other.
E. a clique member who has links with another clique.
F. control information flows.

The uses of communication network concepts

The main use of communication network analysis is for the purposes of improving organisational design — by matching the official organisation chart with data about actual networks. This may help in finding solutions to problems in organisational structure, such as changing the divisional basis of an organisation. It might also be useful in designing options for workplace stations, or in the development of telephone network systems. These kinds of uses of network analysis, however, are constrained practically by the complexity and cost of network measurement.

Since the development and use of computer-based communication network analysis in the 1980s, however, the concept of networks has acquired a range of expanded meanings. First, network ideas have been important in explaining and predicting the role of communications technology in organisations. Second, there is a growing emphasis on intra-organisational network building as effective management. Third, there is a neofeminist concept of networking as a means for people to advance their careers. Additionally, some cross-cultural studies of organisations have highlighted the growing importance of networked forms of enterprise.

Information networking. This is the way that information is used to communicate in organisations. Ideas of the 'networked nation' and a 'wired society' have become part of the folklore of the later twentieth century. It is a fact that modern organisations are the heartland of the new communication technologies. Just as business organisations were the first to acquire telephones in the 1880s, they were the first to introduce mainframe computers to the workplace in the 1950s, and PCs (personal computers) in the 1980s. Currently US, European and Japanese organisations are in the forefront of experimenting with digitally converging forms of information technology. Most important now are ISDN (Integrated Standard Digital Networks) systems — which can combine voice, data, image, text and video — local area networks (LANs) for PCs (personal computers), wide area networks (WANs) for mainframes, and phone-based computerised PABXs (Personalised Automated Branch Exchanges) (Bordow & More, 1991).

The introduction of these technologies is as important for their potential effects on the social nature of work — for example, the shift to home working and more casual and part-time work — as for productivity increases. Whether

information networking
The way that information technology is used to communicate in organisations.

this will really benefit society or further divide it remains to be seen. Australian agencies such as the Commission for the Future, and the South Australian government's Multi Function Polis (MFP), are now concerned that Australians should be both technologically and Asia literate (James, 1990). Some critics, however, have expressed doubts about the ways in which technology is being used to increase employer power and as a potential means of social surveillance, as in debates over a national ID card. There is also the issue of how new technologies differentially affect men and women in the workplace (Hackett, 1991).

Managerial networking. This is how managers build interpersonal influence coalitions within organisations. Managers need to build networks in their organisations and one way of doing this is via information and communication strategies (Irwin & More, 1994: 83–93). This argument applies especially to the managerial communication methods needed to plan, implement and follow through organisational change. The securing of a commitment from an influential cross-section of organisation members by top management is essential if new programs are to be successful. In securing this commitment, managers need to build their own personal influence networks. Conversely, new or junior members of organisations need to understand organisational politics enough to recognise that they may have to take sides in power struggles to retain their own positions.

One study of the uses of networking by managers drew a distinction between those who were 'effective' and those who were 'successful'. Networking was defined here as 'interacting with others' and 'socialising and politicking'. What made effective managers were the perceptions of the managers' performance by their own subordinates, in terms of overall unit performance. In contrast, managers identified as 'successful' were those who had advanced rapidly to a senior managerial position, but did not have the level of subordinate support which effective managers had achieved (Fulop et al., 1992).

Career networking. This is how individuals consciously develop interpersonal networks to advance their professional interests. There is now a neofeminist emphasis on networking for success. A number of prominent Australian women have reasoned that as traditionally men use their 'old boy' networks to advance their careers, so women should use a similar strategy. Women in business, management, administration, the professions and academic life should develop and practise networking strategies of their own. Ideally these associations would not discriminate against men, but actively promote the interests of women (Still, 1990). These loose networks may be specific to particular industries, such as the Australian Women in Publishing group, formed in the mid-1980s along the lines of a British model for women working in book and magazine publishing, or they may be less industry-specific. Such moves for senior women to play mentoring roles towards the development of younger women's careers is a positive means of striving for gender equality in Australian life.

Organisational networking. This is the way organisations form interorganisational networks to defend their business or professional interests. Some analysts see this as a growing trend in Western economies, while others view it as a characteristic of many of the rapidly growing North-East Asian economies. Powell (1990), for example, argues that network forms of organisation have

---

managerial networking
How managers build interpersonal influence coalitions within organisations.

career networking
How individuals develop interpersonal contacts to advance their professional interests.

organisational networking
The way organisations form interorganisational links to defend their business or professional interests.

been adopted in high-tech industries in the US's 'Silicon Valley', as well as in small manufacturing companies in Northern Italy. These forms are more flexible than those of large companies, more open to innovation, and offer greater job satisfaction for their employees.

The network forms of organisation model may also explain the relative success of enterprises in Japan and in the 'Four Little Dragons' — Taiwan, Hong Kong, Singapore and South Korea. Tam (1990), for example, argues that Chinese family firms in Hong Kong have a typically centrifugal growth tendency, in contrast with the centripetal tendencies of large Japanese trading firms. However, what these often diverse Asian societies have in common is the way in which they tend to structure their family-based enterprises along network lines, in contrast to the traditionally individualistic models used in European and American business.

Exercise 10.3 Role-playing a job selection interview
Have two class members spend 15 minutes preparing to apply for jobs they have previously written job application letters for (See Dwyer, 1993: 445). Three class members should prepare to interview them on the basis of their applications and résumés. Appoint two observers — one for the applicants and one for the selection panel. The interviews should be 10-15 minutes each. Afterwards the panel should choose one applicant and explain their reasons. The observers should then report.

Possible questions to be asked (See Dwyer, 1993: 483):
1. Why do you want this particular job?
2. Tell us about yourself.
3. How does your education relate to your ability to do this job?
4. Tell us about your personal strengths and weaknesses.
5. What are your long-term career goals?
6. Do you have any problems working for a woman boss?
7. Have you had much experience working with other people?
8. How would you handle a difficult customer or client?
9. Tell us about your previous boss.
10. What questions would you like to ask us?

Instructions for panel observer
Did the panel . . .
1. Divide questions up appropriately among themselves?
2. Address the selection criteria thoroughly?
3. Record significant information?
4. Make the applicants feel at ease?
5. Give the applicants the opportunity to ask them questions?

Instructions for applicant observer
Did the applicant . . .
1. Make a confident entry and exit?
2. Speak fluently throughout the interview?
3. Deal effectively with questions about selection criteria?
4. Volunteer appropriate favourable additional information?
5. Maintain eye contact with the panel?

Chapter 10

Gender and communication at work

gender-based managerial stereotypes
Negative attitudes about men and women, either as managers or as co-workers, which act as an obstacle to effective communication.

Gender-based managerial stereotypes are negative managerial stereotypes about men and women either as managers or as co-workers, which act as an obstacle to effective communication. These may relate to the ability of men or women to be competent managers, or they may refer to the different attitudes men and women workers may have towards new technology (Hackett, 1991).

Managerial stereotypes and gender-typed organisations

One early US argument used to explain women's lack of business success was the idea that they were afraid of success. More recent cognitively based studies of women's careers by some Australian psychologists have rejected this earlier focus on the internal psychological characteristics of women. Instead, they emphasise the importance of the structural limitations experienced by many women in the workplace. So, for example, the difficulties of child-bearing and possible subsequent role conflict for married and single-parent working women may lead to major discontinuities in their careers and result in fewer promotions (Tharenou, 1990: 366).

Another recent US psychological analysis by Powell et al. (1984) of sex effects on managerial value systems considered the relative perceptions about success for both men and women managers. Based on a random sample of 6000 managers, 10 per cent of whom were women, it used 130 men and the same number of women executives in comparable age, salary and managerial categories. The study cited previous findings which associated 'masculine' characteristics — such as dominance, ambition and independence — with men, and 'feminine' traits — such as nurturance, submissiveness and sensitivity to the needs of others — with women. However, Powell's conclusion was that women managers showed more concern for production-oriented goals, such as high productivity and efficiency (1984: 918).

Whether psychological or sociological research methods are used to investigate workplace attitudes, however, one negative stereotype of women as bad managers persistently surfaces. This is the stereotype of the 'mean and bossy woman boss'. The pervasiveness of this image has been discussed by the US pro-feminist management theorist Kanter (1979). She lists several features of this 'bossy woman boss' stereotype:

1. Women bosses are too jealous ('They're bossy!')
2. Women bosses take things too personally ('They're too emotional!')
3. Women bosses are too concerned with details ('They're petty!')
4. Women bosses supervise too closely ('They don't delegate!')
5. Women bosses find fault more often ('They're too critical!')

Both Kanter and Australian management Professor Leonie Still acknowledge that research does show that many women, like men, dislike women bosses. Still points out, however, that while people can say what they dislike about women bosses, they find it hard to agree on what their desirable qualities are. She also considers that women's managerial styles may offend because they breach conventional expectations that women should be soft and considerate (Still, 1990: 93).

Kanter's explanation of these particular negative projections about women as bosses is that such stereotypes are a perfect picture of powerless people. That is, that women (and men) who feel they are in powerless organisational positions tend to engage in these kinds of negative behaviours. While pre-war theories about the nature of male managerial leadership tended to identify personal traits that good managers were supposed to have, more recent studies of these trait-based explanations have not justified them. That is, ideas that there could be a 'Great Man' or 'Captain of Industry' theory of leadership were just as misleading as some of the current prejudices about women necessarily being bad managers.

In the same way that trait theories of leadership are usually no longer accepted, there has been a move away from the exclusive study of women who are successful managers — or the 'Enterprising Women', as Still's study describes them. One problem with this approach is that it is elitist and fails to address the issue of divisions among women. The great majority of women in the workforce, even in Western countries where generally women have greater freedom, are not managers, but usually work in lower-level managerial, clerical or manual labour jobs (Alvesson & Billing, 1992). Accordingly we will look at the position of Australian secretaries later in this section.

Award-winning University of Canberra teacher Penny Collings in action. (Photo: *Australian Academy of Science*)

A more positive approach to innovative research about gender in the workplace is Wicker and Burley's study (1991) of how husbands and wives work together in establishing new businesses. They describe this trend as 'close-coupling in work-family relationships'. By 'close-coupling' they mean work situations where married couples are obliged to participate together. Their Californian material examined how married couples in business together applied different norms — such as equity and hierarchy — to the overlapping spheres of their home and work activity. It focused on twenty-four new retail and service establishments, such as women's clothing stores, restaurants and car repair shops, where the business was the family's primary way of making a living. They classified the enterprises into male-type (car repairs), female-type (florists) and gender-neutral (video rentals).

The researchers assumed that the decision-making process between the partners had a high potential for tension and conflict, particularly as among US retail and service businesses the two-year survival rate — the time period of their study — was roughly 50 per cent. They also assumed the partners would differentially apply an equity norm in making decisions about the relative effort to be put into the work and family spheres. Wicker's findings confirmed that partners did have different spheres of influence. There was a predictably greater expenditure of hours worked by either the husband or the wife, depending on the gender-type of the enterprise.

In the gender-neutral firms, the spouses worked roughly equal hours. But where the businesses were gender-typed, the other spouse typically chose to do the clerical work. So there was a mutual recognition of a hierarchy of expertise in allocating their efforts to what each could do best. In the businesses that survived, the spouses reported a greater closeness, a sense of sharing and reduced tension in their marriages. Those businesses that had failed, however, had adversely affected the relationships, which sometimes ended in divorce. The successful couples had resolved the division of labour issues between themselves without talking much about the mattter.

What happens in larger organisations, however, especially when they are gender-typed organisations with a traditionally masculine culture, is another story. Researchers in this area of gender and communication at work are only beginning to identify some of the key issues. One possibility is that of **classifying organisations by gender-type.** This was suggested by organisational culture researchers, such as Deal and Kennedy (1982), who talked of particular industries having implicit gender dimensions. So, for instance, they described the banking and insurance industry as being a 'process' culture, where managers were typically cautious and had long-term planning horizons. The mining industry, in contrast, was a 'bet your company' culture, where managers were expected to be entrepreneurial high-risk takers.

A similar classification of organisations by cultural types was pursued in Australia by Pringle (1988) in analysing the work of secretaries. Though her main interest was in the gendered construction of their role as women workers, some of her analysis of companies, particularly private sector ones, suggested the idea of gender-types or styles of masculinity or femininity, which set the prevailing interpersonal climate in those organisations. Pringle studied a manufacturing company, a large national retailer, and a conglomerate trader with interests in transport, travel and finance. She classified companies in terms of their styles of masculinity, which set gender behaviour expectations for both men and women. The manufacturing group she characterised as 'Manufacturing macho', the retailer had a style of 'Retailing paternalism', and the trading company was a '[Patrician] conglomerate' (1988: 104–13).

After comparing gender roles in several public sector agencies, including a union organisation, she concluded: 'A variety of styles of masculinity were constructed ... ranging from working class brutality, gentlemanly sadism, paternalism, liberal rationality, socialist mateship, and fraternal back-slapping'. These were all considered as oppressive to secretaries, while the best employer

gender-typed organisations
Organisations where certain gender-types, or styles of masculinity and femininity, set the prevailing interpersonal climate.

was not the union organisation, but one of the private companies. Pringle's work, along with that of other researchers, such as Game and Pringle (1983), Williams (1988), Still (1990) and Burton (1991), is part of an ongoing effort to apply feminist perspectives to the Australian workplace.

Exercise 10.4   Life goals inventory
One method used by vocational counsellors is to have young people undertake a life goals inventory with the aim of clarifying their possible vocational career paths.

For the life goals listed underneath, write down your own personal preferences, then score their importance to you on a scale of 1 (low) to 10 (high).

Life goals
1. What specific job or career do you want, including a position you would like to hold?
2. What professional, business or community groups do you aspire to belong to and how important is it for you to join them?
3. What importance do you place on personal relationships in your life, with parents, colleagues, friends and people generally?
4. What kinds of leisure activities do you wish to pursue and how important are they to you?
5. What kinds of further educational aims do you have and how important are they to you?

- Now go back through the goal list and score them again in terms of your opinion of how difficult they will be to achieve.
- Next prioritise the five goals in order of their importance to you.
- Finally write down what you think the priorities for the same goals would be for a member of the opposite sex who is your age and from a similar social background.

Gender equity issues in the public and private sectors

One recurrent theme that arises in Australian and British studies of **gender equity programs**, which are designed to equalise the position of the sexes in the workplace, is the importance of the public sector in initiating gender equity reforms. Pringle's study, for example, contrasted the private sector in Australia as a prospective employer for secretaries with the public sector. Working secretaries see private sector employment as more demanding and pressurised than the public sector, but also as more exciting to work in and as a source of greater potential earnings. Secretaries who are in the private sector are more often non-union members than those in the public sector.

Cynthia Cockburn (1991) similarly contrasted employer styles in the British public and private sectors by comparing a large retail company with a branch of the Civil Service. She labels the company 'High St Retail', a large organisation employing 30 000 people in shops, offices, warehouses and distribution centres, with 75 per cent of its workforce female. Tasks within the company were highly gender-segregated — men loaded the goods and drove vans, while women keyed in data and worked as cashiers and sales assistants. Before the introduction of an EO (Equal Opportunities) program in the firm and an intake of new employees with more diverse ethnic origins, High St Retail's culture was family-style caring, but also authoritarian and patriarchal.

By the end of the 1980s a new EO program had been introduced; it was taken

gender equity programs
Organisational programs designed to equalise the position of the sexes in the workplace.

seriously, staffed by feminist members, and supported by one influential family member on the Board of Directors. Some progress had been made in the employment of black staff members, who had been almost non-existent in the firm previously, and more women were being inducted into training positions in branch store management. However, women union representatives considered no significant career gains had been made by manual women employees, who were some 80 per cent of the female staff. Also, though women had moved into the classic route to company managerial career paths as trainee branch store managers, top positions were now going to men with computer and marketing backgrounds.

She contrasts this attempt at the reform of organisational gender equity policies with a more successful program in 'The Service', a branch of the British Civil Service, with thousands of employees in its London Head Office and elsewhere around the country. Staff in 'The Service' traditionally had been in a three-tier pyramid, with an 'elite corps' recruited from universities on top, followed by 'the clerical grades' recruited from schools at about age sixteen, and on the bottom 'unestablished' typists, telephonists and porters.

When this highly inequitable structure was drastically changed in the 1980s, part of the change was a positive employment policy for gender and racial equality. In contrast with the experience of 'High St Retail', civil service unions were closely involved. 'The Service' subsequently introduced a variety of reforms that provided women with better opportunities for selection and promotion and more flexible working hours. Some women still felt that male prejudice against women in senior posts remained. Lastly, others believed that the 'real men' in 'The Service' were now staying long enough to learn valuable management skills but then leaving for higher-paid positions in business.

This suggests that, even in the context of a strongly pro-business government, gender equity reform policies may be easier to implement in the public sector. The Australian experience is similar, where EEO (Equal Employment and Opportunity) programs have been pioneered by the federal and some state public sectors since the mid-1970s. This is not to say that the private sector has always lagged behind, as some companies, notably Esso — a traditionally male gender-typed organisation — under its equity-minded Director, Jim Kirk, became the first to introduce EEO programs and encourage the employment and promotion of female staff.

Australian EEO programs

The legislation that established Australian EEO programs was the *Public Service Reform Act* of 1984, the *Affirmative Action Act* of 1986, which extended policies to the private sector and tertiary education, and the *Sex Discrimination Act* of 1984 prohibiting sexual harassment. EEO programs aim to benefit women and three other designated target groups — migrants, Aborigines, and the mentally and physically handicapped. The overall aim of EEO policies is to eliminate discrimination against those groups. The only exceptions made to EEO provisions are for those jobs where either discrimination may reasonably be required (e.g. minimum age requirements for apprentices), or where the appointment of people from a certain background is desirable (e.g. Aboriginal recruitment).

The supervisory body which administers these Acts is the national Joint

Council on EEO, chaired by the secretary of the Department of Industrial Relations. In most organisations, private and public, there is now an EEO program directed by an EEO officer, who is usually — though not always — a woman. The function of the EEO officer in organisations is to plan, monitor, and evaluate EEO programs for that organisation. There are five main phases in doing this: the preliminary commitment phase, information gathering, planning, implementation and monitoring.

In the preliminary commitment phase, the EEO officer will work closely with a designated senior executive who has been made responsible for the program. At this stage the EEO officer needs to win commitment for the program from this senior executive, who is also her superior, as well as from other organisation members. Staff and union associations need to be involved. Successful organisation change policies can only work properly when supported both by senior management and line and staff employees.

What the EEO officer does then is to draw up a staffing profile of the organisation. This identifies the existing position of women and other target groups in the company hierarchy, and sets targets for improving the representation of those groups at more senior levels. The development, implementation and monitoring of these plans is an ongoing process that may extend over several years. A key factor in its success is attention to staff recruitment and promotion practices, and attention may be given, for instance, to the organisation's methods of advertising job vacancies or its internal promotion interview procedures. Based on a statistical profile of the organisation's staff, the EEO program will undertake forward planning for the career progression of the target groups.

Legislative programs alone, however, are insufficient to change people's attitudes and behaviour. Real progress has been made in the last decade in Australian organisations in redressing gender imbalances, but a Senate Committee 1992 Report *Half Way to Equal* found that less than three per cent of women at work were in senior managerial positions. It remains to be seen whether the Report's recommendation that gender equity provisions be incorporated into the *Training Guarantee Act* will be acted on. However, the position of women in Australian organisations is still better than that of women in Japan. Japanese traditional cultural values, as well as the legacy of the 1947 Labour Standards Law, have firmly kept most Japanese women in domestic roles. The introduction of an EEO law in 1986, as part of the international United Nations program for the elimination of discrimination against women, stopped Japanese companies saying they could not hire women, but so far the Act has had limited effect (Tanaka, 1990).

Exercise 10.5 Drafting an EEO policy statement

Using the outline above and the following information, draft a policy statement (about 500 words) for the Department of Extraordinary Affairs, a medium-sized department, explaining the policy. The statement should briefly refer to:

- The EEO provisions of the *Public Service Act*.
- The Department's commitment to promote EEO for women and other specified groups.
- The benefits to the Department of the program.
- Actions to assign EEO responsibilities to all managers and supervisors.

- The continuing importance of the Public Service merit principle.
- The name of the senior executive responsible for EEO (Carlos Castenada).
- The name and responsibilities of the EEO coordinator (Vera Vincente).
- The five main stages of the program.
- That measurable results and ongoing evaluation are essential to the program.

Power and communication in organisations

empowerment
Ways in which new opportunities for participation can be opened up for women and other minority groups at work.

To participate effectively at work we need to have some appreciation of the way that power operates in and around organisations. The strategies adopted by EEO officers just described are centrally concerned with the issue of **empowerment**, i.e. the ways in which new opportunities for participation can be opened up for women and other minority groups at work. The relationship between power and communication in organisational life therefore requires discussion.

Here Frost's (1987) analysis is helpful. He maintains that in organisations communication needs to be considered both as a medium and as meaning. First, communication channels are the means by which power flows through the organisation. Because of the ways in which organisational members use communication channels and networks to make decisions and allocate resources, the organisational communication medium is never neutral. It is always likely to favour one set of organisational interests over others. When new members enter organisations they bring with them expectations based on their previous experience about how communication practices should work. In reality, however, the organisation will have a history of its own with accepted ways of communicating. If new entrants disagree with these they will have to spend time and energy in working to change them.

Communication practices are also one of the principal means by which organisation members create a sense of shared meaning about their work (Ticehurst et al., 1991). Communicative power is practised through the language and symbols used in the organisation — in the organisational stories, myths, rituals, metaphors and jokes that shape organisational discourse. Frost suggests that this level of the relation between communication and power in organisations reflects the 'deep structure' of the organisation. In contrast, the first level previously discussed, concerning communication channels and networks, is more indicative of the organisational 'surface structure'. This distinction emphasises the historical, dynamic nature of organisations, and signals to us that organisational communication analysis should not be restricted to examinations of message and information flows.

Coalitions, influence strategies and resource dependency

external coalitions
The external coalition in an organisation represents the interests of the company's owners and directors.

internal coalitions
The internal coalition of an organisation represents management and staff.

Another way of thinking about the relationship between power and communication in organisations has been suggested by Mintzberg (1983). He focused on which interests are most likely to be influential in making and communicating decisions. Though his model is that of US private business, part of it is also applicable to Australian experience. Mintzberg labels the two main players in organisational power games **the external** and **the internal coalition**.

The main difference is that the external coalition represents the interests of the company's owners and directors, while the internal coalition represents management and staff.

The external coalition is composed of, first, the owners; second, the company's associates (suppliers, clients, competition, and any partners); third, relevant associations (unions and concerned professional associations); fourth, the organisation's publics (the general public, special interest groups, and all forms of government agencies interested in the company); last, there are the company directors, who are normally a cross-section of the above groups. The company directors occupy a particularly strategic position in the organisation's politics as they are at the interface of the external and internal coalitions.

In practice, however, the daily management of the organisation is most likely to be the business of the internal coalition. This is made up of, first, the CEOs (chief executive officers — the top management); second, the line managers; third, the operators (the workers who produce the goods and services); fourth, the technocratic analysts (the staff specialists in planning systems, such as computing); and last, the support staff (cafeteria, cleaners, postal and so on). Mintzberg's classification reflects his own analysis of how organisations are typically structured. It is most likely to be applicable to large and medium-sized organisations.

The advantage of this concept of coalitions as the main organisational power-brokers is that it emphasises the group nature of organisational dynamics. Individuals in organisations occupy particular positions, but the power and influence they can exert depends on how they interact with other members about communicating and decision making. That is, the exercise of communication and influence in organisations can be understood by identifying, first, what the dominant coalitions are and, second, the individual roles played by persons in those coalitions.

It is also possible to examine the flows of communication and power in organisations from an individual perspective. In discussing how women may develop better career paths, Kanter (1979) argues that new organisational members quickly need to form personal alliances. These may be with their superiors (people in more powerful organisational positions who can assist the newcomer), or with peers (colleagues on the same level) or with subordinates. This sounds straightforward, but for newcomers in a large organisation even the identification of people at these three levels may be difficult.

Further, in considering the new organisational members' options in dealing with power issues, Mintzberg (1983) considers there are only three choices. First, new entrants can choose to stay and contribute to the organisation without criticising it. He calls this the loyalty option (where people tacitly say 'Shut up and deal. Get on with the job'). Second, if they feel strongly disturbed about problems in the organisation, or if they have better employment possibilities elsewhere, they have the option of leaving ('I'll take my marbles and go'). Third, they can decide to stay and change the system; he labels this the 'voice' option (where people take the attitude 'I'd rather stay and fight than leave'). In other words, the person can actively seek to become an influencer and aim to change organisational practices.

Individuals who choose to attempt to become influential in the organisation have a range of persuasive strategies they can adopt (Kaye, 1994). Their success

influence strategies
The persuasive options that individuals have in exercising their organisational influence.

will depend on their goals, their ability to form coalitions with others interested in influencing the organisation, and the particular situation of the organisation. The **influence strategies**, or the persuasive options that individuals have in exercising their organisational influence, have strong similarities to those of the standard strategies of interpersonal persuasion. Some of the most important are:

- the use of reason and logical argument;
- coalition formation through the mobilisation of others;
- ingratiation via the creation of goodwill;
- bargaining via the exchange of benefits and favours;
- assertiveness by taking a direct, forceful approach;
- appealing to higher authorities in the organisation;
- sanctions via the use of organisational rewards and punishments.

The wisdom of pursuing these particular influence strategies can only be judged in the context of the particular situations of individuals in their organisation and the accuracy of their own perceptions of what is appropriate and ethical behaviour. Although any recommendation about how individuals can be influential in their own organisations is necessarily limited by these factors, it is possible to identify two important frameworks that the individual has to work through.

resource dependency
A theoretical perspective that considers that organisational influence is most likely to be won by those who can provide critical resources to other organisation members.

The first of these is recognition of the importance of **resource dependency** in most organisations. Resources in any organisation are necessarily limited and there is ongoing competition between organisational members for the allocation of those resources. It follows that organisational power and influence are most likely to be won by those actors (in the role-playing sense) who can control and provide critical resources to other organisational members. Resources may be expertise, information, personal contacts, money, or whatever else is considered critical for the organisation at that time. Organisations attempt to deal with resource dependency by networking with other organisations. The extent to which organisations pursue these inter-organisational linkages is one of the more hotly debated topics in the literature on organisations. Theorists such as Pfeffer, who see interest group conflicts as an unavoidable result of organisations being powerful, take a pluralist view of this issue. In contrast, critical theorists such as Morgan (1990: 186) argue that organisations use their inter-organisational networks as a means of consolidating positions of market dominance.

Resource acquisition is considered to be one of the main tasks of senior executives in organisations. They are expected, because of their high personal and community status and the depth of their professional and business experience, to be linked with significant others external to their own organisations. Individual power based on the solution of resource dependency issues is likely to be greater when organisations are operating in rapidly changing environments, such as high-tech or mining companies. Conversely, more bureaucratic organisations, such as hospitals, are likely to face more stable environments and are therefore less likely to be open to major organisational change.

The second main factor determining the success of any particular influence strategy is the *personality traits* of the individual. The personality attributes,

Organisational communication (2)

The tasks of senior executives — Don Aitken, Vice-Chancellor of the University of Canberra, opens a new building with Education Minister Kim Beasley and Chancellor Donald Horne. (Photo: *Cecilia Burke*)

interpersonal skills, and life and career experience that people bring to bear on organisational tasks all affect their chances of acting influentially. Here major ethical dilemmas may arise. For example, media figures such as Kerry Packer have often been criticised for the ruthless exercise of their executive power. What may seem ethical business behaviour can also change quickly — in the 1980s Christopher Skase was presented by the media as an entrepreneurial hero, while he is now portrayed as a villain. Exactly how individuals deal with questions about the exercise of their own organisational influence and power is a product of their own ethical choices.

More positively, the term 'intrapreneurs' has been applied to those who have behaved responsibly and creatively in using their personal power to manage organisational change. Those who use their influence positively are demonstrating a high need for achievement as well as a willingness to use power constructively to bring about change in their organisations. Organisational power, then, is not only located in managerial solutions of the resource dependency problem, but also in the personal choices made by individuals in organisations.

Exercise 10.6 Coalition bargaining

Bargaining at work is one of the most important occasions when issues of power and communication become central. Fisher and Ury (1983) claim the best form of bargaining is 'principled negotiation'. This consists of:

(a) separating the people from the problem
(b) focusing on interests, not positions
(c) inventing options for mutual gain
(d) insisting on objective criteria.

Form into three groups — *which must be of unequal size* — and see if you can apply these principles in the following example.

Background

You are the members of Departments Red, White and Blue, which are regional sales divisions of a national retailer of children's toys.

The company, Auntie Jack's Toys Ltd, retails upmarket toys for older teenagers and young adults, notably Zipper remote control cars, John and Marsha talking dolls, and Whizzbang computer games. The organisation is preparing a new sales training program to meet the requirements of the *Training Guarantee Act* (1990), but presently only has the resources to introduce the scheme to two of its three divisions. It has been left to the divisions themselves to negotiate a coalition between two of them. Financial resources in each division currently vary according to department size. Each divisional member in budget terms is worth $30 000.

Your task is to negotiate a coalition between your department and one of the others. The *primary conflict of interest* is how you will agree to divide the existing budgets between the two divisions in their new amalgamated form. Management has said that the original regional divisions will still retain their own identities, though two will amalgamate for purposes of introducing the training scheme, which should be advantageous to those divisions.

Secondary bargaining points you may use are:

(a) the new product ideas your department can generate
(b) the sales experience and confidence of your departmental members

Rules

1. There will first be a 5 minute planning period for all groups to discuss their negotiating strategy.
2. There will then be one round of negotiations between the three teams in this order: red and white, red and blue, white and blue. In each round the non-active group should leave the room.
3. There will then be a second and final planning period for the groups to discuss in confidence the second and final negotiation round, which will be held with all three groups present.
4. At the end of the last round all teams are to submit a written offer to the class instructor, stating concisely the proposed terms of a coalition between two of the departments: e.g. 'Red team will go with white, with red getting $x and white getting $y'.
5. No two teams are permitted to receive the same amount of money.
6. A successful coalition is formed when the instructor confirms that two of the teams have handed in matching written statements.

Industrial Democracy programs

One of the main differences between Australian and US workplaces is the higher level of union membership in Australia. Though there has been a steady decline in union membership recently and now some 70 per cent of private sector workers do not belong to unions, the influence of the Australian Council of Trades Unions and the large public sector unions still make the Australian industrial relations climate significantly different. One result of this is that through the 1980s the federal Labor government has promoted Industrial Democracy plans in both the private and public sector. This was endorsed by the employers' group, the Business Council of Australia, in 1988. These plans are seen as complementing other government policies for workplace reform, such as the *Training Guarantee Act* (1990), job redesign, international Best Practice policies, multiskilling, award restructuring and, most recently, enterprise bargaining. The overall aim is to improve communication in the workplace and to make Australian work practices more flexible and efficient.

In 1987 the responsibility for Industrial Democracy policy was located in the work organisation branch of the Department of Industrial Relations. These plans aim at the involvement of staff and their unions in company decision making. This is to be achieved by management and employee information sharing and joint consultation on important organisational issues, such as working conditions, new technologies, occupational health and safety, EEO policies and personnel practices. The DIR's communication campaign to launch Industrial Democracy included pamphlets to all staff, then to new employees, the appointment of ID action officers, and the requirement for each division to identify and act on its ID information needs.

In 1991 the DIR published the results of a major survey of industrial relations, which had examined some 2400 workplaces in both the public and private sector. Its findings about communication practices were that the major variables related to the level of employee participation were, first, management style and, second, the degree of union control.

The most common employee involvement technique was direct personal communication, such as 'management by walking around' and supervisor, senior manager and employee meetings. Some more specialised problem-solving techniques, such as Quality Circles — where workers involved in a production process are brought together to develop possible workflow improvements — and suggestion schemes, were also used (see Table 10.1). A commentary on the survey concluded that the overall trend towards more decentralised work and management practices would require more comprehensive employee involvement at workplace levels (Marchington, 1992). It seems that company attention to the importance of communication will be an ongoing concern in the 1990s workplace, especially with the move to enterprise bargaining (Ludeke & Swebeck, 1992).

Table 10.1 *The extent of employee involvement by communication technique*

	Employees (%)
Direct personal communication	
Management walkabout	72
Senior management–employee meetings	72
Supervisor–employee meetings	71
Newsletters	69
Upward problem-solving techniques	
Quality Circles	20
Suggestion schemes	33
Representative participation	
Use of consultative committees	30
Employee representative on board	11
Task forces and other committees	41

Source: Callus, R. et al. (1991).

Coming to such an unqualified conclusion, however, would be too ingenuous. Dunphy and Stace's (1991) study of how Australian companies coped with the economic turbulence of the 1980s found that the best way was for managers to use directive, not participative, decision-making styles in implementing organisational change. Companies are also more likely to permit employee participation in areas such as occupational health and safety, rather than in matters of financial planning. On the other hand, the higher level of education of Australian workers will probably reinforce movements towards more genuinely cooperative work practices in future. If employees are to be more motivated, and managers are to act with greater social responsibility, the 1980s reforms concerning gender and ethnic equity and Industrial Democracy need to be seen as essential dimensions of organisational change (Gardner et al., 1988). Similarly, theoretical analyses of organisational communication practices need to consider both structural and cultural dimensions of organisational experience.

Summary

1. Social networks are important in seeking employment. Understanding your own communication networks is a useful introduction to thinking about organisational communication networks.
2. Organisational communication networks are made up of cliques and the individual network roles within those cliques. The better the organisation's informal networks 'fit' the organisation hierarchy, the more effective formal communication should be.
3. Computer-based network analysis is a costly process. Other forms of networking that are equally important are information networking, managerial networking, career networking and organisational networking.
4. Negative gender-based managerial stereotypes may act as barriers to equal opportunity in organisations, especially in occupations where certain styles of masculinity may set the interpersonal climate.
5. One response to employment discrimination is gender equity programs. Australian EEO programs are the responsibility of the EEO Officer in organisations and federally are administered by the Department of Industrial Relations. They aim to empower women and minority groups in the workplace.
6. Power in organisations is negotiated between an external and an internal coalition. Identifying the dominant coalition in organisations is usually the best way to understand the power that individuals hold and also organisational resource allocation decisions.
7. Organisation members have a range of strategies in exercising their personal influence, such as coalition formation. The degree of access which individuals or coalitions have to crucial resources that the organisation needs is their most important bargaining point.
8. While EEO programs seek to empower women and minority groups, Industrial Democracy programs aim to give all workers more of a say in workplace decision making. Federal responsibility for ID programs is also vested in the Department of Industrial Relations.

Discussion questions

1. What are the limitations of relying on informal job search networks in seeking employment?
2. Identify the five main individual roles members may play in organisational communication networks. What is the difference between a liaison and a bridge?
3. Give one example each of information networking, career networking, managerial networking and organisational networking?
4. What is meant by 'close-coupling' in work and family relationships?
5. Are gender equity programs more likely to be implemented in public or private organisations?
6. What are the five phases in the implementation of an EEO program? Give examples of what is done in each.
7. What is the difference between communication as a 'medium' and as 'meaning', in analysing the role of power in organisations?
8. How may the composition and role of the 'internal' and 'external' coalitions differ in large and small organisations?
9. What is 'resource dependency' in organisations and how is it related to the exercise of organisational power?
10. Give three examples of Industrial Democracy initiatives in organisations. What is the most common technique of employee involvement in Australian organisations?

Further reading

Alvesson, M. & Billing, Y. (1992) 'Gender and Organization', *Organization Studies* 13 (12): 73–102.

Frost, P. (1987) 'Power, Politics, and Influence', pp. 505–47 in F. Jablin, L. Putnam, K. Roberts, & L. Porter, (eds) *Handbook of Organizational Communication* Newbury Park, CA: Sage.

Hackett, E. (1991) 'Women's and Men's Expectations about the Effects of New Technology at Work', *Group and Organization Studies* 16 (19): 60–85.

Irwin, H. & More, E. (1994) *Managing Corporate Communication* Sydney: Allen & Unwin.

Kaye, M. (1994) *Communication Management* Sydney: Prentice Hall.

Monge, P. & Eisenberg, E. (1987) 'Emergent Communication Networks', pp. 304–43 in F. Jablin (ed.) *Handbook of Organizational Communication* Newbury Park, CA: Sage.

Morgan, G. (1990) *Organizations in Society* London: Macmillan.

Pringle, R. (1988) *Secretaries Talk* Sydney: Allen & Unwin.

Tanaka, Y. (1990) 'Women's Growing Role in Contemporary Japan', *International Journal of Psychology* 25: 751–65.

Ticehurst, B., Walker, G. & Johnston, R. (1991) 'Issues in Communication Management in Australian Organisations', *Australian Journal of Communication* 18 (3): 81-95.

References

Bordow, A. & More, E. (1991) *Managing Organisational Communication* Melbourne: Longman.
Burton, C. (1991) *The Promise and the Price* Sydney: Allen & Unwin.
Callus, R., Morehead, A., Cully, M. & Buchanan, J. (1991) *Industrial Relations at Work* Canberra: AGPS, DIR.
Carson, E. (1989) 'Social Networks in the Labour Market', *Australian Bulletin of Labour* 15 (4): 287–312.
Cockburn, C. (1991) *In the Way of Women* Basingstoke: Macmillan.
Deal, T. & Kennedy, A. (1982) *Corporate Cultures* Reading, MA: Addison-Wesley.
Dunphy, D. & Stace, R. (1991) *Under New Management* Sydney: Allen & Unwin.
Dwyer, J. (1993) *The Business Communication Handbook* Sydney: Prentice Hall, 3rd edn.
Farace, R., Mange, P. & Russell, H. (1977) *Communicating and Organizing* Reading, MA: Addison-Wesley.
Fisher, R. & Ury, W. (1983) *Getting to Yes* London: Hutchison.
Fulop, L., Frith, F. & Haywood, H. (1992) *Management for Australian Business* Melbourne: Macmillan.
Game A. & Pringle, R. (1983) *Gender at Work* Sydney: Allen & Unwin.
Gardner, M., Palmer, G. & Quinlan, M. (1988) 'The Industrial Democracy Debate', pp. 336–62 in G. Palmer, (ed.) *Readings in Australian Personnel Management* Melbourne: Macmillan.
Ireland, D. (1981) *City of Women* Melbourne: Penguin.
James, P. (ed.) (1990) *Technocratic Dreaming* Melbourne: Left Book Club.
Kanter, R. (1979) 'Power Failure in Management Circuits', *Harvard Business Review* July-Aug: 65–76.
Ludeke, P. & Swebeck, B. (1992) *Enterprise Bargaining* Sydney: Federation Press.
Marchington, M. (1992) 'The Growth of Employee Involvement in Australia', *The Journal of Industrial Relations* Sept: 472–81.
Mintzberg, H. (1983) *Power In and Around Organizations* New Jersey: Prentice Hall.
Powell, G., Posner, B. & Schmidt, W. (1984) 'Sex Effects on Managerial Value Systems', *Human Relations* 37 (19): 909–21.
Powell, W. (1990) 'Network Forms of Organization', pp. 295–336 in B. Staw, (ed.) *Research in Organizational Behaviour* 12 New York: JAI Press.
Still, L. (1990) *Enterprising Women* Sydney: Allen & Unwin.
Tam, S. (1990) 'Developmental Patterns of Chinese and Japanese Firms', pp. 153–85 in S. Clegg and G. Redding, (eds) *Capitalism in Contrasting Cultures* Berlin: de Gruyter.
Tharenou, P. (1990) 'Psychological Approaches for Investigating Women's Career Advancement', *Australian Journal of Management* 15 (2): 363–70.
Tichy, N., Tushman, M. & Fombrun, C. (1979) 'Social Network Analysis for Organizations', *Academy of Management Review* 4 (4): 507–19.
Wicker, A. & Burley, K. (1991) 'Close-Coupling in Work–Family Relations', *Human Relations* 44 (1): 77–93.
Williams, C. (1988) *Blue, White and Pink Collar Workers in Australia* Sydney: Allen & Unwin.

Analysing television

11

Objectives

After completing this chapter you should be able to:

- distinguish between popular TV criticism and specialist TV research;
- classify different types of TV research according to whether it is primarily a policy, production, program or reception study;
- understand some of the basic principles of formal television analysis and apply these to particular programs;
- discuss ways in which TV programs can construct images of cultural identity and difference, in relation to personal, national and gender identity.

Chapter 11

TV came rather late to Australia: 1956 in the cities, later still in the country regions where the distance between towns was immense for the technology of that time. So it was in the early 1960s that in a remote mountain village — where few sounds disturbed the peace except for the mist rolling down to the valley, the murmur of the wireless, the laugh of the kookaburra, the call of the bellbird, the humming of chainsaws and lawnmowers, and the occasional rustle of a snake in the grass — the pervasive silence was shattered by the voice of Lucille Ball.

'Banality in Cultural Studies', in Mellencamp's Logics of Television, *Meaghan Morris*

Television is part of our everyday lives. Australian critic Meaghan Morris, quoted above, goes on to recall her memories of growing up with TV in the 1950s and how her father disliked *I Love Lucy*. She points out how in *Crocodile Dundee* the bushman hero Paul Hogan, on seeing TV in New York for the first time in twenty years, jokes that *Lucy* is still on — in other words, TV doesn't change. Morris then develops a theme about how TV oscillates between the banality of everyday life and being interrupted by 'fatality', or possible crises. That is, there is always the possibility of programs being broken into by 'the latest flash from our newsroom', which may be a cyclone flattening Darwin or the next world war.

This is one way of analysing TV, by criticising it in its cultural context. This chapter will consider a variety of ways of analysing television, with the aim of explaining how we can go about applying communication and cultural theory to TV. Critical TV analysis needs to consider, the structural (formal), contextual (cultural) and institutional (economic) dimensions of television. The economics of the TV industry, however, will not be treated here (see O'Regan, 1993).

TV criticism and TV research

TV criticism
Popular writing about television, found mainly in the press and TV magazines; usually presents reviews or previews of television programs.

TV research
Theoretically based analysis of television intended for a relatively specialist audience.

A broad distinction can be drawn between TV criticism and TV research. TV criticism is popular writing about television that is found mainly in the press and TV magazines and is either a review or a preview of television programs. It is located in the TV guide sections of the weekly television supplements published by the daily papers, as well as in weekly television magazines like *TV Week*. It also exists in a variety of other magazines and in popular books, as well as on television itself. **TV research**, in contrast, is theoretically-based analysis of television intended for a relatively specialist audience. It is published mostly in academic journals and books, in government and private industry reports, and in the broadcasting trade press. Popular TV criticism is aimed at wider audiences, while TV research is mainly intended for educational audiences and sometimes policy-makers.

Popular TV criticism in Australia can be found in the weekly TV guides of the daily metropolitan papers. Preview stories are usually promotional pieces to encourage viewers to watch a program. These are often used as a cover story in the guides to promote a particular show, series or TV personality. Reviews of programs already screened are more likely to be made by a resident columnist who will offer personal and often idiosyncratic opinions of TV shows. Australian Clive James first made his name in Britain as a newspaper TV reviewer. Occasionally the papers will also carry TV criticism as part of their leisure sections, separately from the TV guide, as with Phillip Adams' long-lived column in the *Weekend Australian*.

The limitation of much of this reporting about television is that its main purpose is public relations advocacy. More critical discussions of television are likely to be found in other sources, such as the *Bulletin, Arena,* and the ABC's *24 Hours.* There is also some TV criticism on television itself. Currently the ABC has three programs — *TVTV, Media Watch* and *Backchat. Backchat* is light entertainment, *Media Watch* is often serious, while *TVTV* is somewhere in between. SBS-TV has a weekly feedback show *Hotline* (Wilson, 1994). Commercial TV has no direct counterpart to these programs, except for *60 Minutes'* letters from viewers, used mostly as light entertainment.

Exercise 11.1 The do-it-yourself TV ratings game
In December 1993 *TV Soap* magazine listed its 'Hits and Misses' for the year as follows.

Hits
Baywatch, Beverly Hills 90210, Australia's Funniest Home Videos, The Best and Worst of Red Faces, The Bold and the Beautiful, General Hospital, A Country Practice, GP, Days of Our Lives, Home and Away, Melrose Place, Home Improvement, Movies with Bill Collins, Money, Neighbours, Picket Fences, Northern Exposure, Roseanne, Our House, Police Rescue, Santa Barbara, Seinfeld, Sirens, Donahue, Oprah and Sally, TVTV, The Young and the Restless

Misses
All Together Now, Civil Wars, Bingles, The Comedy Sale, E Street, Class of '96, Jeopardy, LA Law, Paradise Beach, Star Trek: the Next Generation

1. Go through their list and rank the shows in your own order of preference, giving them a numerical ranking from 10 for 'excellent' to 0 for 'pathetic'.
2. Do this first individually and then add your individual scores together to make up a class list.
3. How does the class list correspond to the *TV Soap* list?

There are three Australian media textbooks that cover radio and the press as well as television. These are Bonney and Wilson's *Australia's Commercial Media* (1983), Windschuttle's *The Media* (1984) and, most recently, Cunningham and Turner's *The Media in Australia* (1993). Specifically on television, however, four main kinds of research can be identified.

6First, there are policy studies concerned with the legal, economic, technical and, less often, the social features of the industry. The Australian Broadcasting Authority (ABA, previously the ABT) is the most important originator of these studies, though the ABC, the Department of Transport and Communications, the Australian Film, TV and Radio School (AFTRS), SBS, the Communications Law Centre at the University of New South Wales, and CIRCIT in Melbourne also produce policy research. The commercial broadcasters sometimes make inputs. Academic policy studies have been made by Armstrong et al. on media law (1992), Cunningham on cultural policy (1992), Jacka on TV globalisation (1992) and Davis on the ABC (1988). In New Zealand, the work of Lealand is notable (1988; 1991).

Second, there are production studies of the television industry. These are usually analyses of the financing, production and distribution of television, some of which consider the creative aspects of TV production. Notable overseas studies of this kind are Elliot's (1972) in Britain, Turow's work in the US (1984) and Collins (1990) in Canada. In New Zealand, Winter has written a good account of NZTV during market deregulation (1993). There are fewer Australian production studies, but the work of Cunningham on the Kennedy-Miller group (1988), O'Regan (1993) on TV networking and Jacka (1991) on ABC drama are good examples. Henningham's study of TV news (1988) mainly concerns the organisational nature of journalism, while Moran's (1993) guide to Australian TV series has a wealth of information.

Third, there are TV program studies that examine particular programs or series. These are sometimes referred to as textual studies. The method here is to look closely at the narrative style, content and themes of programs. American studies are the most numerous, with analyses of TV soaps (Allen, 1985) as well as sitcoms, cop shows, TV news, sport and music videos. Some excellent British program studies have also been made, such as that by Brunsdon and Morley on *Nationwide* (1978). Australian work has included Tulloch and Moran on soaps (1986), Cunningham on TV mini-series (1989), Turner on variety shows (1989) and Bell, Boehringer and Crofts (1982) on TV election coverage.

Lastly, there are reception studies, also referred to as audience studies, that consider what television audiences actually do with particular TV programs. Whereas early TV research mostly concerned program and industry studies, curently researchers emphasise the active role of audiences in using television. Australian studies of how children negotiate meaning on kids' TV by Palmer (1986), and of how both men and women view TV sport by Nightingale (1992), have used qualitative research methods. Notable works of this kind have also been made overseas by Ang (1985) in Holland.

This classification of contemporary trends in TV research is necessarily simplified, but it aims at making a convenient paradigmatic representation of approaches to the field. These four kinds of research approaches are broadly representative of the ways that researchers investigate television. In comparative cross-cultural terms, most of the English language research is Anglo-American and European. Traditional American quantitative research, which relies on surveys and content analysis, is still central in US journals such as the *Journal of Broadcasting*, *Journalism Quarterly*, and the *Journal of Communication*.

The influence of cultural and interpretive approaches to media studies since the 1970s, however, can be seen in journals such as *Critical Studies in Mass Communication* and *Communication,* and in some articles in the *Journal of Communication*. British and European approaches, which are inclined to be politically critical and interpretive, may be found in journals like *Screen, Media, Culture and Society,* and the *European Journal of Communication*. In Australia the main journals are *Media Information Australia* and *Continuum*, though TV analyses can be found in some issues of the *Australian Journal of Communication,* the *Australian Journalism Review, Art and Text* and *Meanjin*.

It is also possible to define the field of television studies historically and contextually. As suggested, the trend has been towards the challenge of quantitative research methods by qualitative approaches, such as the ethnographic methods of participant observation and open-ended interviewing used by Nightingale (1992). The advantage of these methods is that more interpretive judgments may be made about a wider range of issues. Previously, content analysis and quantitative audience research were dominant in 1950s and 1960s approaches. Then in the later 1960s these were challenged by different research paradigms, for example the social psychology based 'uses and gratifications' research. US scholars such as Katz were now asking what it was that audiences used media programs for, in order to develop more culturally sensitive theories of TV use, where earlier approaches had been narrowly functionalist or dismissive of television (Lowery & DeFleur, 1988). In Australia this approach was applied to children's television (Noble & Noble, 1979).

Uses and gratifications, however, was just one new trend. Another approach was 'cultivation analysis'. Researchers such as Gerbner and associates (1980) argued that the cumulative representation of certain stock types of characters in TV fiction programs negatively stereotyped women and ethnic minorities. They linked this critique with the perennial television violence issue in arguing that violence in TV fiction in terms of 'who did what to whom' symbolically displayed US culture's unwritten rules about moral order and authority and thereby reproduced the social framework. They called this the 'mainstreaming of America'. The television violence debate, which peaked in the US Surgeon–General's Report of 1972, has since died down though it recurs in arguments about censorship of X-rated videos and new computer software (Rowland, 1983). In 1993 the Australian commercial television industry introduced new program classifications and rules, including the rule that mature adult material containing sex or violence should not be shown before 9 p.m., partly as a result of the personal intervention of the Prime Minister, Paul Keating.

Industry research has been mostly concerned with developing more accurate measures of audience size. Audience research techniques were first developed in the 1930s in the US to measure radio audiences, by ratings companies such as Crossley and Hooper. These were then translated into the Nielsen TV ratings in the 1950s. The essence of the methods used for commercial TV rating (currently conducted by Nielsen in Australia) is that a stratified random sample is taken in various capital cities to represent a cross-section of the viewing audience. This cross-section is based on geodemographic measures, relying on the most recent household census information where viewers are defined in terms of their age, sex and levels of income.

Since the 1950s, the TV ratings method has relied on a mixture of telephone viewer surveys and the keeping of a household viewing diary. Diaries stay in the household for some three years at a time and, though the total sample size is relatively small; it is judged to be statistically significant. Householders agreeing to keep diaries get modest gifts from the ratings company. Now, in the 1990s, the development of Peoplemeters has revised the diary system. A meter is attached to the television set and household members are required to identify their presence each time they view. This information is downloaded by phone to the ratings company computer, where the national data is analysed. In regional aggregated TV markets, programmers are now able to gauge viewer responses on a daily instead of a monthly basis for the first time.

There has been much argument about the technical accuracy of the ratings measurement systems, with a few percentage points difference meaning the possible cancellation of a program, as well as extra costs for the advertising agencies that rely on the ratings to plan their media-buying. The information collected by TV ratings agencies is confidential and current information is made available only to subscribers — mainly the commercial TV stations, though the ABC also subscribes. What industry TV audience research is essentially concerned with is the absolute size and demographic composition of the television audience. Ratings research is purely a technical exercise with a commercial purpose and has no interest in issues concerning the social significance of television (Meehan, 1990).

Exercise 11.2 Recognising differences in TV criticism and TV research

Below are several examples of TV criticism and TV research.

(a) Thursday's baboon-infested and Sir David Attenborough-enriched edition of *Wildscreen* (ABC, 8 p.m.) was a fine illustration of the sorts of things that irritate the learned anti-wildlife documentary lobby whose arguments I have been splashing across these columns in an attempt to generate some debate among my readers; if I have any.

(b) The older men, observed by Peter, demonstrated an intense identification with the players. The intensity of identification was most obvious in the way they commented on the actions of players who held team positions they themselves had held in the past. Peter was surprised at the tendency for some of his mates to take the game 'too seriously'.

(c) As a new domestic season approaches, SBS is cementing its reputation as 'the soccer station' with two new weekly programs. *Soccer on Monday* will screen at 5.30 p.m. for 60 minutes from October 25, while the 30-minute *Goal* will begin a day later at 7.30 p.m.

(d) In TPS 14, the ABT stresses the cultural, rather than the economic, reasons for regulating for Australian content. It acknowledges that the lower cost of imported programs and the need to maintain the domestic production industries have been important factors in the development of such regulations but . . . sees these criteria as inadequate for meeting cultural objectives and objectives of quality and diversity of programming.

(e) The first three decades of Australian TV were characterised by an absence of cheap delivery systems linking the major capital cities to facilitate simultaneous programming. This led to the development of a form of 'networking' . . . based upon the sharing of costs of production. But this did not extend to scheduling practices of programming and advertising.

(f) In a detailed survey of *Asia Report* in 1990, I found that the application of news values was very interesting. The weekly newsreel at the top of the program always carried BBC or Channel 4 reports, predominantly about conflicts in Asia. The *Asia Magazine* at the end of the program presented what was called the lighter side of Asia.

1. First, decide which of these quotations are popular TV criticism and which are academic research.
2. Then, distinguish which of the popular pieces of criticism are previews and which are reviews.
3. Finally, classify the remaining quotations in terms of the several varieties of academic TV research previously discussed.

Analysing TV form

To criticise television seriously a theoretical approach is necessary. Although there is no agreed-on single theory of **television form** — the formal structure of the television image — some suggestions will be made about how a narrative analysis of television can be made, followed by a discussion of several current interpretive approaches to television analysis. Fiske and Hartley's *Reading Television* (1978) remains a good introduction concerning TV form, while Davis' essay 'The Language of TV News' (1991) is an excellent guide, but what will be suggested here instead will treat television as a narrative. Four key terms can help us to undertake a critical analysis of television form — the ideas of media texts, of intertextuality, of narrative discourse, and of TV genres. There is some overlap between these in practice, yet they need to be separated initially for the purposes of definition.

> **TV form**
> The formal structure of the television image.

Media texts and intertextuality

First, there are **media texts**. These may be newspapers, magazines, movies, radio or TV programs, or advertisements. Television occupies a strategic place as a media text because it has both sound and vision and can draw on many of the conventions of print journalism. Formally, media texts are a structured network of codes. Each media text has its own characteristic style and methods of presentation which act as signifying systems to create a range of possible meanings. Discourse is organised in media texts according to the particular conventions prevailing in that medium at the time. Media texts such as film and television differ strikingly from literary texts, previously discussed in Chapter 2, in that they use visual instead of written language to create meaningful passages.

So TV news and the newspapers, for example, both lead with their most important items — even if the news values of TV news are often more trivial and determined by the availability of pictures — and usually put sports news at the end. Radio stations tailor their programs according to the tastes of particular audience segments — 'listener-driven radio'. Innovative pop on JJJ is aimed at young adults, as are commercial radio FM formats, while the 'easy listening' stations are directed at an older age bracket with more sedate tastes. The station's programming style and the DJ's manner are expected to match those formats. Similarly with movies, a number of different film genres are readily recognised by audiences. Current genres may cross over and even radically change their traditional themes — e.g. *Superman IV* had an anti-nuclear weapons theme — but the genre conventions themselves remain.

Second, there is the idea of **intertextuality**. This is more complex. Formally, intertextuality refers to the way that media texts take their meaning from other texts. All media have the capacity to make intertextual references, to themselves, or to different media. *Mad* magazine, for instance, regularly satirises current film and television shows, while comedy programs like *Fast Forward* and *Full Frontal* parody TV advertisements and other TV shows. Television advertisements themselves sometimes parody other TV formats. Many media texts echo previous media texts and television is the most

> **media texts**
> A structured network of codes; media texts act as signifying systems to create a range of possible meanings. Discourse is organised in these texts according to the particular conventions prevailing in that medium at the time.

> **intertextuality**
> All media texts, whether television, film, radio or print, can take their meaning from other texts, and make references to them.

intertextual of all media. Clive James' British television shows, which show many clips from foreign television, are good examples of intertextual TV. Television has the capacity to reproduce formats originating in other media. So TV pop music shows play the same tracks as radio, but with moving pictures. Though the coverage of TV news is much less than that of the daily paper, it originally derived its news agendas from the press. Television also directly broadcasts films. Most recently, television information services, such as Teletext, can carry computer-generated information displays.

There are two more important dimensions of TV's intertextuality — its reflexivity, and its patterns of seamless flow. **Reflexivity** is the tendency of television to refer to itself and to its own method of production. This can take place intentionally or accidentally. Programs such as *Hey Hey it's Saturday* and *New Faces* consciously include the show's production as part of the show itself. Contestants in *New Faces* are at times shown backstage preparing to appear, while compere Bert Newton will ask them on-stage how they feel about being on television.

Similarly, *Hey Hey* often shows its own production, with the camera crew, the musicians and stage hands becoming part of the fun. These shows can also refer, either consciously or unconsciously, to television's own history. Bert Newton, for instance, is one of the great survivors on Australian television. His career began with 'the King', Graham Kennedy, on *In Melbourne Tonight*, then carried on through the *Tonight* show with Don Lane. Two of the *Hey Hey* regulars, Red Symons and Molly Meldrum, are themselves TV veterans, as Symons' 1970s band 'Skyhooks' used to play on the ABC's pop show *Countdown*, compered by Meldrum.

Some TV shows are consciously, and even self-consciously, reflexive, especially comedies like *Fast Forward*. TV advertisements and TV personalities are mercilessly made fun of. At the same time these shows plunder Hollywood history with lovingly crafted satires of classic films and stars. Many TV entertainment and comedy programs that satirise, quote and plagiarise other TV programs have a style of self-conscious parody. There is also accidental reflexivity on television. When we are watching *A Country Practice*, for example, and there is a cut from an operating theatre sequence to an advertisement for a health benefits fund, is this a joke or just a happy coincidence? We can also channel-zap sometimes to find the same star on different channels in different roles.

The other important dimension of TV intertextuality is the seamless flow of its program structure. The idea of television 'flow' was first suggested by Williams (1974). This refers to the variety of techniques and programming strategies that create a sense of continuity in television. He considered it necessary to look at TV as a kind of supertext that was more than the sum of its separate programs. Programs are strictly timed for hour and half-hour slots, but commercial TV fragments this with advertising breaks. What unifies TV is the sound track. Station logos and promos between programs are also used to stitch it all together as if it naturally cohered. The TV sound track is a particularly important feature of TV flow (Altman, 1986) and is more important to television than it is to movies. We may leave the room for coffee in the advertising breaks, but the sound cues us when the program is about to start again.

---

reflexivity
The tendency of television to foreground the methods of its own production and to refer to itself; this can be intentional or accidental.

Narrative discourse and TV genres

The third key element of TV form is **narrative discourse**. This is the signifying techniques and formal strategies that are used to tell a story. Almost everything on TV can be interpreted as a story which has a form of narrative discourse. Narrative discourse takes a plot and elaborates it as a story. The plots and characters of TV soaps, for example, are often predictable as well as discussed in advance in fan magazines. What gives the viewer potential pleasure and involvement is not only the plot of each story, but the way in which the episode is made to unfold. The same could be said of *Eyewitness News*. The formal conventions of soaps or news may change little, but we can still choose to admire or dislike the performance.

Narrative discourse usually creates meaning by establishing a certain point of view. This may belong to the characters in a drama, or to the host in a game show. In establishing this viewpoint the viewer (or 'the spectator' in film analysis terms) is being positioned by the program in a certain way. A story told from a certain viewpoint is expected to bring about a particular audience response. The relationship of the narrator of the story to the characters is a decisive element in the construction of meaning in TV programs (Kozloff, 1989).

In *Australia's Most Wanted*, for instance, program host Ann Sanders, then the studio presenter, distances herself from the criminals the program is tracking down while aligning herself with the authorities. She does this by attempting to enlist audience help in catching the crooks, but also by the presence of a friendly policeman or woman in studio discussion. Unless the audience perversely sides with the criminals, the program's clear intent is for the audience to identify with the viewing position the host has constructed for them. Narrative discourse, then, refers to the sequential development of a story. So to analyse television dramas or current affairs, the show's narrative needs to be analysed to explain how the story has been structured, as well as how it might have been structured differently.

Another essential part of the way TV presents its narratives is via the use of **visual grammar**. This is the set of film and video techniques that are used to construct TV images. Some of these derive directly from film. For instance, they include the basic types of camera shots — long shots, mid-shots and close-ups — and camera angles, as well as the presentation of a certain *mise-en-scène* (i.e. the arrangement of space and objects on the screen) and different styles of editing — the use of fades, wipes, cuts, montages, flashbacks or flash-forwards. What TV has in addition is a number of computer-generated special effects; they are used mainly to create hi-tech station logos, but split-screen windows are common in news bulletins, and a galaxy of video effects are used in music videos and TV commercials.

Fourth, there is the idea of **TV genres**. While TV programs can be considered as individual media texts, they also need to be analysed as part of a broader set of programs of a like kind. TV genres are similar classes of television programs. They are formulas, or structures of narrative conventions. These conventions typify a particular TV format. Where narrative discourse analysis of TV shows explores the development of the story within those texts by breaking them into sequences, that approach needs to be supplemented by genre analysis. The aim is first to distinguish it from other genres, then to explore differences between

---

narrative discourse
The signifying techniques and formal strategies that are used to tell a television story. Narrative discourse takes a plot and elaborates it as a story.

visual grammar
Film and video techniques used to construct television images.

TV genres
Classes of TV programs, such as soaps or news bulletins; formulas or structures of narrative conventions.

programs of the same genre. All soaps are not the same, neither are news nor sports shows. They will each conform to certain genre conventions, but they also try to be sufficiently different to establish a niche of their own.

Genre theory originated in literary and film studies. Analysis of popular films like Westerns found that they contained a regular series of binary oppositions, such as the struggle between the individual and the community in *High Noon* and *Shane*. More recently, Berger (1992) has argued that TV genres should be classified in terms of whether they are 'objective' (concerned with the real world) or 'emotive' (feelings and emotions). So TV news is highly objective and weakly emotive — relative to other TV genres, at least, because it is not so if compared to the quality print media — while sportscasts are strongly emotive and highly objective, while soaps are strongly emotive but not highly objective.

As well as soaps, news and sports, Berger identifies other main TV genres as sitcoms (situation comedies like *Hey Dad!*), documentaries, police shows, game shows, talk shows, and spectacles (e.g. the opening of the Olympic games). Like film genres, TV genres are not static, and some experimental ones, like *Twin Peaks,* may attract large audiences. There are also notable gender differences in the audience composition of TV genres. Soaps and police shows traditionally have been watched by women and men respectively.

To sum up: TV shows can be analysed as media texts and as forms of narrative discourse. To do this we need to be aware of intertextual and reflexive elements in those texts to determine if they are an important part of narrative strategy. We also need to consider how the plot is turned into a story via its formal method of narration. One clue to this is clarifying the point of view a text establishes for the viewers, because that viewpoint is intended to position them in a certain direction towards the characters and the events. Lastly, textual analysis of the narrative discourse of TV programs should be supplemented by locating the show within a particular genre to determine how it meets, and possibly breaks, that genre's conventions.

Exercise 11.3 Analysing TV form

1. *Media texts*
   Collect and compare the formal treatment of the major news story presented in the same city on any one day. Do this either for TV, radio and the press, or for SBS-TV, ABC-TV and one commercial channel.

2. *Intertextuality*
   Locate and analyse a TV show that is either a spin-off from a film or a version of a book. What are the formal differences?

3. *Narrative discourse*
   Locate and view several times a recent Australian TV soap or serial. Analyse how its plot and point of view are developed to narrate its story.

4. *Visual grammar*
   Examine any commercial TV fiction program and compare the different elements of visual grammar used in the program as well as in its advertisements.

5. *TV genres*
   Choose the program schedule from a weekly TV guide for one commercial and one non-commercial station and classify six hours of its programming in terms of the TV genres.

TV, identity and difference

As well as the four kinds of academic research into TV described previously, there is also a body of serious writing about television which is closer to cultural criticism. This draws on recent French media theorists, such as Baudrillard, Barthes, de Certeau, Foucault and others, and refers back to Frankfurt school writers such as Walter Benjamin. These more complex approaches are concerned with the way TV presents images of cultural identity and difference. That is, they deal with how TV produces selective representations of group identity and personal experience, about national identity and ethnic difference, and about gender differences.

TV and personal identity

First, consider **personal and generational identity**. Morse (1990) de-familiarises television by arguing that the experience of TV viewing has important psychological similarities with shopping in suburban malls and driving on freeway systems. Drawing on de Certeau, she claims that these experiences share a psychological sense of 'mobile privatisation'. Malls, freeways and TV can each induce a mental state of distraction: so freeway driving produces a feeling of 'detached involvement', suburban mall shopping can be a form of purposeless yet pleasurable loitering, like 'couch potato' TV viewing. Each of these pastimes can make us feel 'spaced out'.

Her critique leads to several suggestions about the formal nature of TV and its potential consequences for the repression of social and personal change. First, she suggests a modification to Williams' idea of TV 'flow'. TV flow consists of a series of passages between program segments which together create an aesthetic sense of coherence. Morse argues that TV discourse consists of a series of 'stacks' of recursive levels — like a Hypercard program — each of which represents a different kind of reality. The advertisement differs from the program promo, while both may be located in a news bulletin, which itself is composed of stories of different orders of importance. Over-the-shoulder news windows behind the presenter, or advertisements and music videos, condense a range of different worlds into one artificially constructed visual field.

Morse concludes that the psychological and cultural results of television are a form of 'mobile privatisation', where the paradox of living in conditions of mass culture and social isolation are resolved only symbolically. The end result has ideological consequences: narratives which aim to present the possibility of social change are defused by the underlying principles of TV representation. The cultural logic of television is basically static — as suggested by Hogan's joke about the *Lucy* show referred to in the first paragraph of this chapter — either in its fictions or in news, which limits both personal and social change.

This rather bleak interpretation has been questioned by other theorists. Some argue that TV can have positive 'pro-social' effects in promoting public health campaigns (such as the *Grim Reaper* AIDS awareness advertisements), while others maintain that TV texts are read by audiences 'subversively' (Fiske, 1987). These claims have been made about programs which have been traditionally aimed at women. Whereas US soaps, such as *Days of Our Lives,* were previously criticised for their conservatism in presenting women in subordinate

TV and personal identity
How television projects selective representations of personal and generational experience.

TV flow
The techniques and programming strategies that create a sense of continuity; a series of passages between program segments which together create an aesthetic sense of coherence.

domestic roles, recent analyses have argued that soaps can be seen more positively. Cantor's study (1983), for instance, found that, though soaps still expressed traditional family values, they had changed so that women were relatively equal to men in most series.

A similar re-reading of TV melodrama was made in Ang's study of *Dallas*. She argued that women watching *Dallas* were not escaping from their daily lives. Rather, they enjoyed the possibilities *Dallas* characters played out in dealing with complex personal relationships (1985). Another soap positively re-evaluated in these terms was the 1980s Australian series *Prisoner,* which was set in a women's prison. Curthoys and Docker suggested that schoolchildren watching the program enjoyed it as they identified the prisoners' frequent rebellions against the authorities with their own subordinate place in the school system (1989). Turner has also suggested that some formats like game shows are 'transgressive television' (1989). Lastly, in terms of children's TV, which traditionally tended to be slighted by critics, Patricia Palmer (1986) argued that kids were 'active audiences' who were selective and critical in their viewing.

Exercise 11.4 Social identity themes on TV
Spend one hour watching commercial television with a group of class-mates, preferably ones you don't know too well. Half the group should watch with the aim of identifying pro-social themes in TV programs and advertisements, the other half should watch for anti-social themes.

- What genres do these themes mainly occur in?
- What age group are they aimed at?
- What criteria did you use to define 'pro-social' and 'anti-social'?

TV and national identity

Another important question is to what extent television creates images of the **nation and the community**. Hartley (1989), for example, cites a number of TV theorists who maintain that television differs so radically from one country to another that its content cannot be generalised about. He raises the issue of television's difference in what he terms 'marginal places', such as Wales and Western Australia. Television is like the press, in that its most typically local stories, such as current affairs, are not exportable to other countries. However, the initial experience that most countries had of television in the 1950s was usually North American television.

Since then, many countries, especially non-English speaking ones such as Brazil, Mexico, Japan and the larger European countries, as well as Britain and, to a lesser extent, Australia, have developed their own local TV production industries. The exact way in which this has happened has been the subject of an ongoing debate among television scholars, which is referred to alternately as the 'international TV flow' or the 'cultural imperialism' issue. A number of left-wing writers, such as Schiller and Nordenstreng, argued that American programs dominated Third World countries and that this was part of US media imperialism. From the early 1980s, however, this interpretation was questioned by scholars such as Taiwan's C.C. Lee (1980), who pointed to signs of a clear preference for local programs. Most recently, in the Australian setting Jacka and

---

TV and national identity
How television represents the nation and the community, either culturally or politically.

The Americanisation of television.
Source: *G. Pryor, The Canberra Times, 25 September 1992. Used with permission.*

Cunningham (1993) have identified a range of different internationalising strategies being pursued by local producers.

Moran (1989) sums up Australian TV history into three stages. The first was from its beginnings in 1956 to 1965. Then most programming was imported, usually from the US, while the foundations of the national 9 and 7 networks were laid. US westerns, crime shows and sitcoms dominated prime-time schedules, while there was little local content except for news, variety and quiz shows. The second stage was from 1965 to 1975. The third network, the 10 network, was created, while local TV drama began with police shows like *Homicide*. A local production industry was consolidated around the production houses of Grundys and Crawfords. The third stage was from 1975 to around 1990. This saw the introduction of colour TV (1976), the beginning of daily satellite feeds from Visnews in London (1975), the launch of AUSSAT (1986) and the start of SBS-TV in 1980. This was a period of growing internationalisation.

In trying to identify what is distinctive about Australian television, however, we probably need to look no further than the best-known national TV personalities (Hall, 1981). These are not usually exportable. Television in most countries grew up in the shadow of movies, and after radio, so initially some radio personalities crossed over directly into TV, such as Bob Dyer with *Pick-a-Box* and Graham Kennedy. Yet TV personalities never had the same glamour as movie stars. They were more domesticated and more just talking heads. Cleverness and humour were more important for TV personalities, whereas movie stars had a bigger screen presence. 'King' Kennedy epitomised these qualities. His mercurial wit, rubber face, and his larrikin and often crude jokes, endeared him to local TV audiences. His successor was Paul Hogan, who was more self-consciously Australian.

Though local television is now distinctively Australian in its content, debate continues about whether it's worth the trouble. In 1993 the *Independent Monthly* editorialised on the poor quality of local commercial television, suggesting that with new satellite-delivered overseas programs it was doubtful if 'Australianness' was worth protecting. Here one dilemma for the national commercial networks is that it is not possible for them to build a sense of an Australian community as opposed to a sense of the nation. Sydney and Melbourne, location of the head offices of the networks, are too big and too diverse to be targeted as communities. Commercial TV's fictional representations of communities are necessarily idealised and context-free: *A Country Practice* is a small country town somewhere, while *Neighbours* and *Home and Away* float intangibly in suburbia and on the coast.

An emphasis on genuine localism is instead left to the smaller country stations and regional networks, such as the Prime network in New South Wales, Victoria and Queensland, which attempts to create a sense of community identity via local news and weather readers and the promotion of community events. What the national networks do instead is to emphasise the nation rather

Capital Television's Peter Chapman and Greg Robson host the Sportstar of the Year awards. (Photo: *Focus Photography of Canberra*)

Thousands flock to Regatta Point each year for the Capital Television Birdman Rally. (Photo: *Capital Television*)

than the community and promote a corporate image of the networks themselves. They do this in 'celebrity' clips, featuring the networks best-known local and sometimes overseas stars as very happy families.

The national networks also advertise themselves as experts in news and current affairs. Currently the 9 network, troubled by the challenge from 7's news, is playing a *'Who's who of the news'* promotion designed by ad-man John Singleton. This presents the 9 news team, with the emphasis on being a team, headed by long-time bulletin reader Brian Henderson, but featuring sports compere Ken Sutcliffe as prominently. The rest of the team is shown as Jana Wendt, Mike Willesee, Mike Munro, Steve Liebmann, Liz Hayes and Jim Waley, represented as the 'real' news experts. Even the ABC now promotes itself as 'The Newsforce'.

Network TV, however, has been spectacularly successful in promoting an image of Australian nationalism. The commercial stations do this with a commercial emphasis, especially via sports programs such as the football grand finals, while the ABC presents a lower-key but equally nationalist 'Go for Gold' approach. The first major Bicentennial event on 1 January 1988, for example, was a nationwide TV special *Australia Live,* which was saturated with advertisements for paint, beer, cars and the 9 network, while its hosts Ray Martin, Clive James and Jana Wendt tried to piece together the real nature of the nation.

Apart from specials of this kind, international sports events, such as the 1983 America's Cup victory, are other occasions for TV patriotism. The ideology of nationalism can also be seen in patriotic advertising: 'Buy Australian' campaigns, Mr Okimura playing Aussie life-saver on Bondi beach, and even the ghosts of Gallipoli soldiers literally willing to die for a Toohey's Blue. Allen (1993) has cleverly analysed Telecom's massive 1993 TV advertising campaign to show how a discourse of national identity based on physical distance has been constructed by Telecom to represent itself as 'truly Australian'.

The emerging problem in 1990s multicultural Australia is that older and simpler discourses about 'real Australians' are harder to sell. Serials like *Home and Away* and *Neighbours* are widely criticised for their nostalgic and atypical Anglo-Australian casting, despite occasional appearances by non-Anglo characters. As Natt and McKie say, 'Australia . . . emerges from sitcoms as a society with no unemployment, no obvious class structure, no poverty, and no racial tension or significant minority or racial groups' (1993: 118). A 1993 survey of ethnic groups by the Office of Multicultural Affairs came to a similar conclusion — commercial TV was seen as foregrounding American and British programs, there was a weak sense of what Anglo-Australian culture was, while a number of offensive stereotypes of ethnic Australians were transmitted (Coupe & Jakubowicz, 1993). In 1994, the new teenage program *Heartbreak High* was launched with the clear aim of showing more ethnic characters.

TV representation of ethnic and Aboriginal Australians, however, gradually increased through the 1980s. Aboriginals featured in *Women of the Sun* (SBS, 1982), in *Naked Under Capricorn* (9, 1989), and in *Blackout* (ABC, 1989–93), *Heartland* (ABC, 1994), as well as in Ernie Dingo's appearances on *Fast Forward*. ABC-TV ran several earlier series about Italian immigrants, such as *Home Sweet Home* (1980), but the big breakthrough was the spectacularly Greek *Acropolis Now* (7, 1989) featuring Mary Koustas as Effi.

Albert Namatjira being interviewed by Roger Climpson in the early days of Australian television. (Photo: *National Library of Australia*) Used with permission.

These potential contradictions between multiculturalism and nationalism were highlighted by Tulloch's (1989) examination of one episode of *A Country Practice*. By the show's own standards this story was unusual as it concerned migrant exploitation in the context of rural unemployment. Tulloch describes in detail the story as well as the thematic composition of the advertisements in the program. There were two explicitly multicultural ads in the establishing sequence. These Papa Guiseppi pizzas and Kraft cheese advertisements showed unproblematic and then more equivocal images of multiculturalism, with the pizza advertisement representing a happy Italian family situation, while the Kraft advertisement contrasted chaotic Italian emotionality against cool Nordic blondes. Three more advertisements at the end of the program in effect contested the multicultural territory marked out by the show itself and the earlier pizza and cheese advertisements. These included a Paul Hogan spot for tourism, and a Bundaberg rum advertisement featuring a woman diver linked with images of the 'Mean Machine' Olympic swimming team. This set of advertisements presented a trouble-free view of a white Australia, with sun-tanned Aussies enjoying outdoor living. In other words, the construction of 'Australianness' in commercial television drama is ambiguous.

These examples have concerned television and cultural nationalism. There is also the issue of television and nationalism in time of war. Most recently, TV coverage of the Gulf War has been analysed by Tiffen (1992). Unlike the Falklands War, where reporting was severely restricted by the British government, the Gulf battle received saturation coverage from the US cable channel CNN, though security restrictions there too censored CNN reports. The most controversial issue about local TV coverage — which was largely limited to commentary and re-broadcasts of CNN — concerned the less than pro-American remarks made by academic Robert Springborg on the ABC. This drew strong criticism of ABC bias by then Prime Minister, Bob Hawke, and his ministers and by supporters of the war. More TV coverage did not necessarily mean more diverse reporting.

Exercise 11.5 Watching for nationalism on TV
1. What are some current British, American, and Australian comedies on TV? What, if anything, is most distinctive about humour in the Australian ones?
2. How does TV in your city report local, as against national, news and current affairs?
3. What kind of image of Australia do you get from watching *Four Corners* (2), *60 Minutes* (9), *Real Life* (7), and *Hard Copy* (10)?
4. How do the reporters on *Foreign Correspondent* (2) and *Vox Populi* (SBS) position themselves as Australians?

TV and gender identity

US and Australian TV content has changed considerably to reflect the changes in public perceptions of men's and women's roles in the 1990s — their **gender identity**. The never-ending search for the postmodern man and woman goes on in the lifestyle magazines and many more women are in television on and off camera. Arguments still recur about sexism in advertising, but US sitcoms now feature off-beat and independent women, if still in families, in shows like *Roseanne*, while Australian women comedians like Magda Szubanski and Maryanne Fahey are becoming national icons of popular culture.

Roseanne first screened on US television in late 1988. The show broke many conventions of traditional sitcoms, as Roseanne is fat, feminist and blue-collar. Her deadpan, nasal motor-mouth assaults are evenly made against domesticity, femininity and masculinity. With her equally fat and almost equally loud husband Dan playing a central supportive family role, and a close loving relationship with her unmarried sister Jackie, Roseanne Arnold has won over both critics and audiences. She has personal control over the show and many of its producers are women. 'A guy is a lump, like this doughnut,' she reflects. 'Gotta git rid of all this stuff his mom did to him. Then you gotta git rid of all the macho crap from the beer commercials.' This new female assertiveness is also evident in Australian television, though more in comedy sketch programs like *Fast Forward, Full Frontal,* and *Kittson, Fahey*. Other stand-up feminist comics like Wendy Harmer have crossed over from ABC-TV to commercial radio, while Maryanne Fahey, formerly with the *Comedy Company*, is now on ABC-TV.

The gender and ethnic plurality beginning to appear on US and Australian television is not just the result of social change. Network TV in the US is fast losing viewers to the challenge of cable and VCRs. Australia already has a very high home ownership rate of VCRs and pay-TV is belatedly about to begin. This differentiation of audiences and markets is an equally important driving force in changing screen representation. However, some American feminists, such as Mellencamp (1992), argue that TV content still pursues a strategy of social containment that oppresses women. Adapting Freud, she maintains that TV's emphasis on catastrophe (*Real Life, Hard Copy*), on gossip (*Oprah* and *Phil*) and on health and ageing (*Healthy, Wealthy and Wise*) creates an anxiety-ridden social climate.

She sees TV's endorsement of new lifestyle diversity, via fitness, aerobics, sports, high-tech gyms and safe sex campaigns, as reinforcing obsessive-compulsive behaviours in its audiences. Perhaps the agencies have read Mellencamp, for one current Kellogg's Cocopops advertisement shows an anxious middle-aged woman with her face in a shadow next to a packet of

TV and gender identity
How television represents traditional, modern and alternative sex roles for men, women and children.

Cocopops, with a comical Pete Smith 1950s-style male voiceover saying, 'Brave adults are now coming forward to admit it.' What she admits is 'OK, it *is* an obsession'. Back to the male voice: 'Don't all adults love the taste of Kellogg's Cocopops?' TV advertisements like this are stranger than fiction.

In the Australian context Nightingale (1990) has emphasised that the function of commercial TV — which now is becoming the model for SBS-TV and ABC-TV — still identifies women television audiences as oriented towards family and consumption. Watching TV is a form of displaced work, as it is a leisure activity in which viewers are asked to lose themselves and blur the distinction between reality and fantasy. Audiences are asked to see TV advertisements as entertainment, not as a continual reminder of the work of purchasing. With Morse, she points out that shopping and television are culturally inseparable, while the prospect of home shopping via interactive TV is now near. Though women have become more evenly represented on TV, men still own and run the channels and appoint themselves as guardians of family viewing.

Some recent critiques have also examined the changing image of men and masculinity. Joyrich (1990), for example, argues that the later 1980s emphasis on male body display in films and TV carried over into what she calls 'violent hypermasculinity'. This means the social construction of an 'excess of maleness' that makes it possible for men to enjoy and identify with television, though TV is traditionally seen as a woman's medium. If Madonna is the new Monroe with muscles, then Schwarzenegger is Charles Atlas cross-dressed with a machine gun.

There has always been a gendered division in men's and women's reading, film and TV preferences. However, Joyrich sees TV sports and cop shows like *Magnum* and *Miami Vice* as venues for the display of the unwrapped male body, except that Crockett and Tubbs are more *nouvelle* fashion-plates. She argues that North American culture in the aftermath of Vietnam and feminism needs new symbols of masculinity. One of these, also discussed on the ABC's youth program *Attitude*, is the SNAG — the sensitive, new age guy, who is often represented as a figure of fun. But the other option she sees as 'The Savage' — either the angry young men who scream and shout on heavy metal rock videos, like Guns'n Roses, or the screen action hunks, like Schwarzenegger and Van Damme.

Joyrich's feminist critique of TV sport has special relevance to Australia, where sport is more a way of life than in the US. The national TV calendar works around sport. Summer is cricket and tennis, winter is football. Two of these are all-male sports, while men's tennis gets the most coverage and money. As well as live weekend sportscasts, sport is a regular part of all TV news, taking up to ten or fifteen minutes on ABC weekend bulletins. Sport is semi-intellectualised, with Roy Slavin and H.G. Nelson's JJJ broadcasts and TV show, and Elle McFeast on *Live and Sweaty*. SBS has cornered the TV soccer market while, on the commercials, 9's *Wide World of Sports*, with Ken Sutcliffe and Max Walker, is a melange of often bizarre sports from all over the world.

Poynton and Hartley have described AFL (Australian Rules football) as a form of 'male gazing', where women can enjoy watching beautiful male bodies in motion (1990). Football stars like Warwick Capper and Mark 'Jacko'

Jackson represent twin poles of the male 'beauty and the beast' image of sportsmen. Capper's short, tight shorts and his long flowing hair, they argue, disturbed some sports commentators. He has been packaged as a pop star, whereas Jacko's brute force and ugliness got him a good press, an American TV role, and the Energizer battery advertisement. Similarly, writing of State of Origin Rugby League games in Brisbane, Yeates caused controversy by criticising the macho violence of League and the episodes of sexual harassment that marred the records of some players (1992).

If sport is one of the main refuges of real men on TV, there are also many other genres in which men are still dominant. In 1983 Lewis suggested there was a range of male roles on Australian TV — 'soft men' (Ray Martin), 'tough men' (Hinch, replaced unsuccessfully by King-of-the-Talk-Back-Bullies Alan Jones) and 'official men' (Jim Waley). These roles are still in evidence but so, mercifully, are some new ones. All commercial prime-time newsreaders and those on the ABC during the week are still male, as are most current affairs anchors. The TV images of Willesee, Lyneham, Carleton and Munro range from the inquisitorially assertive to very aggressive, while cop shows such as *Police Rescue* continue the TV tradition of series like *Homicide*.

On the other hand, there is now a generation of younger Australian men on TV who are smart, articulate and less macho, such as Andrew Denton and the *Late Show* crew on the ABC, and good-looking, but also not macho, stars like Jason Donovan, Dieter Brummer and Craig McLachlan on the commercials. The characters of Jimmy and Mimo on *Acropolis Now*, though neither smart nor articulate, are also not traditionally macho nor Anglo. There is also a new emphasis on the unclothed male body in advertisements for milk, sports gear and jeans. Gay men or women on TV, however, are still taboo, except for late night programs on SBS or the ABC's *Sticky Moments* with Julian Clary, who is English.

Exercise 11.6   TV's treatment of gender
1. What kind of gender roles do you see young people playing in *Home and Away* (10), *Paradise Beach* (9) and *Neighbours* (7)?
2. How are men's and women's roles shown in *World Sports* (SBS) and *Sports Tonight* (10)?
3. How are gender roles for children positioned in children's television programs like *Blockbuster* (7), *Ship to Shore* (9) and *Totally Wild* (10)?
4. What kind of gender roles are acted out on Australian TV game shows, such as *Sale of the Century* (9) and *Wheel of Fortune* (7)?

The early 1990s will probably prove to be the high-water mark of network television in Australia. Following US trends, the industry in the near future is likely to move into a 'narrowcasting' mode. O'Regan (1993) has described SBS-TV as already being the 'national narrowcaster' and argues that SBS's success will lead to a 'multicultural mainstreaming' of both ABC and commercial TV in future. Whether this is so or not, or if the likely abundance of new channels in the near future will lead to more screen diversity or just more of the same, remains to be seen. In any case, television seems destined to remain the principal leisure-time occupation of many Australians and the most pervasive media form.

Exercise 11.7 Researching and writing a television review

1. Choose either a news or current affairs program or a current TV serial and tape one episode.
2. Research the program by using sources indicated in the chapter and in the references below. Also include reference to previous reviews of the program in the print media. Moran (1993) is excellent background for fictional programs.
3. Then write an extended review of the program using the formal categories of analysis introduced in Exercise 11.3.
4. This exercise may be done either individually or in groups. A group review is best if you choose to analyse TV news or current affairs.

Summary

1. TV criticism and TV research may overlap, but popular TV criticism is usually aimed at viewers and fans and is found in the daily press. TV research is aimed at specialist audiences and has a theoretical basis. The four main types of TV research are policy, production, program and reception studies.
2. The methods used in TV research may be either quantitative — surveys and content analyses — or qualitative, such as participant observation, open-ended interviewing and textual readings. Research conducted by the TV industry is mainly quantitative analysis for measuring audience size and composition.
3. TV can be analysed formally using the ideas of media texts, intertextuality, narrative discourse and TV genres. Intertextuality also involves the ideas of reflexivity and TV flow. Narrative discourse involves the use of signification and visual grammar.
4. TV can also be analysed in terms of the way it constructs images of cultural identity and difference. In practice, formal and contextual analysis are supplementary ways of analysing TV.
5. TV's construction of personal identity may be interpreted negatively, as in Morse's idea of TV as 'mobile privatization'. But it can also be read positively by identifying the pro-social themes and uses of television.
6. TV's construction of national identities may be considered from the viewpoint of the national origins of programs shown, or as how particular images of the nation are projected. TV's image of the nation and society may be either cultural or political.
7. TV also represents men's and women's gender identities. TV programs can be analysed in terms of their targeted gender audiences, as well as how they picture conventional, modern or postmodern gender styles and attitudes.

Discussion questions

1. What are the main differences between TV criticism and TV research in terms of its authors and audiences?
2. Of the four main kinds of TV research, which ones are most likely to overlap with which others?
3. What is the main kind of research conducted by the TV industry and what are its methods?
4. How are radio and TV similar and different as media texts?
5. What are some examples of intertextuality and reflexivity in TV programs and in feature films?
6. What are the main elements in TV narrative discourse and how are these different from film language?
7. How do TV genres compare with different popular novel genres?
8. What is there about TV as a medium that both promotes and prevents social and personal change?
9. How does TV, in different ways, present the cultural and political dimensions of Australian national identity?
10. How do the representations of gender differences between young men and women on TV — in advertisements, and in Australian dramas and serials — compare with those differences in social reality?

Further reading

Berger, A. (1992) *Popular Culture Genres* Newbury Park, CA: Sage.
Cunningham, S. & Turner, G. (eds) (1993) *The Media in Australia* Sydney: Allen & Unwin.
Kozloff, S. (1989) 'Narrative Theory and Television', pp. 42–74 in R. Allen, (ed.) *Channels of Discourse* London: Routledge.
Meehan, E. (1990) 'Why We Don't Count: The Commodity Audience', pp. 117–38 in P. Mellencamp, (ed.) *Logics of Television* Bloomington: Indiana University Press.
Mellencamp, P. (1990) 'TV Time and Catastrophe', pp. 241–65 in P. Mellencamp *Logics of Television op. cit.*
Moran, A. (ed.) (1992) *Stay Tuned: An Australian Broadcasting Reader* Sydney: Allen & Unwin.
Morse, M. (1990) 'The Freeway, the Mall, and Television', pp. 193–221 in P. Mellencamp *op. cit.*
Nightingale, V. (1990) 'Women as Audiences', pp. 25–37 in M. Brown, (ed.) *Television and Women's Culture* Beverly Hills, CA: Sage.
Tulloch, J. (1989) 'Soaps and Ads', pp. 120–37 in J. Tulloch & G. Turner, (eds) *Australian Television* Sydney: Allen & Unwin.
Williams, R. (1974) *Television* London: Fontana.

References

Allen, M. (1993) 'Telecom adverts, Telecom networks, Telecom Australia', *Australian Journal of Communication* 20 (2): 97–114.

Allen, R. (1985) *Speaking of Soap Operas* Chapel Hill: University of North Carolina Press.

Altman, R. (1986) 'Television/Sound', pp. 39–55 in T. Modleski, (ed.) *Studies in Entertainment* Bloomington: Indiana University Press.

Ang, I. (1985) *Watching Dallas* London: Methuen.

Armstrong, M., Blakeney, M. & Watterson, R. (1992) *Broadcasting Law and Policy in Australia* Sydney: Butterworths, 2nd edn.

Bell, P., Boehringer, K. & Crofts, S. (1982) *Programmed Politics* Sydney: Sable.

Bonney, W. & Wilson, H. (1983) *Australia's Commercial Media* Melbourne: Macmillan.

Brunsdon, C. & Morley, D. (1978) *Everyday Television: Nationwide* London: BFI.

Cantor, M. (1983) *The Soap Opera* Beverly Hills, CA: Sage.

Collins, R. (1990) *Culture, Communication and National Identity* University of Toronto Press.

Coupe, B. & Jakubowicz, A. (1993) *Nextdoor Neighbours* Canberra: OMA.

Cunningham, S. (1989) 'Textual Innovation in the Australian Miniseries', pp. 39–52 in J. Tulloch & G. Turner, (eds) *Australian Television* Sydney: Allen & Unwin.

Cunningham, S. (1988) 'Kennedy-Miller: House Style in Australian Television', *Media Information Australia* 50: 177–201.

Cunningham, S. (1992) *Framing Culture* Sydney: Allen & Unwin.

Curthoys, A. & Docker, J. (1989) 'In Praise of Prisoner', pp. 52–72 in J. Tulloch and G. Turner, (eds) *op. cit.*

Davis, G. (1988) *Breaking up the ABC* Sydney: Allen & Unwin.

Davis, H. (1991) 'The Language of TV News', pp. 182–92 in R. Cochrane & D. Carroll, (eds) *Psychology and Social Issues* London: The Falmer Press.

Elliot, P. (1972) *The Making of a Television Series* London: Constable.

Fiske, J. (1987) *Television Culture* London: Methuen.

Fiske, J. & Hartley, J. (1978) *Reading Television* London: Methuen.

Gerbner, G. & Gross, L. (1980) 'The "Mainstreaming" of America', *Journal of Communication* 30 (3): 10–29.

Hall, S. (1981) *Turning On, Turning Off: Australian TV in the 'Eighties* Sydney: Cassell.

Hartley, J. (1989) 'Continuous Pleasures in Marginal Places', pp. 139–57 in J. Tulloch and G. Turner (eds.) *op. cit.*

Hartley, J. (1992) *Tele-ology* London: Routledge.

Henningham, J. (1988) *Looking at Television News* Melbourne: Longman Cheshire.

Jacka, L. (1991) *The ABC of Drama* Sydney: AFTRS.

Jacka, L. (1992) 'Globalisation and Australian Film and Television', pp. 185–92 in A. Moran (ed.) *op. cit.*

Jacka, L. & Cunningham, S. (1993) 'Australian Television: An International Player?' *Media Information Australia* 70: 17–27.

Joyrich, L. (1990) 'Critical and Textual Hypermasculinity', pp. 156–73 in P. Mellencamp *op. cit.*

Lealand, G. (1988) *A Foreign Egg in Our Nest?* Wellington: Victoria University Press.

Lealand, G. (1991) 'Selling the Airwaves', *Media Information Australia* 62: 68–74.

Lee, C. (1980) *Media Imperialism Reconsidered* Beverly Hills, CA: Sage.

Lewis, G. (1983) *Real Men Like Violence* Sydney: Kangaroo Press.

Lowery, S. & DeFleur, M. (1988) *Milestones in Mass Communication Research* New York: Longman, 2nd edn.

Mellencamp, P. (1992) *High Anxiety* Bloomington: Indiana University Press.

Moran, A. (1989) 'Three Stages of Australian TV', pp. 1–15 in J. Tulloch & G. Turner, (eds) *Australian Television* Sydney: Allen & Unwin.

Moran, A. (1993) *Moran's Guide to Australian TV Series* Sydney: AFTRS.

Morris, M. (1990) 'Banality in Cultural Studies', pp. 14–44 in P. Mellencamp *op. cit.*

Natt, H. & McKie, D. (1993) 'Situating Comedies, Plac(at)ing Identities', *Australian Journal of Communication* 20 (2): 114–26.

Nightingale, V. (1992) 'Contesting Domestic Territory: Watching Rugby League on TV', pp. 156–69 in A. Moran *op. cit.*

Noble, G. & Noble, E. (1979) 'Teenagers' Use and Gratification of *Happy Days*', *Media Information Australia* 11: 17–23.

O'Regan, T. (1993) *Australian Television Culture* Sydney: Allen & Unwin.

Palmer, P. (1986) *The Lively Audience* Sydney: Allen & Unwin.

Poynton, B. & Hartley, J. (1990) 'Male-Gazing: Australian Rules Football, Gender and Television', pp. 144–57 in M. Brown, (ed.) *Television and Women's Culture* Beverly Hills, CA: Sage.

Rowland, W. (1983) *The Politics of TV Violence* Beverly Hills, CA: Sage.

Tiffen, R. (1992) 'News Coverage', pp. 114–39 in M. Goot & R. Tiffen, (eds) *Australia's Gulf War* Melbourne: Melbourne University Press.

Tulloch, J. & Moran, A. (1986) *A Country Practice* Sydney: Currency Press.

Turner, G. (1989) 'Transgressive TV', pp. 25–40 in J. Tulloch & A. Moran *op. cit.*

Turow, J. (1984) 'Pressure Groups and Television Entertainment', pp. 142–65 in W. Rowland & B. Watkins, (eds) *Interpreting Television* Beverly Hills, CA: Sage.

Wilson, T. (1994) 'Television and Difference', *Australian Journal of Communication* 21(1): 33–45.

Windschuttle, K. (1984) *The Media* Melbourne: Penguin, 2nd edn. 1988.

Winter, P. (1993) 'News Production at Television New Zealand Ltd 1989–1992', *Australian Journalism Review* 15 (1): 17–29.

Yeates, H. (1992) 'The State of Origin', *Australian Journalism Review* 14 (2): 130–36.

Globalisation/Kokusaika

国際化

12

Objectives

After completing this chapter you should be able to:

- discuss how the idea of modernity was debated in the US after the 1920s in terms of media effects and mass culture;
- appreciate how these arguments were changed by new Latin American and Asian perspectives on development communication;
- consider how globalisation has impacted on several South-East Asian countries;
- understand some of the differences between Japanese and Australian communication policies.

Chapter 12

In Hong Kong they're forcibly repatriating — repatriating: what a word! — Vietnamese refugees. Remember Viet Nam? Now they make self-indulgent films about it and build memorials. The Hong Kong Chinese are doing it; and they *want British passports. 1997 is not far away. If there's no room in the inn, perhaps there will be in the manger. The Queen's Country is taking 250 000 'economic citizens' into Britain while Her Majesty's Government is repatriating 'economic refugees' to Viet Nam. Refugee-blues dreaded like AIDS. Wait for Christmas 1997.*

The Wounded Sea, *Satendra Nandan*

Nandan's ironic comment reflects his own experience as a doubly displaced person. His grandparents were shipped to Fiji by the British and in 1987 he was forced to leave Fiji for Australia as a result of a military coup which overthrew the elected Bavadra government, of which he was a member. This experience of refugee displacement is one of the dominant themes of current discussions about globalisation, whether they come from Fiji, Viet Nam or China.

Pro-democracy protest. The banner proclaims 'Blood on the Great Wall', China, 1989. (Photo: *Anon*)

kokusaika
The Japanese word for 'internationalisation'.

A new global culture is coming into place. The Japanese term for it is **kokusaika**, meaning internationalisation. It is evident in the spread of computer-based information networks and Direct Broadcast Satellites. As well as world tourism and the refugee experience, another factor contributing to a global outlook is the widespread concern with environmental issues. Matters such as the size of the hole in the world's ozone layer and the rate of 'global warming' are a source of concern to all the world's peoples. The attention paid to environmental issues boosted Sydney's successful bid for the year 2000 Olympics. The insight that the economy and ecology of countries are interwoven is a main impetus to thinking of the world globally (Mowlana, 1993).

The concept of globalisation is relatively new in social theory. It has recently been elaborated by cultural sociologists, such as Robertson (1990), who take a different approach to interpreting international communication issues. Previously these have been dealt with more in terms of the spread of world communication systems (e.g. Frederick, 1993). These newer approaches merge some of the concerns of communication and cultural studies in analysing cultural, economic and political questions. Notable Australian communications globalisation analyses have been made by Sinclair (1991) of the advertising industry, by Jacka and Cunningham (1993) of film and television, and by Chitty's reappraisal of development communication (1993). This chapter considers globalisation from a regional Australian communication perspective and relies methodologically on cultural and economic history, comparative political economy and political communication. However, before we can analyse globalisation, we need first to ask what 'modernity' and 'modernisation' mean, then link these debates with globalisation.

Modernisation, the media and development

The twentieth century is often described as 'the age of communication' and as 'the American century'. It is true that it was in America that modern media and communication technologies were first and most fully developed. Many of the ideas about the nature of communication as a social process have also been most carefully worked out by Americans. This link between American pre-eminence as a world power and the centrality of communication in the twentieth century, however, needs to be seen as part of a longer-term trend in Western society towards modernisation. Major Western countries became **modern** after approximately the 1920s. The idea of the modern can be explained in terms of aesthetics and psychology as well as institutionally and is often contrasted with the changes from traditional to modern society (Cooke, 1990). Our concern here, however, is with communications, so we will say that as societies modernise they become increasingly industrialised and urbanised, and more dependent on media and communications.

modernity
A state in which societies become increasingly industrialised and urbanised, and more dependent on the media and communications.

Tradition and modernity, Denpasar, Bali.
(Photo: *Glen Lewis*)

The most visible forms of the new media were radio, movies, and television. Radio began in the US in the early 1920s, organised entirely on a commercial basis, and enjoyed its golden age between 1930 and 1950. Movies began in Europe and the US in the 1900s and Hollywood had its maximum audience reach between 1930 and 1940. Television began in the US in the 1940s then boomed after the 1950s. Radio, movies and TV were only the most visible of the new media. The press and the print media also expanded greatly. Newspaper circulation in the US, however, peaked between 1900 and 1910 and has since declined. More importantly, the growing cultural importance of the press — especially in its tabloid form — and of radio, movies, and TV, were seen as symbols of the development of a 'modern' society. Along with cars and aeroplanes, broadcasting, the film and the popular press irreversibly changed the nature of public communication in Western countries after the 1920s.

Additionally, there was a relatively 'invisible' set of other new technologies, such as the telephone system, undersea cables and wireless telegraphy (Mulgan, 1991). Although central in the expansion of global commerce and in the newspaper business, undersea cables did not capture public attention in the way broadcasting and the movies did. This was not true, however, of the extension of computer systems after the 1950s and the world's first communication satellite in 1962. Each of these technologies tended to spark off a dual response about their potential, both in the US and elsewhere. Their advocates saw many possible benefits they could bring, but their critics were alarmed by their potentially negative effects. Radio, for example, was seen by its advocates as a 'family friend', and as a way of linking isolated communities. Its critics, however, warned about the possible effects of poor speech habits, or of political demagogues influencing mass audiences (Johnson, 1988). A similar cycle of high hopes and fears accompanied the introduction of films, television and, later, computers.

These new media had unprecedented influence because they were re-introducing a traditional, more oral and immediate style that was shifting public communication away from a print-based culture. Additionally, by the moral standards of most Western countries, the new media were speaking in a brash American accent that seemed to convey antiestablishment values. This concern was expressed by more traditional rural and religious groups in the US, while in other parts of the world the media were seen as spreading 'Americanisation'. The 'American way of life' was spread globally by film stars, by jazz, swing, then rock'n roll, and later by images of American affluence on television.

These hopes and fears about the new media and 'Americanisation' came together in a loose body of social theory and criticism about the media and modern life. There were two main strands to this narrative of public concern. First, at the more specialised level of social theory, especially in the US, there developed a body of social science research about 'media effects'. Second, there was a more widely shared set of anxieties about the dangers of 'mass society' that was informed by social and literary criticism.

The main argument in **media effects** discourse in the US between the 1920s and the 1940s was whether the mass media had 'strong' or 'weak' effects on their audiences. Those who argued for a strong effects model included Walter Lippman, who focused on the role of propaganda in the press in World War I in

media effects
A debate originating in the US between the 1920s and 1940s about whether the mass media had 'strong' or 'weak' effects on audiences.

Globalisation/Kokusaika

The Americanisation of outer space.
Source: *G. Pryor, The Canberra Times, 10 December 1993. Used with permission.*

moulding public opinion (Lowery & DeFleur, 1988: 38). Later, in the 1940s, however, social scientists such as Paul Lazarsfeld argued for a 'weak' or 'limited effects' model. Based on the concept of a 'two-step flow' of communication, he maintained that mass media messages were watered down by opinion leaders in various social groups, who filtered out the persuasive effect of the media for their audiences. It was this 'limited effects' model which has remained the orthodoxy in US communication studies.

There was another worry about the power of the media which was of wider public interest. This concerned the degree of monopoly ownership in media industries and their use for the purposes of persuasion, in either politics or advertising. Books such as Vance Packard's *The Hidden Persuaders* (1957) alarmed many with its ideas of how psychology and the media were being used for manipulative purposes. Fears about subliminal advertising, for instance, were expressed. These arguments about the media's role centred around the supposedly degrading effects of **mass culture**. Dwight McDonald detected a division between 'high-brow' and 'low-brow' culture in the media. He argued that the influence of the media led to a deterioration in public taste and standards which undermined people's capacity to exercise their individual judgment. Trivialised news and sensational entertainment were making people vulnerable to advertising and to political propaganda (McDonald, in Rosenberg & White, 1957). This 'mass society' critique also developed in European countries where the charge of 'Americanisation' was added. In 1930s Germany, Theodor Adorno saw jazz as a portent of Nazism, while in 1950s Britain Richard Hoggart lamented the decline of traditional working class communities (Curran & Seaton, 1988).

This debate about the media and modernity ran from the 1920s to the 1960s and still surfaces today. Looking at that argument in the US, Jensen (1990) has

mass culture
The argument that urbanisation and the mass media create a division between 'high-brow' and 'low-brow' culture which undermines people's capacity to exercise their individual judgment.

claimed 'the media' and 'modernity' were being seen as synonymous by both their critics and defenders. That is, much criticism of the media was a displaced critique of a wider dissatisfaction with the many real problems that resulted from modernisation — such as urban pollution, environmental degradation, crime, continued social inequality and virulent nationalism. In her reading, the media became modernity's scapegoat. Tensions in Western societies were expressed in terms of exaggerated hopes and fears about the role of the communications media.

Exercise 12.1   The media's effect on folk culture
'Festivals and the Media — For Good or Bad?'

At times the media can influence whether a ceremony is preserved or dispensed with.

The Nong Kra Temple in Songthanburi County holds a 'river cleansing' ritual during the Monkey Festival each year, which asks the gods to come to purify the river.

Because the temple guardians were concerned last year that their ancient wooden statue of the Monkey God might break, they considered not using it in their annual river cleansing ceremony. However, it had not been realised that a visiting Australian television crew wanted to make a television program about the ceremony and wished to film this rare religious ritual.

After much discussion, the temple guardians agreed to use the sacred symbol in the ceremony. Fortunately, no damage was done.

1. What does this fictional news item suggest about the impact of modern media on a country's traditional folk culture?
2. What foreign countries have you visited where photography was not permitted in certain locations?
3. Does the media in Australia have similar influence in dealing with religious and community cultural events?

From modernity to modernisation: Asia and Latin America

Moving from North American perspectives on how ideas about the media and modernity developed, let us now examine the role of the media in non-Western contexts. The global political agenda in 1945 was set by the US's confrontation with the USSR. The Cold War of the 1950s, which lasted until Gorbachev's *Perastroika* (openness) in the late 1980s, cast the US as the capitalist hero and the Soviets as the villains of world communism. It was against this threatening nuclear-war background that the Third World countries emerged and postwar debates about 'modernisation and development' took place. Whereas concern about the media's role and the nature of mass culture continued in the First World, the issue for Third World countries was one of nation-building and the need for rapid economic development.

India, China and Indonesia emerged as the largest newly independent Asian states after the war. India and Indonesia took the path of 'non-alignment' in the global conflict between capitalism and communism, whereas China chose communism. The 1950s and 1960s, however, saw the formation of a multitude of new Asian and African smaller nations. Algeria, Kenya and Cuba won their independence from Western colonialism, while serious conflict took place in the civil wars in Korea in the 1950s and Viet Nam in the 1960s. Singapore also split from Malaya in 1965 to become a city-state in its own right, while Taiwan and South Korea re-established their independence from Japan.

After 1945 the United Nations replaced the League of Nations and through its agencies, such as UNESCO (United Nations Educational, Scientific and Cultural Organisation), became centrally involved in the new drive for economic development. After the US launched the Marshall Plan for rebuilding Europe in the 1940s, it turned its attention to Third World development. The US was undertaking a global public relations and propaganda campaign to 'make the world safe for democracy'. This had several negative results, such as American support for the corrupt Marcos regime in the Philippines and the Diem government in Viet Nam, and the deposition of the democratically elected socialist President Allende of Chile in the early 1970s.

The more positive side of US involvement in Third World issues was the attempt to boost the economic growth of developing nations. In facilitating this, development communication was established as an academic field of study in its own right with important practical policy implications. The best-known US development communication scholars included Lerner, Pye, Schramm, and Everett Rogers. Their 1950s model emphasised top-down centralised planning and capital-intensive industrialisation via the transfer of communication and production technologies from First to Third World countries. There was an emphasis on measuring per capita income and the level of television and radio ownership as an index of modernisation.

These scholars often worked with the support of international organisations, such as UNESCO and the World Bank, in advising Third World governments, particularly in Asia, to develop modern media systems. The hope was that this would trigger economic growth and encourage popular participation in the development process, notably in agriculture and in family planning projects. Rogers placed special emphasis on the communication strategies needed to diffuse new technologies effectively. This overall agreement on the desirability of national development through communications growth came to be known as **modernisation theory** (Melkote, 1991).

However, in the 1970s, this approach was challenged on two fronts. First, it became clear that some Third World states, such as Mexico and Brazil, as well as Taiwan, South Korea, Hong Kong and Singapore, were rapidly industrialising. Second, a group of Latin American scholars, such as A. G. Frank, Paulo Freire and Luis Beltran, articulated a rival theory of communication and development. Called **dependency theory** (*dependencia*), this argued that Third World underdevelopment resulted from the political and economic constraints of First World dominance. According to this theory, the importation of First World media products by the Third World was perpetuating the cultural dependency of these countries on the 'periphery' on First World countries, which were 'the core'. Whereas 'modernisation and development' theory stressed the democratic intent of Western modernisation programs, 'dependency theory' saw them as means of prolonging cultural and economic imperialism (Atwood & McAnany, 1986).

After the 1970s a review of these theories took place. Some American writers, notably Rogers, revised their earlier views, while new Asian scholars, notably in India and the Philippines, suggested different approaches. Sri Lankan scholar Wimal Dissanayake, for example, criticised both theories and argued that there was a need for local community involvement. The use of native folk traditions to spread development messages — e.g. birth control information in folk dances

modernisation theory
The agreement on the desirability of national development through communications and economic growth.

dependency theory
The view that Third World underdevelopment results from the political and economic constraints of First World dominance.

and songs — was one suggestion. This approach received some support from UNESCO in the 1970s through 'development support communication' programs. There was now to be a new emphasis on 'small technology' rather than 'high technology' (e.g. the use of local radio broadcasting), and wider consultation with local rural communities (Dissanayake, 1984).

These ideas were given special emphasis in the Philippines. Though US influence in Philippines development communication research was strong, a number of women scholars, such as Nora Quebral, outlined a distinctive approach. She identified three related areas of **development communication** — development journalism, development support communication, and the discipline of development communication. The Philippines was one of the first Asian countries to set up development journalism programs in the late 1960s. Unlike Western journalism, these aimed to highlight the positive features of modernisation. Development support communication, in contrast, arose from the needs of UN aid projects such as UNICEF, and was linked with the managerial needs of development organisations in rural areas. Last, development communication studies aimed at constructing a special academic discipline (Quebral, 1986). Her emphasis on community empowerment has been extended by recent writers to argue that new communications technologies can be used as a means of community self-reliance (Chitty, 1992).

Despite efforts to adjust development communication practices to the needs of local communities, the media's role in national politics in many developing countries has often been repressive. By Western standards the practices of many Asian media systems continue to be undemocratic, although this is frequently defended by Asian politicians, such as Singapore's Lee Kuan-Yew (Lee, 1993). There remains an unresolved tension about this issue. At the time of the May 1992 pro-democracy protests in Thailand, for example, despite the existence of five TV channels and three satellite services in Bangkok, nothing was shown locally of these protests at the time. Television news stories concentrated instead on the arrival of entrants to the Miss Universe contest (Hamilton, 1993).

The point here, however, in tracing the links between ideas about modernisation and development in non-Western countries and debates about modernity and mass culture in the West, is that in each case the media's role was often problematic. The tension that exists in Western countries about the media has its counterpart in most Asian countries, except that their debates are conducted with different cultural assumptions (Slade & Applebee, 1993). On the positive side, in Asian countries there is a desire to see the media used pro-socially to promote economic and social progress — this kind of view is rarely expressed in Western countries, where 'bad news is good news' (Glasgow, 1980). On the other hand, the limits on media freedom is not a topic usually open for discussion in many Asian countries.

Exercise 12.2 Women's education in developing countries

A recent news release for a global financial aid agency argued:

'The education of women in developing countries, such as Africa and India, has important potential to securing long-term protection of the global environment.

It does this for several reasons. Women who are educated have less children and that

development communication
The use of communication policy, journalism and research to promote national economic growth in less developed countries.

is good for the environment. Also, women in developing countries often have the responsibility for managing the family's household resources.

It benefits First World countries to fund the education of women in Third World societies because we all share the same global enviroment. More education means less children.'

1. Why might some groups in developing countries not welcome these comments?
2. What kinds of criticisms might First World governments attract by tying their aid programs to family planning projects in developing countries?
3. Is it correct to believe that population control will always benefit developing countries?

From modernisation to globalisation

At some point in the 1980s communication and culture scholars as well as business executives and policy makers started to talk of 'globalisation'. There is no agreed meaning for this term yet. Broadly, however, **globalisation** refers to the process of increased world interdependence brought about by recent changes in the global economy and in communications technology. Globalisation implies something more than internationalisation (Featherstone, 1990). Four trends associated with globalisation will now be considered: deregulation and privatisation, communications technology convergence, deterritorialisation and global cultural flows.

What is implicit in the idea of globalisation is that the influence of nation-states in the world is declining, while the power of transnational corporations (TNCs) such as IBM, Philips and NEC is increasing. In this sense the world is becoming postnational, or as scholars in literary studies say, postcolonial (Hodge & Mishra, 1990). This change in the political and economic order is accompanied by shifts in cultural values and ideas about personal identity. Critics who concentrate on these latter changes say the world is becoming **postmodern**. Postmodernists have several themes, but one of their key ones is that traditional beliefs in 'meta-narratives' — such as science, progress, patriarchy, nationality and even rationality — no longer apply (Milner, 1990). The postmodernist view is one that rejects linear accounts of human knowledge and progress implicit in modernity (Lyotard, 1984). Debates here are very complex, but an excellent account of them from a British viewpoint is available in McGuigan (1992: 207–49).

Four key elements of globalisation

The first key element of globalisation is **deregulation**. This means getting rid of government regulations which are seen to constrain private sector activities. This movement originated in the US as far back as the 1950s, but its greatest impact came with the Reagan Presidency in the 1980s when the airlines, banking and telecommunications were deregulated. The most significant example of communications deregulation was the 1982 break-up of the Bell telephone company AT&T. The rationale was to increase competition in

globalisation
Increased world interdependence brought about by recent rapid changes in the global economy and in communications technology.

postmodernity
The view that in postindustrial societies traditional beliefs in 'meta-narratives', such as science, progress, patriarchy, nationality — and even rationality — no longer apply. Linear accounts of human knowledge and progress implicit in modernity are rejected.

deregulation
The removal of government regulations that are thought to hinder private sector activities.

markets and provide cheaper service. The Bell divestiture was followed in Britain by the privatisation of British Telecom in 1984, then of the National Telephone and Telegraph company in Japan in 1985.

Privatisation is another aspect of deregulation. It is where public sector agencies are either completely or partially sold off to private sector interests. The most striking example of privatisation in Australia so far has been the partial sale of the Commonwealth Bank in 1992. In communications, the biggest change has been the entry of Optus to compete with Telecom in the telephone market. There has also been the introduction of sponsorship advertising to SBS-TV in 1990, while the 1986 changes to the *Broadcasting Act* opened up the Australian media market to allow new 'players' to buy into TV companies. These had previously been controlled by newspaper and magazine owners, such as Fairfax and Packer.

The second main force in globalisation has been the trend towards **communications technology convergence**. This is the interfacing of telecommunications, computers and broadcasting. The specialised meaning of this term refers to the convergence between telecommunications and broadcasting (Westerway, 1990). Telephony, computers and broadcast technologies are combined by digitisation to become broadband ISDN services. In practice, this means the possibility of interactive media — such as home shopping on TV — and the accessing of voice, video and data from home computers (Schaap, 1992).

The third element in globalisation is that of **deterritorialisation**. This is the accelerated physical and symbolic mobility of world populations. Where communications technology convergence refers to the integration of communication systems to move information more effectively, deterritorialisation is about the movement of people. This term seeks to define the social impact of rapid changes in communication and the global economy on world populations. The last decade has seen unprecedented movements of people globally. These are both physical — as tourists, students, immigrants, refugees and guest workers — and symbolic, in terms of the creation of new world markets by global marketing and by the world film, TV and music industries. The first concerns people moving about the world, while the second is about the psychological impact of these movements, resulting in a new symbolic world cultural order.

The last element of globalisation is **global cultural flows** — the circulation across national borders of new ideas, images and values that may clash with traditional cultures. Appadurai (1990) has defined these as ethnoscapes, mediascapes, technoscapes, finanscapes and ideoscapes. Ethnoscapes are the movement of people in the new global system. Mediascapes are the image-centred, narrative-based versions of reality represented in TV, film, video, music and print. Technoscapes are the movement of information and production technologies across national borders by multinational companies. Finanscapes are the internationalisation of world currency markets via the computerised linking of national stock exchanges. Last, ideoscapes are key ideas and ideologies of different political cultures that circulate globally but are often intepreted differently, such as 'human rights', 'democracy' or 'sustainable development'.

---

privatisation
Where public sector agencies are either completely or partially sold off to private sector interests.

communications technology convergence
The interfacing of telecommunications, computers and broadcasting.

deterritorialisation
The accelerated physical and symbolic mobility of world populations.

global cultural flows
The circulation of new ideas, images and values across national borders that may clash with traditional cultures.

Globalisation/Kokusaika

Exercise 12.3 Globalisation quiz
Match the statements on the left side with the correct ones on the right side.

1. Global information flows is
2. Privatisation is
3. Globalisation is
4. Communications technology convergence means
5. Deregulation refers to

A. the process of world interdependence.
B. getting rid of government regulation.
C. the selling off of public sector agencies.
D. the circulation of images across national borders.
E. telecommunications, computers and broadcasting being interfaced.

Globalisation and media politics in South-East Asia

The effects of globalisation in South-East Asia have been dramatic in the past decade. The Association of South-East Asian States (ASEAN) includes Brunei, the Philippines, Thailand, and Indonesia, Singapore and Malaysia. This section of the chapter will consider the experiences of three of those nations — Singapore, Malaysia and Indonesia — with reference to changes in their communications infrastructures and some of the media-related political disputes that have taken place between them and Australia. Compared to Australian relations with Japan, which will be surveyed in the last section of the chapter, several important cross-cultural communication breakdowns have taken place between Australia and its closest Asian neighbours.

Singapore has the most developed telecommunications network in Asia after Japan. Singapore and Malaysia are in the forefront of the communications revolution in the region, while Indonesia lags behind except for its satellite system (Wang, 1993). Malaysia has gone furthest with its privatisation policies in communications. Corresponding reforms in the other two countries have so far been limited. In Singapore the government has a tradition of strong public control that emphasises a 'looking outward' policy, aiming mainly to encourage foreign TNCs to locate in Singapore rather than develop domestic business. In Indonesia, the largest private companies are owned by Chinese groups, so privatisation policies likely to benefit them, rather than native Indonesian business, have not been pursued. In Malaysia, critics argue that privatisation has benefited established Malay businesses rather than new competitors (Milne, 1992).

Issues concerning deterritorialisation and cultural flows are politically sensitive in all three countries. The presence of a substantial Chinese population in Malaysia and Indonesia goes back to the centuries-old migration of the Chinese diaspora. Governments in both Malaysia and Indonesia encourage native Malays and Indonesians via policies favouring the *Bumiputra* (Malay 'sons of the soil') and the *Pribumi* (Indonesian interests). Ethnic conflict of this kind was the motivation for the Chinese in Singapore to secede from Malaysia in 1965.

There are also other deterritorialised groups in both Malaysia and Indonesia. There is a Malay separatist movement, for example, along the Southern Thai border. In Indonesia there are ethnic tensions arising from the dominance of Java over the outer islands. The government has a 'transmigration' policy aimed at reducing population pressure in Java by encouraging settlement in Irian Jaya. It is against this troubled background that the conservative attitudes — by Western standards — of all three governments to their media and communication practices need to be appreciated.

In 1985 the Singapore government consolidated the press into one group, Singapore Press Holdings, with the aim of 'developing common ideals'. Newspapers from Malaysia and Singapore are not allowed into the other country, and currently Singapore private homes and hotels are not permitted to own satellite dishes. Singapore has had many public communication campaigns aimed at bringing about community change. There is a longstanding 'Speak Mandarin' campaign, a National Courtesy campaign, and a Productivity Month. There is a stronger element of state direction in these campaigns than most Western countries would tolerate. Between 1986 and 1988 several US papers and magazines, such as *Time*, were banned for alleged interference in domestic politics (Sussman, 1991; Birch, 1993).

The Malaysian government, too, has often controlled its own and censored foreign media. The New Straits Times newspaper group was formed in 1972 to take control of the press from Chinese and foreign interests, while BERNAMA was made the sole distributor of foreign news in 1984. In 1986 there was a three-month ban on the *Asian Wall Street Journal*, and in the next two years several Chinese and Malaysian papers were banned for reporting sensitive racial issues. Prime Minister Mahathir and his deputies have often criticised Western media for belittling the development efforts of Malaysians, for painting a poor image of Islam, and for being under 'Zionist control' (Lent, 1991). In 1992 he criticised the ABC serial *Embassy* for the unfavourable portrayal of a country

Secular and sacred in Kuala Lumpur.
(Photo: *Robert Hamilton*)

taken to be Malaysia. In the same year, press controversy continued in both countries over the custody dispute about the Malaysian–Australian Gillespie children (Loo & Ramanathan, 1993). Then in December 1993 Malaysia briefly banned all Australian radio and TV program imports because of Prime Minister Keating's comments about Mahathir's 'recalcitrant' absence from the November APEC meeting.

Media freedom is limited in Indonesia as well. There is a policy of Press Pancasila (*Pers Pancasila*) which requires journalists and editors to observe the principles of the national ideology. This means that any divisive ethnic, religious or racial issue should not be reported. There is also a press permit system, the SIUPP, which licenses newspapers and may be revoked if officials consider breaches of standards have occurred. In 1991 the editor of *Monitor*, a monthly magazine, was jailed for five years for publishing opinion poll results which rated the prophet Mohammed eleventh in a list of the country's most popular figures (Kingsbury, 1992). Similar restrictions have been applied to Indonesian television. Commercials in TVRI broadcasts were deleted on services to the outer islands and rural areas to prevent unfulfilled material expectations. The introduction of commercial TV has also seen a limitation on the number of foreign films on TVRI (Kitley, 1992).

There have been several cases of controversial Australian media treatments of these South-East Asian countries. In 1986 *Sydney Morning Herald* journalist, David Jenkins, wrote an exposé of the Soeharto family's business interests that caused diplomatic protests (*SMH*, 10 April 1986). ABC-TV reporters were also banned from Indonesia for much of the 1980s, though Radio Australia traditionally was well-received by Indonesian audiences. Most seriously, the legacy of the killing of two Australian journalists by Indonesian troops in East Timor in 1975 and the Dili massacre in 1991 has promoted regular negative Australian media coverage of the East Timor situation. Australian media treatment has also offended Singapore, with the 1991 banning of the

Street theatre in Brisbane: protest on East Timor, 1976. (Photo: *Glen Lewis*)

ABC/US/Japan documentary *The Big Picture*'s treatment of Singapore (Hodge, 1991).

Australian journalists are expected by their editors to report the more notable evils and conflicts they see in neighbouring Asian countries, just as they are in Australian affairs. Sometimes, reasonably, they complain that they are criticised as culturally insensitive by foreign politicians and officials to distract attention from the real issues (Dobell, 1993). The danger of journalists taking a trouble-shooting attitude to foreign reporting is that it may easily slip over into irresponsible and neocolonialist criticisms of Asian societies. There has been relatively little academic or journalistic writing that seeks to explain the cross-cultural differences of Australia with South-East Asian countries (though see Noesjirwan, 1986; Hardjono, 1992). As one Filipino comments about the role of the Australian media in reporting news about his country:

> [It] tends to adopt a moralistic or 'foreign missionary' attitude whenever things appear to go wrong in the Philippines and therefore are deemed newsworthy ... Television programs such as *60 Minutes* seem to harbour a fascination with prostitutes, paedophiles, murder and slavery ... From most of what one reads in the news or sees on television — and there is not much — the Philippines appears to be the complete opposite of what Australian normalcy is perceived to be. Through the use of clichés and metaphors an 'eternal' Philippines is concocted which is more digestible to the average Australian. A traditional perception of the oriental 'Third World' is thus affirmed (Ileto, 1991).

Exercise 12.4 Satellites and TV violence
Satellite TV blamed for Indian Riots

A 1993 press release reads as follows:

'Police and community leaders have claimed that foreign news satellite broadcasts have aggravated ethnic tensions in India during recent communal riots.

The official policy of Indian television has been to play down religious passions, so domestic news coverage never indicates which members of particular religious groups are involved in the riots. The official news term is that only "a religious community" was involved.

Recent news coverage via satellite from the CNN and BBC services, however, specifies whether Muslims, Sikhs, Hindus or Christians were involved.

Indian authorities consider these foreign reports add to communal hostilities.'

1. What other violent world news has been broadcast by satellite in recent years?
2. Do nations have the legal and moral rights to stop 'satellite spillover'?
3. What kind of communal violence can also be identified regularly in Western countries?

Media and modernisation debates in Japan and Australia

The rest of this chapter will compare Japan's experience of internationalisation with Australia's in further analysing the regional meanings of globalisation for Australia. *Kokusaika* is a Japanese word meaning 'internationalisation'. The modernisation debate in Japan and Australia took a course that was like neither that in Third World countries nor in the US. The arrival of television in both countries had a similar initial result — most programming was imported from the US. Both also developed dual regulatory systems, with Japan's NHK (1926) and Australia's ABC (1932) being state-funded, modelled more on the British BBC than on American networks. However, there were several important differences in their broadcasting culture. Japan's public TV system retained first place over its commercial rivals, unlike in Australia, and also kept its licence fee funding base. Second, the NHK-E channel was devoted to educational broadcasting after 1959 (Stronach, 1989). The ABC, restricted to one channel, made no such commitment.

Third, a clear difference in program content between the two emerged by the mid-1960s. Japan began to produce most of its own programs and in the space of a decade became a media exporter, especially of animated TV shows (Ito, 1990b). The weaker Australian industry, though protected to an extent by local content rules, did not develop an export-oriented local production sector until about the mid-1970s. The Japanese film industry was also one of the world's largest. Between 1954 and the mid-1960s it was the biggest in the world. Its other media exports included pop music (*enka* and *karaoke*), comic books (*manga*) and some worldwide TV successes, such as *The Samurai* (1965) and *Oshin* (1984).

How then did both countries deal with the cultural impact of Americanisation and modernisation? Also, what kind of debates did they have about the role of the media and the growth of mass culture? Perhaps the most striking difference was that Japan developed a version of communication theory that presented an increasingly assertive image of Japan as an 'information society'. In contrast, Australian media debates took a more defensive nationalist line in arguing for protectionist media cultural policies.

The 1950s and 1960s

There were some surprising similarities about these kinds of debates in both countries in the 1950s and 1960s, but then they diverged. One common factor until about the mid-1960s was a quite strong left-wing inflection. In Australia, the wartime Labor vision of a postwar social democratic society carried over into a range of writing, e.g. Vance Palmer, Brian Penton and Brian Fitzpatrick (Moran, 1988). With the election of a conservative government in 1949 this discussion was muted, but retained a left orientation. The debate among Australian intellectuals now took on an increasingly critical attitude to US influences, although Australians fought alongside the US in Korea, then in Viet Nam, while accepting US communication bases linked to the Pentagon's global surveillance system.

In communicating this debate the left-leaning literary journals *Meanjin*, *Overland* and *Nation* were important vehicles for writers such as A.A. Phillips, Ian Turner and Alan Ashbolt. One 1954 issue of *Meanjin*, for instance, critiqued 'Koka-Kola Kulture' by focusing on the supposedly negative effects of American comics and popular culture. In 1967 the same journal ran a 'Godzone' issue lamenting the Americanisation of Australia. Via drive-in cinemas, suburban shopping malls, TV programs and 'juvenile delinquency', Australia appeared to be being Americanised without having resolved its traditional relation with Britain (Bell & Bell, 1993).

Japan's postwar debate about modernisation was more complex. First, there was the thorny issue of war guilt and the related problem of how Japanese nationalism could now be legitimately defined. The broad solution was that cultural, rather than political, nationalism would be endorsed. There was also an element of pacifist internationalism that influenced Japanese postwar thought and for a time 'modernisation' was associated with 'democratisation'. A further complication for left-intellectuals was the emergence of a communist China. Even leading Marxist professors chose to distance themselves from the authoritarian style of the Chinese leadership. Despite these complications, many of Japan's leading intellectuals in the 1950s and 1960s were antigovernment, anticapitalist and anti-American (Hidaka, 1986).

Japanese mass society theory at that time was articulated by liberals and neo-Marxists. Some of the liberal critics, such as I. Shimizu, developed theories of the media as a 'pseudo-environment'. The media were seen as creating an artificial public communication environment where audiences were 'dominated by copies' of real events (Ito, 1990a). Shimizu was then a political activist, who joined in radical student protests against the Japan–US Security Treaty of 1960. Marxist critics of Japanese 'mass society', such as Hidaka, disputed that perspective, but they shared Shimizu's concern with the societal rather than the individual effects of the media.

Exercise 12.5 Japanese culture or Japanese cultural imperialism?
Japanese Comics Craze Hits Korea
'Korean Comics Hit by Japanese Manga Craze'

'Korean parents are complaining about the popularity of Japanese comics (*manga*) among Korean children. They are too violent and too obscene, parents complain.

Community leader Kim Young-sam says that Korean youngsters are preferring to read Japanese instead of Korean comics, as they see them as more exciting.

Local Korean comic-book artists are also worried that pirated versions of Japanese comics are undermining the viability of the Korean comics industry.'

1. What are the most popular children's comics and TV shows in Australia?
2. What, if any, Australian movies have been popular in Japan?
3. What Japanese cartoons and TV shows have appeared on Australian TV?

The 1970s and 1980s

After the end of the 1960s the modernisation and media debates took different paths in Australia and Japan. In both countries American social science methods made an impression, but especially in Japan. In Australia, a range of writers still made critical commentaries on the media in terms of 'cultural imperialism'. Important left analyses, usually couched in anti-American terms, were made, as in studies by McQueen (1977) and Bonney and Wilson (1983). These mostly supported pro-nationalist policies aimed at fostering an indigenous media industry via protectionist local content regulations, which had been first suggested by the Vincent Committee in 1964.

However, a range of factors rapidly changed the local media landscape. After 1983 the Hawke Labor government recklessly internationalised the economy via financial deregulation. Ethnic radio began in 1975, SBS-TV commenced in 1980, and the first communications satellite AUSSAT was launched in 1985.

Feminism and multiculturalism also emerged as important intellectual perspectives to question the masculinist orthodoxy of earlier left positions on social change, while American empirical models of communication inquiry were now themselves being challenged by British and European cultural studies approaches.

In response, new analysts now talked more about the globalisation of the media. Some expressed opposition to the tradition of pursuing nationalist protective cultural policies. Yet, if the tactics of mainstream Australian media criticism had changed, its main strategy remained the same. The new theorists still relied on government policies, except that their emphasis was on developing 'cultural policy', where the media were seen as another cultural industry alongside book publishing, the fine arts, museums and tourism. These still needed to be overseen by government agencies, even if they had to operate in a deregulated setting (Frankel, 1992).

The terms of debate about 'mass society' issues also changed. Ironically, the internationalist rhetoric of many of the new media theorists was at odds with the rise of a media-based commercial nationalism in the 1980s. This kind of 'Aussie' nationalism was exemplified by the campaigns of the Mojo advertising agency and ad-man John Singleton, who became advertising adviser to the federal Labor party. The 1980s 'Ocker' media nationalism began with the sporting hysteria fuelled by Australia's win in the America's Cup yacht race in 1983 and exploded in an orgy of patriotism in the successful 1993 bid for the year 2000 Olympics in Sydney.

Critics of 'mass society' risked seeming elitist and antipatriotic against this background, but they made two main responses. First, the new British-derived cultural theories of postmodernism were taken up to celebrate the popular. Readings of media texts, in this light, were determined by 'active audiences', who were capable of producing 'oppositional readings' of media messages (Fiske, 1987). There was also a tendency to uncritical celebration of 'the popular' as being just as legitimate a cultural pursuit as 'high culture' — the postmodernist point was that the distinction between the two was invalid (Docker, 1991). The mass society critique in its older form continued, but now it was the province of theorists on the right, such as the *Quadrant* group.

This new wave of nationalism affected Japan earlier. The 1970s saw a rebirth of Japanese cultural confidence as the economy boomed, and this was most visibly expressed in the proliferation of **Nihonjinron** writings — a term loosely meaning 'theories of the Japanese'. Much of this was not about the media or modernisation but was concerned with the redefinition of Japanese cultural identity, and had implications for the renegotiation of Japan's relation to America. After an initial phase of anti-Americanism, America came to be looked on with increasing favour. Opinion polls from the 1960s onwards showed that America was for Japan the most admired nation in the world. This lasted till the late 1980s (Chapman, 1991).

A new Japanese approach to communication, however, was emerging which stressed Japan's role as an 'information society' *(Johoka shakai)*. Though it was based on some US and European precedents, this approach became the most distinctive Japanese method of communications analysis. It came to occupy a much more central place in Japan than in Australia. Japan's 'information society' research assumed that people lived in an 'information environment'

Nihonjinron
The Japanese term for theories explaining the uniqueness at Japanese society.

which could be measured. This 'information society' approach had heavyweight institutional support. The Ministry of International Trade and Industry (MITI) had developed an Information Society Plan as early as 1972, and in the later 1980s was experimenting with a range of regional Technopolises. This concept was exported to Australia, with some difficulty, in 1987 (Morris-Suzuki, 1990). The *Johoka shakai* approach reflected the greater centrality of computer technology in Japan than in Australia. Japan traditionally has had a high literacy rate, a regimented education system promoting the sciences and engineering, and an information-oriented culture with some of the highest newspaper circulations in the world (Sugimoto & Mouer, 1989).

So what had happened to the mass society debate in Japan after the 1970s? First, it tended to be subsumed in the proliferation of *Nihonjinron* literature. Second, some of the earlier mass society criticism continued but, as in Australia, the political orientation of this criticism was now conservative instead of radical, as in the move to the political right by Shimizu. Third, more attention was given to 'the art of Japanese management' (Pascale & Athos, 1982). *Nihonjinron* theories focused on the group-centred nature of Japanese society and offered cultural, rather than structural, explanations of 'why Japan is different' (Mouer & Sugimoto, 1986). If Australians were 'true blue' (as in John Williamson's song) then Japanese were so different that only Japanese people could understand themselves.

Current communications policy issues

Of an estimated forty communication satellites in the Asia-Pacific region Japan has seven and Australia three. The recent expansion of satellite broadcasting in both countries has been driven by wider trends to privatisation and deregulation (Hoover, Venturelli & Wagner, 1993). Japan's Nippon Telephone and Telegraph (NTT) service was privatised after 1985. NTT's counterpart, Telecom, was similarly challenged by the entry of Optus into its long-distance market in 1992. Japan launched its first communication satellite in 1984 and AUSSAT followed in 1985. Currently Japan's BS-3 satellite carries NHK 1 and 2 and the Japan Satellite Broadcasting commercial channel WOWOW, though neither carries advertising. Japan inaugurated the world's first DBS service in 1988. By July 1992 four million Japanese households had access to DBS signals, the largest DBS service in the world. NHK also has the world's first satellite-delivered HDTV service, Hi-Vision. JSB has one million pay-TV subscribers, while two other satellite commercial services — Superbird and JCSat — have much smaller market shares (Khushu, 1993).

Between 1985 and 1987 Australia launched three AUSSAT A series satellites, while its new B series was delayed in late 1992 by launch failure in China. The AUSSAT series has been a heavy financial burden on the government, running up a loss of some $700 million by 1991. Currently pay-TV is seen as one way of recouping these losses. Also, the AUSSAT service does not have a footprint capable of reaching towards Asia (Fell, 1992) so, in February 1993, the ABC's new ATVI service was launched via the Indonesian PALAPA satellite. ATVI carries corporate sponsorship — as now does SBS-TV, which in September 1993 began regular morning satellite feeds of US, European, and PRC news to Australian audiences.

Globalisation/Kokusaika

Paying for Aussat.
Source: *G. Pryor,
The Canberra Times,
13 October 1991.
Used with permission.*

'Satellites are a blessing,' said the Director of International Relations of NHK in 1992; 'the age of satellites, regardless of national boundaries, is in the best interests of the public' (Takashima, 1993). These sentiments restate the simplistic techno-idealism that has so often been espoused by the managers who control the new technologies. So far the Japanese government treats satellite transmissions from outside its own borders as illegal, though there are now moves for a Japanese 'open skies' policy, such as Indonesia permitted in 1991. Yet, at the same time, the NHK and JSB satellite signal spills over into Korea, causing controversy and official criticism (Won, 1993).

Concerns about satellite services in Australia have been more about the cost of ATVI. A government grant of $5.4 million was made to the ABC to establish the service, but some critics consider that the successful commercial operation of ATVI — which is by no means assured — may be used as leverage to persuade the ABC into further corporatisation of its domestic service. In addition, the content of ATVI is limited to ABC programs as there has been no cooperation between ABC and SBS about programming. SBS-TV was originally created because the ABC was seen as too Anglophile. ATVI services are therefore unlikely to spread a multicultural message to Asian audiences. Australian society itself has a rather poor historical record of displaying racially tolerant attitudes to people within its own borders. It may be seen as hypocritical if Australians now attempt to set themselves up as apostles of multiculturalism to their Asian neighbours (Lewis & Slade, 1994).

Exercise 12.6   What will the Australian Multi Function Polis be used for? More Sci-Tech Towns in the Making

A recent report in a Japanese financial journal was:

'Japan's Sci-Tech Towns on the Move'

'Suzuki City wants the government to build a "West Japan corridor". This would be a combination of freeways and *shinkasen* (bullet train) railroads to connect the cities between the Pacific Ocean and the Sea of Japan.

The proposed new sci-tech towns aim to involve government, industry and universities.

Local residents hope to build a brand of new internationally-minded cities as part of Japan's committment to *kokusaika* (internationalisation).

The cities will be "hi-tech, hi-touch" enterprises, that will be both economically efficient and environmentally friendly.'

Using APAIS and/or CD-AUSTROM, research and write an essay or discuss in class the most recent developments concerning Adelaide's Multi Function Polis. Questions to consider could include:

1. What is it going to be used for?
2. How many of those proposed uses match the plan for Suzuki City?
3. Why was the MFP built in Adelaide instead of on the Gold Coast?

Globalisation and Australian identity

The rapid changes in communication technologies that have recently brought Australia much closer in time, if not in space, to its regional neighbours have not always meant better understanding in the region. Originally Australia looked deferentially to Britain, then to North America for cultural role models. Now there is a tendency to turn to Asia for economic salvation, if not culturally. This new concern about Asia comes at the same time as a renewed domestic emphasis on multiculturalism.

However, there is not just one 'Asia' and there is more than one 'Australia', despite its much smaller population. Australians will need to become more mindful of their own and their regional neighbours' communication practices and how these reflect different cultural beliefs. Cultural difference cannot always be reduced to cultural plurality. In this text, we have looked at how our concept of self is determined by those with whom we interact, by our language, cultural practices and the national, local and global influences on us. Our argument is that we need to look more carefully than we usually do at the contexts in which we communicate. As this not-so-brave new postmodern world shifts and changes, it is essential to realise that *how* we communicate is often just as important as the *content* of our communication.

Summary

1. The idea of modernity was associated with industrialisation and urbanisation and increased media and communications dependence. Debates about modernity in the US after the 1920s centred around the issues of media effects and mass culture. In other parts of the world, 'Americanisation' was also an issue.
2. Concerns about modernisation in non-Western countries were more about the needs for economic development and national unity. American scholars argued that national development could be increased via the

transfer of Western communication technologies — this was referred to as 'modernisation theory'. Latin American and Asian scholars argued that Third World underdevelopment resulted from First World dominance — this was labelled 'dependency theory'.

3. Debates about globalisation have tended to replace the earlier modernisation arguments. Globalisation is the process of increased world interdependence resulting from changes in the global economy and in communications technology. The cultural effects of globalisation include the growth of a postmodernist outlook, deterritorialisation and global cultural flows. The economic basis of globalisation is deregulation, privatisation and communications technology convergence.

4. Globalisation in South-East Asia has had the effect of accelerating national development in telecommunications and the media. It has also highlighted the region's sensitivity to its own media's coverage of potentially divisive racial, ethnic and religious issues. The role of the Australian media in reporting the domestic affairs of countries like Singapore, Malaysia, Indonesia and the Philippines has often been controversial.

5. Postwar modernisation in Japan and Australia had some similarities in its initial anti-Americanism, but then diverged. Japan developed a view of itself as an 'information society' bent on internationalisation (*Kokusaika*), whereas Australia took a more defensive line in arguing for protectionist media cultural policies and only recently began talking about becoming 'part of Asia'. Japan has stressed its cultural uniqueness via its *Nihonjinron* literature, whereas Australia has become committed to multiculturalism.

Discussion questions

1. What distinctive features make a society 'modern'?
2. Apart from the mass media, what are the main technologies used in international communication?
3. Modernisation debates in the US revolved around the issues of 'media effects' and 'mass culture'. What do these terms mean?
4. What different meaning did 'modernisation' have in many Asian and African countries?
5. What is the difference between 'dependency theory' and 'development communication'?
6. What are four key factors in globalisation?
7. What kind of media-related disputes has Australia had with Malaysia, Indonesia and Singapore in the past decade?
8. What were the main differences in modernisation debates in postwar Japan and Australia?
9. How are communications satellites used differently in contemporary Japan and Australia?

Further reading

Bell, P. & Bell, R. (1993) *Implicated: The US in Australia* Melbourne: Oxford University Press.

Birch, D. (1993) *Singapore Media* Melbourne: Longman Cheshire.

Chitty, N. (1992) 'Development is Communication: Self-Reliance, Self-Empowerment', *Telematics & Informatics* 9(1): 21–41.

Featherstone, M. (1990) 'Global Culture: An Introduction', *Theory, Culture and Society* 7: 1–14.

Fell, L. (1992) 'International TV in the Asia Pacific Region', pp. 38–63 in E. More & K. Smith, (eds) *Case Studies in Australian Media Management* Sydney: AFTRS.

Ito, Y. (1990a) 'Mass Communication Research in Japan', *Media, Culture and Society* 12(4): 49–85.

Lent, J. (1991) 'Telematics in Malaysia', pp. 165–200 in G. Sussman & J. Lent, (eds) *Transnational Communications* Newbury Park, CA: Sage.

Schaap, R. (1992) *A Dictionary of the Australian Communications Debate* Canberra: Glovebox.

Slade, C. & Applebee, A. (eds) (1993) *Media Images of Australia/Asia* Canberra: University of Canberra.

References

Aboud, J. (1992) 'Japan as a TV Culture', *Japanese Studies Bulletin* 12 (2): 32–44.

Appadurai, A. (1990) 'Disjuncture and Difference in the Global Cultural Economy', *Theory, Culture and Society* 7: 295–310.

Atwood, R. & McAnany, E. (eds) (1986) *Communication and Latin American Society* University of Wisconsin Press.

Bonney, B. & Wilson, H. (1983) *Australia's Commercial Media* Melbourne: Macmillan.

Chapman, W. (1991) *Inventing Japan* New York: Prentice Hall.

Chitty, N. (1993) 'Vocabularies of Globalisation', Paper at AMIC Conference on Communication, Technology and Development. Kuala Lumpur.

Cooke, P. (1990) *Back to the Future* London: Unwin Hyman.

Curran, J. & Seaton, J. (1988) *Power Without Responsibility* London: Routledge, 3rd edn.

Dissanayake, W. (1984) 'Buddhist Approach to Development', pp. 39–53 in G. Wang & W. Dissanayake, (eds) *Continuity and Change in Communication Systems* New Jersey: Ablex.

Dobell, G. (1993) 'The Makings of a Story in Another Country', pp.45–57 in C. Slade and A. Applebee, (eds) *op. cit.*

Docker, J. (1991) 'Popular Culture versus the State', *Media Information Australia* 59: 7–26.

Fiske, J. (1987) *Television Culture* London: Methuen.

Frankel, B. (1992) *From the Prophets Deserts Come* Melbourne: Arena.

Frederick, H. (1993) *Global Communication and International Relations* Belmont, CA: Wadsworth.

Glasgow University Media Group (1980) *More Bad News* London: RKP.
Hamilton, A. (1993) 'Video Crackdown: Censorship and Cultural Consequences in Thailand', *Public Culture* 5 (3): 515–31.
Hardjono, R. (1992) *White Tribe of Asia* Melbourne: Hyland House.
Hidaka, R. (1986) 'The Crisis of Postwar Democracy', pp. 228–47 in G. McCormack & Y. Sugimoto, (eds) *Democracy in Contemporary Japan* Sydney: Hale and Iremonger.
Hodge, E. (1991) 'The Impact of the ABC on Australian–Indonesian Relations since Timor', *Australian Outlook* 45 (1): 109–21.
Hodge, R. & Mishra, V. (1990) *The Dark Side of the Dream* Sydney: Allen & Unwin.
Hoover, S., Venturelli, S. & Wagner, D. (1993) 'Trends in Global Communication Policy-Making: the Asian Case', *Asian Journal of Communication* 3 (19): 103–33.
Ileto, R. (1991) 'The Philippines: Developments and Prospects', pp. 125–39 in D. Ball & H. Wilson, (eds) *Strange Neighbours* Sydney: Allen & Unwin.
Ito, Y. (1990b) 'Japan's Shift from an Information Importer to an Information Exporter', pp. 430–65 in *Communication Yearbook 13*, Newbury Park, CA: Sage.
Jacka, E. & Cunningham, S. (1993) 'Australian TV — an International Player?' *Media Information Australia* 70: 17–28.
Jensen, J. (1990) *Redeeming Modernity* Newbury Park, CA: Sage.
Johnson, L. (1988) *The Unseen Voice* London: Methuen.
Khushu, O. (1993) 'Satellite Communications in Asia', *Media Asia* 20 (1): 3–10.
Kingsbury, D. (1992) 'Agendas in Indonesian Responses to Australian Journalism', *Australian Journalism Review* 14 (2): 58–68.
Kitley, P. (1992) 'Television and its Audiences in Indonesia', *Rima* 26 (1): 71–110.
Lee, K. (1993) 'Democracy and Human Rights for the World', *Media Asia* 20 (19): 33–38.
Lewis, G. & Slade, C. (1994) 'Australia, Japan and Globalisation', *Media Information Australia* 71: 31–39.
Loo, E. & Ramanathan, S. (1993) 'Soured Relations: Press Coverage of the Bahrin-Gillespie Custody Dispute', *Media Information Australia* 70: 3–9.
Lowery, S. & DeFleur, M. (1988) *Milestones in Mass Communication Research* New York: Longman.
Lyotard, J. (1984) *The Postmodern Condition* Manchester: Manchester University Press.
McGuigan, J. (1992) *Cultural Populism* London: Routledge.
McQueen, H. (1977) *Australia's Media Monopolies* Melbourne: Widescope.
Melkote, S. (1991) *Communication for Development in the Third World* New Delhi: Sage.
Milne, R. (1992) 'Privatization in the ASEAN States', *Pacific Affairs* 65 (1): 7–30.
Milner, A. (1990) 'Postmodernism and Popular Culture', pp. 46–57 in S. Alomes & D. den Hartog, (eds) *Post Pop* Melbourne: VUT.
Moran, A. (1988) 'Media Intellectuals', pp. 109–27 in B. Head & J. Walter, (eds) *Intellectual Movements and Australian Society* Melbourne: Oxford University Press.

Morris-Suzuki, T. (1990) 'Futuristic Cities in Japan: Lessons for Australia', pp. 178–93 in P. James, (ed.) *Technocratic Dreaming* Melbourne: Left Book Club.

Mouer, R. & Sugimoto, Y. (1986) *Images of Japanese Society* London: KPI.

Mowlana, H. (1993) 'The New Global Order and Cultural Ecology', *Media, Culture and Society* 15(1): 9–29.

Mulgan, G. (1991) *Communication and Control* Cambridge: Polity Press.

Nandan, S. (1991) *The Wounded Sea* Sydney: Simon & Schuster.

Noesjirwan, J. (1986) 'Behavioural Differences between Australians and Indonesians', pp. 19–30 in A. Zainu'ddin, (ed.) *Nearest Southern Neighbours* Melbourne: Monash University.

Packard, V. (1957) *The Hidden Persuaders* London: Penguin.

Pascale, R. & Athos, A. (1982) *The Art of Japanese Management* London: Penguin.

Quebral, N. (1986) 'Is it Government Communication or People Communication?' *Media Asia* 13 (2): 79–85.

Robertson, R. (1990) 'Mapping the Global Condition', *Theory, Culture and Society* 7: 15–30.

Rosenberg, B. & White, D. (eds) (1957) *Mass Culture* West Drayton: Free Press.

Sinclair, J. (1991) 'The Advertising Industry in Australia', *Media Information Australia* 62: 31–40.

Stronach, B. (1989) 'Japanese Television', pp. 127–67 in R. Powers & H. Kato, (eds) *Handbook of Japanese Popular Culture* New York: Greenwood Press.

Sugimoto, Y. & Mouer, R. (eds) (1989) *Constructs for Understanding Japan* London: KPI.

Sussman, G. (1991) 'Singapore's Niche in the New International Division of Communication and Information', pp. 279–309 in G. Sussman & J. Lent, (eds) *Transnational Communications* Newbury Park, CA: Sage.

Takashima, H. (1993) 'The Age of Satellites in the Asia-Pacific', *Media Asia* 20(1): 21–24.

Wang, G. (1993) 'Satellite TV and the Future of Broadcast TV in the Asia-Pacific', *Media Asia* 20 (3): 140–52.

Westerway, P. (1990) *Electronic Highways* Sydney: Allen & Unwin.

Won, W. (1993) 'The Impact of Satellite Broadcasting in Korea', *Media Asia* 20(1): 15–21.

Teaching appendix

This appendix is intended mainly for the course instructor and explains some of the teaching strategies recommended for use in this book, as well as supplying additional material for several chapters. We appreciate that lecturers prefer to structure their courses to meet their own students' needs and we have written this text in a way that encourages this.

The book contains more than sufficient material for a two-semester, year-long introductory course. The first six chapters could be delivered, for example, in first semester, followed by the remaining chapters in second semester. Alternatively, if the course must be limited to one semester, we recommend you use Chapters 1, 2 and either 4 or 8, and two or three other chapters that best suit your needs. Those courses with a focus on interpersonal communication could begin with Chapter 1, followed by chapters 5, 6, 7, 8 and then returning to 2. Each chapter takes at least two teaching weeks to cover.

As communication courses become more specialised it seems important that first year courses should expose students to as wide a range as possible of learning experiences which are both creative and functional, assuming that their chosen specialisations will give them expertise in researching, writing, or producing in one particular area. The exercises in this text are therefore diverse and alternately stress discussion and class activities.

The initial exercises in most chapters are intended to raise awareness, via class discussions and sometimes role-plays. Several of the chapters then have a major revision exercise at their end which often requires a longer piece of written work. Any of these major writing exercises could be highlighted to meet the needs of particular courses. There are also several longer exercises (e.g. 5.8, 9.7, and 10.1) which aim to introduce students to questions of survey construction and use. As well as several essay-type exercises (e.g. 1.5, and 11.7), there are a number of others which require students to write more technically (e.g. 9.5 and 10.5). The longer research assignments (e.g. 12.6) also refer to students to database searching.

The teaching strategy we normally pursue is to raise the main features of the text in lectures, varied by relevant videos, overheads and guest lecturers, then use the exercises as the basis for workshops and tutorials. Class workshops work well when the class is divided up into smaller subgroups for particular exercises after a preliminary explanation of the purpose of the exercise. For many exercises of this kind, the use of observers with clear instructions as to what they should observe is also important. Giving neutral, accurate and detailed feedback is a difficult observational skill that needs practice. The class should then be re-formed at the end of the session to assess the value of the exercise and also to engage in debriefing, especially in giving feedback to class members who performed well, or explaining ways of improving for others who had difficulty with the task.

The following material is supplementary to the chapter exercises. Unless stated otherwise, the exercises are for class discussion. Exercises that may be used as writing and/or research assignments are indicated.

Chapter 1

The exercises in this chapter are introductory. They are designed to make students aware not only that the evidence of their own experience is useful in communication studies, but also to apprise them of standards of discussion and scholarly presentation. There is a difference between the style of articles and surveys found in weekly magazines and those used in communication studies, and students need to be aware of this and the fact that reading academic articles will not always be easy.

Exercise 1.1 Communication breakdowns and Exercise 1.2 Models of communication
These exercises should encourage an analytical approach by students to their own experience and their own expectation of communication studies.

Exercise 1.3 Chinese Whispers
There is nothing derogatory about the name of this game. Feedback in this game is the final member's interpretation as received by the originator. The conduit is either the voices carried by the sound waves or, more tendentiously, the minds of those in the chain.

Exercise 1.4 Language and meaning
The questions in this discussion are very complex, but students should be encouraged to think of their own experiences — grandparents whose mother tongue is no longer spoken in the family, for instance. The canonical response to Humpty's claim to be able to use words as he chooses is that languages are social and cannot be altered at will. While we could make up a new language as a variant of a natural language, it is impossible to create an entirely new language. Wittgenstein argued that there could be no such thing as a language used by only one person. Such a private language would, he argues, have no criteria for when words are used correctly and hence would fail of coherence. While there are those that disagree, the argument must be countered.

Exercise 1.5 The conduit metaphor
Lenin appears to assume that ideas can be injected into people, which is the extreme version of the transmission model, known as the hypodermic needle view of communication. It is an instance of the conduit metaphor, with ideas interpreted as objects to fight with. Lakoff and Johnson (cited in Chapter 2) call this the metaphor of 'Argument as War'.

Exercise 1.6 Two views of communication
This is designed as an exercise in brevity and clarity. Students should be encouraged to talk over their ideas, both in their group and together in class. It is useful to restrict them to a 500 word limit. This leaves room only for the most concise of summaries, not new research. The exercise does not require references or scholarly apparatus, but does require clear thinking.

Discussion questions
8. Can a dog make a mistake and know that it has?
Many argue, with Wittgenstein, that without the concept of a language, there can be no concept of a mistake.

Chapter 2

This chapter deals with language and the exercises are designed to make students aware of the language they use and, at the same time, to allow them to recognise that the language of communication studies, both spoken and written, has its own conventions, which they will need to acquire. There is an intentional dovetailing between the theory in the final section of Chapter 2 and the application to the genre of academic writing in Exercise 2.4, which should be brought to the attention of the students.

Exercise 2.1 Pronunciation
See pages 35–39 for a summary of regional differences in pronunciation in Australia. The point to be made is that while we do judge socioeconomic status by accent (a point very easy to make if you have access to a tape of one person talking in a variety of accents and ask students to judge SES, since the broader the accent, in general, the lower the SES attributed to the speaker), it is not by any means a reliable guide. The accents of NESBs are also deceptive in this regard. It is worth noting how politicians vary their accent according to the audience — Mrs Thatcher in Britain, for instance, from a family of grocers, could sound like the Queen when she chose, and Bob Hawke in Australia could range from sounding like a wharfie to sounding like the Rhodes scholar he had been in his youth.

Exercise 2.2 Jargon and specialised language
Medical and academic jargons, like slang, serve to set aside a group, but they also involve a level of abstraction which it may not be possible to translate into simpler terms. The mistake of the plain English movement is to think that simple, non-metaphorical, non-technical language serves all purposes.

Exercise 2.3 Sign languages
This exercise is designed to draw a link between the model of generativity in the text and the idea that language makes possible ways of thinking. The example of the deaf shows that preverbal sign languages do not allow people to think in the complex way full structured languages do. Of course, once a sign language is developed with structure, new structures can emerge which were not possible in spoken language — e.g. American Sign Language apparently uses space for syntactic forms, rather than, as in spoken languages, either prefix, infix or temporal progression. Far too often in communication theory the uniqueness of language is forgotten.

Exercise 2.4 Determining meaning
This exercise emphasises paralinguistic features of utterances. Students should become aware of the impact of their own paralinguistic behaviour, particularly rising sentence intonation.

Exercise 2.5 The genres of writing
This gives an opportunity to introduce referencing conventions and the models of presentation suitable for the group. Instructors can adapt the exercise to favour an approach to communication suitable for their students.

Exercise 2.6 Analysing language in a cartoon
Gum nut babies are signifiers of a certain childishly romantic view of the bush and of Australia itself — a bush in which there are no Aboriginal people, and in which the exotic vegetation is personified. The Greens' view of Australia takes on these meanings in the cartoon — a sort of babyish ('very, very, very . . .') romanticism.

Exercise 2.7 Analysing radio talk
This exercise is a demanding group exercise, leading in to a major individual essay in the next question. The differences may be illustrated by using taped segments or transcripts. A full analysis of such differences will be beyond the scope of this exercise, but it is illuminating for groups of students to attempt the analysis.

Exercise 2.8 Media texts
This is designed to focus attention on particular linguistic styles in the media, as a focus of study, and on one style suitable for writing in communication studies, for the presentation of the essay. The topic can be modified to suit the focus of a particular course — for instance, a series of articles on the health system for those in health communication.

Chapter 3

This chapter gives a preliminary introduction to techniques of observation. The exercises are graduated for increasingly complex observations. It will be necessary to introduce ethical guidelines for observation: each university has such guidelines and a new set of guidelines are now being developed for Australia.

Exercise 3.3 Observing nonverbal codes in public
This exercise is designed to show the difficulty of observation, and the sensitivity needed for accurate reporting.

Exercise 3.4 Breaking nonverbal conventions
This exercise introduces a shorthand model of a report in the social sciences.

Exercise 3.5 Analysing a cartoon
This exercise requires a review of the definitions from semiotic theory from this chapter and Chapter 2. Students should be made aware of the context of the debate in Australia about the possibility that Australia could become a republic, and of the relevance to that debate of a flag that includes the flag of the United Kingdom. They should also be aware of the constant harping in the press about the 'identity' of leaders.

Exercise 3.6 Smiling
This exercise is an investigation of smiling. The project is to describe the practice of smiling. The context of the study could be narrowed down to suit particular approaches. Health communication students could be directed to investigate the difference in smiling behaviour of doctors and nurses with patients, for instance, on one ward in the morning session over three days. Alternatively, students oriented to design could look at representation of the smile in a limited context: such as the work of a major designer.

Those attempting a semiotic analysis could be made aware of the complexity of cultural studies and of writings in that tradition dealing with the notion of the body, such as Irigaray, Kristeva or Foucault's *History of Sexuality*. However, such material is difficult.

Students attempting a preliminary observation study should be encouraged to take a very limited focus. The results should be written up in a formal fashion, possibly not that described in the exercise, but with a clear structure.

Chapter 4

Exercises in this chapter are designed to put into practice some of the concepts developed in the chapter. The answers here are brief, and there are correct alternatives. As there is no formal machinery in the chapter, there are no proofs of validity — merely an appeal to intuitive judgments.

Exercise 4.1 Presuppositions
In a strict sense, there are few presuppositions in the letter. The writer assumes that the reader disapproves of prostitution. She also confounds a set of expectations about the educational level of those in that profession. When she says 'Something must be done

about the present archaic law which does demean me', there is implicit the view — a presupposition of the argument — that the law should not demean anyone. There is also a presupposition that laws regulating prostitution resemble those regulating seat belts and that therefore they will eventually be accepted in the same way.

Exercise 4.2 Fact or inference
1. ? Not sure there was a thief. 2. T; 3.T; 4 ?; 5.? ; 6. T;
7. ? The lecturer might have been a woman. 8. ?; 9. F; 10. ?

Exercise 4.3 Deductive or inductive?
Whether an argument is inductive or deductive depends in part on which premises (P) are identified and the formulation of the conclusion (C). The clue to **inductive** form is in italics in the premises.

(a) No degree can guarantee a job P
   Unless a degree can guarantee a job it's worthless P
   All degrees are worthless C
                 Deductive

(b) The galaxies we've *observed so far* exhibit a red shift P
   The most likely explanation is that it is a Doppler shift brought
   about by their movement away from us. P
   So, the universe is expanding (ie all galaxies are moving away from us) C
                 Inductive

(c) We've been travelling now for 30 years P
   We travel 185 million kilometres a year P
   So we've gone 5550 million kilometres C
                 Deductive

   Our sensor reveals the presence of intelligent life P
   Seven Platonians are friendly, humanoid, purple-skinned P
   another Platonian humanoid will be purple too C
                 Inductive

(d) I can't get away until half an hour before class P
   When I arrive the parking area is *usually* full P
   I have trouble getting to this class on time C
                 Inductive

(e) *Some* people who stayed on the dole for
   over 9 months in the past were dole bludgers P
   All people who stay on the dole after 9 months are bludgers C
                 Inductive

Exercise 4.4
Facts/inferences   Induction/deduction   Necessary/sufficient
Definitions in Glossary

Argument 1
   Wilson's right hand is a size larger than his left P
   He has worked with it, and the muscles are more developed P
   Most people with developed muscles are labourers (suppressed premise)
   He has done manual labour C

Inference, on **inductive** grounds, and a larger right hand is neither **necessary** nor **sufficient** evidence for being a labourer.

Argument 2
    Wilson's right cuff is shiny for five inches **P**
    The left sleeve has a smooth patch where he rests upon the desk **P**
    Most people with such cuffs and sleeves are writers (suppressed premise)
    Wilson is a writer **C**

Inference, on **inductive** grounds. A rubbed right cuff and rubbed left elbow is **neither necessary** nor **sufficient** evidence for being a writer. (In these days of word processors, it is not even evidence.)

Argument 3
(a) The fish that Wilson has tattooed above his right wrist has
    stained fish scales of a delicate pink **P**
    Delicate pink-stained fish scale tattoo is only done in China **P**
    Wilson has been to China **C**

This is also an **inference**. If Holmes is right that the tattoo can only be done *in* China then the two first premises are **deductive** grounds for the conclusion and hence offer **sufficient** evidence, although not **necessary** grounds for the conclusion, since people go to China and do not get tattooed.

(b) A Chinese coin hangs from his watch-chain **P**
    Most people with Chinese coins have been to China (**suppressed premise**)
    Wilson has been to China **C**

Inference, on **inductive** grounds. Having a Chinese coin is neither **necessary** nor **sufficient** evidence for having been to China.

Exercise 4.5 Contradictions
The contradictions of each sentence are below:
1. Some dog does not have its day.
2. Some non-aerobic exercise keeps you fit.
3. Some possums are not a pest in New Zealand.
4. Rain is not rare in the Western Plains.
5. Most immigrants to Australia are not of European origin.
6. Some dead may speak.
7. Some of the king's horsemen could put Humpty together.
8. Some employed are lazy.
9. All men are happy.
10. Squinks are never ginks.

Exercise 4.6 Valid arguments
(a) Invalid: affirming the consequent. She did not say she would leave if she got a job, only that she wouldn't leave *unless* she got another job.
(b) Appeal to tradition.
(c) Appeal to authority — may be valid in this case, since he is expert.
(d) Causal fallacy.
(e) Invalid: affirming the consequent.
    Everyone may be on holidays on credit.
(f) Possible overgeneralisation. However, it is reasonable, given that restaurants are expensive and tend to be consistently good or bad, to act on the generalisation.
(g) Valid, seen by rearranging premises:
    All babies are illogical **P**

Illogical persons are despised **P**
Therefore, all babies are despised (suppressed C, & P — next step)
No one is despised who can manage a crocodile **P**
Therefore, no babies can manage a crocodile **C**

Exercise 4.7 Critical appraisal
This is a writing exercise designed to focus attention on different ways that arguments are presented. Note that students are asked to prepare two different sorts of written version of the arguments, one in which the arguments are stated almost in premise/conclusion form and another in which the impact of the argument is the major aim. Instructors might like to teach memorandum conventions for the first approach and tie in journalistic conventions to the second.

Discussion questions
3.
A   Capitalism requires continuing and limitless exploitation of natural resources **P**
    Without this, it must break down **P**
B   Greenies claim that 'space ship earth' is a closed system, whose natural resources are finite and limited **P**
    If natural resources are finite and limited then there can be no limitless exploitation of natural resources (**suppressed premise**)
C   If the greenies are right then capitalism must be wrong (**intermediate suppressed conclusion**)
D   *Some* events (in the Soviet bloc) show that capitalism is the one true form of economic organisation **P**
    Capitalism is not wrong **C**
E   So the greenies are not right **C**
Notice that sub-argument D is **inductive**, but the structure of the argument is **deductive**, at least as presented above, where it is valid, since C and D together yield E. However, the premises are debatable.

4. The Mayan Empire, an advanced complex American civilisation, collapsed about six centuries before the Spanish invader came across the Atlantic **P**
       Ninety skeletons unearthed by a university expedition to Guatemala had numerous lesions due to syphilis and vitamin deficiencies **P**
       Some skeletons unearthed by a university expedition to Guatemala had other disorders, including parasitic infestations and childhood infections **P**
       The decline of the Mayan civilisation was to be explained by the ravages of malnutrition and disease **C**
Inductive argument, since the evidence base was a number of skeletons, not the entire population. Is this a sufficient evidence base? Can we hope to do any better?

5. Definitions in the Glossary.
A   Monica's huge oyster-coloured eyes, today slightly bloodshot, behind her dark glasses. **P**
    Bloodshot eyes are *sometimes* evidence of crying (suppressed premise)
    Crying is *sometimes* evidence of bereavement (suppressed premise)
    A breakdown; a bereavement **C**
Inference, on inductive ground.
B   If someone is a smoker and has a patch on the lung then they are forbidden to smoke (suppressed premise)
    Monica smokes **P**
    Monica is forbidden to smoke **P**
    Monica has a patch on a lung **C**

Inference, which is, as described above, an **invalid deductive** argument, affirming the consequent.

While the sort of evidence in A and B above is not **sufficient** grounds for the conclusions, which are eminently revisable, drawing such conclusions may well be rational. We all use such forms to draw our conclusions about others.

Chapter 5

Exercise 5.4   Alternative role-reversal interpersonal perception exercise
Ollie has lived in an affluent North Shore suburb in Sydney for most of his life though he was born of poor but honest Italian parents in Melbourne. He completed his school leaving exam recently at an exclusive private boys school and is now enrolled at the University of Canberra in a communications course. Ollie is very popular and has many friends of both sexes. He also has several gay friends. Till now he has got his way by smiling frequently and basically doing what he thought others wanted him to do. He is very conscious of his appearance and how he is seen by others. He likes to be liked by everyone. Not wanting to seem uninformed he often seeks help from a group of friends who did the same course. Sometimes they help him with assignments and let him use their last year's work. Among his women friends Ollie has the reputation of being a bit of a lad after a few drinks. How do you see Ollie?

Exercise 5.5   Gender differences: Answers
1. F, 2. N, 3. M, 4. M, 5. F, 6. N, 7. F, 8. M, 9. N, 10. N, 11. F, 12. F, 13. M, 14. M.
F = female, M = male, N = neutral.
Adapted from the Bem sex-role inventory. S. Bem (1974) 'The Measurement of Psychological Androgony', *Journal of Consulting and Clinical Psychology* 44: 155–62.

Exercise 5.6   Evaluating student friendships
Possible major group research and survey design exercise.

Chapter 6

Exercise 6.7   Reading the ethnic press
Possible major group or individual research and writing exercise.

Chapter 7

Exercise 7.3   Aboriginal culture and conservation
Possible research and writing exercise.

Exercise 7.4   Differences in white and aboriginal group decision making
This is intended as a role-reversal exercise which positions Aboriginals rather than whites as the dominant group.

Exercise 7.6   Recognising generational differences in ethnic groups
Possible major research and writing exercise.

Chapter 8

Exercise 8.1   Current awareness of group membership
An awareness exercise to help students appreciate which groups they are already members of.

Exercise 8.2   The effects of goal clarity on group performance
The rationale is that undefined group tasks are much less manageable.
The task:
Group A: Develop a plan of how you would go about improving the quality of university life.
Group B: Develop a plan of how to improve university life, specifically in terms of parking facilities, public transport services, library services, cafeteria standards, safety and security on campus, social, cultural, and sporting activities, and bar rules.
Observer's chart: Both observers use the same categories: 1. Assessment of the climate of the group — was it cooperative or uncooperative? Score for the start, middle and end of the exercise. 2. Score the number of times members asked for goal clarification or made clarifying statements. 3. Score the frequency of verbal and nonverbal behaviours not directly related to the task. 4. Rate the progress the group made in completing the task from 1, low, to 10, high.

Exercise 8.3   Stages of group development and group size
This is intended to clarify the effect of size and uncertainty on group task performance by having one larger and one smaller group perform the same task. Note that the instructor needs to decide the exact six letter squares choice of letters. Each sealed envelope must include one participants' instruction sheet, and one calculation chart.

INSTRUCTION SHEET FOR PARTICIPANTS: WORD-BUILDING GAME
Do *not* open the envelope until:
1. You have agreed on the best method of calculation of potential profit by studying the calculation charts.
2. You have given the information required to the instructor.
The sealed envelope contains six squares with a different letter of the alphabet on each one. One or more of these is a vowel. *Your group task is to make up and write down as many three or five letter words as you can using the six letters*. The goal of your group is to make as large a profit as possible in doing this.

Before beginning you must give the following information to the instructor: (a) the profit you expect to make, (b) the time you nominate to take, (c) the number of words you expect to make.

You have a maximum planning time of 15 minutes, then a maximum of 10 minutes to do the task. Keep your own time.

No questions may be asked of the instructor or the observers.

INSTRUCTION SHEET FOR OBSERVERS: WORD-BUILDING GAME
The expectation here is that the larger group will take longer to go through its stages of development in dealing with their task and probably experience greater difficulty in agreeing on it.

The stages of development you should seek to identify are those of Bales and Strodbeck, namely, an orientation stage, an evaluation stage, and a control stage. In the first, basic questions about the task will be asked; in the second, the group will focus more on the central issue required by the task; and in the third they will put their analysis of the task requirement into practice.

Take brief notes on the following: (a) who picked up the instructions first, (b) who best explained the charts to the group, (c) who took the initiative in giving the information to the instructor, (d) who divided up task procedures within the group, (e) how actively each member participated.

Keep track of the time as well and see if you can nominate when the group moved from the orientation, to the evaluation, then to the control stage. Lastly, at the end of the exercise make a brief verbal report to the group about your observations. This should be an objective description of group interaction. Be careful not to make negative personal judgments about particular group members.

CALCULATION CHART

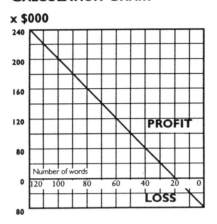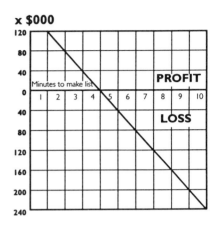

Exercise 8.4 Recognising individual members roles
This exercise is intended to allow participants to practise a particular group role and test the observers' abilities to categorise those roles. It is advisable to tell the participants not to openly declare their nominated roles before beginning.

Member roles Group A
1. Sydney — Task role.
2. Melbourne — Maintenance role.
3. Adelaide — Task role.

Member roles Group B
1. Perth — Maintenance role.
2. Hobart — Task role.
3. Brisbane — Maintenance role.

The remaining members of these groups will not be allocated particular roles. They should support or oppose the suggestions of others or advocate their own choices.

FIRST OBSERVER SHEET
Categorise the statements and behaviours of the three individual members nominated by the instructor to advocate particular cities in terms of whether they are task or maintenance behaviours.

SECOND OBSERVER SHEET
Categorise the statements and behaviours of the individual members nominated by the instructor not to support particular cities in terms of whether they act as:
(a) information and opinion giver, (b) direction and role definer, (c) tension reliever, (d) information and opinion seeker, (e) process observer, (f) summariser, (g) direction and role definer.

Exercise 8.5 Individual styles of conflict resolution
This is a simple bridging exercise to lead students into recognising individual styles of conflict resolution and link with the next exercise. After students complete it individually, ask them to compare choices and discuss with their neighbour prior to final class discussion.
Answers: (a) Smoothing over, (b) Confrontation, (c) Integration, (d) Avoidance, (e) Accommodation, (f) Compromising.

The best choice is (c) Integration. Then probably (f) Compromising, (b) Confrontation, (a) Smoothing over and (e) Accommodation. The worst is (d) Avoidance.

Exercise 8.6 Choosing alternatives in group conflict resolution
These three examples illustrate group conflict arising from the use of inappropriate humour, from individual over-involvement, and from 'group-think'. Be sure class members list all the options, not just the first. After individual completion ask them to compare answers and discuss with their neighbours before general class discussion. It is important to focus on the best and worst options to clarify why they are so.

Answers
1. Best is (e) ('Get the discussion back . . .), worst is (c). Options (a), (b), and (d) are 4th, 2nd, and 3rd best.
2. Best is (c), worst is (e). Options (a), (b), and (d) rank as 2nd, 4th, and 3rd best.
3. Best is (e), worst is (a). Options (b), (c), and (d) are 3rd, 4th, and 2nd best.

Exercise 8.7 Group problem solving and decision making
This exercise is best done either in a three-hour time slot or over a three-week period and is meant to consolidate the range of group skills practised in earlier exercises. In allocating roles it is advisable to have back-up persons (possibly the observers) ready to take on those roles in case of non-attendance. The instructor should determine specifically what behaviours the observers should watch for in light of the group's level of competence. Only the principal roles are detailed here — the student roles need filling in.

1. *Union President* — This is an extraordinary meeting and you need to say so at the start. Your task is to draw up the meeting's agenda and direct the meeting. You will be issued with the previous meeting's minutes. The agenda should list these as the first item of business, then the major item of business — the issue of raising students' fees — and, last, an 'other business' final category. You are open-minded about the issue and should make up your own mind purely on the basis of the arguments presented at the meeting. *Your objective is to have the meeting resolve the issue themselves, rather than you having to record your vote on the issue.* You may still have to do so if the vote is split, or if you are convinced the meeting is pursuing the wrong option. Procedurally you should anticipate the following: the moving of motions (which must have a mover and seconder); the amendment of motions (ditto); the splitting of motions (which must be agreed to by the original mover and seconder); points of order and points of information (you may ask your secretary for help with these); direction of all remarks to the meeting through you as chair; ensuring the secretary has an accurate written version of the motions; being conscious of the time and prepared to put motions to the vote while still allowing maximum time for discussion, or to limit debate which is irrelevant or personally offensive; to disallow any motions for postponement or the appointment of further subcommittees on the matter; finally, to fix a time for the next meeting and formally close the meeting.

2. *The Secretary* — Your job is to circulate the attendance record, to accurately record the motions put, and if necessary to advise the Chair on procedures and information points. You need to record motions, and their movers and seconders accurately and be prepared to read these back to the meeting before a vote is made. When votes take place you need to record 'fors' and 'againsts'. If a point of information arises concerning the right of the Union to levy extra charges on academic members, you must regretfully advise members this is not possible as the Union Constitution does not allow it. The Constitution would have to be changed. If a point of order re student reps is raised, you

should advise the Chair that, provided this has been announced as an extraordinary meeting, then the reps may participate and vote.

3. *Student Union Treasurer* — In the first 10 minute pre-meeting period you should discuss the financial position of the Union with students and show them the minutes of meeting on 9.6.1999 and the financial survey. Your options are to (a) increase fees, (b) to close the student paper, or to reduce the number of issues (c) to raise cafeteria prices (d) to reduce staff numbers at the Sports Association, (e) to cut Travel Association charges. After listening to general discussion, you should attempt to move a motion that fees will be increased and that one of the above options should be chosen. This will be opposed, so be sure to appeal to the interests of other Union members. If your motion is accepted it may later be split into sections — which you are not opposed to. (There is no truth in the vicious rumour that you are indirectly related to two of the Union part-time secretaries: this is a lie that has been planted to discredit your determination to solve the Union's financial problems).

4. *Travel Association Representative* —You have heard on the grapevine that the Treasurer may be planning to raise Association travel charges to balance the Union budget. You don't think this is desirable, as this will mean fewer customers for the Travel Association, but you will listen to reason. During the initial discussions you wish to ask for a point of information through the Chair if it is true that travel services at other universities are subsidised by the academic staff as well as the students. If this is so, you intend to move that a separate additional charge be made on non-student users of the Travel Association. You are opposed to any moves to shut down the paper as it is an important means of advertising your own operation.

5. *Newspaper Editor* — You are tired of what you see as the thoughtless attitudes of many of the Union executive. They do not appreciate that the student newspaper is an important source of vocational training for journalism students at the University, and that the paper is now covering its costs, which it had not been doing until recently. In your opinion, the executive has been overindulgent in employing four part-time secretaries, and you have heard a rumour that two of these are distant relations of the Treasurer. You also consider that the cafeteria and the sports association are badly managed, and that they are the real loss-makers in the Union's services. You are more sympathetic to the travel service, as they advertise in your paper. You intend to move for the closure of the sports association, the reduction of cafeteria services, and the dismissal of two of the part-time secretaries.

6. *Sports Association Representative* —You have heard that the Treasurer may be seeking to increase charges for sports association users and you are determined to resist this. The sports association is linked to accredited sports management courses at the University, and any reduction in the Association's services could reflect badly on these courses. You also dislike the newspaper editor's high-minded talk about the importance of the paper, and consider that his/her attitude towards you is offensive in assuming that you are only interested in sport. You intend to support closing down the paper.

7. *Cafeteria Representative* — You are concerned that the Treasurer may have a plan to increase cafeteria charges. You consider it is the Union's function to subsidise cafeteria charges, as it is running at a relatively small loss. Further, a number of students work part-time there and this is an important source of work experience and money for them. You are also doubtful of the value of the student travel association and the newspaper. You have heard unfavourable reports about the management of both of these, and you feel that good food is the one really essential thing that hard-working students need. The

EEO officer has also advised you that it may be necessary in future to provide a much wider range of food to cater for students of different religious backgrounds, and this is likely to increase your operating costs further.

8. *Student Representative A* — a vocal supporter of the Sports Association.
9. *Student Representative B* — a strong supporter of the travel service.
10. *Student Representative C* — considers the cafeteria service by far the most important of the Union's services.
11. *Student Representative D* — supports the student newspaper at all costs.
12. – 20. *Student Representative E* — open-minded. You are prepared to listen to reason.

Minutes of previous Students' Union meeting
Present: The President, the Treasurer, the Committee
Date: 9 June 1999

1. This meeting urged that student fees should be increased by instalments by $7.50 a year.
2. It was also recommended that a survey should be made before the next meeting concerning the financial position of Union services.
3. It was proposed as an option to 1 that cuts across the board should be made to all Union services.
4. It was also agreed that the meeting for Week 7 should permit Student Representative to attend and vote at the meeting.
5. It was agreed that 1 and 2 should be held over till the Week 7 meeting, but that 2 should be carried out.

Survey of the Union's financial position

	Revenue		*Expenditure*
Union dues	100 000		
Union costs			100 000
Salaries			
4 part-time secretaries		40 000	
2 part-time managers		40 000	
Rents		20 000	
Paper	5 000		5 500
Cafeteria	20 000		25 000
Travel Association	15 000		20 000
Sports Association	5 000		10 000
Totals	145 000		160 000
Current debit	—		$15 500

Sample Agenda

1. Notice of extraordinary meeting.
2. Minutes of previous meeting (distributed).
3. Major item of business: Should fees be raised?
   (a) Travel Association representative's report.
   (b) Sports representative's report.
   (c) Cafeteria representative's report.
   (d) Newspaper editor's report.
   (e) Treasurer's response.
4. General discussion from floor.

5. Any other business.
6. Date of next meeting.

Chapter 9

Exercise 9.1 Presentational speaking
This exercise may extend over a period of weeks with one or two speakers weekly, or be used in concentrated sessions. After each presentation the speaker should leave the room while the class discusses the strengths and weaknesses of their talk. A different student in the audience each time should be appointed to convey the class's feedback to the speaker after class discussion.

Exercise 9.3 Writing a job application
Possible short individual written assignment that can be linked with subsequent job-selection interview in 10.3.

Exercise 9.4 Quiz on organisational structure
Answers: 1. E, 2. D, 3. B, 4. A, 5. C.

Exercise 9.5 Prioritising organisational information flows
Possible group writing exercise.

Exercise 9.7 Surveying organisational culture
Possible major group survey design exercise. A different approach is taken in Goldhaber (1993).

Chapter 10

Exercise 10.2 Quiz on communication networks
Answers: 1. F, 2. C, 3. B, 4. E, 5. D, 6. A.

Exercise 10.3 Role-playing a job selection interview
This ideally requires the prior writing of job application letters as in 9.3. This exercise works well when the applicants are physically out of the room in the interview preparation period. After each is interviewed they may remain present to watch subsequent interviews. They should then leave the room while the panel discusses their performance before deciding.

Exercise 10.5 Drafting an EEO policy statement
Possible individual writing exercise. A sample statement is in *EEO Programs Guidelines 1 and 2* Canberra: AGPS (1990): 82–83.

Exercise 10.6 Coalition bargaining
With a mixed-sex class it is useful either to balance gender representation in the teams, or divide it entirely. The observer's guidelines are the four Fisher and Ury principles.

Chapter 11

Exercise 11.2 Recognising differences in TV criticism and TV research
(a) I. Warden, 'I Saw' *Canberra Times TV Guide* 1 November 1993. Popular program review.
(b) V. Nightingale, 'Watching Rugby League on TV', p. 159 in Moran (ed.) (1992) *Stay Tuned*, Sydney: Allen & Unwin. Audience research.
(c) E. Simper, *Weekend Australian* 9–10 October 1993, p. 44. Popular program preview.

(d) T. Flew, 'Foreign Ownership and Australian Content', *Media Information Australia* 62: 26. Policy research.
(e) T. O'Regan, 'The Background to TV Networking', p. 135 in E. More & G. Lewis, (eds) (1988) *Australian Communications Technology and Policy* Sydney: AFTRS. Industry research.
(f) K. Seneviratne, 'Multicultural Television', *Media Information Australia* 66: 54. Program research.

Exercise 11.3 Analysing TV form and 11.7 Researching and writing a television review
Possible individual or group research and writing exercises.

Chapter 12

Exercise 12.3 Globalisation quiz
Answers: 1. D, 2. C, 3. A, 4. E, 5. B.

Exercise 12.6 What will the Australian MFP be used for?
Possible major individual or group research and writing exercise.

Comment on Further reading and References

Each chapter designates what we consider the most essential sources as Further reading. Additional material cited in the chapter is listed under References. There are more extensive references provided in the later chapters. This is intended to reflect students' increasing research capacities towards the end of the program. An exception is Chapter 7, the second intercultural chapter. Particular effort was made there to give an extensive list of sources as this remains a difficult area to find good Australian material on.

We would welcome any comments that instructors or students may wish to pass on to us to help us improve the usefulness of the second edition. These should be sent to the Humanities Acquisition Editor, Prentice Hall of Australia, 7 Grosvenor Place, Brookvale New South Wales, 2100.

Glossary

1 Theories and models of communication

administrative communication models Models that draw on traditions of US communication research that aim at applying the results to the benefit of business or government.
code A system of signs.
communication The sharing of ideas, knowledge or feelings.
communication model A simplified representation of some feature of communication which is similar in some crucial and specifiable respects to an original; models simplify, aid in prediction or explain complex events.
communication studies The disciplinary field concerned with the study of communication.
communication theories Extended representations of communication processses that seek to explain or classify essential features.
communications The technologies and media used to transmit ideas, information and entertainment.
context dependence of communication The fact that the setting of communicative acts affects the import or meaning those acts have.
contexts The setting of communicative acts.
contextualised research methods Those that consider communicative acts in the physical, social or cultural context of which they form a part.
conventions The behaviour arising when a group adopts a form of activity either by explicit agreement, or by implicit and possibly unconscious accord.
critical communication models Models that take the purpose of communication research to criticise in the public rather than in the private interest.
cultural relativism The view that meaning is relative to a culture.
culture The ideas, beliefs and practices of a group and the products they engender.
decontextualised research methods Those that consider communicative acts in isolation from their social context.
feedback The message the source receives when their original message is received, interpreted and responded to by a receiver.
functional models of communication Models that define the communicative process in terms of the functions or effects of communicative acts.
linguistic relativism The claim that each language embodies a way of conceptualising the world, and no one way is correct.
meaning-based theories of communication Accounts that give a central place to the notion of meaning in communication.
mechanistic models of communication Models based on the idea that human communication resembles communication between machines.
medium The particular channel through which messages, converted into signals, are sent.
methodologies Views of how research should be conducted.

noise Any element that interferes with the successful reception of a message.

process models of communication Models that identify communication as a series of messages to which the receiver responds, and to which the sender may then in turn respond.

qualitative research Research that uses non-numerical techniques for understanding society.

quantitative research Research that uses statistical measures for understanding society.

receiver The person or object that receives a transmitted message.

reflexive research methods Those that take the researcher to be part of the research and see the researcher's purposes as crucially affecting the data.

sender The transmitter or source of a message.

transmission models of communication Models that map the pathways communication takes, and assume that information, understanding and thoughts travel along those paths as if they were objects.

2 Language in context

connotation The overtones, or colouring, of a word.

deconstruction The laying out of oppositions and displacement or reversal of the privileged one of the pair.

denotation The core object to which a word refers.

discourse (1) Extended passages of language use.

discourse (2) A systematically organised set of statements that describes and delimits what it is possible to say.

discourses The ways of knowing which are the products of social, historical and institutional frameworks.

elaborated code Language used with strangers or in formal situations, in which ideas are made fully explicit.

gender differences in language use Those differences in use of language which cannot be traced directly to biological difference.

icon A sign that resembles its object.

implicature Conclusions derived from a statement based on contextual knowledge.

index A sign that indicates or points to its object.

language A system which gives resources for people to assign meanings to words, sentences and discourse structures, by virtue of being used in interaction.

language transformation The systematic alteration of the syntactic form of sentences.

linguistic genres The set of principles governing discourse in a particular context of interaction.

metaphor Where the literal meaning of a word is not so much altered as used falsely.

morphemes Those sounds or sound complexes that are meaningful in a language.

paradigmatic relations Those defined by contrasts within a set of members of a category.

paralinguistic features of utterances Those features that alter or change the unmodified conventional meaning.
phatic communication Communication that serves purely social purposes.
phoneme A sound which makes a significant difference in a language.
pragmatics The study of features of utterances which depend on the linguistic and non-linguistic context.
referent The object referred to.
register Differences in linguistic style deriving from contextual constraints on language.
restricted code Language that makes assumptions about shared knowledge.
semantics The study of meanings.
semiotic theories of language Theories that treat language as a system of signs.
sense The particular way a name identifies an object.
sentences The smallest complete unit in language.
sign This consists of two components, the signifier, or actual token of a sign, and the corresponding signified concept evoked by its use.
signified The concept evoked by the use of a signifier.
signifier The actual token of a sign.
social semiotics Linguistic theories that describe the role of signs in society and how social practices constitute signs.
symbol A representation of an object or idea where the connection between the object and the sign is arbitrary.
syntagmatic relations Those relations which bind elements of the sentence together.
syntax The structures that bind words into sentences.
texts The smallest meaningful passages of social language.
utterance The spoken analogue of a sentence.

3 Codes of nonverbal communication

adaptors Nervous, unconscious nonverbal displays.
affect displays The way our facial expressions, or sometimes our body movements, reveal our emotions.
body language The entire range of nonverbal codes circumscribed by the use of the body.
chronemics The code relating to the use of time.
emblems Gestures that have a direct verbal translation and are performed quite consciously.
haptics The code relating to the use of touch.
illustrators Nonverbal behaviours we use to illustrate what we are saying.
kinesics The study of gesture and body movement as a meaning system.
nonverbal code One that is independent of spoken forms; nonverbal codes are conventional and culturally specific.
proxemics The study of the use of space as a meaning system.
regulator Nonverbal signals that provide cues for verbal interaction.
structuralist theories Theories that consider that the meanings of signs derive from the contrasts within a paradigm or structure.

territoriality The tendency to defend an area of space.
visual codes Codes that use the arrangement of visual elements to communicate.

4 Critical thinking

ad hominem argument One that is directed not at ideas but at the identity of the speaker.
analogy Argument by analogy infers from the basis of a similarity in some respect a similarity in other respects.
appeal to authority An argument where the evaluation is based not on logical content but on the recommendation of a supposed authority.
appeal to tradition An argument that suggests that it is worth behaving in a certain way because it is traditional to do so.
argument A logically interwoven set of statements, one of which, the conclusion, rests on or follows from the others (the premises).
causal fallacy Where an event that is prior to another is wrongly supposed to cause it.
conclusion The logical outcome of an argument.
conditional statement One which has the form 'if ... then'; the antecedent follows the 'if', and the consequent follows the 'then'.
contradiction The contradiction of a proposition is such that if the proposition is true then the contradiction cannot be true and vice versa.
deductive argument An argument that purports to lead from the premises (either particular or general) to a conclusion (either particular or general) by necessity.
enthymematic argument One in which the premises are suppressed, or evidence or grounds not mentioned.
equivocation The intentional use of a form of words that is ambiguous.
facts In any state of information, some statements will count as facts; they are the propositions held true in that state of information.
fallacies Errors of argument, whether inductive or deductive, which may be the result of invalid argument forms or misguided strategies.
fallacy of moderation or compromise Where it is argued that extremes are necessarily wrong.
inductive argument An argument in which a generalisation is based on observed particular instances.
inferences In any state of information, other statements will require argumentation to be ascertained; those statements are inferences.
invalid argument An argument in which the premises can be true and the conclusion false.
necessary condition A proposition is necessary for another if, when the latter holds, the former must.
premise The grounds or statements assumed to be true that are used as the basis of an inference to the conclusion.
presupposition A statement (question ...) p, presupposes another, q, if, whether p is true or false, q is true.

proposition A statement abstracted from a particular language; e.g. English, French and Spanish statements that are translations of each other, express the same proposition.

sufficient conditions A proposition is sufficient for another if, when the former is true, the latter must be.

valid argument One in which, if the premises are true, the conclusion must be true. It is impossible for the premises to be true and the conclusion not to be.

5 Interpersonal communication

assertiveness The capacity to stand up for your own rights while respecting the rights of others.

attentiveness The selective directing of attention towards information relevant to the ongoing interaction.

communication apprehension A sense of anxiety associated with either real or anticipated communication with others.

empathy The ability to take another person's viewpoint.

interpersonal communication Engaging in meaningful face to face interactions with others.

interpersonal perception How we see other people.

interpersonal stereotypes Rigid perceptions of members of one group that are widely shared by others in a different group.

intrapersonal communication Creating a sense of meaning for yourself.

perceptiveness The integration of meanings of self in relation to another in the course of interpersonal communication.

prejudice Holding a strong dislike for people who are seen as members of a particular out-group.

reflexivity Understanding that research involves the researcher as much as the subjects.

responsiveness The capacity to be sensitive to the communication behaviours of others.

self-concept The relatively stable set of perceptions you hold of yourself.

self-disclosure The intentional disclosure of personal information about yourself to someone else, usually in a one-to-one situation.

self-esteem The extent to which you approve of and accept yourself.

self-image How you perceive yourself at a particular time.

self-monitoring The extent to which you are aware of consciously projecting a particular image of yourself.

self-presentation The way you choose to present yourself in a specific social context.

social involvement Maintaining a positive level of social relationships with other people.

stereotyping Judging others by their labels or roles.

Glossary

6 Intercultural communication

acculturation How immigrants learn to identify, then internalise, the significant symbols of the host culture through communication.
communication accommodation theory (CAT) People may adjust their speech styles with respect to others as a way of expressing their values, attitudes and intentions.
cross-cultural communication Face-to-face communication between representatives of business, government and professional groups from different nations.
discrimination Taking harmful action against individuals on the basis of their different religious or political beliefs, ethnic origins, or their gender or sexual preference.
ethnic stereotypes Relatively fixed negative conceptions of an ethnic group.
ethnocentrism Considering one's own social groups as 'normal' and judging others' as abnormal or inferior.
host culture The mainstream culture in any one particular country.
intercultural communication Face-to-face communication between people from differing cultural backgrounds.
intracultural communication Shared interpersonal communication between members of the same culture.
minority cultures Cultural groups that are smaller in numerical terms in relation to the host culture.
multiculturalism The official recognition of Australia's cultural and ethnic diversity.
prejudice A negative attitude towards ethnic or minority groups.
social distance Every society has a tacit scale that is used to rank other ethnic groups in a social hierarchy.
subculture A smaller, possibly non-conformist, subgroup within the host culture.

7 Communicating in multicultural Australia

Aboriginality Aboriginals' sense of their being the original inhabitants of the continent, their belief in the Dreamtime, and their distinctive beliefs about the land.
Anglo-Australian culture The culture that white Anglo immigrants have established in Australia since settlement.
assimilationism The process whereby immigrants become more similar to the host population as a result of social interaction.
chain migration Immigrants sponsor family members, relations, neighbours and friends, usually from their own geographical place of origin, for immigration.
core values and behaviours The social values and sense-making practices that the mainstream culture sees as normal.
cultural heritage Any group's own distinctive history and language.
culture Distinctive national pattern of social behaviours that develops over time.

ethnic pecking order How each ethnic group has to take its place in a queue while waiting for acceptance into the host culture.

intracultural communication networks Social and familial bonds that exist between members of the same ethnic group and act as channels of cultural interaction.

pluralism A situation where immigrants retain their original sense of cultural identity while supplementing it with selective adaptation from the norms of the new host culture.

postcolonialism The cultural and political consequences of decolonisation.

8 Small group communication

brainstorming A method of group problem solving that aims at initially generating as many ideas as possible.

constructive controversy A positive approach to dealing with group disagreement.

forming The orientation stage of group development.

group attractiveness The degree of individual members' attraction to other members and the whole group.

group cohesiveness The extent to which members perceive external forces as influencing them to remain in the group.

group conflict episodes Latent conflict, emergent conflict, explicit conflict, and a conflict aftermath period.

group consensus A method of reaching a decision, in which all group members have the opportunity to express their views, to challenge and re-define the views of others, and work towards a reformulation of the problem.

group decision making What the group finally decides to do about the problem.

group effectiveness The extent to which the group's interaction patterns results in a positive outcome.

group interdependence The extent to which individual group members need each other to achieve group goals.

group problem solving The process a group has to work through in recognising, exploring and solving a problem.

group satisfaction The evaluation that members make of the worth of their membership in the group and of the group's overall effectiveness.

hidden agendas When members pursue aims of their own which they do not disclose to the group.

interpersonal conflict styles Individuals have their own orientations towards group conflict that can be expressed in avoiding involvement, competing, compromising, accommodating others, or collaborating.

leader mandate Where a final decision is made by the group leader.

majority vote Where a final decision is made by a formal or informal vote of all group members.

negative membership roles Roles that suit the particular needs of individual group members, but which are not necessarily compatible with the group's overall needs.

norming The stage of group development when feeling and cohesiveness increase.

performing The stage of group development when the group concentrates on the completion of the task.

positive membership roles Roles that facilitate group cohesion and group task completion.

small group A collection of individuals in contact who act interdependently as they work towards a common goal.

standard problem-solving agenda This identifies six steps for groups to work through: problem recognition, problem description, problem analysis, problem solution proposal, problem solution selection, and implementation.

storming The conflict stage of group development.

task leadership A leadership style concerned with getting the job done.

team leadership A leadership style concerned with how well group members are working together; sometimes referred to as social-emotional or climate leadership.

9 Organisational communication (1) Structure and culture

career path The normal route an employee travels through an organisation in a particular vocational role.

centralisation The extent to which decision making is concentrated in an organisation.

complexity The degree of specialisation in an organisation's hierarchy.

external environment The set of contextual factors outside the organisation that it is vitally concerned with.

formalisation The extent to which work roles are closely defined by the organisation.

functional theories of organisation Theories that stress 'bottom line' factors in organisations, measured in quantitative terms based on performance indicators, e.g. productivity, profit or staff turnover.

internal environment An organisation's climate and culture.

levels of organisational culture analysis The different levels at which organisational culture can be studied: the level of the national culture; the particular industry context; and the subcultural variations within an organisation.

meaning-centred theories of organisations These theories consider that people work most effectively through a shared sense of meaning and purpose about their goals.

message flows The ways in which written, oral and electronic messages move through the organisation. There are three kinds: downwards, from superior to subordinates; upwards, from subordinates to superiors; and laterally, between workers on the same level of the organisational hierarchy.

official goals The mission statements of the organisation.

operational goals Targets that are specific, functional and measurable; different departments may be given goals they have to reach in a set time period.

organisational communication climate The current feelings that organisation members have about how satisfying it is to communicate with others in the organisation.
organisational culture The values and interpretive frameworks used to construct a unique sense of shared meaning in an organisation.
organisational goals The shared aims that the members of an organisation develop over time.
organisational heroes Dominant people who imprint their vigorous personalities on the company culture.
organisational outcomes Outcomes that are defined in terms of profits, services or products.
organisational resources The factors an organisation uses as its raw materials.
organisational rites and rituals In-house ceremonies by which the organisation validates its own cultural meanings.
organisational structure The formal design of the prescribed chain-of-command in the organisation.
organisational technologies The information, equipment and techniques that are used to transform organisational inputs into outputs.
organisational values Shared beliefs about organisational activities that members use to make judgments about events in organisational life.
organisations considered as open systems A theoretical perspective that considers that organisations have an external and an internal environment.

10 Organisational communication (2) Networks, gender and power

career networking How individuals develop interpersonal contacts to advance their professional interests.
empowerment Ways in which new opportunities for participation can be opened up for women and other minority groups at work.
external coalitions The external coalition in an organisation represents the interests of the company's owners and directors.
gatekeepers Organisation members who are positioned in networks so that they can control information flows into, out of, or across the organisation.
gender-based managerial stereotypes Negative attitudes about men and women, either as managers or as co-workers, which act as an obstacle to effective communication.
gender equity programs Organisational programs designed to equalise the position of the sexes in the workplace.
gender-typed organisations Organisations where certain gender-types, or styles of masculinity and femininity, set the prevailing interpersonal climate.
influence strategies The persuasive options that individuals have in exercising their organisational influence.
information networking The way that information technology is used to communicate in organisations.
internal coalitions The internal coalition of an organisation represents management and staff.

managerial networking How managers build interpersonal influence coalitions within organisations.

network bridge A clique member, most of whose communication links are within his or her subgroup, but with one or more links to a member of another clique.

network clique A subgroup in the network, composed of members who have at least half their contacts with each other; a clique must have at least three members.

network isolate A person with few communication links in the organisation.

network liaison A person who links two or more cliques within the work unit.

network star The person who receives the highest number of nominations as a communication link by other organisational members.

organisational communication fit The extent to which an organisation's informal communication networks match its official hierarchy.

organisational communication networks Regular patterns of interaction and interdependence among organisational members.

organisational networking The way organisations form interorganisational links to defend their business or professional interests.

resource dependency A theoretical perspective that considers that organisational influence is most likely to be won by those who can provide critical resources to other organisation members.

11 Analysing television

intertextuality All media texts, whether television, film, radio or print, can take their meaning from other texts, and make references to them.

media texts A structured network of codes; media texts act as signifying systems to create a range of possible meanings. Discourse is organised in these texts according to the particular conventions prevailing in that medium at the time.

narrative discourse The signifying techniques and formal strategies that are used to tell a television story. Narrative discourse takes a plot and elaborates it as a story.

reflexivity The tendency of television to foreground the methods of its own production and to refer to itself; this can be intentional or accidental.

TV and gender identity How television represents traditional, modern and alternative sex roles for men, women and children.

TV and national identity How television represents the nation and the community, either culturally or politically.

TV and personal identity How television projects selective representations of personal and generational experience.

TV criticism Popular writing about television, found mainly in the press and TV magazines; usually presents reviews or previews of television programs.

TV flow The techniques and programming strategies that create a sense of continuity; a series of passages between program segments which together create an aesthetic sense of coherence.

TV form The formal structure of the television image.

TV genres Classes of TV programs, such as soaps or news bulletins; formulas or structures of narrative conventions.

TV research Theoretically based analysis of television intended for a relatively specialist audience.

visual grammar Film and video techniques used to construct television images.

12 Globalisation/Kokusaika 国際化

communications technology convergence The interfacing of telecommunications, computers and broadcasting.

dependency theory The view that Third World underdevelopment results from the political and economic constraints of First World dominance.

deregulation The removal of government regulations that are thought to hinder private sector activities.

deterritorialisation The accelerated physical and symbolic mobility of world populations.

development communication The use of communication policy, journalism and research to promote national economic growth in less developed countries.

global cultural flows The circulation of new ideas, images and values across national borders that may clash with traditional cultures.

globalisation Increased world interdependence brought about by recent rapid changes in the global economy and in communications technology.

kokusaika The Japanese word for 'internationalisation'.

mass culture The argument that urbanisation and the mass media create a division between 'high-brow' and 'low-brow' culture which undermines people's capacity to exercise their individual judgment.

media effects A debate originating in the US between the 1920s and 1940s about whether the mass media had 'strong' or 'weak' effects on its audiences.

modernisation theory The agreement on the desirability of national development through communications and economic growth.

modernity A state in which societies become increasingly industrialised and urbanised, and more dependent on the media and communications.

Nihonjinron The Japanese term for theories explaining the uniqueness of Japanese society.

postmodernity The view that in postindustrial societies traditional beliefs in 'meta-narratives', such as science, progress, patriarchy, nationality — and even rationality — no longer apply. Linear accounts of human knowledge and progress implicit in modernity are rejected.

privatisation Where public sector agencies are either completely or partially sold off to private sector interests.

Name index

n *indicates a reference note*

Adams, P. 244–245
Adorno, T. 271
Allen, M. 257, 264n
Allende, S. 273
Altman, I. 115, 118n
Anderson, C. 154, 168n
Ang, I. 246, 254, 264n
Appadurai, A. 276, 288n
Aristotle 12, 13, 93
Armstrong, M. 245, 263n
Asuncion-Lande, N. 123, 141n
Ashbolt, A. 281
Atlas, C. 260
Austin, J. 33, 48n

Bales, R. 175, 179, 180, 181, 193n
Bandura, A. 17
Barnlund, D. 138, 142n
Barthes, R. 66, 67, 68, 72n, 115, 253
Bartol, K. 182, 193n
Baudrillard, J. 253
Bavadra, T. 268
Beazley, K. 285
Beck, B. 214, 217n
Beethoven, L. 92
Bell, P. 139, 142n, 168n, 246, 264n, 288n
Bell, R. 110, 111, 117n
Beltran, L. 273
Bem, S. 107, 118n
Benjamin, W. 253
Benne, K. 179, 180, 193n
Bennett, S. 155, 168n
Berger, A. 252, 263n
Berger, P. 13, 22n
Berne, E. 110, 118n
Bernstein, B. 36, 48n
Bishop, B. 64
Blixen, K. 52
Blainey, G. 125
Bonner, N. 131–132
Bonney, B. 245, 264n, 282, 288n
Borges, J. 13
Boynes, R. 6
Brookner, A. 95
Bruce, L. 132
Brummer, D. 261
Brunsdon, C. 246, 264n

Calwell, A. 148
Cantor, M. 254, 264n
Capper, W. 260–261
Carey, J. 9, 22n
Carleton, R. 261
Carmody, K. 152
Carson, E. 220, 242n
Castles, S. 152, 168n
Castro, B. 146, 168n
de Certeau, M. 253
Chang, H. 113, 117n
Chang, V. 132
Chi, J. 152
Chapman, P. 256
Chipman, L. 151–152
Chitty, N. 269, 288n
Chomsky, N. 32, 40, 48n
Clary, J. 261
Coates, J. 42, 44, 47n
Cockburn, C. 231–232, 242n
Collins, R. 246, 264n
Condon, J. 129, 141n
Connell, W. 149, 169n
Coombs, H. 153, 169n
Corris, P. 98
Cottee, K. 127
cummings, e.e. 28
Cunningham, S. 245, 246, 263n, 264n
Curthoys, A. 254, 264n

Davis, G. 245, 264n
Davis, H. 249, 264n
Deal, T. 211, 212, 217n, 230, 242n
Denton, A. 261
Derrida, J. 42, 48n
Dessler, G. 8, 22n
DeVito, J. 103, 118n
Dewey, J. 183
Diem, N. 273
Dingo, E. 257
Dissanayake, W. 16, 22n, 273, 288n
Donovan, J. 261
Downs, C. 209, 217n
Dunphy, D. 240, 242n
During, S. 166, 168n
Dyer, B. 255

Eco, U. 67
Ekman, P. 61, 72n

Elliot, P. 246, 264n
Ellis, C. 115, 118n
Emery, F. 199
Evered, R. 214, 217n

Fahey, M. 259
Fairfax 103, 276
Fairclough, N. 39, 48n
Fayol, C. 198
Feather, N. 149, 167n
Fisher, R. 237, 242n
Fiske, J. 147, 169n, 249, 264n
Fitzgerald, T. 150–151, 169n
Fitzgibbon, M. 67
Fitzpatrick, B. 281
Flaubert, G. 26
Folb, E. 123, 142n
Ford, H. 212
Forgas, J. 149, 169n
Foucault, M. 26, 42, 48n, 253
Frank, A. 273
Freud, S. 52, 69
Frege, G. 30, 48n
Freire, P. 273
Frost, P. 234, 241n
Furnham, A. 139, 142n

Gallois, C. 134–135, 141n, 142n
Game, A. 231, 242n
Geertz, C. 137, 142n
Gerbner, G. 247, 264n
Gibbs, M. 42
Gilbert, K. 153, 169n
Giles, H. 135, 141n
Goffman, E. 13, 23n, 45, 48n, 62, 102, 109, 115, 118n
Goldhaber, G. 206–207, 217n
Goolagong-Cawley, E. 131
Gorbachev, M. 54, 272
Grice, H. 33, 48n, 54, 73n
Grossberg, L. 165, 169n
Gudykunst, W. 135, 142n, 165, 169n

Hall, E. 58, 73n
Harmer, W. 259
Harre, R. 115, 118n
Hartley, J. 254, 264n

319

Name index

Hawke, R. 41, 85, 89, 258, 282
Hayes, E. 257
Hazzard, S. 88, 196
Henderson, B. 257
Henningham, J. 246, 264n
Hidaka, R. 282, 289n
Hill, S. 214, 217n
Hinch, D. 261
Ho, R. 150, 168n
Hochschild, A. 61, 73n
Hodge, R. 41, 48n
Hofstede, G. 149–150, 169n
Hogan, P. 244, 253, 255, 258
Hoggart, R. 271
Holmes, J. 43, 48n
Holmes, S. 88
Howard, J. 125

Ireland, D. 220
Irwin, H. 139, 142, 197, 218n
Ito, Y. 138, 142, 288, 289n

Jablin, F. 199, 201, 217n
Jacka, E. 245, 246, 254–255, 264n, 269, 289n
Jackson, M. 260–261
James, C. 244, 250, 257
James, H. 76
Jayasuriya, N. 126, 142n
Jenkins, D. 279
Jensen, J. 271–272, 289n
Johnson, D. 184, 191, 193n
Jones, A. 261
Jones, R. 154, 169n
Jourard, S. 102
Joyrich, L. 260, 265n
Jupp, J. 151–152, 169n

Kahn, R. 199
Kalantzis, M. 137, 143n
Kanter, R. 228, 229, 235, 242n
Katz, D. 199
Katz, E. 247
Keating, P. 69–70, 103, 247, 279
Kendon, A. 62, 70, 72n, 73n
Kennedy, G. 250, 255
Khomeini, Ayatollah 15
Kim, Y. 135, 142n, 165, 169n
Kincaid, L. 135, 143n

Kirk, J. 232
Knapp, M. 111, 115, 117n
Koustas, M. 257
Kress, G. 12, 22n, 27, 47n, 48n

Lakoff, R. 43, 49n
Lane, D. 250
Langley, E. 28
Lasswell, H. 9, 23n
Lawrence, P. 199
Lazarsfeld, P. 271
Lealand, G. 245, 265n
Lee, C. 254, 265n
Lee Kuan-Yew 274
Leeds-Hurwitz, W. 114, 118n
Lenin, V. 15
Lerner, D. 273
Lewis, D. 27, 49n
Lewis, G. 261, 265n
Liebmann, S. 257
Likert, R. 198
Lippman, W. 270–271
Lloyd, G. 45
Lorsch, J. 199
Lyneham, P. 261

MacKinnon, C. 45, 49n
Madonna 260
Mahathir, M. 278–279
Malouf, D. 2, 3, 14
Marcos, F. 273
Martin, D. 122
Martin, M. 68
Martin, R. 257, 261
Maximenkov, V. 78
Mayle, P. 60
Mayo, E. 198
McCroskey, J. 109, 118n
McDonald, D. 271
McFeast, E. 260
McGregor, D. 198
McGuigan, J. 275, 289n
McLachlan, C. 261
McLuhan, M. 15, 23n
McQuail, D. 6, 22n
McQueen, H. 15, 23n, 282, 289n
Meldrum, M. 250
Mellencamp, P. 259–260, 263n, 265n
Mintzberg, H. 235, 242n
Mitchell, A. 38, 49n
Mitchell, W. 70
Moffat, T. 152
Monroe, M. 260
Moran, A. 246, 255, 262, 263n, 265n

More, E. 214, 217n
Morgan, G. 236, 241n
Morgan, S. 152
Morris, Mark 68
Morris, Meaghan 244, 265n
Morrison, G. 127
Morse, M. 253, 260, 263n
Moyal, A. 18, 23n
Munro, M. 257, 261
Murdoch, R. 212

Namatjira, A. 258
Nandan, S. 268
Natt, H. 257, 265n
Nelson, H. 260
Newton, B. 250
Nightingale, V. 246, 260, 263n, 265n
Nomura, M. 63, 73n
Nordenstreng, K. 254

O'Regan, T. 166, 170n, 244, 246, 261, 265n
O'Grady, J. 132–133
O'Shane, P. 130
Ouichi, W. 210–211, 218n

Packard, T. 212
Packard, V. 271
Packer, K. 237, 276
Palmer, P. 246, 254, 265n
Palmer, V. 281
Pascale, R. 211, 218n
Pascoe, R. 147, 170n
Peirce, C. 40
Penton, B. 281
Phillips, A. 281
Powell, G. 228, 242n
Powell, W. 226–227, 242n
Poynton, B. 260–261, 265n
Poynton, C. 43, 49n
Pringle, R. 230–231, 241n
Pryor, G. 7, 18, 43, 64, 85, 89, 103, 132, 162, 255, 271, 285
Pye, L. 273

Quebral, N. 274, 290n

Ramsey, S. 63, 73n
Rawlins, W. 112, 114, 119n
Reagan, R. 275
Reddy, M. 11, 22n
Roberts, T. 2, 68
Robertson, R. 268, 290n
Robson, G. 256
Rogers, E. 273
Rudder, J. 59, 73n

Name index

Rue, L. 8, 23n
Rushdie, S. 15
Ruxton, B. 151–152

Sacks, O. 33, 49n
Sanders, A. 251
Saussure, F. 40, 41, 49n, 66
Schein, E. 213, 218n
Schiller, H. 254
Schramm, W. 273
Schwarzenegger, A. 260
Schopenauer, F. 94
Schutz, W. 176, 194n
Searle, J. 33, 49n
Seymour, A. 147
Shakespeare, W. 79
Shannon, C. 9, 23n
Sherif, M. 130–131, 143n
Shimizu, I. 282, 284
Sinclair, J. 269, 290n
Singleton, J. 257, 283
Skase, C. 237
Slade, C. 191, 194n
Slade, D. 37, 48n
Slavin, R. 260
Smircich, L. 213, 218n
Snyder, G. 103, 118n
Soeharto, President 279
Sontag, S. 66, 73n

Spender, D. 44, 49n
Sperber, D. 34, 49n
Springborg, R. 258
Stanner, W. 153, 170n
Still, L. 228, 231, 242n
Sutcliffe, K. 257, 260
Symons, R. 250
Szubanski, M. 259

Tajfel, H. 115, 119n, 136
Tam, S. 227, 242n
Tannen, D. 43, 47n
Taylor, F. 198
Thatcher, M. 39
Ticehurst, W. 209, 218n
Tichy, N. 222, 242n
Tiffen, R. 258, 265n
Trist, E. 199
Tuckman, B. 175, 176, 194n
Tulloch, J. 246, 258, 263n, 265n
Turner, G. 246, 254, 265n
Turner, I. 283
Turow, J. 246, 265n

Van Damme, J. 260
van Dijk, T. 39, 49n
Viviani, N. 163, 170n
Von Sturmer, J. 155, 168n

Waley, J. 257, 261
Walker, M. 260
Walsh, M. 138, 142n
Ward, R. 147, 170n
Warumpis 152
Weber, M. 198
Weick, K. 211, 218n
Weir, P. 124
Wendt, J. 257
Wheeless, V. 110, 119n
Whorf, B. 13, 24n
Wicker, A. 229, 242n
Willesee, M. 257, 261
Williams, C. 231
Williams, R. 250, 253, 263n
Williamson, John 284
Williamson, Judith 67, 73n
Willis, A. 166, 170n
Windschuttle, K. 15, 24n, 245, 265n
Winter, P. 246, 265n
Wittgenstein, L. 39, 49n, 93, 96n

Yang, W. 158
Yeates, H. 261, 265n
Yothu Yindi 152
Yum, J. 135, 143n

Subject index

d *indicates a definition*

ABA 245, 248
ABC 281, 284, 285, *see* Television
Aboriginals 13, 14, 32, 59, 128, 232, *see* Intercultural communication
Abortion 115
ACTU 41, 239
Advertising 15, 67, 78, 249, 285, *see* Television advertising, *and* Reasoning
AFTRS 245
AIDS 66, 164, 253
Americanisation 15, 128, 269–272, 281, 283, 286
AMIC 16
ASEAN 277
Asian Wall Street Journal 278
AT&T 275
ATVI 284–285
AUSSAT 255, 284
Austrade 127
Australian identity 67–69, 147, 152

Bali 139
BCA 239
BERNAMA 278

Canada 126, 134, 214, 246
Chaos theory 7
China 113, 131, 282, 284, *see* Intercultural communication
Commonwealth Bank 276
Communication 4d–22
and culture 15d
communication studies 5d
contexts 5d, 10d, 17, 18
conventions 12d
cultural relativism 14–16, 15d
cultural studies 5, 15, 16, 165–166, 282
globalisation 15
language 13–14
linguistic relativism 13d–14
postmodernism 12, 16
power 14–16
persuasion 16
group *see* Small group communication
intercultural *see* Intercultural communication
international *see* Globalisation
interpersonal *see* Interpersonal communication
mass *see* Television
models of 6d ff
administrative 16d
critical 16d
functional 10d
mechanistic 4d
process 10d
research methods 17–20
administrative and critical 16d
and methodologies 17
contextualised and decontextualised 17d
feminist 15, 16, 18, 199, 228–229, 253, 259–260
qualitative and quantitative 17d–19, 248
reflexive 18d
studies 5d
American 9, 16, 43, 45, 101, 102, 107, 110, 112–113, 115, 131, 138, 149–150, 165–166, 179, 191, 198–199, 206–207, 210–212, 214, 222, 228–229, 234–236, 246–247, 269–273, 282
Asian 16, 113, 227, 254, 273–274
Australian 15, 18, 136, 138–139, 148, 150, 164–165, 191, 209, 214, 226, 230–231, 240, 245–246, 254, 257–258, 261, 280–285
British 135–136, 226, 231, 246, 250
European 13, 16, 229, 246, 253, 275
Japanese 63, 138, 233, 280–285
Latin American 273
New Zealand 43, 150, 151, 245–246
theories 7d
meaning-based 12–14, 12d, 18, 20
transmission 8d–11, 12, 18, 20
Communications 4d
and development communication 274d
and technology 2–3, 9, 17, 19, 173, 204, 214, 225
code 9d
feedback 10d
medium 8d
noise 8d
receiver 8d
sender 8d
technology convergence 276d
and telecommunications deregulation 275d
and transport 8
satellites 284–285

East Timor 279
Environment 68, 153, 268

Feminist theory 15, 18, 159, 283
Fiji 268

323

Subject index

Foreign reporting 277–280
France 53, 60, 66

Globalisation 15, 122, 128, 164, 268–287, 275d
  and Australia 280–285
    ABC 279–280, 281, 284, 285
    cultural policy 283
    multiculturalism 283, 286–287
    nationalism 283
    satellite broadcasting 284–285
  and cultural flows 276d
    communications technology convergence 276d
    deregulation 275d, 282
    deterritorialisation 276d, 277d
    postmodernity 275d
    privatisation 276d–277
  and development 272–274
    development communication 274d
    Human Rights 268, 276, 279
    media freedom 274, 277–280
  and Japan 280–285
    johoka shakai 284
    kokusaika 268d, 280
    Marxism 282
    media exports 281
    MFP 283–284, 285–286
    NHK 281, 284
    Nihonjinron 283d, 284
    satellite broadcasting 284–285
  and modernisation 269d–273, 274
    Americanisation 281
    communications technology 270, 274, 276
    dependency theory 273d
    in Asia and Latin America 272–273
    in the US 269–272
    media effects debates 270d–272, 281
    mass culture debates 270, 271d–272, 274, 282
    modernisation theory 273d
  and South-East Asia 277–280
    Indonesia 277, 279, 284
    Malaysia 272, 277–278, 279
    Philippines 273, 274, 277, 280
    Singapore 272, 273, 274, 277, 279–280
    Thailand 274, 277
    Viet Nam 268
  and the United Nations 273–274
Greece *see* Intercultural communication
Gulf War 30, 130, 258

Hong Kong 268, 273
Human rights 268, 276, 279

IBM 275
Independent Monthly 255
India 57, 280
Indonesia 277, 279, 284
Intercultural communication 122d–168
  and Aboriginals 130, 132, 138–139, 147, 152–157
  and Aboriginality 153d
  and Anglo-Australian culture 146, 147d–150
  and foreign students 129, 130, 133, 134
  and immigration 125, 127
    British 124, 146–147, 148, 149, 150, 165
    Chinese 129, 132, 134, 157–158, 161–164
    Greek 123, 132, 134, 136, 164
    Indochinese 129, 134, 149, 161–164
    Italian 123, 133, 134, 137, 158–159, 164
    Lebanese 134, 159–160
    New Zealand 125, 129, 131, 134, 150–151
    Turkish 134, 159–161
    Yugoslav 130
  and Maoris 129, 131, 150–151
  and media
    ethnic radio 125–126, 130, 134, 153
    ethnic press 130, 139–140, 159, 165
    ethnic television 125–126, 134–135, 165, 166
  and multiculturalism 125d–127, 139, 150–152, 157–167
  and tourism 127
  and White Australia 125, 147, 150
  in a global context
    China 131, 149
    Germany 123
    Indonesia 126
    Japan 123, 128, 138
    Malaysia 126
    New Guinea 149
    Philippines 163–164
    United States 123, 124, 128, 131, 134, 136, 138, 149, 151
  principles of
    accommodation theory 135–137
    acculturation 133d–135, 159, 161, 163
    assimilationism 151d
    chain migration 160d
    competence 137–139
    core values and behaviours 149d–150
    cross-cultural communication 127d–128
    cultural heritage 147d
    culture 146d
    culture shock 133

Subject index

discrimination 132d, 158, 161–162
ethnic networks 123, 131, 134, 135, 158–159, 160, 162–163
ethnic pecking order 157d
ethnic stereotypes 131d
ethnocentrism 131d
host culture 123d
intermarriage 160, 163–164
intracultural networks 163d
language barriers 129, 135–137, 148, 162
minority cultures 123d
pluralism 151d
prejudice 132d
religious differences 129–130, 132, 148, 159–161
social distance 131d
subcultures 124, 125d
Interpersonal communication 98d–117
and American research 102, 112–113, 115
and cultural differences 113
and gender differences 107–108
and intrapersonal communication 98d
and self-concept 99d, 102
self-disclosure 101d –102, 110, 138
self-esteem 100d–101, 103
self-monitoring 102–103d
self-presentation 102d–103
social identity 102–103
and perception 13, 104d–109
attribution 105
constructs 104–105
judgments 105–106
prejudice 107d
reflexivity 114d
stereotyping 105d–109
and social involvement 109–111
assertiveness 110d

attentiveness 111d
communication apprehension 109d
empathy 109d
friendship 112
loneliness 110
perceptiveness 111d
relationship development 111–114
responsiveness 110d
shyness 101
yuan fen 113
Interviewing 3, 57, 63, 227
Iran 15
Italy *see* Intercultural communication

Japan 57, 272, *see* Globalisation, *and* Organisational communication, *and* Intercultural communication

Korea, South 272, 273, 282

Land Rights 153–154
Language 12, 26, 27d–47
context 27, 32–33, 34, 35, 36
foreign 26, 28–29, 38, 43
level of discourse 35–39
elaborated code 36d
register 36d
regional variations 29
restricted code 36d
level of sentences 31d–33
semantics 31d, 32
sign language 33
syntax 32d
transformation 32d
utterances 31d
level of pragmatics 33d–35
implicature 34d
paralinguistics 34d
level of words 28–31
connotation 30d
denotation 30d
jargon 29, 31
metaphor 30d–31
morphemes 29d
phonemes 29d
phonetics 28–29
referent 30d
sense 30d
and Aboriginal society 155–157

and Australian English 3, 13, 29, 34–35, 38
and classroom talk 44
and cultural difference 26, 38
and deconstruction 27, 42d
and discourse 35–39, 35d, 39d, 42d
and gender differences 42d–45
and linguistic genres 36d, 39
and linguistic relativism 13d–14
and literacy 129
and media 29–30, 41, 45
and New Zealand English 29, 43
and power 36, 43
and semiotics 39, 40d, 41d, 43, 65–69
icon 40d
index 40d
paradigmatic relations 41d
sign 40d
signifier 40d
signified 40d
structuralism 41, 66
symbol 40d
syntagmatic relations 41d

Mabo 7, 42, 152, 153
Malaysia 272, 277, 278
Maoris 43
Marxism 16, 236, 254, 282
Masculinity 67, 107, 147, 148–150, 260, 282
McDonalds 61
Meanjin 281
Mexico 80
MFP 128, 226, 283–284, 285–286
Middle East *see* Intercultural communication
MITI 284
Monitor 279
Multiculturalism 286–287, *see* Intercultural communication

Nation 281
New Guinea 149, *see* Language, *and* Intercultural communication
New Straits Times 278

325

Subject index

New Zealand 55, 246
Nonverbal communication 52d–71
    adaptors 61d
    affect displays 61d
    emblems 61d
    illustrators 61d
    regulators 60, 61d
    and Aboriginal society 59, 66
    and advertising 67–68, 70
    and animals 54, 58
    and art 68
    and body language 53d, 55, 56, 64
        eye movement 56, 62
        kissing 53, 62
        smiling 54, 70
        touching 57
    and children 54, 58, 64, 65
    and context 62
    and cultural conventions 53–57, 60, 65
    and deception 61
    and fashion 66
    and gender differences 60, 63–65, 70
    and interviewing 57, 63
    and Japan 63
    and nonverbal codes 52d ff
        chronemics 59d
        haptics 57d
        kinesics 56d, 59
        proxemics 58d, 59
        visual 65d
    and Parliament House 68–69
    and power 63, 65
    and pronunciation 28
    and semiotics 65–69
    and structuralism 66
    and television 58
    and territoriality 58d–59
NTT 276, 284

Olympics 34, 268, 252, 283
Optus 276
Organisational communication 196–241
    and career paths 199–201d
        bargaining 275–276
        job selection interviews 227
        life goals analysis 231
        line and staff positions 199
        motivation 201, 209
        organisational socialisation 201
        personal and positional roles 199
        presentational speaking 197
        supervisor–subordinate relations 200
        writing a job application 201–202
    and contexts 196ff
        BHP 196
        Coles 203
        DAS 196
        DIR 233, 239
        Esso 232
        IBM 197, 210
        NZI 214
        SBS 197
        USN 214
    and Japanese companies 199, 210, 212, 227, 233
    and organisational change 212, 214, 227, 230–231, 239, 240
    and organisational culture 208–216, 211d
        climate 208d–210, 215–216
        heroes 212d
        language 214
        levels of analysis 213d
        rites and rituals 212d
        values 212d
    and organisational leadership 213, 214, 226, 229, 236, 240
    and organisational structure 202–207, 205d
        centralisation 206d–207
        complexity 205d–206
        external environment 203d
        formal and informal communication 207
        formalisation 206d
        goals 203d
        internal environment 204d
        message flows 200, 206d–207, 234
        open systems 202d
        outcomes 203d
        resources 204d
        technology 204d, 214, 224
    and power in organisations 234–237
        external and internal coalitions 235d
        enterprise bargaining 239
        Industrial Democracy programs 238–240
        influence strategies 236d
        resource dependency 236d
    and the *Training Guarantee Act* 233, 238, 239
    gender differences and 199, 221, 226, 228–34, 235
        EEO programs 232–234
        empowerment 234d
        gender-based managerial stereotypes 228d
        gender equity programs 231d
        gender-typed organisations 230d
    networking 225ff
        career 226d
        information 225d
        managerial 226d
        organisational 226d
    networks 220–227, 222d
        analysis 221–224
        bridges 223d
        cliques 223d
        fit 224d
        gatekeepers 225d
        isolates 223d
        liaisons 223d
        stars 223d
    theories of 198ff
        American theories 198–199, 210–212, 228
        communication measurement 210, 215–216, 233
        functional theories 198d, 208

meaning-centred
theories 198d, 208
Overland 281

Pay-TV 284
Pers Pancasila 279
Philippines 163–164, 273, 275, 277, 280, *see* Intercultural communication
Pornography 45
Postcolonialism 166d
Postmodernism 12, 16, 41, 114, 115, 165, 283
Press censorship 278–280
Propaganda 93
Prostitution 78

Quadrant 283
Quality Circles 191, 239

Radio 45
Reasoning 76–96
and advertising 78, 79, 80, 85, 87, 90, 93
and argument 83d
ad hominem argument 90d
analogy 83d–84
contradiction 89d
deductive argument 86d
enthymematic argument 81d
inductive argument 86d
inferences 81d
invalid argument 84d
irrelevance 81, 82
premise 83d
valid argument 84d–85
and conditionals 86–87
necessary and sufficient conditions 86d, 87d
and conversations 93
and critical thinking 76–77, 91–94
and children 77
and equivocation 79
and gender differences 93
and journalism 79, 80, 94
and legal procedure 82
and persuasion 78
facts 81d, 82
fallacies 88d

appeal to authority 90d
appeal to tradition 90d
causal 90d
of moderation 90d
and presupposition 77d, 78
and proposition 80d
and statement of fact and value 80
and vagueness 80
Refugees 268, 276
Russia 15, 54, 78

Samoa 43
SBS-TV 276, 282, 285, *see* Television
Sexual harassment 57, 261
Singapore 272, 273, 274, 277–78, 279–80
Singapore Press Holdings 278
Small group communication 172d–192
and decision making 182, 183d–184
agendas 183–184, 186
brainstorming 185d
consensus 190d
Japanese 191
leader mandate 189d
majority vote 190d
and goal clarity 174
and group effectiveness 174d
attractiveness 174d
cohesiveness 174d
interdependence 174d
satisfaction 174d
size 175, 178, 181–182
stages of development 178, 183–184
and Interpersonal Process Analysis 176, 179
and problem solving 182, 183d–184, 190
and task leadership 178d–181
and team leadership 178d–181
conflict in 185–189
conflict episodes 188d
conflict styles 188d
constructive controversy 184d
hidden agendas 188d
gender differences in 182
goal setting in 179
in work groups 172–173

negative membership roles in 180d
positive membership roles in 179d–181
theories of 191
Syria 3

Taiwan 272, 273
Telecom 257
Telegraph 9
Telephone 18, 65
Television 244–262
and gender identity 259d–261
and national identity 254d–258
and personal identity 253d–254
and radio 249
censorship 247
criticism 244d–245, 248
form 249d–252
flow 250, 253d
intertextuality 249d–250
media texts 249d
narrative discourse 251d–252, 253
reflexivity 250d
visual grammar 251d
genres 251d–252
advertising 247, 249, 250, 253, 257, 258, 259, 260–261
drama 251, 252, 258, 260
news 15, 249, 257, 258
sports 251–252, 260–261
programs
A Country Practice 250, 256, 258
Acropolis Now 132, 257
Attitude 260
Australia Live 257
Australia's Most Wanted 251
Backchat 245
Blackout 257
Comedy Company 259
Countdown 250
Dallas 128, 254
Days of our Lives 253
Donahue 138, 259
Embassy 278

Subject index

Eyewitness News 251
Fast Forward 249, 250, 257, 259
Full Frontal 249, 259
Hard Copy 259
Healthy, Wealthy and Wise 359
Heartbreak High 257
Heartland 257
Hey Dad! 252
Hey Hey, It's Saturday 250
Home and Away 256, 257
Home Sweet Home 257
Homicide 255, 261
Hotline 245
I Love Lucy 244, 253
In Melbourne Tonight 250
Kittson, Fahey 259
Live and Sweaty 260
Magnum PI 260
Media Watch 245
Miami Vice 260
Naked Under Capricorn 257
Neighbours 256, 257
New Faces 250
Pick-a-Box 255
Police Rescue 261
Prisoner 254
Real Life 259
Roseanne 259
60 Minutes 55, 245, 280
Sticky Moments 261
The Late Show 261
TVTV 245
Twin Peaks 252
Wide World of Sport 260
Women of the Sun 257
ratings 17, 247–248
research 18, 244d–248
   audience 15, 18, 246
   children and television 18, 246, 247, 254
   content analysis 246, 257
   cultural imperialism 254
   history 255
   uses and gratifications 247
   violence and television 17, 19, 247

satellite (DBS) 255, 284
stations
   ABC 245, 246, 248, 259, 260, 261
   CNN 258
   commercial broadcasters 247, 249, 251, 255–257
   SBS 125, 130, 245, 249, 255, 257, 261, 276
Thailand 57, 139, 274, 277
Time 91, 128, 278
Tourism 276
TVRI 279

United Nations 273–274
USA 123, 124, 128, 270–271, 272, 273, 278, 280–281, 282, 282, 283

Viet Nam 268, *see* Intercultural communication
Vincent Committee 282

World Bank 273

About the authors

Both authors currently are Senior Lecturers in the Faculty of Communication at the University of Canberra. They have published articles and presented papers in national and international journals and conferences.

Glen Lewis is author of *Real Men Like Violence, Australian Movies and the American Dream*, co-editor of *Australian Communications Technology and Policy*, and co-author of *Communication Traditions in 20th Century Australia*. He has been a guest editor of the *Australian Journal of Communication* and is now an advisory board member of the *Journal of International Communication*.

Christina Slade has published widely in English and French on reasoning in groups, children and philosophy, and language and cooperation. She was a founding member of Philosophy for Children in Australia and is active in the international movement. She has worked as a foreign policy journalist, ran the Asian Study Group of Islamabad, contributed to *A Traveller's Guide to Pakistan*, and co-edited *Media Images of Australia/Asia: Cross-cultural Reflections*.